JOYS of IRISH HUMOR

Henry D. Spalding

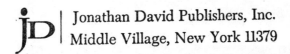

Jonathan David Publishers, Inc.
Middle Village, New York 11379

JOYS OF IRISH HUMOR

Address all inquiries to:

JONATHAN DAVID PUBLISHERS, INC.
68-22 Eliot Avenue
Middle Village, New York 11379

Original title: *Lilt of the Irish*

Library of Congress Cataloging in Publication Data
Main entry under title:

Joys of Irish Humor.

Bibliography: p
Includes index.

1. Irish wit and humor. I. Spalding, Henry D.
PN65178.16L5   827′.008   77-24307
ISBN 0-8246-0337-0

Printed in the United States of America

Table of Contents

Malin Head
Rathlin I.
Giant's Causeway
L. Swilly
Innishowen Peninsula
Garron Point
L. Foyle
ANTRIM MTS
Aran I.
Derryveagh Mts
Letterkenny
Derry
LONDONDERRY
Dungiven
Ballymena
Larne
Strabane
Antrim
Carrickfergus
Bango
DONEGAL
Ards Peninsula
Donegal
NORTHERN
TYRONE
Omagh
Lough Neagh
Belfast
Ballyshannon
Dungannon
IRELAND
DOWN
Strangfor
Downpatrick
Donegal Bay
L. Erne
FERMANAGH
Enniskillen
Armagh
ARMAGH
Monaghan
Portadown
Mourne Mts.
Dundrum Bay
Sligo
LEITRIM
CAVAN
Dundalk
Ballina
SLIGO
Cavan
Monasterboice
Blacksod
Lough Conn
ROSCOMMON
Shannon
LOUTH
Mellifont Abbey
Drogheda
Achill I.
Carrick-on-Shannon
MEATH
Kells
Clare I.
Clew B.
Castlebar
Longford
Slane
MAYO
Westport
LONGFORD
Longford
L. Ree
Mullingar
Trim
Tara
Lambay I.
Partry Mts
Roscommon
WESTMEATH
Boyne
Howth Head
L. Mask
Athlone
Maynooth
Dublin
Connemara
L. Corrib
Tullamore
DUBLIN
Dún Aengus
GALWAY
Galway
Clonmacloise
OFFALY
Kildare
KILDARE
WICKLOW MTS
REPUBLIC
OF
Aran I.
Galway Bay
Birr
The Curragh
Wicklow
L. Derg
Port Laoise
CLARE
IRELAND
LEIX
BARROW
Arklow
Ennis
Carlow
CARLOW
Shannon Airport
TIPPERARY
Thurles
KILKENNY
Cahore Point
Limerick
Cashel
Kilkenny
Nore
WEXFORD
Mouth of Shannon
LIMERICK
Tipperary
Slaney
Wexford Bay
Listowel
Clonmel
Wexford
Tralee
Knockmealdown Mts
Waterford
Hook Head
Dingle
KERRY
Blackwater
WATERFORD
Dingle Bay
Lismore
Dungarven
Killarney
Boggeragh Mts
Blarney
Youghal
Glengariff
Lee
Cork
Bantry

Ireland today

A Word About Words

The older jokes, anecdotes, and poems in this volume, that is, those that originated in pre-twentieth-century Ireland, contain a fair number of Gaelic expressions. They have been retained so that they might correspond as closely as possible to the original telling, thus preserving their unique Irish flavor and authenticity.

The modern name for Ireland is Eire, but we can only conjecture about the source of the name. Aristotle referred to Ireland as "Iernia." Plutarch called the country "Ogyia." Little is known of the original inhabitants of Ireland, let alone their language. We do know, however, that the first of the main colonizers, Gaelic Celts from France and northern Spain, settled on Irish soil about 350 B.C. Their Druid influence can be seen in the old Celtic name, Eriu, the sun goddess, which they gave to Ireland, in deference to the sun worshippers who already lived there. Eriu, it is believed, finally evolved into Eire.

Among the earliest to influence the Gaelic language were the Norsemen—Swedes, Norwegians, and Danes—who began their invasions of Ireland in the ninth century. The Danes, it will be remembered, constructed a fortress atop a hill, around which a Danish town grew. This town, located near a "dark pool"—*dubh linn,* in Gaelic—became Dublin.

Ireland's eight-hundred-year struggle against the British began in the year 1155, when Pope Adrian IV named King James II of England as the sovereign ruler of Ireland.[1] The succession of monarchs who followed, instituted many important changes in the culture of Ireland, among them the cruelly enforced abandonment of their Gaelic tongue. The English language was thrust upon the Irish people, with dire punishment meted out to violators who dared speak in Gaelic. All contracts, indeed all legal documents and judicial proceedings were conveyed in English. Nearly all

---

[1] Pope Adrian IV, whose name was Nicholas Breakspeare, remains the only Englishman ever to become Pontiff.

1

2

education of children was prohibited, and the little that was permitted was taught in English.[2]

When we speak of the Gaelic language, we are referring to the Celtic tongue, often called "Old Irish," or just "Irish," and the terms are used interchangeably in modern Irish literature. Ireland, of course, is an English-speaking country, and has been one for many centuries. Nevertheless, an abundance of Gaelic expressions have survived as Anglo-Irish terms, and have been accepted as part of the English language. A few of such words are shillelagh, leprechaun, blatherskite, smithereen, whiskey, blarney, brogan, colleen, spalpeen, pooka, and others far too numerous to mention here. The Gaelic words and phrases have been italicized in these pages. The Anglo-Irish words have not.

Nearly all of the Irish emigrants to America were unfamiliar with the Gaelic language. Its use was confined to sporadic tag words and old sayings. Very few could master whole sentences in the ancient language. But it was their use of English, laced with Gaelic idiom, that gave the Irish immigrants an immediate advantage over the other newcomers to the United States. True, it was also spiced with "brogue," but easily understood.

A "brogue" is simply an Irish accent in the pronunciation of English. There are several such accents, or brogues, in Ireland, differing somewhat according to geographical area, just as accents differ in various parts of the United States. Depending upon their locality, some Irish writers employ the word *iv* for "of," and *av* for "if," while others transpose them, doing just the opposite. The use of the long *a* in place of the long *e* in Irish pronunciation is another illustration of the brogue. Such words as *aisy* for "easy," *tay* for "tea," and *belave* for "believe," come to mind. The use of the letter *h* to soften the sound of *t*, as in "throuble," or in the letter *d*, as in "murdher," are further examples of brogue, and hark back to the gentler sounds of the people's native Gaelic tongue. The letter *r* has a rolling sound, as in *wurrld,* for "world," *wurrk* for "work" and *burrd* for "bird."

There are numerous other types of accented English words that stem from the earlier use of Gaelic. The Celtic vocal chords, for instance, do not seem able to cope with the letter *j,* just as the Slavic and other people have difficulty pronouncing the letter *w*. Hence, the Irish made Shawn of John, or Shamus of James. The name O'Shay, is the Irish equivalent of Johnson. The pronunciation of Gaelic names, however, cannot always be determined by the spelling. The great Irish warrior from Derry who marched against the hated Cromwell (only to be poisoned by Cromwell's agents), was named

---

[2]One result of the forced conversion to the English language proved to be an unexpected boon to the Irish. Their fluency with the adopted tongue enabled them to enter the English-speaking world of letters and commerce, and to exert an influence on world thought which Ireland, isolated as it was, might not otherwise have attained. However, it is important to note that the Irish success with the English language must, in part, be attributed to Saint Patrick who introduced the Roman alphabet to Ireland, some 1,000 years earlier. Prior to Patrick's teachings, the Gaels employed a twenty-letter alphabet called "Ogham." The sounds were represented by a combination of vertical or slanting lines, and read from top to bottom, as in the Chinese.

Eoghan Ruadh O'Neill, pronounced "Owen Roe," in English. Dublin's most popular resort, Dun Laoghaire, is pronounced "Leary."

Many Irish authors, of course, wrote in perfect English. But some of Ireland's most eminent writers, humorous or otherwise, employed the brogue because of its naturalness and identification. Certainly, there is nothing pejorative in its use, provided it is authentic and in good taste. And no one enjoys the old familiar expressions as much as the Irishman himself. He greets them with the smile of recognition usually reserved for old friends.

The reader will find it helpful to consult the Glossary at the end of the book which contains the definitions of the Irish terms used in this volume, in addition to the Anglo-Irish words and English colloquialisms employed.

Meanwhile, *cead mille failte, ma achora* (a hundred thousand welcomes, my friend), to the homes and lives of the very pleasant Irish and Irish-American men and women you will meet in the following chapters.

—H.D.S.

Preface

Once upon a time, ever so long ago, before Saint Patrick brought scholarship and Christianity to the Emerald Isle; long before the mighty King Brian Boru drove the Norsemen from Irish soil; even long before the magnificent epic of *Táin bô Cúalnge* (the Cattle-Raid of Cooley), in which Maeve, Queen of Connaught, sallied forth to capture a famous bull and which ended in the single-handed defense of Ulster by the legendary Cuchulain—yes, even before all of those, there lived two opposing factions: the leprechauns of the south of Ireland and the pookas of the north.

Very good. The pookas of the north were given to mischief-making and all sorts of shenanigans. They were never really vicious, mind you. But, oh, how they did love to tase the leprechauns. Now the leprechauns, for their part, were no angels, either. They loved to play practical jokes and were just as great a nuisance to the pookas as the pookas were to them. What is more, they enjoyed certain advantages over the pookas: leprechauns, as everyone knows, can wish themselves anywhere, at any time, in the twinkling of an Irish eye. Indade, they can wish for anything they plase.

Very well. One day in those remote times, Paeder Og, king of the pookas, weary of the continual warfare between the spirit forces, challenged Rory, king of the leprechauns, to battle. The winner of this hand-to-hand combat would become king of both the pookas *and* the leprechauns. Thus united, the fighting, year in and year out, would come to an end. The only stipulation made by Paeder Og—oh, he was a sly one!—was that Rory would refrain from his dirty Irish thricks, such as disappearing and then emerging behind his back in the midst of combat. King Rory quickly accepted the challenge, including the unfair terms, confident that he could bate the livin' bejabbers out of his old rival.

Fine. They met on a battleground beneath an overhanging laylac bush, Paeder Og with a stout *kippeen* that made Rory nervous, but only for a moment. King Rory himself was armed with an iron-tipped shillelagh, the sight of which brought a quick gasp from Paeder Og.

"The back o' me hand to ye, ye spalpeen!" shouted Paeder Og.

"The toe iv me boot to *ye*, ye scalawag!" yelled Rory.

4

And with that, they sprang at aich other, with the "wee people" of both sides cheering their own champions. Ah, but it was a grand fight while it lasted, *kippeen* and shillelagh banging and clashing, and with that much shouting from all the pookas and leprechauns, the din could be heard from Dunqueen in the west of Kerry to Cashel. They stopped only twice; for a bit of mountain dew, to take a few bows, then another thrifle of mountain dew, and then back to fighting again.

Very good. But all that fighting and banging and yelling was most displeasing to the Creator, who was at that very time trying to take a little nap. "I'll put a sthop to those ructions," he said. And he did, indade. In fact, all Three of Him did.

So it was that the Creator sprinkled the stardust of forgetfulness on both the pookas and the leprechauns so that their bad habits would be banished...well, some of them. And with that stardust, the Creator gave to all Irishmen the gift of imagination to compensate them for what they are not, and a sense of humor to console them for what they are.

Now, whether you believe my little folk tale or not—and I give you my assurance that every single word is true—from that day to this, the imaginative humor of the Irish people has been a factor in human experience everywhere in the civilized world and Great Britain. Unfortunately—and heartbreaking it is, too—the pookas of the north and the leprechauns of the south are again at each other. But the fact remains that the funny story you just heard on television may have stemmed from an episode in Irish mythology or may well have originated in the sixth century when Saint Patrick, among his other gifts, brought a new dimension to Irish folkways: that of finding a hurt and healing it through laughter.

Perhaps it was the anger and humiliation of a proud people who were forced to suffer a foreign power on their soil, or the famines and general poverty throughout the land, or the unvarnished severity of everyday existence that brought into Irish literature that sense of comedy which is one of its marked characteristics. Almost everywhere in Irish prose and poetry, there twinkles and peers the merry eye and laugh of a people who had little to laugh about in real life. Swift's humor is savage, Synge's is tragic, Stephen's impish, Wilde's sophisticated, Shaw's trenchant, and Lover has the schoolboy touch. But they all share the common characteristic of using humor to illustrate a point.

The only offset to unhappiness is happiness, so it was undoubtedly some divine law of compensation that gave to the Irish the ability to squeeze laughter out of an existence from which they could extract little else. The people they wrote about lived in a state of dire want, preoccupied with food, a roof over their heads, and concerned with the elementals of making ends meet. Of course, there were many people who got along comfortably in the Ireland of yesteryear. But there were enough of the less fortunate kind so that no writer, humorous or not, could remain unaffected by their straits. The tragedies of Irish writings were more likely to be those of starvation, or death itself, than those of the divorce court.

Despite the near absence of obscenity (or perhaps because of it), true Irish humor, in some of its aspects, is second to the wit and humor of no nation on earth. Judging it by its average specimens, it manages to convey an idea fully. But, in its haste to express itself, the metaphors get mixed and the thoughts transposed or reversed. This is especially true of those' uniquely Irish products, the bull and the limerick, both of which are discussed in the introductions to their respective chapters.

The thoughts which give rise to Irish mirth may be compared to a crowd all trying to get out of a doorway at the same time, the result being chaos, and sometimes a spill. This is not because of a poverty of thought, but from a wealth of ideas which the warm nature of the Irishman is unable or unwilling to control, so eager is he to share his thoughts with another. But when he is serious, when his impulse to share his thoughts is held in control, the Irish writer has displayed a talent for creativé output that once made Dublin the center of the literary world—and, indeed, shows healthy signs of doing so again. He is well aware that, for sheer playfulness, for satirical keenness, for gracefulness, and for red-hot scornfulness, few things are more effective than his own wit and humor. Even when an Irish joke, told by a rustic, initially appears to be inane, we later realize that it cloaked a native shrewdness whose only fault was that the storyteller was untrained, and therefore the joke was unpolished; or that the teller was in too great a hurry to speak—his ideas all trying to get out of the doorway at the same time.

The legend of the pookas and the leprechauns indicates that the humor of Ireland is more imaginative than that of most other countries. And it is probably more good-natured as well, although the Irish do have a special aptness in the saying of things that wound. The most illiterate of Irish farmers can put more scorn into a comment than some of the most highly educated of other nationalities. I am reminded of an old farmer of Galway who described the timid assault by a British platoon against a *Sinn Fein* stronghold: "They were halted by a sign that ordered KEEP OFF THE GRASS." There seems to be a half-pathetic strain in the best Irish humor writers. Just as in their saddest moments the people are inclined to joke, so it is that in many of their writings where pathos predominates, the touch of humor is easily recognizable in all its buoyancy and expression of heart.

Naturally enough, the chief themes of the Irish humorists have been courting and drinking, with the occasional relief of a fight. The amativeness (not to be confused with sexuality) of the poets, who have supplied much, if not most, of classic Irish humor, is little short of marvelous. Men, like the aptly-named Lover (who has seldom been surpassed as a humorous love-poet), usually confined their humor to that sphere; others, like Maginn, kept to the tradition that liquor is the main attraction in life.

There can be no question, it seems to me, of Ireland's supremacy in the humorous literature devoted to drinking, prior to that nation's independence from England. Still, all the Irish bards were not as fierce as Maginn in their likes and dislikes when liquor was on the table. It may, in fact, justifiably be said of them that their enthusiasm for the flowing cup was more often mere boastfulness. It is difficult to believe Tom Moore in his raptures about the joys of the bowl. He was no roisterer, and his Bacchanalian effusions lack that reckless abandon of the more bibulous school.

A glance at the lives of the Irish poets and humorists—often one and the same—shows that the Irish inclination to wit was indeed stimulated by drinking long and deep of *poteen*—the Irish equivalent of America's "white lightning." According to humorist Patrick Ireland, *poteen* may also be described as the *magnum cum laude* of "mountain dew," as unlike the American hillbilly concoction as champagne is to Appalachian joy juice. *"Poteen,"* avers Mr. Ireland, "is comprised of fifty per cent shillelagh splinters, forty per cent broken knuckles, nine per cent crushed blarney stone, and one per cent remorse. For centuries, it has been the favorite drink of Irish heroes. Only an Irish hero would venture to drink it."

To return to their love of hard liquor, the Irish poet-humorists were often pictured as very gloomy, gnawed by care, and tortured by remorse. But the opposite seems to be true. The writer did not, as a rule, extract a pessimistic philosophy from tippling; he was "elevated," not depressed, and did not deem it essential to the production of a humorous piece that its author be a prophet of gloom. He considered himself a follower of Bacchus, a convenient deity invented by the early Celts as an excuse for getting drunk. As of the present writing, the Roman Catholic Church in Ireland has not yet granted formal recognition to Bacchus.

One of the best attributes of Irish humor is its constant expression of the natural emotions. Prior to the close of the seventeenth century, it is said, drunkenness was seldom if ever suggested as being common by the poet-humorists in Ireland. But the popularity of drinking songs since that date seems to prove that the vice eventually became a virtue. Maginn, in the nineteenth century, was the noisiest of his contemporary revelers, and easily roared the others down. Real drollery in Anglo-Irish literature, however, seems to have begun with Steele, founder of *The Tattler* and *Spectator*. Steele was rarely offensive; his tenderness, in fact, akin to Oliver Goldsmith's. A direct contrast is seen in Sterne, who could often be malicious and sly, full of *doubles-entendres,* and dependent upon the morbid tastes of his readers. But the paradox lies not in the fact that this dour, unlikable man could be hilariously funny on occasions, but in the knowledge that he was a teetotaler, while the sweet-tempered and eminently likable Steele and Goldsmith were heavy drinkers. Perhaps the god of *poteen* is trying to tell us something.

The treatment of sacred subjects by Irish wits differs from that of most Catholic countries. Saint Patrick is hardly regarded as a conventional saint by Irish humorists, and it is curious that even Saint Peter is accepted as a legitimate object of pleasantry. If, however, Irish humorists occasionally seem to lack reverence for things that are holy in their eyes, "it is only for fun," as Charles Lamb suggested. Only those who are in the closest intimacy with objects venture to treat them familiarly, and the Irish find it easy to joke, without disrespect, of that which is dearest to them. However, only an Irish-*American* could ever have conceived the idea of Saint Patrick as an editor of *Prayboy* magazine.

Many of the contributors who speak in these pages were poets as well as writers, playwrights, and humorists, which is reason enough why one cannot imagine an anthology of Irish humor without its rhymers. Included in this volume are such notables as W. B. Yeats, George Moore, J. M. Synge, Oliver St. John Gogarty, and A.E. (George Russell). And here, too, you will meet Sean O'Faolain, Frank O'Connor, and Patrick Kavanagh.

But the main body of Irish humor is represented by the old masters of the eighteenth and nineteenth centuries: Lover, Lever, Maginn, Luttrell, Fahy, Goldsmith, Sheridan, Curran, Boyle, and many others who made Ireland, and then the world, laugh through their scintillating and very funny lines.

The Biographical Index of Authors at the end of this book gives a brief sketch of the lives of these illustrious contributors. Some of the post-Yeats writers, however, who are better known to American readers, have not been included in the necessarily abridged Index; their biographical references may be found in most modern encyclopedias.

But what of the Irish-*American* joke? Can a "Pat and Mike" story be considered "Irish" because of the names used? Hardly! Technically, an Irish joke is one that is ordinarily told by one Irishman to another, and which revolves around a theme usually associated with Ireland or the Irish people. Granted, that definition is restrictive. But, thanks to one Joe Miller and the "Americanization" of Irish humor, much of what might once have been considered authentically Irish has been so diluted that it is now scarcely recognizable. The result is about the same as if someone had watered good Irish whiskey, weakening its potency, smothering its bouquet, and destroying its original flavor. In one instance, Pat and Mike, a couple of undertakers, decide to raise their burial price because of the increased cost of living. It isn't a bad joke, but it will never set the world afire. And it cannot be considered "Irish" because it was first told as a Scottish story, and divil the likes iv Pat and Mike iver enthered into it.

The avalanche of pseudo-Irish jokes in the United States may be ascribed to the aforementioned Joe Miller, a comedian whose name was used to promote a "jestbook" assembled from earlier humorous works by a hack writer, John Motley. First published in 1739, it was titled *Joe Miller's Jests: or The Wit's Vade-Mecum.* With a title like that, one would think the book destined for eternal anonymity. Not so. The book went into edition after edition, until the original 247 jokes grew to more than 1,500. It was said that during the eighteenth and nineteenth centuries, *Joe Miller's Jests* had more readers than Chaucer, Milton, and *Pilgrim's Progress* combined. Of course, if you have ever labored through those works, you will be hard put to blame your great grandparents too much. It is easier, and certainly more pleasant, to remember a book about Diamond Jim Brady who preferred to die with his boots on, so he wouldn't stub his toe when he kicked the bucket.

Many of the original anecdotes and quips in the first edition of *Joe Miller's Jests* were based on Irish tales, and rewritten (very poorly) for non-Irish readers. Gone were the graceful phrasings, the truly clever wit, the imaginative humor of the Irish creators. Later editions carried a few pseudo-Irish words, and, by the end of the 1840s, the book was replete with "greenhorn" stories, describing the Irish immigrants to American shores. The term "greenhorn," later used to describe the immigrants of other nationalities, originally referred to those Irish men and women who sailed to America's Pacific Coast from the Emerald Isle. Having rounded the Horn at the southernmost tip of Latin America (the Panama Canal had not yet been built), the sobriquet, "greenhorn," came into being.

In the corrupted humor of the day, the "greenhorns" were almost invariably named Pat and Mike: ignoramuses whose "brogue" was so farfetched and ridiculous as to make the so-called Paddy jokes downright insulting. As a rule, their shenanigans would bring them before a stern judge who accepted only two pleas: "Guilty" and "Guilty, Your Honor." By the 1870s, the jokes had lost whatever iota of genuine Irish humor they might ever have possessed. The terms "Paddy" and "paddy wagon" stem from the Irish name Patrick, or its Gaelic form, Padraic. (See *Paddy* and *paddy wagon* in the Glossary of this book.)

The ambitious, hard-working immigrants did not remain "greenhorns" for long. They were soon represented in nearly all fields of industry and service. The Irish lassies quickly graduated from "domestic service" as maids and cooks, eventually becoming Women's Liberation enthusiasts, going so far as to post a sign in a Senate Office Building washroom: THIS MEN'S ROOM DISCRIMINATES AGAINST WOMEN! Many of the menfolk found jobs as police officers, firemen, and mail carriers, after attending Delehanty's Civil Service School, or voting as suggested by the local ward boss—usually another Irishman. Politics was a popular occupation, since schooling was neither necessary nor desirable. A few became motormen in New York's subway system.

The motorman! Now *there* was a fine broth of a lad! Nearly all of them were Irish at the turn of the present century. Until they became accustomed to their jobs, New York became the only city in the world where the passengers had to take the I.R.T. to get to the B.M.T. The Lexington Avenue Express could often be observed making all the local stops on the Eighth Avenue tracks. The Broadway trains rumbled happily along the Third Avenue Elevated, or the "El," as it was popularly called. It wasn't until many years later, when the former motormen were finally running the entire transportation system in New York, that they finally acceded to the demands of the people and got the El out of there.

Before concluding this Preface, we must ask, "What is an Irishman?" The obvious answer is that he (or she) is a human being like anyone else. But Irish humorists see themselves in another light. "An Irishman," declares Patrick Ireland, "is a native of Ireland, or an American facsimile thereof, who is composed of two parts—a front and a back. The front part is used mainly for talking, fighting and drinking. The back part is that area it is your privilege to contemplate when proclaiming the virtues of busing or abortion." Sports columnist and outstanding humorist Jim Murray, in chapter one, *Blarney—Oh Thou Irish Baloney!* offers one of the most delightfully funny descriptions of an Irishman to appear in print.

The Irish-American bride does not escape the attention of the humorist. She serves corned beef and cabbage to her new hubby, we are told, not because it is especially nutritious, but because she read somewhere that this is the staple of proper Irish cuisine. It is a belief that comes as a surprise to the residents of the Emerald Isle, who apparently are not as Irish as the Irish in America. The citizen of Ireland is well aware of the advantages of corned beef. It needs no refrigeration, for one thing. Whatever may be expected to happen to unrefrigerated corned beef has already happened to it. As to cabbage, the only time a true Irish housewife cooks it is when she is determined to annoy her neighbors who keep their windows open. How-

10

ever, cabbages do grow to a good size in Ireland: about as large and wise as a congressman's head.

Aah! The time has come for us to heave a grateful sigh of relief: the best part of this Preface is at hand—the end! Having maintained my sobriety until these last few pages of writing, and being in lubricated voice, I would like to entertain you with a rendition of "Too-ra-loo-ra-loo-ral: It's an Irish Lullaby." But there is an ancient Gaelic proverb whose translation warns, "Melodious is the closed mouth." So, instead, I leave you with one of the loveliest of the old Irish blessings:

> May the road rise to meet you.
> May the wind be always at your back.
> May the sun shine warm
> upon your face,
> the rains fall soft
> upon your fields
> and
> May God hold you in the palm of His hand.

Now, let us raise the curtain on the grandest theater of all—Irish laughter.

And a cheery top o' the mornin' to ye!

HENRY D. SPALDING

January 15, 1978
Northridge, California

Chapter One

Blarney—Oh, Thou Irish Baloney!

Introduction

*"Baloney is flattery so thick it
cannot be true; blarney is flattery
so thin we like it."*

—Monsignor Fulton J. Sheen (1895-)

Paradoxical though it may seem, the verbal skill known as blarney was born of illiteracy and subjugation. To understand the first of these causes, we must remember that, for hundreds of years, almost until the establishment of the Republic of Ireland, formal education was suppressed by the British interlopers, and schools were very few. As a consequence, much of the Irish population could neither read nor write. It was in such an atmosphere that the oral arts of poetry, oratory, and storytelling took root and flourished.

The other factor that contributed to the development of the Irish gift for words can be attributed to the injustices heaped upon them by the British courts that were maintained throughout Ireland. Many of the infamous judges were ignorant, corrupt, and brutal men. The sentences they meted out were incredibly harsh, and virtually no Irishmen brought before them were ever found innocent. During one term of a judicial circuit in rural Ireland, the British judge heard one hundred criminal cases, found ninety-eight defendants guilty, and ninety-seven were summarily hanged![1]

In order to cope with the hostile legal machinery that had been forced upon them, another Irish national type came into being—the politician skilled in law, best-personified by Daniel O'Connell, Ireland's greatest man of the early nineteenth century. These lawyers-turned-politicians were the vanguard of those who developed the Irish genius for storytelling into a hybrid form of communication that employed the art of soft deception—blarney.[2]

The original purpose of blarney was to preserve the fiction of compliance while maintaining one's own ideas of justice. To speak out directly against the system imposed by the British was a dangerous activity. The alternatives, then, were either discreet silence or skilled speech. But silence, discreet

---

[1]Casey McDougal, *For the Wearing of the Green* (Dublin, Donohugh & Sons, 1931).
[2]Sean O'Faolain, *King of the Beggars: A Life of Daniel O'Connell* (Viking Press, New York, 1938), pp. 98-99.

11

or otherwise, has never been numbered among the Irish virtues, so they cultivated what Sean O'Faolain called "that so typically Kerry-ish form of silence, an affluence of volubility."[3] Thus, "soft deception," cloaked in elaborate evasiveness, became one of the main features of that unique phenomenon called Irish blarney.

The word "blarney" stems from a sixteenth-century incident when Queen Elizabeth attempted to wrest the castle which rightfully belonged to Cormac Carthy, the Lord of Blarney. It was Elizabeth's quaint notion that Carthy would agree to renounce his ancestral claim to his land by accepting the proposition that he would henceforth hold title at the pleasure of the Crown. The title, of course, could be canceled any time at the Queen's pleasure. Cormac Carthy recognized the futility of outright refusal. He pretended to agree to Elizabeth's demands, but repeatedly postponed its fulfillment "with fair words and soft speech," until she exploded in outrage, "This is all Blarney! What he means he never says; what he says he never means!"[4]

From that incident sprang the tradition that whoever kisses the stone at Blarney Castle will be blessed with the gift of eloquence. One unsung bard expressed it this way:

> The stone this is
> Whoever kisses,
> He never misses
> To grow eloquent.
> 'Tis he may clamber
> To my lady's chamber,
> Or be a member
> Of Parliament.

Most dictionaries define blarney as "flattering or wheedling talk; cajolery"—a simple definition that hardly begins to do justice to that noble word, as any Irishman will attest. The only universally accepted rule is that blarneying must be done with a straight face, because:[5]

> He must not laugh at his own wheeze;
> A snuff box has no right to sneeze.

Blarney, for example, may be used to ingratiate one's self into a lady's good graces: "Please don't think of me as a witty, wealthy, handsome, sensitive, intelligent man. Try to think of me as just another guy."

Another form of blarney is the glib, spontaneous retort, but only when it is witty, and whatever malice it may contain is more or less hidden. To illustrate: A proud father boasts, "That boy of mine just graduated with straight A's." The boy's uncle retorts, "I believe you. It goes to prove that heredity has nothing to do with a kid's intelligence!"

---

[3]*Ibid.*, p.41.
[4]William Carleton, *Traits and Stories of the Irish People.*
[5]An anonymous poem, quoted in John Gibson Lockhart's *Life of Sir Walter Scott.*

What happens when *two* experts in the art of blarney confront each other? A classic example occurred one day when a clerk in the Irish Legation in New York slipped this note under the windshield wiper on his car: "I realize my car is too close to the fire hydrant, but I have circled the block ten times, and if I don't park here I'll be late for work and lose my job. Forgive us our trespasses."

When he returned to his car that evening, he found a parking ticket under the wiper, together with a note from the Irish cop on the beat:

"I have circled the block for ten *years,* and if I don't give you a ticket I'll lose *my* job. Lead us not into temptation."

We have seen, now, that the gift of eloquence, whether in its long form or in its brief and terse nature, or even when it is expressed in poetry, may still fall within the area of blarney. But there is yet another category—a combination of blarney and malarkey, and probably the most enjoyable. Assuredly, its telling requires the most skill. Malarkey is an English-Irish word meaning "to obscure, mislead, or impress." In short, "bunkum." That, at least, is the technical definition. Informally, however, it has also come to mean exaggerated truth—not quite an outright falsehood, but not something you would take your oath on, either. It is hyperbole scented with wit. For want of a better descriptive work, this fusion of blarney and malarkey may be termed "blarkey." John F. Kennedy was among the foremost exponents of the short form. Here is an example containing all the truth the traffic will bear:

In 1952, John F. Kennedy ran for the Massachusetts Senate seat against Republican Henry Cabot Lodge. During the course of his successful campaign, the future president enjoyed telling the story of Mrs. O'Hurley, a sweet little old lady whose husband had recently passed away. The city bureaucrats had refused to accept her explanation as to the cause of her late husband's death, and she was unable to collect a pension. So she went to the ward leader in her district with her problem.

"They kape askin' what me owld man died of," she complained.

"That's a perfectly normal question," observed the ward leader. "What did you tell them?"

"Sure an' I towld thim over an' over agin—he died of a Monday!"

There are still shorter forms of blarkey than enjoyed by Kennedy; among them such snide but sunny snappers as, "The louder he spoke of his honesty, the faster we counted the spoons." The undisputed master of the long form of blarkey, however, must be Jim Murray, sports columnist for the *Los Angeles Times,* who employs the technique daily in his reportage. Murray has been voted "Sportswriter of the Year" for three consecutive years (as of 1977), and the indications are that his colleagues in the National Sportswriters and Sportscasters Association will continue to bestow the title upon him in the years to come. In 1976, the Masquers Club of Hollywood named him the "Irish Man of the Year." Murray's reaction, published in the *Times,* is a masterpiece of blarkey, and serves as the first selection in this chapter.

In the final analysis, it makes little difference whether the Irish gift of soft deception is expressed in the long or short form; whether it is used to make a point in law, as a glib comment to gain a lady's favor, or any other of the multiple uses that the witty Irish mind can and does conceive—it is still covered by that marvelous umbrella word: blarney!

—H.D.S.

"Away with yer blarney, Mike," she said,
"Go tell it to Mother Machree,
To Nancy or Kate Clancey—
To annywan ilse, Mike, but me!"

—Patrick Ireland (1915-   )

"Irish Man of the Year"[6]

It will come as a great surprise to all of you—to say nothing of Saint Patrick, I am sure—but tomorrow night, on the natal day of all Irishmen, I am to be honored by the Masquers Club of Hollywood as (get this!) "Irish Man of the Year."

I can understand their admiration. Being Irish and not making a muck of things by my age calls for a testimonial of some kind, an achievement kind of like overcoming a clubfoot.

It grieves me they had to settle for a mere sportswriter, but that's what's happened to the ancestral land of poets, saints and scholars. They've all become harbor commissioners. You see, you usually have to get an Irish author young. Before he dies of the drink, that is. If an Irishman says he's a writer, give him a sobriety test. If he flunks, he's a writer.

They'll be needing to know a few things about the Irish if they want to keep from making fools of themselves. An Irishman is a guy who:

—May not be sure there's a God, but is damn sure of the infallibility of the Pope.

—Won't eat meat on Friday, but will drink gin for breakfast.

—Believes everything he can't see, and nothing he can.

—To paraphrase Cleveland Amory, is someone who's very good at weekends, but not very good in the middle of the week.

—Is against abortion, but in favor of hanging (or vice versa).

—Has such great respect for the truth, he only uses it in emergencies.

—Is irrational in important things but a tower of strength in the trivial.

—Get married for life, but not necessarily for love.

—Can argue either side of a question, often at the same time.

—Sees things not as they are, but as they never will be.

---

[6]Jim Murray, *Los Angeles Times,* Copyright, 1976. Reprinted with permission.

—Believes in leprechauns and banshees and considers anyone who doesn't to be a heathen.

—Can lick any man in the house he is sole occupant of.

—Cries at sad movies, but cheers in battle.

—Considers funerals a festivity, but weddings sad events to be put off as long as possible, preferably forever.

—Says he hates the English, but reserves his greatest cruelty for his countrymen.

—Is not afraid of dying—in fact, he might prefer it.

—Gets more Irish the farther he gets from Ireland.

—Believes that God is Irish, or, at least, Catholic.

—Believes in civil rights, but not in his neighborhood.

—Is against corruption, unless it's a Democrat.

—Takes the pledge not to drink at the age of twelve—and every four years thereafter.

—Believes that to forgive is divine—therefore, doesn't exercise it himself.

—Believes salvation can be achieved by means of a weekly envelope.

—Considers anyone who won't come around to his point of view to be hopelessly stubborn.

—Loves religion for its own sake, but also because it makes it so damnably inconvenient for his neighbors.

—Considers a bore to be someone who keeps constantly interrupting.

—Scorns money, but worships those who have it.

—Considers any Irishman who achieves success to be a traitor.

Well, you can see we are a very perverse, complex people. It's what makes us lovable. We're banking heavily that God has a sense of humor.

I, myself, have much of the good humor of the Irish, but fortunately few of their faults, or, as my grandfather preferred to call them, "inconsistencies," and I know the Masquers will want to know that I was (a) a fine altar boy who never watered the wine like Mick Kingsley to cover up his samplings; (b) winner of the Latin medal in grade school over a field of three others; (c) the best speller in my class on the boys' side and the 73rd overall; (d) a good citizen who always cooperated with the police whenever we got caught sneaking into the Rivoli Theater, because I wanted to save my companions from a life of crime, and not, as they suggested, myself from a whipping; (e) a Boy Scout who would have made Eagle Scout except I flunked helping old ladies across the street, and whenever I rubbed two sticks together I got sawdust.

And you ask, how are things in Glocca Morra?!

—Jim Murray (1919-   )

*

New enrollments are now being accepted at Leary's College of Blarney. The freshman course revolves around the subtle art of getting acquainted with "aloof, hard-to-meet females of the opposite sex." Introductory samples of the art are as follows:

—"Yes, miss, I know we haven't met before. I could never be this lucky twice in one lifetime."

—"I quite agree, lovely lady. No respectable daughter of Erin should talk to strangers. Allow me to introduce myself."

—I'm positive I've seen you before—perhaps on television. Weren't you Miss America last year?"

—"I'm going to be perfectly frank with you, miss. A lovely girl like you deserves only the very best—me!"

—"I wanted to talk to you many times before, you gorgeous creature, but my doctor advised me to watch my blood pressure."

—"As beautiful as you are, miss, you really shouldn't be out all alone on a dark night like this. Let me go with you, so if you're attacked I'll be right there to make a citizen's arrest."

—"I could just stare at your pretty face for hours, *macushla*. Let's go to my apartment where the light is better."

*

"The most outrageous blarney I ever heard was foisted on me last summer," averred John Peter Toohey, the man who gave *The New Yorker* magazine its name. "I was approached by a panhandler outside our office building who asked me for thirty cents for a cup of coffee.

" 'Thirty cents!" I protested. 'A cup of coffee is only fifteen cents!'

"The panhandler had the audacity to look surprised. 'Oh,' he replied glibly in a Kilkenny brogue, 'won't ye be afther joinin' me?' "

*

At the turn of the century, theatrical producer Samuel Foote was known to be generous to his actors and much liked by them. In fact, he was much more considerate and businesslike than some of his habits would lead one to suppose.

An actress named Judith O'Neal once complained to him of the low salary she received from Garrick, another famous producer of the day at Drury Lane.

"Why did you go to Garrick?" asked Foote. "You must have known you would get a better salary at the Haymarket."

"I don't know what I could have been thinking," replied Judith, almost weeping. "Oh, that man and his blarney! He talked me over by telling me he would make me immortal."

"Did he indeed?" retorted Foote. "Well, then, I suppose I must outbid him. Come to me when you are free and I'll pay you two pounds a week more. And I'll charge you nothing for the immortality!"

*

'Tis the divil's own work when a wee lad cannot indulge in a bit o' blarney of his own, when the motivation is strong upon him. Let this little missive warm the spirit within you:

Dear Grandpa,
I hope that when I grow up I will be as smart and handsome and nice as you.
Your loving grandson,
Willie.
P.S. Friday is my birthday.

*

In Massachusetts, the Lowell Hibernian Society decided to honor their oldest member, ninety-nine-year-old McGuiness, with a banquet.

Numerous toasts were made to the guest of honor, and when his fellow Irishmen eased up a bit, a young man of twenty or so approached him.

"Mr. McGuiness," he said warmly, "I only hope that I can be here next year to toast your hundredth birthday."

"Sure, an' there's no rason a'tall why ye can't," replied McGuiness airily. "A foine broth iv a young bucko like you should make it, aisy!"

*

Trying to score with a sensitive young lady can be a trying experience, even when you suspect that her mind is in the bedroom and you are intent on getting the rest of her there. Her delicate sensitivity must be respected, especially when she has been on the receiving end of blarney from the experts. According to *McNulty's Manual of Strategic Romance,* the cautious approach is the best; *i.e.,* "I know just how you feel, Miss O'Gilvie. I'm tired of being considered a sex object myself."

*

This story had its birth in September, 1949, and has been doing yeoman service ever since. It should. It's a classic.

An aspiring young writer named Terence O'Toole brought his new brainchild to Arthur Dunne, the off-Broadway producer, a man widely known for accepting only logical plays. Terence, convinced that his was the most logical play ever written, began to extol its virtues.

"This is the greatest play you ever heard," he said modestly, opening to the first page of his manuscript. "It'll be greater than *Gone With the Wind.* And every scene is absolutely logical—just the way you like it."

"You don't have to read all of it," interrupted the trapped producer, clearly alarmed. "Just tell me about it...as briefly as you can."

"Well," began Terence, "it starts out in a stately, hundred-year-old mansion in Ireland, long before the potato famine, when the British had not yet destroyed the old Irish aristocracy, see. Suddenly a British officer breaks down the front door, see; and inside is this beautiful lassie, see; but is she terrified; No, not a'tall! She jumps behind the harpsichord, see, and then up she comes with a big saw in her hand."

A blistering look of disgust spread across the producer's face. "Tell me," he snapped, his sense of logic outraged, "how the hell did a saw get behind the harpsichord?"

But Terence O'Toole was prepared.

"The carpenter left it there when he finished building that old mansion!"

*

Overheard at O'Banion's Beer Emporium:
"Pardon me, darlin', but I'm writin' a telephone book. C'n I have yer number?"

*

Let the bells peal the glad tidings—Bar Harbor is checking in with one! A seedy-looking character sidled up to Grace Cudihy of *the* Cudihy family! After a quick appraisal of her furs and diamonds, he asked, "Lady, could you spare four thousand seven hundred dollars and thirty cents for a new Chevvie?"

"What!" snapped Mrs. Cudihy indignantly. "Why, I never heard anything so outrageous!"

"Yeah, you're right, lady," agreed the moocher. "That's exactly what I told the car dealer."

*

Tom McCauley, one of the "Fightin' Irish" who made up the famous Forty-second (Rainbow) Division in World War I, was one of three others in his platoon to receive the Medal of Honor for outstanding heroism in capturing several hundred Germans. The division commander held a party for his men that Saturday night, and the prettiest girls in the nearby town were invited. Of them all, the loveliest was a French ma'mselle named Yvette.

"Oh," she cooed to the first of the medal winners, "an' 'ow many Jarmaines you capture?"

"Sixteen," replied the soldier.

"An' wiz wheech 'and you 'old ze gun?"

"Why, I held it in my right hand."

Yvette promptly took his right hand and kissed it. Then she turned to the second soldier.

" 'Ow many Jarmaines you catch?"

"Eighteen," responded the soldier.

"Wheech 'and you use to 'old ze gun?"

"My left."

Yvette grasped his left hand and lifted it to her pretty lips. Now she turned to Private Tom McCauley.

"An' 'ow many Jarmaines *you* capture, *mon cher*?"

"Twinty-wan," said Tom.

"An' wheech 'and you 'old ze gun?"

"Nayther," said Tom, puckering his lips, "I bit 'em into surrenderin'!"

*

For a whole year after her boyfriend had sailed away to Vietnam, Maureen had not heard a single word from him. Now, at last, the postman finally delivered the first letter from her love, written from "Somewhere in the South Pacific area."

Hastily, Maureen tore open the envelope, but inside, instead of the expected letter, she found a thin strip of paper bearing a brief message:

"Your boyfriend still loves you, but he talks too much."

(signed) J. L. Smith, Censor.

*

The *Hibernian Clarion* of Donegal carried this gem in its Lost and Found column:

> *Bird or Hat*—Flew in or blew in out of car passing Coniff's Petrol Station, Roscommon Street. It's sorta round and pointy on top, with pink and yellow polka dots, and with feathers or something in it. Whether or not you lost this hat or bird, drive by and see it—it's funny.

*

Father Gerald Phelan, head of the Pontifical Institute of the University of Toronto, was in his office one day when a young country boy entered, his hat held diffidently in his hand. "Father," he began, his voice hesitant, "may I ask a question?"

"Of course, my son. What is it?"

"Well, sir, can I lead a good Christian life in Toronto on twenty-five dollars a week?"

"My boy," replied Father Phelan, "on twenty-five dollars a week, that's *all* you can do!"

*

In Boston, during the 1920's, there was a popular singer named Arthur O'Dwyer who billed himself as "O'Dwyer, Singer of Sweet Ballads." But the truth is that his billing was far more impressive than his vocal talents.

It so happened that the renowned Irish tenor, John Charles Thomas, was giving a concert in Boston when he chanced to hear O'Dwyer's uninspired rendition of "'Mollie Malone." Mr. Thomas, infuriated at this assault upon his sensibilities, immediately went backstage after O'Dwyer had finished his act and confronted him in his dressing room.

"Do you call that singing?" he stormed. "Here. This is the way 'Mollie Malone' should sound." His melodious voice rang out, demonstrating in just two or three bars all the beauty of the song. Two minutes later, he stalked out of the room just as abruptly as he had entered.

The next day, the Boston vocalist changed his billing to: "O'Dwyer—Pupil of John Charles Thomas."

*

This one is old—good and old!

General Sheridan was having an afternoon brandy with a fellow Union officer named O'Brien, when an interesting question was posed.

"Did you ever stop to think how a person's name indicates his nationality?" asked O'Brien.

"No, not really," said Sheridan. "Does it?"

"Certainly. Take the Italians, for example. Their names usually end with an *i* or an *o*."

"You mean," grinned Sheridan, "such names as Levi and Shapiro?"

The officer joined in the laughter. "Very well, take yourself, for a better illustration. You are a member of an illustrious Irish family. Don't you think it strange that your name has no *o* as a prefix?"

"Yes, Mr. O'Brien, it is strange indeed," blarneyed Sheridan, "considering that no family has a better right to it. We *owe* everybody!"

*

The late Frank Coniff had been up all night, struggling over a new musical arrangement for his orchestra. As dawn broke, still sleepless and with his arrangement not yet completed, he decided to go out for breakfast. Hollow-eyed, in a gloomy and depressed state, he entered Maggie's Shamrock Restaurant on Eighth Street and Ninth Avenue. Maggie hurried over to serve her old friend.

"Maggie, all I want is some scrambled eggs and a few kind words," he said, gazing up at her with his melancholy eyes.

"Sure, Frank," she blarneyed cheerily. "I'll bring the eggs in a minute, and my kind words are—don't eat 'em!"

*

John L. Sullivan, the famed pugilist of a bygone day, sported a broken nose, which he acquired, of course, during his usual business hours. He was scarcely aware of its misshapen appearance, until one day, when an elderly lady whom he had just met brought the matter to his attention.

"Sure, an' you're a marvelous prizefighter," she said with the kind of candor old ladies are entitled to express, "but I can't get over that nose o' yours."

"There's no wonder to it a'tall—I can't get over it meself," he laughed. "The bridge is gone!"

*

The glib rejoinder is an essential part of blarney, especially when it is used to conceal inner resentment. An example is offered in the brief anecdote about the worried patient and the witty physician.

"Doctor Delaney," asked the patient, "is it absolutely sure ye are that I'm sufferin' from terminal dandruff?"

"That's my diagnosis."

"Faith, it's sorry I am to hear the bad news, Doc, but to tell the truth, I'd like to have another medical opinion, beggin' yer pardon."

"I don't mind at all, my boy!" boomed the good doctor. "Come back again tomorrow and I'll take another stab at it!"

*

As they were leaving the theater after witnessing one of Hollywood's super colossal premieres, Pat O'Brien met James Cagney in the lobby.

"What did you think of that picture?" O'Brien asked his friend and fellow film star.

"To tell the truth," averred Cagney in his usual emphatic tones, "I thought it stank!"

"I can't say I liked it that well," said O'Brien shortly.

*

When Pat Rooney, Sr., the tap-dancing entertainer of several decades ago, reached his ninetieth birthday, he invited a few old friends to his home for a quiet celebration. One of the guests brought his granddaughter, a lovely young lady with a figure that dreams are made of.

"Oh," sighed Pat, after a quick appraisal of the girl's manifest charms, "what I wouldn't give to be thirty again—or even seventy!"

*

True or not, it's a good story. One rainy afternoon, Orson Welles arrived in Ireland, where he was scheduled to lecture at Dublin University Hall. But, because of the inclement weather, the audience was almost non-existent. Glancing around at the empty seats and noting the small attendance, he proceeded to open his remarks with a brief sketch of his career:

"I'm an actor of the stage and motion pictures. I'm a director of plays and a producer of plays. I'm a writer and producer of motion pictures. I write, direct, and act in radio and for television. I'm a magician and painter. I've published books. I play the violin and piano."

At this point, Welles paused and surveyed his tiny audience.

"Isn't it a pity," he concluded, "there's so many of me and so few of you!"

*

A little Irish impudence can sometimes go a long way, as this little anecdote illustrates.

Some years ago, an ambitious youth, who aspired to become a writer, sent his first manuscript to F. Scott Fitzgerald, asking the distinguished author and playwright to become his collaborator. Fitzgerald, to put it mildly, was astounded at the impertinence. Angrily, he seized his pen and wrote: "How dare you, sir, yoke together a noble horse and a contemptible ass?"

He received a reply by return mail:

"How dare *you*, sir, call me a horse?"

*

Bear stories were the stock in trade of the old-time Alaskan sourdough— and when he happened to be a transplanted son of Erin, his added blarney produced some tall tales. Hark:

Old Red Mulvaney, lately of the Emerald Isle, was down at the general store, where he was swapping stories around the warm stove.

"I recollec' the time I come face-to-face with a giant Kodiac bear. He was a monsther if iver there was wan. That bear was all iv two tons an' tin feet long. Well, he just riz up an' came at me. Then me rifle jammed, an', faith, I headed fer th' nearest tree, but it had only wan limb, an' that was thurrty feet off the ground. I got to that tree not more'n a foot ahead of the bear an', bejabbers, he took a swat at me just as I was gatherin' meself for the leap. The spalpeen tore me britches but didn't quite get me."

Mulvaney paused for a moment to lend a little more drama to his tale.

"Well, that bear scairt me so bad I missed that wan an' ownly limb...."

"What happened, ye ask?

"I caught it on me way down!"

*

A red-headed, freckled-face beggar was at his accustomed place in front of City Hall one morning when a prosperous-looking gentleman got out of his Lincoln Continental and passed by, on his way to his office.

"May the graa-a-cious mother iv th' gintle Jazus pour her blessin's on ye," the beggar called out. "May the graa-a-cious mother follow ye foriver, bringin' ye all manner iv good luck."

The affluent gentleman continued his purposeful stride without so much as turning his head.

Glaring malevolently, the beggar yelled after him:
"And may the graa-a-cious mother niver catch up with ye!"

*

Sign on the back of one of McGuire's Hauling Company trucks in Boston:

THESE LETTERS SEEM
TO BE GETTING LARGER
BECAUSE I'M BACKING UP!

*

Harrigan had just returned from a vacation in the old country, and he was now besieged with questions about the Emerald Isle. But, as the incessant queries went on and on, the usually patient traveler grew irritated—especially with some of the more inane questions that were put to him. The final, exasperated retort was almost inevitable.

"Mr. Harrigan," asked a young lady, smiling brightly, "did you see any of the old ruins in Dublin?"

"Madam," replied Harrigan, his voice cold, "I not only saw the ruins, but two of them wanted to marry me!"

*

Minor accidents happen to everybody, but everybody doesn't have the Irishman's gift of blarney to avoid the usual stumbling apologies.

Lawrence O'Brien, the former Chairman of the Democratic National Committee in Washington, D.C., was hastening down Pennsylvania Avenue, his mind on weighty matters. Approaching from the opposite direction came a pretty lady, also walking rapidly.

They met head on. Both veered abruptly to the left, and then to the right, confronting each other in a vain effort to untangle themselves and pass. Inevitably, the dodging and weaving finally stopped and they made ready to continue on their respective ways.

"Good-bye," murmured O'Brien, tipping his hat and bowing, "it's nice to have known you!"

*

Old John, a farmer of Louth, in arrears on a loan, was summoned to the bank to explain why the payment on his note was so long overdue.

The banker had one of those faces that really looked like a banker's. "John, your account is now more than thirty days past due," he said in a voice usually reserved for the poor but seldom for the rich.

"Thurrty days, is it now?" replied old John in slow, measured tones. "Sure, and this bein' January there's a good rason fer me lateness."

"What has that got to do with it?" snapped the banker.

"Sor," explained John with a straight face, "I had no idea iv the time passin' so quick. Thurrty days durin' the winter fly by faster than in the summer—the days are that shorter!"

*

At a banquet in which the late actor, Victor Moore, was the after-dinner speaker, the toastmaster made the mistake of introducing him with a quip of his own, one which Moore felt was somewhat slighting: "I am pleased to present a gentlemen who has a very glib tongue. All you need do is put a dinner in his mouth, and out comes a speech."

Glowering, Moore rose from his seat and, facing the large audience, he replied:

"Your toastmaster's ability, I must confess, is greater than mine. All you have to do is put a speech in *his* mouth and out comes your dinner!"

*

What did yesteryear's Irishman think of Americans in general? Here is one almost forgotten assessment:

> He'd kiss a queen till he'd raised a blister,
> With his arms round her neck and his old felt hat on:
> Address a king by the title of mister,
> And ask the price of the throne he sat on.'

*

Martin had just settled down to watch the six o'clock news on TV when the telephone jangled. Reluctantly, he arose from his chair and picked up the receiver. "Yeah?" he growled.

"This is Miss Patterson, at Dr. Williams' office," said that lady in severe tones. "You missed another payment on your bill. Frankly, the doctor is quite upset about it."

"Upset, is he now?" exploded Marty, his Irish dander bouncing off the ceiling. "Well, my professional advice is that he take a couple of aspirins before bedtime, and if he isn't feeling better in the morning have him call me again!"

*

One Saturday evening, while the late Morton Downey was appearing in New York, a letter was addressed to him, the envelope simply stating: To America's Greatest Irish Tenor.

"I decline to accept this letter," he said stiffly, handing it back to the

---

'James McCloud, *O'Cullen's Complaint* (Belfast, 1909).

postman. "I am not America's greatest Irish tenor. I am the *world's* greatest Irish tenor!"

*

Dennis, a freshman at Georgetown University in Washington, D.C., considered himself something of a literary man now that he had learned to read the football number on his sweatshirt. Unfortunately for Dennis, however, his professor of English harbored no such illusions.

At the next examination, just before Christmas, the hero of the gridiron stared blankly at the questions and then, grinning, he wrote across the top of the test paper: "God only knows the answer to these questions. Merry Christmas!"

The professor returned the paper with a notation of his own: "God gets an A. You get an F. Happy New Year!"

*

Anne Sullivan, the remarkable lady who gave "ears" to Helen Keller, was one of the most sympathetic of souls, but she once lost all patience with a rude, loud-mouthed news reporter.

"Sir," she murmured as he was about to leave, "don't think it hasn't been charming meeting you, because it hasn't!"

*

The First Lord Liftinant[8]
(As related by Andrew Geraghty, of Philomath)

"Essex, me haro," said Queen Elizabeth, as the two of them sat at breakwhist in the back parlor of Buckingham Palace, "I've got a job that I think would suit you.... Do you know where Ireland is?"

"I'm no great fist at jography," says his lordship, "but I know the place you mane. Population, three million—exports, emigrants."

---

[8]This fanciful story by William P. French was, for many years, among the most popular blarney tales in Ireland, and still remains a classic. However, it does have historical significance insofar as the characters are concerned. Queen Elizabeth knew that she would have to destroy the Irish aristocracy if she were ever to achieve her ambition to dominate Ireland. But the Irish nobility, rather than allow themselves to be driven off the land, fought back with outstanding courage. In 1570, Pope Pius V issued a Papal Bull depriving Elizabeth of her claim to rule Ireland—and England as well. From that time, the Irish cause and the Catholic faith were indissolubly linked. Elizabeth's armies defeated numerous insurrections, but she died before England achieved the decisive victory by crushing the revolt led by Hugh O'Neill, the Catholic Earl of Tyrone. That year, 1603, marked the downfall of the Irish aristocracy. The Irish had lost their last good opportunity to reverse the tide of English conquest. O'Neill's stronghold was Ulster, in northern Ireland. The English government "planted" this domain with thousands of Lowland Scots, most of them Presbyterians. Within two generations, Scottish settlers owned 3,000,000 of the 3,500,000 acres in the northern counties. The political and religious division between Ulster and the rest of Ireland that still vexes the country had been established.

"Well," says the Queen, "I've been reading the *Dublin Evening Mail* and the *Telegraft* for some time back, and sorra one o' me can get at the truth of how things is goin'. The leadin' articles is as conthradictory as if they wor husband and wife."

"That's the way with papers all the world over," says Essex. "Columbus told me it was the same in Amerikay when he was there, abusin' and conthradictin' each other at every turn—it's the way they make their livin'. May I throuble you for an egg-spoon?"

"It's addled they have me," says the Queen. "Not a know I know what's goin' on. So now, what I want you to do is to run over to Ireland like a good fella and bring me word how matters stand."

"Is it me?" says Essex, leapin' up off his chair. "It's not in airnest ye are, ould lady. Sure, it's the height of the London saison. Everyone's in town, and Shake's new fairy piece, *The Midsummer's Night Mare* is billed for next week."

"You'll go when ye're tould," says the Queen, fixin' him with her eye, "if you know which side yer bread's buttered on. See here now," says she, seein' him chokin' with vexation and a slice o' corned beef, "you ought to be as pleased as Punch about it, for you'll be at the top o' the walk over there as vice-regent representin' me."

"I ought to have a title or two," says Essex, pluckin' up a bit. "His Gloriosity the Great Panjandhrum, or the like o' that."

"How would His Excellency the Lord Liftinant of Ireland sthrike you?" says Elizabeth.

"First class," cries Essex. "Couldn't be betther. It doesn't mean much, but it's allitherative, and will look well below the number on me hall door."

Well, boys, it didn't take him long to pack his clothes and start away for the Island of Saints. It took him a good while to get there, though, not knowin' the road; but by means of a pocket compass and a tip to the steward, he was landed at last contagious to Dalkey Island. Going up to an ould man who was sittin' on a rock, he took off his hat and, says he:

"That's great weather we're havin'."

"Good enough for the times that's in it," says the ould man, cockin' one eye at him.

"Any divarshun goin' on?" says Essex.

"You're a sthranger in these parts, I'm thinkin'," says the ould man, "or you'd know this was a 'band night' in Dalkey."

"I wasn't aware of it," says Essex. "The fact is, I only landed from England just this minute."

"Ay," says the ould man bitterly, "it's little they know about us over there. I'll hould you," says he, with a slight thrimble in his voice, "that the Queen herself doesn't know there is to be fireworks in the Sorrento Gardens this night."

Well, when Essex heard that, he disremembered entirely he was sent over to Ireland to put down rows and ructions, and away with him to see the fun and flirt with all the pretty girls he could find. Compared to English girls, *all* Irish girls are pretty, so he found plenty of them—thick as bees they wor, and each one as beautiful as the day and the morra. He wrote two letters home next day, one to Queen Elizabeth and the other to Lord Montaigle, a playboy like himself. I'll read you the one to the Queen first:

Dame Sthreet, April 16th, 1599

Fair Enchantress,
I wish I was back in London, baskin' in your sweet smiles and listenin' to your melodious voice once more. I got the consignment of men and the post-office order all right. I was out all mornin' lookin' for the inimy, but sorra a taste of Hugh O'Neil or his men can I find. A policeman at the corner o' Nassau Sthreet told me they wor hidin' in Wicklow. So I am makin' up a party to explore the Dargle on Easther Monday. The girls here are as ugly as sin, and every minute o' the day I do be wishin' it was your good-lookin' self I was gazin' at instead o' these ignorant scarecrows. Hopin' soon to be back in ould England, I remain, your lovin' subjec',

Essex.

P.S. I hear Hugh O'Neil was seen on the top o' the Donnybrook tram yesterday mornin'. If I have any luck the head'll be off him before you get this.

E.

The other letter read this way:

Dear Monty:
This is a great place all out. Come over here if you want fun. Divil such playboys ever I seen, and the girls—oh! don't be talkin'—'pon me secret honor you'll see more loveliness at a tay and supper ball in Rathmines than there is in the whole of England. Tell Ned Spenser to send me a love-song to sing to a young girl who seems taken with my appearance. Her name's Mary, and she lives in Dunlary, so he oughtent to find it hard. I hear Hugh O'Neil's a terror, and hits a powerful welt, especially when you're not lookin'. If he tries any of his games with me, I'll give him in charge. No brawlin' for yours truly,

Essex.

Well, me bould Essex stopped for six months in Dublin, purtendin' to be very busy subjugatin' the country, but all the time only losin' his time and money without doin' a hand's turn, and doin' his best to avoid a ruction with "Fighting Hugh." If a messenger came to tell him that O'Neil was campin' out on the North Bull, Essex would up and away for Sandycove where, after a bit o' fishin', he'd write off to Elizabeth, saying that "owing to their superior knowledge of the country, the dastard foe had once more eluded him."
The Queen got mighty tired of these letters, especially as they always

ended with a request to send stamps by return, and told Essex to finish up his business and not be makin' a fool of himself.

"Oh, that's the talk, is it?" says Essex. "Very well, me ould sauce-box" (that was the name he had for her ever since she gev him the clip on the ear for turnin' his back on her), "I'll write to O'Neil this very minute and tell him to send in his lowest terms for peace at ruling prices."

Well, the threaty was a bit of a one-sided one, the terms being—

1. Hugh O'Neil to be King of Great Britain.

2. Lord Essex to return to London and remain there as Viceroy of England.

3. The O'Neil family to be supported by Government, with free passes to all theatres and places of entertainment.

4. The London markets to buy only from Irish dealers.

5. All taxes to be sent in stamped envelope, directed to H. O'Neil, and marked "private." Checks crossed and made payable to H. O'Neil. Terms cash.

Well, if Essex had had the sense to read through this treaty, he'd have seen it was of too graspin' a nature to pass with any sort of respectable sovereign, but he was that mad he just stuck the document in his pocket and away with him hot foot for England.

"Is the Queen within?" says he to the butler when he opened the door o' the palace. His clothes were that dirty and disorthered with travelin' all night, and his boots that muddy, the butler was for not littin' him in at first, so he says very grand:

"Her Meejesty is abow stairs and can't be seen till she's had her break-whist."

"Tell her the Lord Liftinant of Ireland desires an enterview," says Essex.

"Oh, beg pardon, me lord," says the butler, steppin' to one side. "I didn't know 'twas yourself. Come inside, sir, the Queen's in the dhrawin'-room dhrawin'."

Well, Essex leps up the stairs and into the dhrawin'-room, muddy boots and all, but not a sight of Elizabeth was to be seen.

"Where's your missus?" says he to one of the maids-of-honor that was dustin' oft the chimbley-piece.

"She's not out of her bed yet," says the maid with a toss of her head. "But if you write your message on the slate beyant, I'll see...." but, before she had finished, Essex was up the second flight and knockin' at the Queen's bedroom door.

"Is that the hot wather?" says the Queen.

"No, it's me—Essex. Can you see me?"

"Faith, I can't," says the Queen. "Hould on till I draw the bed curtains. Come in now," says she, "and say your say. I can't have you stoppin' long, you young Lutharian."

"Bedad, yer Majesty," says Essex, droppin' on his knees before her (the delutherer that he was), "small blame to me if I am a Lutharian, for you have a face on you that would charm a bird off a bush."

"Hould your tongue, you young reprobate," says the Queen, blushin' up to her curl papers with delight, "and tell me what improvements you med in Ireland."

"Faith, I taught manners to O'Neil," cries Essex.

"He had a bad masther then," says Elizabeth, lookin' at his dirty boots. "Couldn't you wipe yer feet before ye desthroyed me carpets, young man?"

"Oh, now," says Essex. "Is it wastin' me time shufflin' about on a mat you'd have me, when I might be gazin' on the loveliest faymale the world ever saw?"

"Well," says the Queen, "I'll forgive you this time, as you've been so long away, but remimber in the future that Kidderminster isn't oilcloth. And now," says she, "let's have a look at that threaty I see stickin' out o' your pocket."

Well, when the Queen read the terms of Hugh O'Neil she just gev him one look, an' jumpin' from off the bed, she put her head out of the window and called out to the policeman on duty:

"Is the Head below?"

"I'll tell him you want him, ma'am," says the policeman.

"Do," says the Queen. "Hello, what's this?" says she, as a slip o' paper dhropped out o' the dispatches. "'Lines to Mary!' Ho-ho! me gay fella, that's what you've been up to, is it?"

> "Mrs. Brady's
> A widow lady,
> And she has a charmin' daughter I adore;
> I went to court her
> Across the water,
> And her mother keeps a little candy store.
> She's such a darlin'
> She's like a starlin',
> And in love with her I'm gettin' more and more;
> Her name is Mary,
> She's from Dunlary,
> And her mother keeps a little candy store."

"That settles it," says the Queen. "It's the gaoler you'll serenade next."

When Essex heard that, he thrimbled so much that the button of his cuirass shook off and rowled under the dhressin' table.

"Arrest that thraitor," says the Queen, when the Head Constable came to the door, "and never let me set eyes on him again."

And indeed she never did. Soon after that, he met his Maker from the skelp of an axe when he happened to be standin' on Tower Hill.

—William Percy French (1854-1909)

＊

"Kitty of Coleraine, and
Blarneyin' Barney McCleary"⁹

As beautiful Kitty one morning was tripping
    With a pitcher of milk from the fair of Coleraine,
She saw me and stumbled, and the pitcher down tumbled,
    And all the sweet buttermilk watered the plain.
"Oh, what shall I do now?—'twas looking at you, now!
    Sure, sure, such a pitcher I'll ne'er see again;
'Twas the pride of my dairy—O Barney McCleary,
    You're sent as a plague to the girls of Coleraine!"

I sat down beside her and gently did chide her,
    That such a misfortune should give her such pain;
A kiss then I gave her, and ere I did leave her
    She vowed for such pleasure she'd break it again.
'Twas hay-making season—I can't tell the reason—
    Misfortunes will never come single, 'tis plain;
For very soon after poor Kitty's disaster
    The devil a pitcher was whole in Coleraine.

—Anonymous

*

"Widow Machree"

Widow Machree, now the summer is come,
    Och hone, Widow Machree,
When everything smiles, should a beauty look glum?
    Och hone, Widow Machree.
See the birds go in pairs,
    And the rabbits and hares,
Why even the bears
    Now in couples agree;
And the mute little fish,
    Though they can't speak, they wish,
    Och hone, Widow Machree.

Widow Machree, when the winter comes in,
    Och hone, Widow Machree,
To be poking the fire all alone is a sin,
    Och hone, Widow Machree.
Why the shovel and tongs
    To each other belongs,
And the kettle sings songs

---

⁹This anonymous song, very popular in nineteenth-century Ireland, is based on an old story. The original tale was quite proper, as evidenced by the above poetic version, but the songs that followed were anything but respectable.

Full of family glee,
While alone with your cup,
    Like a hermit you sup,
Och hone, Widow Machree.

And how do you know, with the comforts I've told,
    Och hone, Widow Machree,
But you're keeping some poor divil out in the cold?
    Och hone, Widow Machree.
With such sins on your head,
    Sure your peace would be fled,
Could you sleep in your bed
    Without thinking to see
Some ghost or some sprite
    Come to wake you each night
Crying, *och hone,* Widow Machree.

Then take my advice, darling Widow Machree,
    Och hone, Widow Machree,
And with my advice, faith, I wish you'd take me,
    Och hone, Widow Machree.
You'd have me to desire
    Then, to stir up the fire,
And sure hope is no liar
    In whispering to me
That the ghosts would depart
    When you'd me near your heart,
Och hone, Widow Machree.

—Samuel Lover (1797-1868)

*

"To a Young Lady
Fanning a Turf Fire
With Her Petticoat"[10]

Cease, cease, Amira, peerless maid!
    Though we delighted gaze,
While artless you excite the flame,
    We perish in the blaze.
Haply you, too, provoke your harm—
    Forgive the bold remark—
Your petticoat may fan the fire
    But, O! beware a spark!

—Anonymous

---

[10]Included in *The Shamrock, or Hibernian Caresses* (1772), a collection of poems edited and mainly written by Samuel Whyte, the schoolmaster of Moore, Sheridan, and others.

"Blarney Is a Two-way Street"

(Biddy spakin')
"Terry O'Rourke, 'tis your presence that tazes me;
   Haven't I towld you so often before?
If you've the smallest regard for what plazes me,
   Never come prowlin' round here any more.
Why you persist in this game's what amazes me;
   Didn't I tell you I'd beaus by the score?
There's Rody Kearney would give twenty cows to me
   Any fine day that I'd let him be spouse to me."

(Terry spakin')
"Biddy, *asthore,* an' 'tis you that is hard on me,
   Whin 'tis me two wicked legs are to blame;
Troth, I believe if you placed a strong guard on me,
   They'd wandher back to this spot all the same.
Saving the gates of the prison are barred on me,
   You might as well try to keep moths from the flame,
Ducks from the water, or bees from the flowers,
   As thim same legs from your door, be the powers!

Come now, me darlin', 'tis no use to frown on me;
   Though I've no cows, but two mules an' a car.
You wouldn't know, but I'd yet have the gown on me,
   Ringing the tunes of me tongue at the Bar.
Whin I've won you, who despised and looked down on me,
   Shure 'tis meself that might come to be Czar;
What are you smilin' at? Give me the hand of you,
   I'll make the purtiest bride in the land of you."

—J. DeQuincy (1856-1920)

•

"I'll Haunt You,
Molly Carew"

Och hone, and what will I do?
   Sure, my love is all crost
   Like a bud in the frost,
And there's no use at all in my going to bed,
For 'tis dhrames and not slape comes into my head;
   And 'tis all about you,
   My sweet Molly Carew—
And indeed, 'tis a sin and a shame;
   Your complater than Nature
   In every feature,
   The snow can't compare
   With your forehead so fair;
And I rather would see just one blink of your eye
Than the purtiest star that shines out of the sky—
   And by this and by that,
   For the matter of that,

You're more distant by far than that same!
Och hone! wirrasthrue!
I'm alone in this world without you.

Och hone! don't provoke me to do it;
For there's girls by the score
That love me—and more;
And you'd look very quare if some morning you'd meet
My wedding all marchin' in pride down the sthreet;
Throth, you'd open your eyes
And you'd die with surprise,
To think 'twasn't you was come to it!
And, faith, Katty Naile
And her cow, I go bail,
Would jump if I'd say,
"Katty Naile, name the day."
And tho' you're fair and fresh as a morning in May,
While she's short and dark like a cowld winther's day,
Yet if you don't repent
Before Easther, when Lent
Is over I'll marry for spite;
Och hone! wirrasthrue!
And when I die for you,
My ghost will haunt you each night.

—Samuel Lover

*

"Bandying Blarney Back and Forth"

He: Be the fire, *alanna,* sittin',
       Purty 'tis you look and sweet,
    Wid yer dainty fingers knittin'
       Shtockin's for yer daintier feet.

She: It's yer tongue that has the blarney,
       Yis, and impudence galore!
    Is it me to thrusht ye, Barney,
       When yer afther half a score?

He: Shure, I ne'er, in all I thravelled,
       Found at all the like's o' you.
She: Now my worsted all is ravelled
       And whatever will I do?

He: Might I make so bould to ask it,
       Shure I know the girl o' girls;
    And I'd make me heart the casket,
       And her love the string iv pearls.
She: Ah, then, Barney dear, I'm thinkin'
       That it's you're the honeyed rogue.

He: Faix, I'd be the bee a-dhrinkin'
      From yer rosy lips a *pogue.*

She: Is it steal a colleen's kisses,
      When it's all alone she's left?
He: Wor they all as sweet as this is,
      Troth, I'd go to jail for theft.

She: Barney! Barney, shtop yer foolin'!
      Or I'll soon begin to scould.
      Shure, I'd like to know what school in
      Did ye learn to be so bould?

He: Och! It's undher Masther Cupid
      That I learned me A. B. C.
She: That the scholar wasn't stupid,
      Faith,* is very plain to see.

He: Ah, then Eileen, but the blush is
      Most becomin' to ye, dear!
      Like the red rose on the bush is—
She: Sir! you needn't come so near!

He: Over lane and road and *boreen,*
      Troth, I've come a weary way,
      Jusht to whisper ye, *asthareen,*
      Somethin' that I've longed to say.
      I've a cozy cottage which is
      Jusht the proper size for two—
She: There, I've tangled all me stitches,
      And it's all because iv you!

He: And, to make a sthray suggestion,
      Maybe you me wish might guess?
She: Shure, an' av ye pressed the question,
      Somehow—I—might answer—Yes!

—Patrick J. Coleman (1867-1936)

---

*The exclamatory word "faith," used by the female, and the Gaelic pronunciation "faix," as used by the male, would indicate that they came from different counties. In any event, the meaning is the same.

Chapter Two

Woojings and Weddings

Introduction

Irish attitudes toward courtship and marriage have been largely influenced by a persistent lack of economic opportunity which has its roots in centuries of English oppression. The same, as we shall see, also accounts for Ireland's enormous loss of population.

There are, today, some 23 million Americans of Irish descent in the United States, about five times the population of Ireland itself. In a century of "population explosion," the Emerald Isle, whose Catholicism absolutely forbids birth control, has nevertheless seen its numbers fall by 50 per cent, due to the extreme decline in marriages and to heavy emigration. This outward flow reached its peak during the famine years of the 1840s, and continued well into the early twentieth century. However, it was not the fear of starvation alone which accounted for this exodus. The vast majority of immigrants came from farm country rather than from such large cities as Dublin; and rural life was almost unrelievedly drab and hard. Unlike many of the more educated in metropolitan areas, the country people were simply too close to the problem, recognizing only the symptoms instead of the causes. They blamed the falling marriage rate, not on external factors, but on each other, with such frivolous complaints as "immature men" and "greedy women."

In his book, *The Vanishing Irish,* the late Sean O'Faolain observed that Ireland is one of the few nations on earth where men outnumber the women, and yet, the marriage rate is one of the lowest in the world. A full quarter of the population never marries at all, while the average age of those who do marry is thirty-three for men and twenty-eight for women.

Many an Irish girl has admitted that her main reason for going to the United States was to find a man who was not already a confirmed old bachelor. The point was well taken. The girls, seeing marriage and motherhood postponed indefinitely by impersonal economic considerations, feared that their reproductive years would slip away, empty and barren. Another problem was the custom that called for parents to marry off their daughters strictly in order of age. Irish folklore is replete with sad

35

stories of the pretty young girls who could not marry until their plain-faced older sister was wed. The understandably restless Irish girl decided she would rather join relatives in an overcrowded tenement in Chicago or New York, or wash dishes for three dollars a week in "cold roast Boston," than live out her life in an unequal race with time and fate.

As for the eligible young men, plagued by frustration and fear, they saw nothing but bleak years ahead, waiting for a small farm of their own. Older men and women, squeezed or displaced entirely by the exactions of the landlord or by land consolidations, decided in middle life that it was not too late for them to take the great gamble. And at times of famine, whole families, from infants to grandparents in desperation made the journey. Thus, the decline in Ireland's population went on, and with it, the continuing fall in marriages and births.

One of the humorous stories that was popular among the Irish immigrants just before the turn of the present century will be found in this chapter. The anecdote concerns the Irish immigrant girl who lost her certificate of character on the ship to the United States. When she arrived, a friend helpfully provided her with another document. He wrote: "She had a good character before she left Ireland, but lost it on shipboard coming over."

The significant feature of this joke is that it was just that—a joke. Historians everywhere agree that the women which Ireland contributed to America were almost universally virtuous. Many immigrant names were to be found in the rosters of the red-light houses of America's pre-Civil War cities, but seldom Irish names. The Irish servant girl—Irish immigrant women were "girls" even in their sixties—may have been unlettered and unfamiliar with nineteenth-century amenities, but she could be trusted, and she was virtuous. As one contemporary said, she might be bold in answering her mistress back (as the jokes about Rosie the upstairs maid illustrate elsewhere in this book), but she was safe when men were about. And the pillowcases wouldn't disappear.

Irishmen, too, were strait-laced in matters of morality. At any rate, the Irish, given to grog, song, and long hours of hard work, seldom got into trouble over women. This virtue served them well during the immigration years. The Catholic Irish developed a successful system for the care of unescorted single women in the crowded quarters of immigrant ships. Before an unmarried girl left home, her parents entrusted her to the care of a male friend of the family in whom they had complete faith. He saw to it that she was not molested. There is no record that the system gave rise to any impropriety.

Today, Ireland's strict rules against divorce, lower living standards, and a shortage of pleasant, modern apartments are often blamed for the lack of interest in marriage, but similar conditions do exist in other countries and marriage has somehow retained its popularity. O'Faolain believed that a native Puritanism bolstered by rigid censorship laws must be to blame.

When the Irish do marry—and they do—they raise large families, probably because of Church bans on birth control, but also due to a natural love for big households with many children. The birthrate of Ireland is one of the highest in the world—more than twice that of the United States—so any fear that the "Irish" Irish will vanish from the earth in the near future is probably unfounded.

The anecdotes, quips, and poems in this two-part chapter reflect the various facets of Irish-American and "Irish" Irish humor as it pertains to courtship and marriage. Some are modern and probing; others, such as the ancient folk tale, "Often-Who-Came," are whimsical; a few are sardonic; but in the main they are warm accounts of actual people, not merely characters in a book. Finally, the stories and poems which follow were selected so as to portray the Irish people in their many moods and attitudes—at their sunniest and funniest best.

A hundred years ago, a man from Cork said, "I believe in matrimony, but not for single people." This chapter, however, is meant for everyone—single people as well as the less fortunate.

—H. D. S.

Part One

Courtin' Daze and Errant Knights

"Maggie Was a Lady"

> Please don't ask me to marry you yet,
> Mother would just have a fit!
> Besides, it was only today that we met,
> Can't you be patient a bit?
> You know how people will talk about things,
> I mean, if they're not in good taste;
> Besides, I don't think a girl, if she's nice,
> Would marry a man in such haste.
> I'll marry you tomorrow, dear, if you like,
> And use the same toothbrush and comb;
> But, darling, if you keep teasing me now,
> I'll get up, get dressed, and go home!

*

"Often-Who-Came"[1]

There was once a man who had a beautiful daughter, and many men were in love with her. Among them were two lads who came courting. One of them pleased her; the other did not. The youth she disliked was very rich. He visited her father's house often, just to see the lass and to be in her company. But the fellow she liked was very poor, and he came but seldom.

The girl's father preferred that she marry the rich boy who constantly came to see her. In an effort to advance the fellow's good cause, the father

---

[1] A literal translation from the Old Irish (Gaelic) by D. J. O'Donoghue, Dublin, 1894. The age of the original tale is unknown, but probably stems from the fourth or fifth century.

38

arranged a lavish dinner party and sent everyone in the village an invitation.

"Drink a drink now," says he to his daughter, "on the man you like best in this company." He waited with a smile on his face, thinking she would drink a toast to the man he liked best himself.

She lifted the glass in her hand, stood up, looked round, and then recited:

> "I drink the good health of Often-Who-Came,
> But who often comes not I also must name;
> Who often comes not I often must blame
> That he comes not as often as Often-Who-Came."

She sat down when she had spoken her quatrain and said not another word that evening. But the rich youth, Often-Who-Came, understood that it was not he whom the lass wanted, and he did not visit her again.

So, with her father's consent, she married the poor but honest man of her choice, and forever after she lived to regret it.

*

Mary, the fairest rose of Tralee, had two suitors and could not make up her mind which one to marry. The question, however, was settled by a thoughtful Providence in the guise of a village priest.

It all started in a delightfully pleasant June month, when romance and whispered promises filled the balmy air. Six months later, in the dead of winter, Mary awoke one night with a wild craving for strawberries. The next morning her ankles started to swell, to say nothing of her abdomen, and, in due time, she gave issue to an eight-pound miniature Irishman.

Now a problem arose. Which of her two suitors was the father? Was it Shemus, the dashing soldier with the wooden leg? Or could it be gentle Jamie, the sensitive wagon driver who hauled potatoes for the farmers in the area? The troubled young lady sought the counsel of wise and elderly Father Fitzgerald.

"Which of the two lads do you love the most?" asked the shrewd old priest.

"I—I—think," stammered Mary, "that I love Jamie the best."

"Then go in peace and marry your Jamie," said Father Fizgerald warmly. "You have chosen correctly."

"But how can you tell?"

"No difficulty at all, my child. You have a perfectly normal baby, therefore the father must be Jamie. If the soldier had fathered the child, it stands to reason it would have been born with a wooden leg."[2]

———

The difference in style and content between the thousand-year-old Gaelic tale, above, and the Irish-American stories that follow, will be quickly

---

[2]*Ibid.*

perceived. The gentle humor of a long bygone day has evolved into the pointed, satirical, sometimes trenchant joke of the modern post-Yeats era. Both types are equally appealing, however: Irish humor has retained its continuity over the centuries, whether in the Emerald Isle or transplanted by its scattered sons and daughters in the United States, Canada, Australia, or England.

"Sir, I love your daughter and she loves me," began the young fellow in a faltering voice. "We want to get married—with your blessing."

"Well, you know how we Irish Catholics are," replied the girl's father thoughtfully. "Do you earn enough money to support a large family?"

"Oh, yes, sir!" exclaimed the anxious suitor, his eager face lighting up.

"Fine!" said the father, smiling as he shook the young man's hand. "Including my daughter, there are seven of us!"

*

"Did you meet the young man who just moved into the house next door?" asked Eileen's mother.

"Yes, this morning," snapped Eileen, obviously annoyed with her new neighbor. "He passed by while I was in the front garden and grinned as if all he had to do was smile and I'd come running to him. Oh, the impudence of the man! Then he asked me, as brazen as you please, 'Colleen, what is your favorite flower?' "

"So I told him—'Pillsbury!' "

*

Some of the boys were bending their elbows at the corner tavern when old John interrupted the third rendition of "Irish Washerwoman" to mention the news that Peggy MacNamara had gotten married. Peggy, it seems, had been a steady habitué of the tavern and had often joined them in their revelries, but had not been seen for the past two weeks.

"I heard that she told her new hubby all about her previous affairs," said John.

Now that's what I call frankness," chuckled one of the group.

"And that's what I called honesty," grinned another.

"Well," concluded John admiringly, "that's what *I* call a *memory!*"

*

Oh, those devious Celts!

"Sure I believe an equal opportunity for women, honey. Let's go to *your* apartment!"

*

The late Eileen McManus, author of some twenty books, was enjoying "a wee drop o' the sperits that cheer" with a few friends, in celebration of her eightieth birthday. The conversation got around to current events.

"Have you joined the Women's Liberation movement?" asked one of the guests.

"Liberation, is it?" snorted old-maid Eileen, downing her fourth or fifth whiskey. "Hell, I'm still hoping to get caught!"

❋

Mick had been seriously contemplating marriage when he happened to overhear a conversation that almost shocked him out of the notion of matrimony. Several women were discussing their husbands, concentrating mainly on their vices and how they had succeeded in curing their bad habits.

"By the way," said one of the ladies to a very pretty matron standing beside her, "I hear that your Patrick has given up smoking and drinking—and after all these years, too! That must have taken a strong will."

"It certainly did," acknowledged the young matron in grim tones, her steely voice in marked contrast to her frail features. "But that's the kind of will I've got!"

❋

At a recent dinner, an elderly spinster complained sadly to Monsignor Fulton J. Sheen that she was lonely.

"Have you ever thought of getting married?" asked Dr. Sheen.

"Thought?" answered the old lady with some asperity. "I *worry*!"

❋

Grandpa was not exactly enamored of the young Holy Cross graduate his granddaughter had brought home to meet the family. Throughout dinner the old man listened to the youth expound on world politics, the nuclear situation, and domestic problems affecting the economy until his ears ached. When the scholar finally left, the girl turned to her grandfather.

"Isn't he a perfectly marvelous conversationalist?" she asked proudly.

"That he is," growled the old-timer. "Faith, I could sit and listen to him for minutes!"

❋

Irene could hardly wait until her sister returned home from the blind date which she had arranged.

"How did you like him?" cried Irene the moment her sister opened the door.

"Sis, don't ever make another date for me," she sighed. "The only thing we had in common was that we're both Irish."

❋

William Flanagan, professor of English at Notre Dame, arrived home early and called his housekeeper into his study. There, he presented the lady with a lovely engagement ring.

"Miss O'Malley—er—darling—I have something important to ask you," he began hesitantly.

"Oh, this is so sudden," gasped Miss O'Malley, who was very good at coining original phrases. "I'm that nervous."

"It's all right," the professor gently assured her, "I won't use any big words."

"Faith, professor darlint," she answered sweetly, "you c'n be afther usin' all the big wurrds you want—fer the time bein'!"

*

"Well, *macushla,* it's glad I am to hear that you're engaged," said the girl's father. "But tell me, does the lad have any money?"

"Oh, Daddy, why do you men always have to mention money?" replied the daughter, pouting. "That's exactly what he asked me about you!"

*

Some years ago, the keyhole columnists who delight in journalistic peeping gleefully reported the courtship of banker Terence Hartigan. It seems that Hartigan fell in love with Bubbles McGrath, a *danseuse* in Billy Minsky's burlesque. For several months, he squired her about in the fashionable circles of New York and Connecticut, and showered her with gifts. Deciding to marry her, and being a cautious man, he prudently hired a private detective to look into her antecedents and check on her current activities and associates. Hartigan was not about to make any rash mistakes. At last, he received the detective's report:

"The lady in question enjoys an excellent reputation, despite her burlesque career. Her past is spotless. Her associates outside the burlesque house are irreproachable. The only breath of scandàl in her life is that, in recent months, she has frequently been seen in the company of a banker of doubtful reputation."

*

It is generally accepted, and correctly so, that folk tales stem from anonymous sources and are kept alive by the storytellers who hand them down from one generation to the next. As usual, the exceptions are always with us. The following pieces owe their longevity, not to verbal transfer, but to written literature. With the exception of one piece, "First Love," none are anonymous. Now considered classics of folk humor, they were written by some of Ireland's greatest writers.

Widow Wadman's Eye

"I am half distracted, Captain O'Shandy," said Mrs. Wadman, holding up her cambric handkerchief to her left eye as she approached the door of my uncle Toby's sentry box. "A mote—or sand, or something—has gotten into this eye of mine. Do look at it. It is not in the white part."

Mrs. Wadman then edged herself close in beside my uncle Toby and, squeezing herself down upon the corner of his bench, she gave him an opportunity of examining her eye without rising. "Do look into it," she said again.

(Honest soul! thou didst look into it with as much innocence of heart as ever a child looked into a rare showcase, and 'twere as much a sin to have hurt thee. Yet, if a man will be peeping on his own accord into things of that nature, I've nothing to say about it.)

My uncle Toby never peeped into a female eye before, and I will answer for him that he would have sat quietly upon a sofa from June to January (which, as you know, takes in both the hot and cold months) with an eye as fine as the Thracian Rhodope's beside him, without being able to tell whether it was a black or blue one.

The difficulty was to get my uncle Toby to look at one at all!

(But now the difficulty is surmounted and I see him yonder with his pipe pendulous in his hand and the ashes falling out of it—looking—and looking —then rubbing his eyes—and looking again with twice the good nature that ever Galileo looked for a spot in the sun.)

In vain! For, by all the powers which animate that organ, Widow Wadman's left eye shines as lucid as her right. There is neither mote nor sand nor dust nor chaff nor speck nor particle of opaque matter floating in it.

(There is nothing, my dear paternal uncle, but one lambent delicious fire, furtively shooting out from every part of it, in all directions into thine. If thou lookest, Uncle Toby, in search of this mote one moment longer, thou art undone!)

"It is not in the white," said Mrs. Wadman once more.

My uncle Toby looked with might and main into the pupil.

Now, of all the eyes which ever were created, including those of Venus herself, which certainly were as erogenous a pair of eyes as ever stood in a head, there never was an eye of them all so fitted to rob my uncle Toby of his repose as the very eye at which he was looking. It was not a rolling eye—a romping or a wanton one—nor was it an eye sparkling, petulant, or imperious—of high claims and terrifying expectations which would have curdled at once that milk of human nature of which my uncle Toby was made up. But it was an eye full of gentle salutations and soft responses— speaking—not like the trumpet-stop of some ill-made organ (in which many an eye I talk to holds discourse), but whispering soft, like the last low accents of an expiring saint.

"Oh, Captain O'Shandy," say her eyes—especially her left one—"how can you live comfortless and alone, without a bosom to lean your head on, or trust your cares to?"

But I shall be in love with it myself if I say another word about it.
It did in my uncle Toby's business.

—Laurence Sterne (1713-68)

*

How Paddy Fret, the Priest's Boy, Won Katty Tyrrell's Hand—and Foot

Paddy Fret, who worked for Father Maher, mounted to his bedroom over the stable and proceeded to array himself with unusual care. He then surveyed himself in the cracked mirror imbedded in the wall, and the scrutiny satisfied him that there was not a handsomer young fellow in the whole parish of Croagh. So, in love with himself and at least part of the world, he stole cautiously down the rickety step-ladder, and gliding like a snake between the over-bowering laurels which flanked the chapel house, he emerged on the high road.

"I'm afeerd, Paddy, that my father will never listen to a good word about you," said pretty Katty Tyrrell, as the priest's boy took a stool beside her before the blazing peat fire that burned on the stoveless hearth. "He's a grave man, wanst he takes a notion into his head."

"All ould men has got notions," said Paddy, "but they dhrop off with their hairs. Lave him to me, and if I don't convart him, call me a souper. Sure, if he wants a son-in-law to be a comfort in his ould age he couldn't meet with a finer boy than meself."

"Well, Father Maher's housekeeper, Mrs. Gavin, says that it would be a morchial sin to throw me and my two hundherd pounds away on the likes o' you. 'A good-for-nothin' *bosthoon,*' says she, 'that I wouldn't grease the wheel iv a barrow with.' "

"Katty dear, the poor woman is out iv her sivin sinsis, and all for the want of a gintleman to make a lady of her, as I'm goin' to make wan o' you."

The splendor of the promise bewildered Miss Tyrrell. She could only rest her elbows on her knees, hide her face in her hands, and cry, "Oh, Paddy!"

"Yes, me jewel," continued the subtle suitor, "I'm poor today, perhaps, but there's noble blood coursin' through my veins. Go up to the top of Knock-meil-Down some fine mornin' and look down all around you. There isn't a square fut o' grass in all you see that didn't wanst belong to my ancisthors. In the time of Cahul Mohr, wan o' my grandfathers had tin thousand min and a hundherd thousand sheep at his command, not to spake of ships at say and forthresses and palaces on land."

"Arrah, how did you get robbed, Paddy?" asked Katty.

"Well, you see, my dear, they were a hard-dhrinkin' lot at the time I'm spakin' of. The landed property wint into the Incumbered Estates Coort and was sould for a song; the forthresses were changed into Martello towers, and the army took shippin' for France, but they were wrecked somewhere in the South Says, where they all swam ashore and turned New Zealandhers."

Katty was profoundly interested in this historical sketch of the Fret family, which Paddy rolled out without hitch or pause—indispensable elements of veracity in a spoken narrative. She allowed her lover to hold her hand, and fancied she was a princess.

As they sat in this delightful abstraction—the ecstasy known as spooning—they were startled by the sound of wheels in the farmyard. Katty, with one swift glance at the window, exclaimed in the wildest anguish, "Oh, Paddy, Paddy, what'll become o' me? Here's my father and mother come back from market already!"

"Take it aisy, darlint," replied Mr. Fret. "Can't I hide in the bedroom beyant?"

"In the *bedroom*!" gasped Katty in terror. "Not for all the world! Oh, dear! Oh, dear!"

Katty glanced in agony round the kitchen, and suddenly a great hope filled her to the lips. Over the fireplace was a crude platform [common to Irish farmhouses] on which saddles, harnesses, empty sacks, old ropes, boots, and sometimes wool, were stored away indiscriminately.

"Up there—up with you!" she cried, placing a chair for him to ascend.

Paddy lost no time in mounting, and having stretched himself at full length, his terrified sweetheart piled the litter over him until he was completely hidden from view.

The hiding was scarce effected when Katty's parents, Andy Tyrrell and old Mrs. Tyrrell, and Mrs. Gavin made their appearance. They each drew stools around the fire in order to enjoy the blaze, which was most welcome after their inclement ride.

"Are you yit mopin' over that blackguard, Paddy Fret, *ma colleen*?" asked Mrs. Gavin, the priest's housekeeper. " 'Tis a bad bargain you'd make o' the same *daltheen*, honey."

Katty, profoundly concerned in the mending of a stocking, pretended not to hear.

"She's gettin' sense, Mary," said Mrs. Tyrrell. "Boys'll be boys, and girls'll be girls, till the geese crow like roosters."

"I tould the vagabone at the last fair," remarked the old man, "that if ever I caught him within an ass's roar of this door I'd put him into the thrashin' machine and make chaff of his ugly bones. Bad luck to his impidince, the *aulaun*, to come lookin' afther my daughter."

A bottle of whiskey was now produced, and Katty busied herself in providing glasses for the party. Mrs. Gavin at first declined to "touch a dhrop, it bein' too airly," but once persuaded to hallow the seductive fluid with her chaste lips, it was wonderful how soon she got reconciled to potation after potation, till her inquisitive eyes began to twinkle oddly in the firelight.

The old man's attention had been fixed for some moments on the creel, or platform, above the fireplace. "What the divil is the matther with the creel?" asked Tyrrell. " 'Tis groanin' as if it had the lumbago."

"The wind, my dear man; 'tis the wind," replied Mrs. Gavin.

"Faith, I think 'tis enchanted it is," observed the lady of the house. "Look how it keeps rockin' and shakin', as if there was a throubled sowl in it."

Katty's heart went pit-a-pat during this conference. She knew that the creel was not the firmest of structures, and she shivered at the bare idea of Paddy making a turn which might send it to pieces.

Again the whiskey went round, mollifying the hard lines of Mrs. Gavin's unromantic countenance. Old Tyrrell, meanwhile, kept a steady eye on the creel, which had relapsed by this time into its normal immobility.

"Have a dhrop, Katty," he said, handing his daughter his glass.

The girl, who knew the consequences of disobeying his slightest command, touched the rim of the glass with her lips, and returned it with a grateful "Thank you, father." At the same time, on lifting her eyes to the creel she saw Paddy's face peering out at her and was honored with one of the finest winks that gentleman was capable of.

"Well, here's long life to all of us, and may we be no worse off this day twelvemonth," said the old man as he replenished the ladies' glasses and then set about draining his own. "Give me your hand, Mrs. Gavin. There isn't a finer nor a better woman in.. "

The sentence was never finished, for while he was speaking the creel gave way, and Paddy Fret, followed by the miscellaneous lumber which had concealed him, tumbled into the middle of the astonished party. The women shrieked and ran, whilst poor Katty, overcome by the terror of the situation, fainted into a convenient chair.

Paddy rose to his feet, unabashed and confident. "Wasn't that a grand fright I gave ye all?" he asked with superb indifference.

Tyrrell, pale as death and trembling in every limb, went to a corner, took up a gun, and pointed the muzzle at the intruder's head.

"Swear you'll make an honest woman of my daughter before another week," he hoarsely exclaimed, "or I'll blow the roof off your skull!"

"I'll spare you all the throuble," said Paddy. "Send for Father Maher and I'll marry her this minute, if you like." He then turned to the now-conscious girl. "Will you have Paddy Fret for your husband, Katty?" he asked.

The whiskey was finished, and on the following Sunday Father Maher united Paddy Fret and Katty Tyrrell in the little chapel of Croagh. Mrs. Gavin danced bravely at the wedding and was heard, more than once, to whisper that "only for her 'twould never be a match." Oh, the gall of some Irish women!

—John Francis O'Donnell (1837-74)

"First Love"

> I remember
>   Meeting you
> In September
>   'Sixty-two.
> We were eating,
>   Both of us;
> And the meeting
>   Happened thus:

Accidental,
  On the road;
(Sentimental
  Episode).
I was gushing,
  You were shy;
You were blushing,
  So was I.

I was smitten,
  So were you;
(All that's written
  Here is true).
Any money?
  Not a bit.
Rather funny,
  Wasn't it?
Vows we plighted,
  Happy pair!
How delighted
  People were!
But your father,
  To be sure,
Thought it rather
  Premature;
And your mother,
  Strange to say,
Was another
  In the way.

What a heaven
  Vanished then!
(You were seven
  I was ten.)
That was many
  Years ago—
Don't let any-
  body know.

—Anonymous, Kilkenny (circa 1889)

"O'Shanahan Dhu"

O'Shanahan Dhu, you're a rover, and you'll never be better,
  I fear;
A rogue, a deludherin' lover, with a girl for each day in
  the year;
Don't you know how the mothers go frowning, when a village
  you wander athrough,

For the priest you'd not seek were you drowning?—
>"That's the truth," says O'Shanahan Dhu,
>"For I'm aisy in love and divarsion,"
>Says the ranting O'Shanahan Dhu.

O'Shanahan Dhu, now you'll vex me; let me go, sir,
  this moment, I say!
I'm in airnest, and why so perplex me? See, I'm losing
  the work of the day!
There's my spinning all gone to a tangle, my bleached clothes
  all boiled to a blue,
While for kisses you wrestle and wrangle—
>"That's the truth," says O'Shanahan Dhu,
>"I own I've a weakness for kisses,"
>Says the ranting O'Shanahan Dhu.

O'Shanahan Dhu, here's my mother! If you don't let me go,
  faith, I'll cry;
Why, she'll tell both my father and brother, and with shame
  maybe cause me to die;
And then, at your bedside I'll haunt you, with a light in my hand
  burning blue,
From my shroud moaning, "Shemus, I want you"—
>"That's the truth," says O'Shanahan Dhu,
>"But, ah, darling, say that while you're living,"
>Says the ranting O'Shanahan Dhu.

—James J. Bourke (1837-94)

*

"Barney O'Hea"

Now let me alone, though I know you won't,
  I know you won't,
  I know you won't,
Now let me alone, though I know you won't,
  Impudent Barney O'Hea.
It makes me outrageous when you're so contagious—
  You'd better look out for the stout Corney Creagh!
For he is the boy that believes me his joy—
  So you'd better behave yourself, Barney O'Hea.
  Impudent Barney—
  None of your blarney,
    Impudent Barney O'Hea!

But as I was walking up Bandon Street,
Just who do you think 'twas myself should meet
  But impudent Barney O'Hea!
    He said I look'd killin',

I call'd him a villain,
And bid him that minute get out of my way.
He said I was jokin',
And look'd so provokin'—
I could not help laughing with Barney O'Hea!
   Impudent Barney—
   'Tis he has the blarney,
      Impudent Barney O'Hea!

He knew 'twas all right when he saw me smile,
For he is the rogue up to every wile,
   Is impudent Barney O'Hea!
      He coax'd me to choose him,
      For, if I'd refuse him,
He swore he'd kill Corney the very next day;
   So for fear 'twould go further,
   And—just to save murther—
I think I must marry that madcap O'Hea.
   Botherin' Barney—
   'Tis he has the blarney
      To make a girl Misthress O'Hea!

—Samuel Lover

"The Widow Malone"

Did ye hear of the widow Malone,
                     Ohone!
Who lived in town of Athlone,
                     Alone?
Oh! she melted the hearts
Of the swains in them parts,
So lovely the widow Malone,
                     Ohone!
So lovely the widow Malone.
Of lovers she had a full score,
                     Or more;
And fortunes they all had galore,
                     In store;
From the minister down
To the clerk of the Crown,
All were courting the widow Malone,
                     Ohone!
All were courting the widow Malone.

But so modest was Mrs. Malone,
                     'Twas known
No one could see her alone,
                     Ohone!

Let them ogle and sigh,
They could ne'er catch her eye;
So bashful the widow Malone,
Ohone!
So bashful the widow Malone.

Till one Mr. O'Brien from Clare—
How quare,
It's little for blushing they care
Down there—
Put his arm round her waist,
Gave ten kisses at laist—
"Oh," says he, "you're my Molly Malone,
My own"—
"Oh," says he, "you're my Molly Malone!"

And the widow they all thought so shy,
My eye!
Ne'er thought of a simper or sigh—
For why?
But "Lucius," says she,
"Since you've now made so free,
You may marry your Molly Malone,
Ohone!
You may marry your Molly Malone."

There's a moral contained in my song,
Not wrong;
And, one comfort, it's not very long,
But strong;

If for widows you die,
Learn to *kiss,* not to sigh,
For they're all like sweet Mistress Malone,
Ohone!
Oh, they're all like sweet Mistress Malone.

—Charles J. Lever (1806-72)

Part Two
Martyrs in Marriage

**Women's faults are many,
Men have only two:
Everything they say—
And everything they do.³**

*

Dr. Frank Curley, the famous mathematician of Dublin University, was once asked why his wife had never borne him any children.

"I know this may sound odd for an Irish scholar to confess, and it grieves me to say it," he commented ruefully, "but I'm afraid I cannot multiply."

*

To raise money for the new annex to Chicago's Sacrament High School, the ladies decided to hold a Saint Patrick's Day "White Elephant" sale. The chairwoman urged her fellow workers of the congregation to bring anything that was of no further use to them.

Some brought old lamps, various items of furniture, household utensils, and bric-a-brac. Others brought old coats and even shoes that were no longer of any use.

Mrs. O'Grady brought Mr. O'Grady.

*

The new father was visiting his wife in the maternity ward of Georgetown Hospital in Washington, D.C., where they had been animatedly discussing possible names for their infant daughter.

"I've made up my mind what we'll call the baby," announced the young woman. "We'll call her Maureen, after my mother."

The name at once evoked some dark thoughts in the father's mind, but he altered his face so that it would look halfway agreeable.

"Maureen, is it?" he cried, as though it was the best choice imaginable. "Now there's a fine Irish name! The girl I almost married before I met you was named Maureen. Ah yes, the name recalls some pleasant memories!"

---

³*Mrs. O'Banion's Lament,* circa 1890. Translated from the Old Irish by Y. W. Clancey, of Cork.

51

The wife maintained a stony silence for a whole minute before she made her final decision:

"We'll call her Pegeen, after my favorite aunt!"

*

Rory, the racetrack tout, and Sadie, the shady lady, were seized with a sudden urge for respectability, and got married. The honeymooners spent two happy weeks in Florida, where they not only enjoyed the sanctity of wedded bliss but picked up a little money on the side. Now they were back in Boston.

"Sweetheart," gushed the cooing bride as she carried Rory across the threshhold of their apartment over Sullivan's Saloon, "here we been married fer fourteen whole days, an' ta think ivrywan said it wouldn't last!"

*

"They say that it's all a myth about Irish women always talking on the telephone," sighed the knowledgeable husband wearily. "But it seems to me they're no different than other women. My Maggie, for instance, calls her friends every morning and talks for three or four hours without drawing a breath....Then she has her breakfast!"

*

At the turn of the century, when Jimmy and his wife first arrived in the United States from Ireland, he quickly became a labor agitator, or "walking delegate." He was prominent for his chronic idleness and was called "Jaws" by the working men, a testimony to his long-winded exhortations. Unfortunately for his family, he concentrated far more energy on these rabble-rousing speeches than he did upon honest toil. As a result, his wife, in an attempt to stave off actual hunger, resorted to the washtub as a means of support.

One day, the elegant Mr. "Jaws" entered the kitchen where his wife was perspiring over a customer's laundry.

"I tell ye, Biddy," he began, "the ownly way for a man to kape these slave-dhrivin' capitalists from realizin' the profits iv our labor, an' for wurrkers to kape their liberty, is to sthrike while the iron's hot."

"Jimmy," replied Biddy, a dangerous flash in her eye, "I've heard enough o' this whang-doodle. I can't sthrike while the iron's hot—I'm 'bliged to iron while the sthrike's hot, an' if ye come here with yer grievances I'll interduce ye to the argymint iv th' broom handle!"

*

A tattered bum accosted Haggerty on the Bowery.

"Misther," whined the panhandler in an unmistakable brogue, "could ye be afther sparin' a dollar fer a meal?"

"No, not for a meal," said Haggerty from long experience with street beggars, "but I'll give you a dollar for a drink."

"Thankee kindly," said the bum, "but it's not a dhrinkin' man I am. I just want somethin' to ate."

"You don't drink?" exclaimed the surprised Haggerty. "Then I'll give you a dollar for cigarettes—or buy yourself some cigars."

"I don't smoke, ayther."

"Then take this dollar and spend it on your girl."

"There's no intherest I have in women," said the man stubbornly. "It's just a meal I'd be wantin.' "

Haggerty eyed the shabby derelict for a long moment, and then, carefully choosing his words, he said, "All right, I'll give you a dollar—in fact, I'll give you two—but first I'd like you to come home with me."

"Why?" asked the bum suspiciously.

"For a very good reason," replied Haggerty. "I want my wife to see what happens to an Irishman who doesn't drink, smoke, or chase women."

*

At Pete's Bar one evening, Jimmy was unburdening his marital woes with complaints that grew more voluble with each shot of joy juice.

"I tell ye, Pete, that wife o' mine has a nonstop, no-skid tongue," he grumped. "Faith, that woman can talk fer sivin hours on anny subjec' in the wurrld."

"Count yer blessin's Jimmy," growled Pete. "My owld lady don't even nade a subjec'!"

*

The wedding sacraments were completed, and the groom slipped the gold band on his bride's finger. There were smiles and congratulations everywhere in the church. Especially joyous was the bride's father.

"Me b'y," enthused the father, slapping his new son-in-law on the back, "you're the second happiest man in th' wurrld!"[4]

*

Kathleen had been in the United States for only a month when she met Patrick. It was love at first sight—or whatever you call that sort of chemistry. After a whirlwind courtship of some seventy-two hours, they eloped and were married. In their honeymoon hotel room, they made ready for their wedding night, but when the bride removed her shoes and stockings, the husband's gaze was fixed on her feet.

"Darlint," he gasped, "sure an' ye niver towld me ye had six toes on aich foot!"

"But, Pathric, honey," she cooed, "ye niver asked me."

---

[4]*Mrs. O'Banion's Lament,* Ibid.

*

While shopping downtown one day, Madelaine happened to run into Catherine. They decided to have lunch together.

"I have a confession to make," said Madelaine as they sipped their after-dinner coffee. "I'm having an affair with a married man."

"You don't seem to be very happy about it," observed Catherine.

"I'm not," sighed Madelaine. "He's very careless about his appearance, he hates to shave, he's always broke, he drinks too much, he's lazy, and he's inconsiderate."

Later that evening, Catherine confronted her husband, a grim look of hostility in her narrowed eyes.

"I had a talk with Madelaine today," she said coldly. "She told me she was having an affair with you!"

*

The denizens of Hollywood, according to popular belief, do not take their marriage vows as seriously as do the folks in other parts of the United States. Actually, the belief is not founded on any known statistics, but Irish wit being what it is, it provides an abundance of humorous anecdotes. For example, where else but in Hollywood would anyone wonder why the groom always wears black?

"My son has been absent from school so many times to attend my weddings," fibbed one movie star, "he was listed as an habitual truant."

*

"Well, well, so you finally got a divorce," sympathized Jack. "I hope you had a good lawyer."

" 'Twas me owld lady's lawyer we used," explained Frank unhappily.

"But at layst he divided our propherty ayvenly—fifthy-fifthy, right down the line."

"You mean you sold your house and split the proceeds?"

"No, not a bit iv it," signed Frank. "She got the house and, faith, I got the mortgage!"

*

Trying to get the last word with an Irishwoman is like playing basketball with your pants down—you can't win. Not because her logic is superior to yours, but because female logic, in general, is just plain illogical. Here is a version of the Garden of Eden—Irish style:

Adam had wandered off in search of some new fruit, or, perhaps, he was birdwatching (the poor man had little else to do, considering that there was not a drop to drink in the place, and he hadn't yet heard about that other thing). But when he returned to his little cottage under the apple tree, Eve met him with a stony glare.

"Where've ye been?" she demanded.

"Why, takin' a walk, *macushla*," he replied.

"Don't ye *macushla* me, ye scalawag. Ye've been with anither woman!"

"Faith, Eve, an' where would I be afther findin' anither woman?" protested Adam. "Sure you're the ownly woman on airth."

"Ahah!" she shrieked. "So that's why I'm *macushla*!"

*

When Francis X. Dooley became Ireland's first cultural attaché to Mexico in the 1920s, he often wondered why the peons of that country always rode on burros while their wives walked behind. One Sunday, while strolling the countryside, he stopped a peasant and asked him the reason.

"But, *señor*," protested the Mexican, obviously surprised at this childish question, "my wife does not own a burro!"

*

Mr. Grogan, the middle-aged, balding insurance executive, may have been approaching his autumn years, but he was young at heart. Too young! his wife sometimes thought.

One afternoon, since she had finished her shopping and was in the business district, Mrs. Grogan decided to have lunch with her husband. They left his office together and entered the "down" elevator. But when they got inside, a very attractive girl called out a warm greeting:

"Top o' the mornin' to ye, *macushla*!" she cried, flashing a gay smile at the vastly uncomfortable Mr. Grogan.

Mrs. Grogan placed a proprietary hand on her husband's arm, and returned the girl's greeting:

"How do you do?" she said in an ice-cold voice. "I'm *Mrs. Macushla*!"

*

A newcomer to the neighborhood was sitting at the bar and chatting idly with Mike, the bartender. A woman entered the tavern.

"Bedad!" exclaimed the new patron. "There's an ugly wan fer ye!"

"Misther, that's me wife," snapped the bartender. "And it might be a good idee fer you to remimber that beauthy is ownly skin dape."

"Then fer Heaven's sake," retorted the stranger, "skin her!"

*

"Before a man agrees to a divorce, he should weigh the consequences carefully," declared Muldoon the amateur marriage counselor, whose office is located between the first three bar stools at Dinty's Place.

"Divorce should be seen for what it is—a matter of give and take: the husband gives and the wife takes," Muldoon continued, downing an Irish whiskey between two shots of Eyetalian vino. "True enough, she may not have married you for your money, but the chances are that she'll divorce you for it. The only ray of sunshine in any marriage breakup is that the wife usually gets custody of her mother.

"Fortunately, it is possible to detect the approximate time that a marriage begins to slide downhill," concluded madman Muldoon. "It starts when the husband unthinkingly says 'I do!' "

*

You need not put too much credence in this one—but here it is, direct from the neighborhood gossips in Hyannisport. It is a story with an old Irish moral: Excessive loyalty can sometimes prove embarrassing.

One night, before she became the nation's First Lady, Jackie Kennedy waited and worried until five o'clock in the morning for her husband to return home. Finally, at noon of the new day, when he still hadn't come home and she was at a loss as to what to do, she sent a telegram to five of her husband's closest friends: "JACK NOT HOME. WORRIED. DID HE SPEND NIGHT WITH YOU?"

Back came five wires with the single identical word: "YES!"

*

Songwriter Arthur Connelly's frequent use of off-color language always irritated his wife, who had tried for years to cure him of the habit. While shaving one day, he cut himself, and then launched into a series of cuss words that nearly exhausted his entire lexicon of profanities. When he finished, his wife decided to teach him a lesson. so she repeated every obscene word he had uttered. But songwriter Connelly was far from dismayed.

"You have the words right, honey," he commented in a mild voice, "but you sure as hell have no ear for the tune!"

*

Two important business executives were discussing their wives as they sipped their after-luncheon coffee.

"I'm ashamed to say this, Joe," sighed the older man, "but my wife won't tolerate my having a good-looking secretary."

"I feel sorry for you," said Joe, his voice full of sympathy. "My wife doesn't care how good-looking my secretary is—just as long as he's efficient!"

*

Pat and Eileen, an elderly couple who were on their way back to Ireland for a nostalgic visit, arrived early at the airport. The wife had insisted on packing innumerable outfits and a wide assortment of casual wear, accessories, and sundry articles for the trip. Struggling manfully under the heavy burden, the rather frail husband finally staggered to a halt and set down the suitcases and boxes.

"Faith, Eileen," he said wearily. "It's wishin' I am that we'd remimbered to bring the dinin' room table."

"I naded ivrything I packed!" snapped Eileen in a cold voice. "Ye nadn't be so sarcastic. Dinin' room table indade!"

"It's not sarcastic I'm bein', me dear wife," he explained sadly. "I was afther lavin' the tickets on it!"

＊

"On the Quay at Galway Bay"

Have I wife? Bedad, I have!
    But we was badly mated:
I hit her a great clout one night,
    And now we're separated.

And mornin's, goin' to me work,
    I meet her on the quay:
"Top o' the mornin' to ye, ma'am," says I;
    "To hell with ye," says she.

—L. A. G. Strong (1896-1971)

＊

"Conjugal (dis)Affection"

When Elliott (called "the Salamander")
    Was famed Gibralter's stout commander,
A soldier there went to a well
    To fetch home water to his Nell;
But fate decreed the youth to fall
    A victim to a cannon ball.
One brought the tidings to his spouse,
    Which drove her frantic from the house;
On wings of love the creature fled
    To seek her dear—she found him dead!
Her husband killed—the water spilt—
    Jude, ye fond females, what she felt!
She looked—she sighed—and melting, spoke:
    "Thank God, the pitcher is not broke!"

—Thomas Cannings (1770-1840)

Chapter Three

Small Fry and Aggravating Adolescents

Introduction

The Irish passion for knowledge has always been a factor in the shaping of the people's humor. In times of academic freedom, the Irishman's witticisms clearly reflected his learning. Conversely, his jokes were of the simple peasant variety when he was denied formal learning. For a thousand years, before the educational facilities of Ireland were obliterated by the English, the Emerald Isle had earned scholastic renown throughout the civilized world. Irish missionaries and other teachers carried the lamplight of learning to the continent during the Dark Ages. So intense was the Irish urge to pass along their accumulated knowledge to succeeding generations that, even after the British smashed Ireland's school system, Irish children furtively attended the legendary "hedgerow" schools.[1]

In the United States, the Irish immigrant hoped that his children would receive the education that had been denied him in his occupied homeland. But, for many, this was not to be. With the Penal Laws still vivid in his mind, the Irish Catholic wanted no part of the Protestant-oriented public schools where daily readings of the King James version of the Bible were conducted, Protestant hymns sung, and the Protestant form of the Lord's Prayer recited. But only a miniscule number of parochial "schools" existed, usually crude classes in church basements. In 1840, about a quarter of the 12,000 Catholic school-age children in New York City attended such parochial classes, another quarter went to secular schools, and half attend-

---

[1]The prohibition of all education, imposed by the British upon Ireland's Catholic children, reached full force after the imposition of the new Penal Laws of 1691. Schools were abolished. Children were forbidden to learn the very basics of reading and writing. The Gaelic language was prohibited. Yet, there were courageous teachers who conducted the forbidden classes in wooded glens; sometimes behind hedgerows—giving rise to the term "hedgerow" schools. When apprehended by their oppressors, the schoolmasters were exiled to what was then the wilderness of America, or banished to the Indies as indentured servants, where plantation owners were glad to accept the new field hands.

ed no schools at all. The condition was little different in Boston. A report in the *New York Post* of October 8, 1877, revealed that 9,000 of Boston's 43,000 Catholic youngsters were not in school. Thus, many a first generation Irish-American remained as illiterate as his immigrant parents.

The relationship between widespread education and a people's humor is readily apparent, whether in Ireland or the United States. Prior to the 1840s, when there were sufficient parochial schools for the relatively small enrollments, Irish humor flowered, and the classic humorists of Ireland were often quoted by the long-established Americans of Irish descent. Few disparaging jokes about them appeared in the press. But when education among Irish Catholics suffered its sharp decline from about 1851 to the turn of the present century, so too did the quality of the jokes. Along the Atlantic seaboard, the degrading anecdotes of the illiterate Pat and Mike were popular, as were others in that vein. In Ireland, the former peasant-type of humor soon lost its national character after the establishment of the Irish Republic and the institution of free, public education for all. And because the Irish never do anything by half measures, the humor of northern Ireland also gained a degree of intellectualism it had not known for generations. Much of the humor of the old masters in both the Irish Free State and in Ulster, men such as Lever, Sheridan, Fahy, Curran, and others who are represented in this book, enjoyed a healthy revival. Today, Ireland need not depend upon a few of its intellectuals for its primary source of entertainment as it had for so many dark years. Its mass humor is now as sophisticated and clever as it is in the United States—perhaps more so in its modernized folk stories.

Another factor that has exerted a strong influence on Irish humor is the people's strong sense of cohesiveness. Originally dwelling in clans, the Irish have remained clannish to this day. Long after other immigrant groups in the United States had divided their political loyalties, every large community could still rely on a solid Irish vote. And when other foreign-born Americans left their moribund nationality clubs and joined the Elks, their Irish neighbors remained staunch members of their beloved Hibernian Society.

All of these shared experiences, in addition to the cement of their religion which discouraged marriage outside the Church (and which further helped to limit outside contacts), contributed to the continuing "Irishness" of the Irish. Even now, such festive occasions as Saint Patrick's Day, for example will evoke a nostalgic tear in the eyes of an American of Irish descent for a land he has never seen, and in most cases never will.

Inevitably, Irish adult humor exerted its influence upon that of the children. In Ireland, where history, customs, and social mores play a larger and more personal role in family life, juvenile humor has retained its traditional uniqueness. Moreover, the jokes told by or about the youngsters of the Emerald Isle seem to be gentler and less critical than those of their counterparts in America. An explanation may lie in the fact that the humor expressed by American children of Irish descent has been influenced by the various other cultures in the United States. True enough, some of it may be indistinguishable from the humor enjoyed by native Irish children, but the difference does exist. For that reason, and for the sake of authenticity, the jokes told by or about Irish-American children are presented separately in

Part One of this chapter, while those referring to "Irish-Irish" youngsters are offered in Part Two.

The differences between both types may be apparent to only a few, but the *similarity* will be recognizable in the current of Celtic warmth that runs through each. And we can be forgiven if we find pleasure in these simple stories and poems that remind us of our own childhood. As that beloved Irishman of yesteryear, George M. Cohan, fervently remarked "Thank God for that glow of the child that remains in each of us."

—H. D. S.

Irish-American Seedlings

"When Willie Wet the Bed"

When Willie was a little boy,
    Not more than five or six,
Right constantly he did annoy
    His mother with his tricks.
Yet not a picayune cared I
    For what he did or said,
Unless, as happened frequently,
    The rascal wet the bed.

Closely he cuddled up to me
    And put his hand in mine,
Till all at once I seemed to be
    Afloat in seas of brine.
Sabean odors clogged the air,
    And filled my soul with dread,
Yet I could only grin and bear,
    When Willie wet the bed.

'Tis many times that rascal has
    Soaked all the bed-clothes through,
Whereat I'd feebly light the gas
    And wonder what to do.
Yet there he lay, so peaceful-like,
    God bless his curly head!
I quite forgave the little tyke
    For wetting of the bed.

Ah, me! those happy days have flown,
    My boy's a father too,
And little Willies of his own
    Do what he used to do.
And I, ah! all that's left for me
    Are dreams of pleasures fled;
My life's not what it used to be
    When Willie wet the bed!

—Eugene Field (1850-95)

Little Kevin, at his grandmother's house, sullenly expressed his displeasure at the dinner placed before him. But the old lady was adamant. As a girl in Ireland, she had often listened to the tales told by her own grandparents about the terrible famine of the 1840s, and the very thought of wasting food was abhorrent to her. Besides, back in the old country, a young spalpeen would not dare to defy his elders so rudely.

"Kevin," admonished the grandmother, "ate yer spinach. It will put color in yer chakes."

"Who wants green cheeks?" muttered the lad. "Green's fer shamrocks."

"Don't ye be gettin' rude with me, young man. Ate it—*now!*"

"But I don't like the damn stuff!"

"Kevin! If ye iver use that wurrd agin in this house, I'll take a shillelagh to yer bottom, ye hear?"

"Aw, Gran'ma, the Bible uses it all the time!"

*

In catechism class, Sister Marguerite had been emphasizing the blessedness of humility, explaining that strength of character was more important than physical strength, and that might does not always triumph over right. To illustrate her thesis, she told the inspiring Bible story of David and Goliath.

"Now, Michael," said Sister Marguerite to one of her pupils, "what important moral have you learned from that story?"

Little Michael, a junior edition of the proverbial fighting Irishman, thought for a moment and then offered his studied opinion: "Ya gotta remember ta duck!"

*

Not that Tim was a bad boy, mind you, or that he was particularly good, either. But the lad did have his moments when a hearty whack to the seat of his britches would have had beneficial results. So it was with a sigh of relief that his long-suffering parents deposited him at his grandmother's house for a two-week visit. That dear old lady, may the seven saints of Ireland protect her, insisted that she was well able to handle the boy. The parents, however, had their private misgivings; and well they should, as they realized when their darling Tim sent them his first letter:

> Dear Mom and Pop,
>
> It sure is nice here and we're having lots of fun. This morning me and Grandma played cops and robbers, and she's gonna bake me a whole bunch of cookies as soon as I untie her.
>
> Love,
> Tim.

*

In the third grade at Saint Joseph's, in Chicago, the teacher happened to notice that young Francis had not lifted his head once during the discussion of her revered Saint Patrick. Curious, she approached his desk to see what had so absorbed his interest. Francis, it seems, was busily engaged in drawing a picture with crayons.

"May I ask, Mr. 'Rembrandt,' what you are drawing?" she asked in a grim voice.

"I'm drawin' a pitcha of God," he explained.

"That's not possible," she retorted. "Nobody knows what God looks like."

Francis held his masterpiece aloft. "Well," he announced proudly, "they do now!"

*

Addressing the Sunday School class of his church, Father Brophy told of his experiences during his recent visit to the Vatican. "While I was there," he said to the children, "I went to all the shrines. But my proudest moment came when I saw the Holy See."

Little Mary was greatly impressed. That evening, at the dinner table, she bubbled over with the exciting news.

"Guess what, Mama," she cried excitedly. "When Father Brophy was at the Vatican, he saw the Holy See-saw!"

*

Editorial in the Boston Irish Gazette:

It's no wonder today's teenager is so confused, what with half the adult population exhorting him to "find yourself" and the other half telling him to "get lost!"

*

The Yuletide holidays had just passed. Mrs. Dugan heaved a sigh of relief as she finished cleaning up the post-Christmas mess in the house. Mrs. O'Rourke, her neighbor, dropped in for a chat.

"An' how was yer holiday?" asked Mrs. O'Rourke.

"Faith, I'm that glad it's over," said Mrs. Dugan wearily. "I got a visit from a jolly, bearded fellow with a grea-a-t big sack...me son came home from college with his laundry!"

*

The late Ed Sullivan was noted for his perpetual look of Celtic gloom, a trait shared by many other Irishmen, but the following joke, told to him by comedienne Patsy Kelly, evoked one of his rare grins.

According to Miss Kelly, the Christmas season was approaching, and teenage Danny, a student at Immaculate Conception High School, knew exactly what he wanted as his Yule gift.

"What I need is another alarm clock," he told his father.

"What's the matter with the one you have?" queried the father. "Doesn't it work?"

"Yeah, sorta," mumbled Danny. "It wakes me up, but it don't turn me on!"

*

Irish-Americans, as a whole, are loyal to Catholic institutions and dogma. In southern California's movieland, however, a few have taken issue with the strict prohibition of divorce, as enunciated by the chief producer-director at the Vatican. These Hollywood multiple marriages also result in confusion among the small fry as well as among the adults. Film director Will Ryan relates the tongue-in-cheek episode about his little son's confrontation with another boy in Beverly Hills.

"Betcha a dollar my father can lick your father," challenged the other kid.

"Don't be silly," retorted master Ryan. "My father *is* your father!"

*

Grandma Doherty and her little grandson, Mickey, arrived early at Disneyland. For several hours they had a happy time together, but it was an exhausting experience for Grandma. About noon, she decided to sit down and rest her aching feet. Realizing it was lunch time, she handed Mickey some money.

"Here, *avick,* take this and get somethin' to eat," she instructed. "But first, tell me what ye'll be afther buyin'."

"Oh boy, two whole dollars!" exclaimed Mickey, glancing at the bills. "I'm gonna buy cotton candy, jelly beans, peanuts, popcorn, hot dogs..." He stopped short for a moment, detecting the ominous gleam in Grandma Doherty's eye..."and a green vegetable!"

*

Miss Abigail Tierney, for many years the assistant librarian at the University of Dublin, had long cherished the dream of living in the great metropolitan city of New York, where she could enjoy the artistic and cultural opportunities she had heard and read so much about. Upon her retirement, Miss Tierney journeyed across the ocean and settled in a small apartment in the West Seventies. But disillusionment and boredom soon overcame her. New York, she belatedly realized, was far less relaxing for a well-mannered spinster than Dublin. So she decided to move to the far suburbs. With a full-page real estate advertisement in her hand, she got off the train on the outskirts of Westchester County. She was totally unfamiliar with the area, so she stopped a boy of twelve or thirteen to ask for directions.

"How do I get to the Shady Lane block of houses?" she asked.

"Well, there ain't no buses this time o' day," responded the lad. "You'll hafta walk. It's about twenny blocks f'm here."

"Twenty blocks from this railroad station?" echoed Miss Tierney incredulously. "But it says right here in the newspaper ad that it's no more than five!"

"Lady," said the boy, shrugging his shoulders, "you kin b'lieve me or you kin b'lieve the ad—but I ain't tryin' ta sell ya nothin'!"

*

According to humorist Patrick Ireland, one of the differences between Irish-American kids and their counterparts in the "old country" is the impertinence of the Americans. In the Emerald Isle, for example, when Mother tells Junior to put his hand over his mouth when he yawns, he does so. In the United States, Junior retorts, "What! And get my hand bit?"

Father doesn't fare any better. In Ireland, he will wait until Mother is out of the room and then, hesitantly, address his thirteen-year-old son: "I suppose it's time I told you about the birds and the bees." Father is assured of a respectful and attentive hearing. But in America, little Junior grumbles, "Aw, Pop, you told me about them bugs last year. Now I wanna hear about girls!"

*

The American grade school system has earned innumerable plaudits for its "progressive" educational activities, its "head start" programs and psychology-oriented teaching methods designed to launch the children into intellectual heights ordinarily expected of much older students. Some of its supporters tend to look down their scholastic noses at the educational systems of other countries, who, in turn, view the American method as permissive rather than progressive, and often frivolous, as well.

In Ireland, for example, not everyone speaks with a Pat and Mike brogue, nor do they all speak or even understand the Gaelic tongue. Some of the grammar schools, in fact, teach Latin and Greek prefixes, suffixes, and root words to their little pupils to foster a better grasp of the English language. Occasionally, an American educator will lose his or her aplomb and air of condescension when confronted with one of these pint-size immigrants who have not had the "advantage" of a "head start" in the United States. A case in point is five-year-old Kathleen who had just left Ireland with her widowed mother to live in the City of New York. The child's proud mother insisted on entering her daughter in the first grades, rather than in kindergarten.

"I'm sorry," said the disapproving principal, "but your little girl would miss our 'head start' program. It would be some time before she could catch up with the other children who have had that advantage. Anyway, the age requirement for the first grade is six years."

"But she can easily pass the test for six-year-olds," protested the mother. "She was at the head of her first grade class in Dublin."

"Oh, all right!" snapped the exasperated principal, turning to the child.

"Let me hear you say some words."

"Which kind of words, sir?" asked Kathleen sweetly. "Germane to the subject of immediate concern, or purely irrelevant?"

*

Elsewhere in this book, Jim Murray states that the farther an Irishman gets from Ireland, the more Irish he becomes. There is more than a kernel of truth in Murray's assertion, as witness the Irish-American father who was discussing his ancestral land with his little son, Jamie. As most boys are, Jamie was full of questions.

"Daddy," he asked, "when was the potato famine in Ireland?"

"Well, now I really don't recall at the moment," replied the father, "I think it was before World War II, though."

A little later, after some more conversation about the "old country," Jamie inquired, "Daddy, why is the Irish Free State and Ulster mad at each other?"

"I never did understand that myself," said the father. "They should try to get along better."

"Daddy," asked Jamie again after a thoughtful pause, "what's a leprechaun?"

"Why a leprechaun is a—well—it's a little—uh—hmmm, I guess I don't know that either."

Several more questions followed with much the same results, until little Jamie realized at last that he might be pestering his tolerant father.

"Gee, Daddy, I hope you don't mind my asking so many questions."

"Not at all, son," replied the father genially. "How else will you ever learn anything about the old homeland?"

*

From the cheery pages of the *Catholic Digest* comes this bit of immortal whimsy:

> Michael McGoohan of Saint Thomas Aquinas Grade School in the Bronx, has just put his first grade on the literary map with two riddles:
>
> "What is a fireman's son? *A little squirt!*
> "What causes forest fires? *Mountain ranges!*"
>
> Master McGoohan's talent might eventually surpass those of such fellow Irishmen as Shaw, Yeats, Goldsmith, or Sheridan, but he will have a lot to answer for when he finally meets them in Irish Heaven.

*

"When I was a girl in Ireland I had too much respect for my parents to talk back the way American children do," sighed Mrs. Grogan. "I don't know what this generation is coming to. Only the other night, my teen-age daughter was leaving for a party and I called out to her, 'Have a good time, honey.' And my daughter yelled back, 'Don't tell me what to do!' "

*

Teenager Jimmy Flaherty, he of the unshaven cheeks, bare feet, torn blue jeans, and unfragrant odor, was finally taken to task by his outraged father, a state assemblyman who started out as a policeman and worked his way down.

"Now look here, me bucko," began Mr. Flaherty, "I'll not be havin' a son o' mine drifthin' along like a will-o'-the-wisp, dhressin' like a refugee from the potato famine an' ignorin' his school wurrk. Faith, Jimmy, it's almost a man ye are now, an' ye owe it to yersilf to take life a little more seriously."

"Aw, what the hurry?" responded Jimmy in a sullen voice. "I got plenty of time."

"Do ye now?" snapped Mr. Flaherty. "Just stop an' think fer a minute: if I were to die tonight, where would ye be?"

Jimmy thought of his father's political deals and campaign promises. His reply was to the point:

"I'd still be right here with Mom and Sis. The question is, Dad, where would *you* be?"

*

The Three Stages of Man[2]

THE CHILD. "My papa can lick your papa."
THE ADOLESCENT. "Aw, Pop, you don't know nothin'!"
THE ADULT. "Well, according to my father..."

*

As the Twig Is Bent[3]

Rory was on his knees beside his bed, saying his nightly prayers. His father listened to the boy's "Now I lay me down to sleep," and patiently waited through all the blessings his little son bestowed upon each member of the family, sundry neighbors, friends, and the family cat, dog, and goldfish. But the man's composure was jolted when Rory earnestly concluded with—"And please, Jesus, send some clothes to those poor ladies in my daddy's magazines!"

*

Here is another of those apochryphal anecaotes about New York Senator Patrick Moynihan. Whether true or not, it is worth repeating.

As a schoolboy, young Patrick was not noted for his tidiness. His mother *sent* him to school as spotless as a snowflake, but his *arrival* caused her, and

---

[2]*The San Francisco Shamrock*, Vol. 6, No. 8 (Aug. 1931).
[3]*Ibid.*

his teacher, a bit of consternation. Finally, in despair, the teacher warned him that if he appeared just once more with such dirty hands, she would be obliged to thrash him. Well, you know kids. He did indeed reappear at school in the same condition.

"Patrick," snapped the teacher, "hold out your hand for inspection."

The boy obligingly spat on his palm, rubbed it on the seat of his trousers, and held it out.

The teacher surveyed it with disgust.

"Young man," she said, "if you can show me another hand anywhere in this school that is dirtier than that, I'll let you off."

Without a word, Patrick held out his other hand.

*

The Muldoon family—father, mother, and six-year old Terence—boarded their ship and set sail for their new life in America. At the time of their departure from Galway, there were three Muldoons, as noted, but when they arrived at Boston Harbor, there were four—the latest addition being baby Kathleen, born on the high seas.

Burdened with all the cares attendant to settling in a new house and caring for an infant, Mrs. Muldoon sent Terence to the corner variety drugstore to get some supplies for his tiny sister. He went to the counter where they were sold, stated his wishes, and, in the space of a few minutes the salesgirl returned with his package.

"That will be four dollars for the diapers and twenty-four cents for the tax," she said.

"Faith, lady," protested Terence, "we'll not be nadin' anny tacks! In Oireland, ivrywan uses safety pins!"[4]

*

Summer was over and the children were back in school, their vacation a fast-fading memory. Miss Dooley, the fifth grade teacher, decided to bring her students abreast of the academic world with a practical example. On the blackboard, she chalked the sentence, "I didn't do nothing last Saint Patrick's Day, I didn't do nothing last New Years Eve, and I didn't do nothing during my summer vacation."

"Now, Dennis," Miss Dooley called out to one of her pupils, "tell the class, please, how that should be corrected."

Dennis gave the problem his serious consideration. "Seems to me," he answered at last, his Irish sense of romance kindled, "you oughtta get a boyfriend!"

*

---

[4]The San Francisco Shamrock, Vol. 6, No. 9 (Sept. 1931).

Part Two
"Irish"-Irish Sproutlings

When Daniel Patrick Moynihan was Ambassador to the United Nations, and probably the most eloquent representative America ever had in that organization, he had occasion to visit Ireland on a brief diplomatic mission. Just outside the Shannon airport, he bought a paper from a young newsboy who charged him the equivalent of five cents.

"My, that's cheap!" Moynihan declared. "I'd have had to pay double the price for this paper in the United States."

"Faith, sor," remarked the little businessman, "you can pay me dooble if it'll be makin' ye feel betther!"

*

Millicent was a sweet child, but she had one fault that was the despair of her mother. Millicent was an "exaggerator," a "distorter," to quote a couple of gentler phrases.

Upon her urgent pleadings, Millicent was given a cute puppy for her sixth birthday, provided that she stop telling tales. Millicent agreed. But habit flourishes strong within the human heart, and Millicent was soon about the neighborhood informing the other children that she had been given a lion.

"Now see here, young lady," said her mother when she heard the news, "I want you to march right upstairs and ask God to forgive you for telling a falsehood. A lion indeed!"

Meekly, the little girl went upstairs, and, when she finally returned, she wore a beatific smile on her face.

"Did you ask God to forgive you?" asked the mother suspiciously.

"Yis, mama, that I did," replied Millicent, "but he towled me not to be worryin' about it. He can hardly tell the diffunce himself!"[5]

*

[5]Shawn O'Gilvie, *At the Poteen Party* (Cork: O'Donohugh & Sons, Ltd., 1881).
69

Silence may be golden, but for the McNeil family it was anything but agreeable. Their only son, Padraic, had never uttered a single word in his nine years of life. The distraught parents had taken him to a dozen specialists in Dublin, Belfast, and London, but never a sound did the lad make.

One evening, as they were at dinner, Padraic finished his pork and *praties,* looked across the table at his mother, and calmly said, "Mama, I'll be afther havin' anither helpin' o' pork."

Both of his parents gaped at him in astonishment.

"You can talk!" cried the amazed father.

"Iv coorse," replied Padraic.

"Faith, son, an' why have you niver spoken a wurrd until now?"

"Because," explained the laddie, his eyes on the pork and *praties,* "I niver naded nothin'!"[6]

Rosemary had reached the grand old age of seven, and for her birthday her grandfather presented her with a doll.

"Mommy, Mommy! Look at the beeyootiful doll Gran'pa gave me!" she cried ecstatically. "He's the bestest gran'pa in all Ireland. When I grow up I'm goin' to marry him!"

"I'm afraid you can't do that, honey," said the mother, laughing. "You'd be marrying my father."

"But, Mommy," protested Rosemary, "you married mine!"[7]

•

While this little vignette had its birth in Ireland, it strikes a responsive chord in the female breast wherever it is repeated—in Dublin, London, Paris or, doubtlessly, in Addis Ababa.

Theresa, the mother of seven children, and Colleen, who had five, were discussing their domestic problems as they sipped their mid-morning tea.

"Theresa, I've been meaning to ask you something," began Colleen. "How in the world do you always manage to get your children's attention the way you do?"

"Nothing to it," explained Theresa. "I just sit down and look comfortable."

•

"During World War II," reports Elaine McAllistair, former secretary to the late president of Ireland, Eamon de Valera, "I was sent to London to deliver some papers to the military authorities there. The Nazis had been bombing the city unmercifully. But, at the moment, my thoughts were far

[6]Shawn O'Gilvie, *Larking With Laddie* (Dublin Univ. Press, 1884).

[7]Oliver St. John Gogarty, *Start from Somewhere Else* (New York: Doubleday & Company, Inc., 1955).

away—back home in Ireland with my grandchildren. Suddenly a particularly loud clap of thunder startled me so much that I jumped a foot in the air. A passing urchin stopped and offered his sympathy.

" 'Hit's all right, lydy,' said the boy in soothing tones. 'Hit ain't 'itler; hit's Gawd!' "

*

Cynthia returned home from her Sunday School class in Donegal, one day, with a disconcerting question.

"Mama, where did I come from ?" asked the little girl.

"Wh-why," stammered the surprised mother, "the stork—well, that is, God....Cynthia dear, why do you ask?"

"Because a new girl in our class said she came from County Monaghan, and I just wondered where *I* came from!"

*

Harry Lauder, a famous Scot entertainer of half a century ago, once declared that no one tells jokes in northern Ireland. Lauder himself was joking, of course, as this Downpatrick anecdote will attest.

Danny came home from Bible class one Sunday and confronted his parents with the surprising news that Biblical children used profanity. "Even babies swore," asserted the boy.

"Sure an' there's not a bit o' truth in it," averred Danny's mother firmly. "Little boys an' girls niver used durrty wurrds, an' it's not afther sayin' so in the Bible, nayther. As fer babies cursin' in Owld Testament days, that's ridic'lous!"

"But, Mother," argued Danny, "didn't I read it meself, this very mornin'? It says that Job cursed the day he was born!"

*

Two small boys of Dungannon, one a Catholic and the other a Protestant, were playing in the square one morning when a minister of the Church of England, new to the town, happened to pass by. "Good morning, Father," said the Catholic boy respectfully, mistaking his clerical garb for that of a priest's.

As soon as the minister passed, the Protestant boy turned on his companion with an exclamation of deep scorn.

"Father?" he jeered. "He ain't no Father—he's got five kids!"

*

Yes, Virginia, there really is a town in Ireland named Dingle, and this is Dingle's contribution to Ireland's cornucopia of humor.

A little schoolgirl in English class was told to write an essay about King Alfred, but was warned by the teacher not to elaborate too much on the familiar story of the cakes. The youngster wrote her composition, summing up the historical facts about the monarch, and then concluded with a rather startling paragraph:

"There is another incident in King Alfred's life. One day, he visited a home where a certain lady lived—but the less said about that, the better!"

*

The light snow that had started to fall in Coleraine shortly after school opened that morning was now growing heavier. Dismissal time was approaching, and Miss McGrath, the third grade teacher, felt duty-bound to warn her little charges against playing too long in the snow.

"Now, children," she began, "you must be careful about colds and overexposure. I had a darling little brother once, only seven years old. One day, he went out in the snow with his new sled and caught cold. Pneumonia set it, and a few days later he died."

The room was silent for a few moments when, in the back row, Mickey raised his hand.

"Miss McGrath," he asked anxiously, "where's his sled?"[8]

*

Crises in the Classroom

"I have a problem," sighed teacher McGrath of Coleraine, "Either I lost one of my little girls or a pair of rainboots walked to school by themselves!"[9]

*

The "permissive society" was frowned upon in pre-Republic Ireland, to put it conservatively. Schoolteachers got their message across with stern injunctions, whacks to the rump of obstreperous pupils, and dire warnings of the consequences that invariably followed moral lapses. Proof, you say? Hark!

Back in the 1890s—I'd go so far as to say 1893 if I was that sure—a dedicated schoolteacher had just spent the better part of an hour instructing his students on the benefits of pursuing Godly ways, with ample and gory details of what happened to bad boys when they forsook the straight-and-narrow for the primrose path to you-know-where.

"Now, Master Timothy Malone," said the teacher, "tell the class what is meant by an unclean spirit."

"Plase, sor," replied Timothy promptly, a grin on his freckled face, "an unclane sperit is a dhurty divil!" He glanced around the room for signs of approval for his little joke.

The teacher fixed a stony eye on the class jester. "Master Timothy, kindly step forward to the front of the room and bend over the chair," he ordered in a deadly monotone.

---

[8]*Wexford Times,* April 1926.
[9]*Ibid.,* August 1926.

As Timothy assumed the correct posture over the chair, the teacher reached under his desk for the shillelagh which was kept handy for just such emergencies. "And now, about that divil, me young bucko, we're about to do a little exorcisin'!"

*

Junior Wisdom from Glengariff

Willie tumbled into bed, leaving his room in a characteristic state of disorder. His mother came into the room to hear his prayers and kiss him good night. She took one look at the messy room and chided him gently:

"Now, I wonder who didn't hang up his clothes before going to sleep."

"Adam," said Willie.

*

The Reverend John O'Shay, of Ballyshannon, stands sponsor for this one.

Whoever said that small boys can't be kindhearted didn't know youngsters. We have for our authority a nice old lady and a very small boy who were seated side by side in church. As the collection plate was being passed, the little boy noticed that the lady seemed to be fumbling fruitlessly in her purse.

"Here, Mum," he whispered, "take my offerin'. I'll hide under the seat."

*

The eminent Irish composer, Victor Herbert, was fond of telling the story about the two little girls he met while visiting Galway. There they were, as alike as a pair of ears, standing in front of a small house, hand in hand. He was immediately taken with the children, and he asked their names.

"I'm Patricia, she's Rosemary," said one.

"You're twins, aren't you?" he asked.

"No, sir," they replied.

"But aren't you sisters?"

"Yes."

"Well, how old are you?"

"We're both six."

"In that case," he laughed, "if you're both six and you're sisters, you *must* be twins."

"No, sir," explained one of them politely, "we're triplets. Maggie is in the house!"

*

Gracie's daddy was a purser on a vessel plying the waters between Ireland and England. Today was her ninth birthday and her father had purchased a couple of gifts in Liverpool for the occasion. Little Gracie was almost over-come with joy when she opened the package to find the two gifts she had most ardently desired: a wristwatch with a tiny alarm bell, and a vial of per-fume. She chattered about her new possessions all day long, wearying her parents with the subject. Father O'Malley, of Saint Paul's Church, was ex-pected for dinner and Mother gently admonished her daughter in advance.

"Now, Gracie dear, everybody knows about your watch with the bell, and the perfume, too. We're all happy for you. But, faith, you mustn't be talking about them all the time—especially in front of our nice priest this evening."

At dinner, the child held her peace throughout the greater part of the meal, with her exciting news just bursting to be told. Finally, a lull in the conversation occurred and, unable to control herself a moment longer, yet mindful of her promise to her mother, she tugged at Father O'Malley's sleeve.

"Father," she cried, "if anyone hears anything or smells anything, it's me!"

*

At Dublin University, that cradle of Ireland's famed scholars and sages, the professor was discoursing on an important topic when he was interrup-ted by the sound of the bell signifying the close of the period. His annoy-ance mounted when the students noisily prepared to leave, even though he was in the very middle of his lecture.

"Just a moment," he barked. "I have a few more pearls to cast!"

*

The *Athlone Gazette* reported this sad tale in June 1928:
Mother was in the kitchen preparing dinner and Father was out in the rear of the house where he was performing some amateur carpentry work. Sud-denly the tranquility was shattered when seven-year-old Michael came sob-bing to his mother.

"What's the matter?" asked the child's mother. "Why are you crying?"

"B-b-because D-d-daddy hit his finger with the hammer," blubbered Michael

"Oh, you needn't cry about that," said the mother, smiling. "Daddy does that all the time. Why didn't you just laugh?"

"I did!" sobbed Michael.

*

Modern-day Americans will recognize a familiar theme in this medical story of today's Ireland.

The insistent ringing of the telephone jarred the physician from a deep and much-needed sleep. He looked at the clock beside his bed. It was three in the morning. He picked up the receiver.

"Dr. Byrnes here," he said grumpily.

"Oh, Doctor," responded a frantic voice at the other end of the line, "this is Mrs. Fannon. My little boy got up in the middle of the night and found some of his father's hunting cartridges. He just swallowed a bullet!" Her voice now bordered on hysteria. "Oh, what shall I do?"

"I'll be over later in the day," replied Dr. Byrnes calmly. "Meanwhile, try not to point him at anyone!"

*

It is said, with good reason, that Irish-American children are lazier than their "Irish"-Irish counterparts. If that is true, then Irish youngsters certainly learn quickly, given the opportunity.

A Fermanagh boy spent two years in the United States with his aunt and uncle, and returned to Ireland with a new outlook on life. On his first Sunday at home, his Bible class teacher called upon him to answer a question.

"Do you know the parables?" she queried.

"Yes, mum."

"Then tell the class about the one you like best."

"That's aisy," said the pride of Fermanagh. "I like the wan where somebody loafs an' fishes!"

*

There is a story circulating in Roscommon about an incident which occurred at the Church of Our Lady of the Bountiful Beads.

According to the gossips, young Timmie posed this question in catechism class: "What did Jesus mean in the Bible when he said, 'Call no man father,' Father?"

*

If it weren't for the habit of biting her nails, Kathleen would have been the nicest little girl in Donegal. The day inevitably came when her mother caught her at it again, after repeated scoldings.

"Now see here, Kathleen," the mother exploded, "do you know what happens to little girls who bite their nails? They swell up like a balloon!"

Considerably impressed with this revelation, Kathleen made a supreme effort to desist from the habit. A week or so later, her mother's sister, who lived in Letterkenny, appeared for a visit. She waddled into the room, clearly pregnant.

Kathleen took one look at the visitor and shouted with glee:

"Oh, Auntie, I know what *you've* been doing!"

*

The O'Keefes of County Clare had long contributed to the scholarship of Ireland. However, in the United States, their transplanted descendant, twelve-year-old Francis, was having some difficulty in maintaining the family tradition. Actually, Francis was a fair student at Saint Paul's, but his great weakness was grammar: he always muddled his past and present participles.

"Francis," scolded his teacher, "you've been told repeatedly not to say 'I HAVE WROTE.' Now, I want you to write, 'I have written' one-hundred times."

Dutifully, Francis finished the task and left the completed pages on the teacher's desk—together with an explanatory note:

"I have wrote 'I have written' one-hundred times like you said, and I have went home."

*

Martha had been naughty at school and was sent home with a note to her mother. By way of punishment, she was compelled to eat her dinner alone at a little table in a corner of the dining room. The rest of the family deliberately ignored her; until, that is, they heard her audibly delivering grace over her own meal.

"I thank thee, Lord Jesus," she intoned, "for preparing a table before me in the presence of mine enemies!"

Nineteenth-Century Children's Folk Riddles
(from the Gaelic—North and South Ireland)[10]

There's a garden that I ken,
Full of little gentlemen;
Little caps of blue they wear,
And green ribbons very fair.
(Flax)

I tossed it up as white as snow;
Like gold on a flag it fell below.
(An egg)

I ran and I got,
I sat and I searched;
If I could get it
I would not bring it with me;
As I got it not I brought it.
(A thorn in the foot)

From house to house he goes,
A messenger small and slight;
And whether it rains or snows,
He sleeps outside at night.
(Boreen)*

---

[10]Translated from the Old Irish by Douglas Hyde (1860-1949) and Francis A. Fahy (1854-1931).
*A lane, or path.

On the top of the tree
See the little man red,
A stone in his belly,
A cap on his head.

(Haw)†

A bottomless barrel,
It's shaped like a hive,
It is filled full of flesh
And the flesh is alive.

(A thimble)

As I went through the garden,
I met my Uncle Thady, ‡
I cut his head from off his neck
And left his body "aisy."

(A head of cabbage)

Out in the field my daddy grows,
Wearing two hundred suits of clothes.

(Large head of cabbage)

Snug in the corner I saw the lad lie;
Fire in his heart and a cork in his eye.

(Bottle of whiskey)

My daddy on the warm shelf,
Talking, talking to himself.

(Pot simmering on the hob)**

Out she goes,
And the priest's dinner with her.

(Hen with an egg)

Up in the loft the round man lies,
Looking through two hundred eyes.

(A sieve)

---

†The fruit of the Old World hawthorne.
‡In some versions, this riddle took the feminine gender. "Auntie Daisy" is recited instead of "Uncle Thady." Although seldom heard by the 1900s, this variant may well have been the original, as it rhymes more realistically with "aisy."
**A projection, or shelf, at the back or side of a fireplace, used for keeping food warm.

Chapter Four

Working, Struggling, and Goofing Off

Introduction

The identity of the first Irishman to reach the New World is unknown. Perhaps he was Saint Brendan of Clonfert who, according to an ancient Vatican manuscript, sailed westward from Ireland in the sixth century. At the "edge" of the world he sighted a vast, unknown land. This new continent, named *Insula Sancti Brendani,* appeared on nearly all maps for several centuries thereafter. Nine hundred years later, another Irishman, William from Galway, was listed among the crew who sailed with Christopher Columbus.

Neither Saint Brendan nor William of Galway settled in the New World; but we do know that the earliest colonial settlements were well represented by the sons and daughters of Ireland. In 1609, Francis Maguire of Virginia wrote (in Gaelic) an account of life in that colony. In the first official census of 1790, the number of Irish immigrants was placed at 44,000; about 100,000 other Americans were classified as "Irish descent."

From those early days to the present, Irish-Americans have been in the vanguard of those who built this nation and broadened its frontiers. Robert Fulton, for example, born in 1765 of poor Irish parents, invented flax- and rope-making machines which later helped introduce the industrial revolution in the United States. In 1807, he launched his famous steamboat, *Clermont.* Fulton has often been called the father of the American canal system, but he shares that distinction with another Irishman, Christopher Colles, a navigation director of the River Shannon before emigrating to colonial America in 1766. It was Colles who introduced the lock system for canals and who drew up the plan for the Erie Canal. The technical breakthrough paved the way for the construction of the many great canals that were to follow.

New York's Governor DeWitt Clinton pushed through the building of the 350-mile Erie Canal in 1817, and by the time it was finished in 1825, more than three thousand Irishmen had labored on the project. The first private company organized for canal building after the American Revolution was headed by George Washington. Employing Irish workmen almost exclusively, the Chesapeake and Ohio Canal was completed in 1840.

Tens of thousands of Irish-Americans moved to the building of the nation's railroads. The work was as backbreaking as it was dangerous. It was estimated at the time that the average working life of the Irish railroader was only seven years. Many thousands of others labored in the coal mines for as little as a dollar a day, sometimes for sixty cents and a ration of whiskey. The working life of the miners was even shorter than the railroaders,. being a scant *six* years! They were cruelly exploited, yet their history is one of accomplishment as they fought to improve their economic and social conditions. In the end, the "fighting Irish" succeeded, but their struggle was long and filled with agony.

For the most part, the early Irish emigrants were a fairly skilled and adventurous people, some even prosperous. But when catastrophe engulfed Ireland in the 1840s, the most unskilled and the poorest of the poor were driven by sheer hunger from their native land. This catastrophe was the terrible ordeal of the potato famine, from 1845 to 1850, in which a million Irish starved to death—a fifth of the entire population of Ireland. Untold thousands of others—hollow-eyed, walking skeletons—barely survived. There was plenty of food in Ireland, but not for them. The starving Irish could only watch helplessly while their cereal grains and meat were shipped off to the hated absentee landlords in England. When they resisted (as many did), they were dispossessed from their homes, imprisoned, and even put to death. Their defiant display of a shamrock, "the wearing of the green" as a protest, was sufficient cause for dire punishment.

The catastrophe struck suddenly in the summer of 1845, when a blight destroyed the one crop the Irish were permitted to keep—the lowly potato. Other crops remained unaffected by the plant disease. For four more years the blight attacked the potato crop, leaving the Irish little or nothing to eat, even as England sent its ships for the wheat, corn, barley, flour, oatmeal, beef, and pork that would have saved the lives of the starving masses. So the Irish people died, just as their last and only hope—the potato—died.

The story of the modern Irish in America is a direct result of that famine. In its first year, 1845, more than 50,000 people migrated to the United States from Ireland. The number of immigrants increased each year until 1851, when 216,000 reached America. In the ten-year period between 1845 and 1855, more than 2½ million Irish men, women, and children were driven by the famine to the United States to find a new and better life.

Unlike other immigrants, the Irish were fortunate in that they spoke English; with a brogue, perhaps, but they were readily understood. They soon found employment as construction laborers, just as their countrymen had before them. Wherever they went—to New England, New York, south to New Orleans, west to Chicago and San Francisco—they wielded the picks, shovels, and hammers that transformed towns into cities. Others accepted any job that would feed their families. They worked as bartenders, janitors, longshoremen, peddlers, and livery-stable helpers. Saving their pennies, many of the laborers became contractors; bartenders opened their own saloons; wagon drivers went into the transportation and haulage business. Their combative nature and love of excitement impelled still others to whatever employment offered a uniform in addition to security: they became policemen, firemen, motormen, and conductors. The women went into domestic service, doing their part as maids, laundresses, cooks, charwomen, and the like. So it was that those intrepid Irish made their way in hustling, bustling, fiercely competitive America. Inch by inch, they advanced in every trade and profession, until they reached the White House itself with John F. Kennedy, a president of the United States whose ancestry they shared.

Bereft of worldly goods though he was, the Irish immigrant brought with him two precious possessions that were not noted by U.S. Customs inspectors: his religion and his keen sense of humor. Both have prevailed. His religion is discussed in another chapter, but looking back at the hardships he had experienced, it seems incredible that he could find anything to laugh about. Yet, laugh he did, just as the Irish have always managed to use laughter as an emotional safety valve in the face of adversity. It is that lighthearted, sunny nature, revealed in his workaday jokes, that we will now enjoy. Some of the amusing anecdotes go back a great many years, to seventeenth-, eighteenth-, and nineteenth-century Ireland; others to nineteenth- and twentieth-century America. Read between the funny lines and you may discern the barest trace of the well-known Celtic temper as the "throubles" involved with earning a livelihood are recounted. But it is quickly smothered by that grand and famous lilt of Irish laughter which is, even now, the Emerald Isle's proudest export.

Yes, today's transplanted sons and daughters of the "ould sod" can finally sing out, "It's a great day for the Irish!"

—H.D.S.

"The Dignity of Labor"

Labor raises honest sweat;
  Leisure puts you into debt.

Labor gives you rye and wheat;
  Leisure gives you naught to eat.

Labor makes your riches last;
  Leisure gets you nowhere fast.

Labor makes you swell with pride;
  Leisure makes you shrink inside.

Labor keeps you fit and prime;
  But give me leisure every time.

—Robert Bersohn (1890-?)

•

Shemus, newly arrived from Ireland, searched hard and long for a job in the United States. The great day finally arrived when he found employment as a bailiff in San Francisco's Chinatown area.

"Faith now, Yer Honor," confessed Shemus, "it's not a blessed thing do I know about bailiffing. What must I do?"

"You needn't worry," said the kindly judge, himself an Irishman and sympathetic to his countryman. "I'll just give you some simple orders and you merely follow my instructions."

On the first morning in court, the judge turned to his new crier and ordered him to summon an Oriental witness to the stand. "Call for Ah Song," he instructed.

Shemus looked puzzled for a moment, then shrugged and faced the spectators:

"All right now, let's look lively and thry 'Kathleen Mavoureen'—and, if ye don't know the wurrds, hum!"

*

In his younger days, before James Cooley became a railroad mogul, he was employed as a traveling salesman for the Baldwin Locomotive Company. Of all his prospective customers, he was most anxious to establish a business relationship with Terence Jackson, then Sales and Purchasing Manager of the Delaware and Lackawanna Railroad. But Jackson was a difficult man to get to see, especially for an obscure salesman like Cooley. Nevertheless, he decided to make the effort.

"I would like to see Mr. Jackson," the ambitious salesman told the secretary in the executive's outer office. He handed her his card.

Cooley's business card was taken into the man's inner sanctum, but the girl had left the door slightly ajar, and through it he saw Mr. Jackson tear his card in half and throw it into the wastebasket. The secretary returned and stated that her employer would not see him.

"May I have my card back?" asked Cooley innocently.

Embarrassed, the girl fled into Jackson's office. In a minute or two, she returned with a nickel and a curt message.

"Mr. Jackson says to tell you that your card was destroyed, and he hopes the five cents will repay the cost of printing it."

More than equal to the occasion, Cooley drew another card from his wallet and gave it to the girl.

"Take this back to him," he said smoothly, "and tell him I sell *two* cards for a nickel!"

*

The steel tycoon, Charles M. Schwab, maintained a certain comradeship with some of his long-time employees in the mill. Coming into the open hearth section one morning, he recognized a brawny old worker, naked from the waist up, his rippling muscles glistening with sweat and shining in the lurid glow of the furnace.

"Mick Dugan," exclaimed Schwab admiringly, "you look like an old Rembrandt!"

"Hell, Charlie," barked Dugan, "you don't look so hot yourself!"

*

The story is still told about Tim Clancey, the laziest cook ever employed by the old Santa Fe. Clancey's problems arose during those early days when the railroad was battling the elements and laying new track at a prodigious rate. It was Clancey's duty to feed the crews who worked against time to beat the winter snows and the thaws that brought on mud slides, and to fight off the Indians through whose reservations the roadbed was penetrating.

After a hard day, the men were hungry and in no mood for delays. But Clancey never seemed to have supper ready on time. The growling finally rose to such a crescendo that Mr. Hogan, the superintendent, at last called the errant cook into his shack.

"Tim," he began evenly, "I'm afther raisin' yer wages a hundred dollars a week."

"A raise, is it?" gulped Clancey, obviously astonished. "Tharkee, thankee kindly."

"And now," added Hogan, with a sudden change of voice, "you're fired!"

"Fired?" gasped Clancey. "Why, ye durrty spalpeen, what the hell's the idee iv givin' me a big raise like that and then firin' me?"

"That's so you'll always be remembrin'," explained Hogan, "what a damn good job you lost!"

*

Michael, from a rural village in Ireland, had only been in America a few weeks when it began to dawn on him that thirty-five cents an hour for driving a truck was somewhat below the standard wage scale. He approached his boss.

"Faith, sor, why can't ye pay me what I'm wurrth?" he complained.

"Because," replied the old skinflint, "you ain't worth it."

*

The Bricklayers, Hod Carriers, and Cement Finishers Union was having its annual convention in Holyoke, a city in Massachusetts. At the same time, and in the same city, another convention was being held by the New England Association of Trial Judges.

Now, Holyoke has not won world renown as a convention center, and its hotel accommodations are somewhat less than those of, say, New York, Chicago, or Los Angeles. So, it occasioned no surprise when Judge O'-Casey, arriving tardily at the Holyoke Hotel, was asked by the management to share a room occupied by Sean McCarthy of the aforementioned labor union—the other five rooms having been filled to capacity; that is, four to a room.

O'Casey, it was soon apparent, had forgotten his own humble origins and spoke to Sean McCarthy in what was clearly a tone of condescension.

"Well, my good man," observed His Honor, "I must say, you'd have remained in the old country for a long, long time before you could ever have shared a room with a judge."

"Yis, Yer Honor," replied Sean smoothly, "and 'tis you that would have been in the ould counthry a long, long time before ye could iver have been called a judge!"

*

Senator Daniel P. Moynihan, he of estimable United Nations fame, tells of the time he overheard his maid as she answered the telephone:
"Yis, this is where Dr. Moynihan lives; but, faith, he's not the kind iv docthor that does annywan anny good!"

*

Addressing a convention of teachers in Washington, D.C., George Meany, president of the AFL-CIO, posed a disturbing question:
"Doesn't it make you a bit uneasy that some of the colleges that are teaching our kids how to make a living are going broke?"

*

It had been a hard day at the plant and now, at the end of the day, old man Quigley pushed into a subway train and sank into a seat with a sigh of relief. He had hoped to take a short nap before reaching his station, but he was jolted wide awake by a white-haired fellow sitting quietly in front of him. The man was reading his newspaper and paying no attention whatever to a pair of pigeons that were perched on his shoulders.
Several stations further on, when the crowd had thinned out, Quigley, unable to suppress his curiosity a moment longer, stepped across the aisle and addressed the peculiar stranger.
"Beggin' yer perdon, misther," he said politely, "but would ye be afther telling me what those pigeons are doin' on yer shoulders?"
"How would I know?" snapped the stranger. "They got on at Fourteenth Street!"

*

Sean Murphy, the Boston roofer, fell from a housetop where he had been working, and was quickly taken to a hospital. Fortunately, he was not badly injured.
"Can you give me an idea about when the accident occurred?" asked the doctor in the emergency ward.
"That I can, indade," replied the patient. "It wor six o'clock."
"How can you be so sure?"
"Because I looked through a window and saw people at dinner on me way down."

*

In the old country, McGill had worked as a plumber and general handyman. So, when he came to America, he naturally sought a job in a similar field. Hearing of employment opportunities in New York's Sanitation Department, he applied for a Civil Service test. The examination for this type of work, he soon learned, was conducted orally.

"Mr. McGill," began the examining officer, "what we want here is not so much theory as practical experience. Now then, let's suppose that you were called upon to clear out a sewer that was 180 feet long and 4 feet in diameter, and blocked up at both ends. What's the first thing you'd do?"

"Go home!"

*

At the construction site of a new church, the contractor stopped to chat with one of his workmen.

"Paddy," he asked casually, "didn't you once tell me that you had a brother who was a bishop?"

"That I did, sor."

"And you are a bricklayer! It sure is a funny world. Things in life aren't divided equally, are they?"

"No, that they ain't, sor," agreed Paddy, as he proudly slapped the plaster along the line of bricks. "Me poor brother couldn't do this to save his life!"

*

It was past midnight when Dr. Abercrombie Sitzbath discovered, to his dismay, that his toilet drain was stopped up. Despite the lateness of the hour, he immediately went to the phone and called Dooley the plumber:

"Mr. Dooley, this is Dr. Sitzbath. I have an emergency here at my house. Can you come right over? My drain is stopped up."

"Doctor," counseled Dooley in his best bedside manner, "try to keep calm and don't get excited. Just take two aspirins every four hours and drop them into the bowl. If the drain isn't cleared up by morning, call me at the office between nine and five."

*

There are still a few Pat and Mike jokes around. This one dates back seventy years or more, and illustrates the economic fallacy that unemployment results from technology.

Two laborers on a big construction site were watching a huge steam shovel as it scooped up a ton of earth with every bite.

"I tell you, Pat," growled Mike, "if it weren't for that blasted scoop, five hundred of us would be working with shovels."

"Sure," replied Pat, "and if it weren't for our shovels, a million of us would be working with teaspoons!"

*

The difference between the rich Houlihans of Penobscot Bay and their poor relations, the Houlihans of Tenth Avenue, was not so much a matter of money as of culture and creative imagination. For proof, consider the incident in which the Penobscot Bay Houlihans decided to build a mansion.

After having the floor plans drawn up by a famous architect, the head of the rich family wrote to his poor relation, Andy Houlihan, a bricklayer and carpenter by trade, and offered him a construction job. Happy to get the employment, Andy arrived in the rarefied atmosphere of Penobscot Bay. But when he saw the blueprints, he was aghast.

"Cousin," he objected, "there's not a brick I'm layin' or a board I'm nailin' till you get these plans straightened out. They're all wrong!"

"What's wrong with them?" demanded the rich Houlihan. "These plans were drawn up by Frank Lloyd Wright himself."

"Wright's wrong!" snapped the poor Houlihan. "Why, if I followed these foolish plans the way they're laid out, do you know what you'd wind up with? *Two bathrooms!*"

*

"Ah, this is the life!" sighed the chubby old-timer who had just cashed his unemployment check and was now in the kitchen, comfortably attired in his undershirt and quaffing beer. "What more could a man ask for? I've got a wife and a TV set—and they're both working!"

*

Soon after Big Bill Brady arrived in the United States from Ireland, he found employment in Macy's as a floorwalker. Excusably enough, Bill indulged in some self-congratulation: his future in America seemed assured, the job paid tolerably well for a newcomer and the hours weren't too bad. But a few months later he quit in disgust and applied to the New York Police Department for a new job.

"Why do you want to become a policeman?" asked the department's personnel manager.

"Sivril rasons," replied Bill. "For wan thing, the hours an' the pay are betther than me ould job, but the best part is that the custhomer is always wrong!"

*

The prices mentioned in this vignette will bear testimony to its venerable age.

In a tavern in Boston's "southie," a recent arrival from the Emerald Isle paid another ten cents for a glass of whiskey—his sixth thus far—and basked in warm nostalgia for the "ould counthry."

"Ah, 'tis the cheapness iv the whiskey in Ireland that I'm afther missin' most iv all," he sighed, brushing an alcoholic tear from his eye. "Just think iv the prices back home: a salmon could be bought for sixpence, and a dozen mackerel for ownly twopence."

"Then tell me," growled the bartender, who had been listening to this same recitation for years, "why did you leave Ireland if every thing was so cheap?"

"Faith, man, is it mad ye are?" argued the new arrival to these shores. "And where would a dacent, self-respectin' man get the twopence—let alown the sixpence?"

＊

Irish immigrants blended into the American mainstream more quickly than those of other nationalities because they were already familiar with the English language—or, as Mr. Dooley put it, "at laste as she is spoke in the U.S. of A."

But even the Celtic newcomers ran into language difficulties on occasion. Padraic, who had arrived in this country only a few weeks earlier, found a job as an apprentice electrician. On the very first day his boss sent him to a hardware store to make a purchase.

"Misther," Padraic asked the hardware clerk, "would ye be afther havin' a four-volt, two-watt bulb?"

"For what?"

"No, two."

"Two what?"

"Yes."

"No."

＊

Someone once said there is no such person as a "dumb Irishman." That assertion is indeed true: there are only some Irishmen who are not as informed about most things as are 99 per cent of the population. Take the case of Naughton, known affectionately among his friends and family as Noodlehead.

For the past several months, Noodlehead had been employed as a sweeper in the Bethlehem shipyard in Baltimore. The constant bedlam, the ear-splitting sound of riveting machines, air hammers, and the clashing and clanging of metal on metal, soon affected our hero's eardrums.

One Sunday, after mass, Noodlehead rushed down to the shipyard clinic, a towel wrapped around his hand.

"What seems to be the matter?" asked the harried, seven-day-week intern.

"Docthor, it's somethin' wrong there is with me finger," gasped Noodlehead. "Ivry time I put it in me ear, I can't hear!"

＊

Old Mike Reardon, janitor at the headquarters of the Pennsylvania Railroad, was mopping the floor in the luxurious offices of the railroad's chief executive when an important-looking man flung open the door and strode into the inner sanctum.

"I want to see Cornelius Vanderbilt," he said imperiously. "Is he here?"

"No, sor, beggin' yer pardon, but Misther Vanderbilt's in Europe, he is," explained Mike, swishing his mop around in the water bucket.

"Well, then, I'll see his secretary."

"Sure an' he's in Newport, he is."

"Then can I see the first vice president?"

"He's just afther lavin' fer Albany."

"How about the second vice president?"

"He an' the thurrd vice prisidint are in Washin'ton, sor, explainin' sartin matthers to the Investhigatin' Committee."

"Where's the superintendent?"

"I'd not be knowin', sor."

"How about the general passenger agent?"

"In jail."

"Dammit!" exploded the visitor furiously. "Who the hell is running this railroad, anyway?"

Old Mike Reardon carefully withdrew his mop from the pail of dirty water, and closed one eye as he contemplated the question.

"Sor," he replied slowly as the sense of his crushing responsibility dawned on him, "I guess 'tis meself that's runnin' this road!"

*

Dr. Dudley Moore of New York tells this one on himself:

"My kitchen faucet wouldn't work one morning, so I called the neighborhood plumber, a fellow named Haggerty. He came over to my place in a jiffy and within five minutes he located the trouble and fixed the pipe.

" 'That'll be one hundred dollars,' he said.

" 'What!' I fairly yelled. 'A hundred dollars for five minutes work? Why, that comes to twelve hundred an hour! You must be crazy! I'm a brain surgeon and even I don't make that kind of money.'

" 'Yes, I know,' said Haggerty, putting his tools back into a little black bag. 'I didn't make that kind of money either, when I was a brain surgeon!' "

*

Bridget Malone, seeking better opportunities in the New World, journeyed from the Emerald Isle to New York. There, she found employment as a chambermaid in a large hotel. On her first day off, bursting with the news of America, and especially about her first job here, she wrote a letter to her sister in Ireland, using the hotel's stationery.

Imagine the surprise of the manager when, two weeks later, he found a letter from Bridget's sister, the envelope addressed in commendable detail:

Miss Bridget Malone
c/o Astor Hotel
All Modern Improvements—Rates on Application
All Rooms with Bath
New York, U.S.A.

*

"Da Greenpernt Irishman"

> I'm a six foot t'ree from Brooklyn,
> A hunnert eighty when I'm bare.
> Me hand is big as hammers
> An' me chest's a mat o' hair.
> I useter be a boxer,
> In da Dead End I wuz tops.
> I wuz raised on lemon extract,
> T'hell wid whiskey slops.
> Da Moider, Inc. boys wuz me pals,
> I scare guys wid me puss.
> To your sixty-four buck question,
> I'm a typist, pal, t'ank youse.

> —*The Stars and Stripes* (Italy, 1944)

We have witnessed some of the "thrials" and "thribulations" that plagued wage-earning Irish-Americans. Now let us be "thransported" on faerie wings for a nostalgic visit to the "ould counthry." There, we will tarry for a while with the "Irish"-Irish as they go about earning their daily bread and "butther." Some of these classic tales go back a hundred years, a few much more, but sure, they are as appealing today as they were when first told.

*

O, th' dayception that lies in th' hearts iv Man! Not us women, mind ye— *Man!* 'Tis enough to make a mortial wape. I take fer me horrible example, Sean Rafferty, manager iv th' Shamrock Restaurant near th' Shannon airport. Wan Saddy mornin' he called all iv us waitresses togither an' he made a little spache.

"Ladies," says Rafferty, "I'm askin' ye to look yer prettiest today. Greet ivery custhomer with a swate smile. Be sure yer hair is smooth an' atthractive, and ye might try wearin' a leetle extra makeup."

"An' who may ye be expectin' today?" asked wan iv th' girls. "Saint Pathrick?"

"No, I'm not afther expectin' annywan important," said Rafferty, "Th' steak's tough!"

*

The American artist, George O'Brien, had just arrived in Ireland to find scenes for his pastoral paintings and to pay a nostalgic visit to the village of his forefathers. In a small town, one morning, he stopped at a rustic inn for breakfast. The waitress, an apple-cheeked lass, came forward to take his order.

"Ye naden't tell me," she said with a cheery smile. "I know what you

Americans are afther navin' fer breakfast—ham and eggs.''

"I'll take the ham," said O'Brien, "but please eliminate the eggs."

The girl disappeared into the kitchen and, in due time, she was back again with a plate of sliced ham and two lovely fried eggs, sunny side up.

"Now see here, Miss," objected O'Brien, "I distinctly told you I wanted the eggs *eliminated*."

"Yis, sor, that you did, sor," agreed the waitress, thinking quickly. "And it's sorry I am, too, but it's all the fault of that dhrunken cook, it is. Ye'd not believe what that spalpeen did, sor, beggin' yer pardon, sor—he dhropped the 'liminator, he did, and broke the handle!"

*

Labor Relations in Ireland, June 1910

"Top o' the mornin' to ye, Mrs. Doyle."

"The same to you, I'm sure, Mrs. O'Grady."

"I see Mr. Doyle is takin' his aise, lollin' on the grass outside. Is it sick he is?"

"No, he's afther sympathizin' with the coal sthrike."

"And how's that, Mrs. Doyle?"

"Not a lump iv coal will the man touch while the sthrike lasts. So I have to build the fire meself, bad cess to it!"

*

In the year 1881, or thereabouts, an order was sternly given and scrupulously carried out—to the great amusement of the neighborhood. The anecdote is cheerfully revived for posterity.

Dr. Marlay, Bishop of Waterford, ordered his Irish coachman (in the absence of the footman) to fetch some water from the well.

"Sor," objected the coachman, his dignity thus offended, "it is my business to dhrive, not to be afther running errands."

"Well, then," said the Bishop, his voice hard as flint, "bring out the coach and four, set the pitcher inside, and *drive* to the well!"

*

"Never trust a Scotsman," observed the gentleman from Offaly, "especially if he's an educated one. Thirty years ago, as I recall it, I bought a mare from a thieving Scot horse dealer who assured me that the animal was without fault. But I soon learned that the poor beast could not see out of one eye and was almost blind in the other. I made heavy complaint to the dealer and reminded him that he had represented the mare as being without fault.

" 'Yes, that I did,' confessed the rascally Scot, 'but you will agree, I'm sure, that the poor creature's blindness is not a *fault*—it is her *misfortune!* ' "

*

Two ambitious sons of Erin pooled their money and purchased a keg of whiskey. Then they set out for the Derby races, where they planned to sell it. Being businessmen as well as connoisseurs of good Irish whiskey, they agreed that neither should have a drink without paying for it. They had journeyed a fair distance toward the racetrack when one of them had a manly drink of the whiskey and paid for it with his last threepence, which was all he had left after paying for his share of the keg.

By and by, the other fellow, who had nothing at all left after paying for his share of the keg, also grew thirsty. So he had some whiskey and paid for it with the threepence he had just received from his partner.

Thus they continued on their way, first one paying, and then the other, till all the whiskey was drunk.

Then, they started to count the receipts.

"Faith, is that all we've earned?" exclaimed the first imbiber, completely astounded. "Why, ivry dhrink was paid for!"

"I cannot belave it!" gasped the other one. "All that business—and all we have to show for it is threepence!"

*

The Towers of Clonmacnoise[1]

Have you ever wondered why one of the two round towers of antiquity, at Clonmacnoise, is incomplete? Here is how grandfather McQuail explained it to his granddaughter, Kathleen:

"The two towers at Clonmacnoise are fine wans, *macushla,* with wan on top iv the hill and wan close beside the plashy bank iv the river. The wan down at the riverside was built first and finished entirely, with the roof on it, as annywan can plainly see. But when that was built, sweet Kathleen, the bishop thought that another'd look very purty up on the hill. So he bid the masons to start work and build another tower up there.

"Well, they set to work at wance, busy as nailers. Troth, it was like a beehive, ivry man with his hammer in his hand, and the tower was complated in due time. But when the last stone was laid on the roof, Kathleen darlin', the bishop axes the masons how much he was to pay them, and they ups and towld him their price. But the bishop, they say, was a skinflint—God forgi' me for saying that word of so holy a man!—and he said they'd axed too much and he wouldn't pay them.

"With that, my little jewel, the masons said they would take no less. But the bishop—oh, the cunnin' av the man!—took away the ladders that was reared up agin the tower.

---

[1]Translated from the Old Irish (Gaelic) by W. H. Howe, *Everybody's Book of Irish Wit and Humor* (London: Brindley & Howe, Ltd., circa 1880). Edited by the present author.

" 'And now, me fine buckos,' says he, 'the divil a down out o' that you'll come until you learn manners and take what's offered to yiz,' says he. 'And when you come down in your price you may come down yourselves.'

"Sure enough, he kept his word, and wouldn't let man or mortyel go nigh the place to help them get down; and faith, the masons didn't like the notion of losing their honest airnins—and small blame to them. But sure they wor starvin' all the time and didn't know what in the wide world to do.

" 'Twas cold and hungry they were when a simple farmer—a stranger from distant parts—chanced to pass by and sees them.

" '*Musha,* but you look well there,' he says like the fool he is.

" 'Not much the better av your axin',' says they.

"So he questioned them and they towld him how it was with them, and how the bishop took away the ladders and they couldn't come down.

" 'I am called a fool,' says the farmer, 'but you are even bigger fools. Sure, isn't it aisier to take down two stones than put wan up?'

"With that, my dear sowl, no sooner said nor done. The masons began to pull down their work, and when this went on for some time, the bishop bid them stop, and he'd let them down. But faith, before he gev into them, they had taken the roof clane off.

"And that's the raison wan tower has a roof, *macushla,* and the other has none."

*

"I Was a Bustle-Maker Once, Girls"

> When I was a lad of twenty
>   And was working in High Street, Ken,
> I made quite a pile in a very little while—
>   I was a bustle-maker then.
> Then there was work in plenty,
>   And I was a thriving man;
> But things have decayed in the bustle-making trade,
>   Since the bustle-making trade began.
>
> I built bustles with a will then;
>   I built bustles with a wit;
> I built bustles as a Yankee hustles,
>   Simply for the love of it.
> I built bustles with a skill then,
>   Surpassed, they say, by none;
> But those were the days when bustles were the craze,
>   And now those days are done.
>
> I built bustles to enchant, girls;
>   I built bustles to amaze;
> I built bustles for the skirt that rustles,
>   And bustles for the skirt that sways.
> I built bustles for my aunt, girls,
>   When other business fled;

But a bustle-maker can't make bustles for his aunt,
    When a bustle-maker's aunt is dead.

I was a bustle-maker once, girls—
    Once in the days gone by;
I lost my heart to the bustle-maker's art,
    And that I don't deny.
I may have had the brains of a dunce, girls,
    As many men appear to suppose;
I may have been obtuse and of little other use,
    But I could build a bustle when I chose.
I built bustles for the bulging;
    I built bustles for the lithe;
I built bustles for the girls in Brussels
    And bustles for the girls in Hythe.
I built bustles for all Europe once,
    But I've been badly hit.
Things have decayed in the bustle-making trade,
    And that's the truth of it.

                —Patrick Barrington (1905-)

          *

Leave the flurry
To the masses;
Take your time
And shine your glasses.

        —Old Irish Verse

Chapter Five

Down on the Farm

Introduction

It seems strange, in retrospect, that the Irish farmer could have developed so keen a sense of humor in view of the centuries of struggle he has endured. From the earliest times, he has fought Norsemen, Normans, Gauls, and others to hold on to the bit of land he needed to sustain his family. Wave after wave of invaders seized his fertile fields and drove him into barren wastelands where he had little chance to harvest enough to feed his loved ones. Among the worst of these massive land grabs was the hated policy of Plantation, which led to the formation of Ulster, or northern Ireland.

Plantation, introduced by Mary Tudor in the sixteenth century, was a convenient euphemism for the confiscation of Irish lands by English settlers. Mary, whose military forces were met by relatively unarmed and unorganized Irish farmers, confiscated the territories of Leix and Offaly, renaming them Queen's County and King's County. Following in Mary's footsteps, Queen Elizabeth I, upon ascending the throne, seized thousands of acres in Munster. But these acquisitions were not enough to satisfy another British monarch, King James I, first of the Stuarts. Learning that Hugh O'Neill, Hugh Roe O'Donnell, and other Irish leaders who had fought the British from their stronghold in Ulster, had escaped to Europe, James correctly surmised that the time was ripe to move in on the leaderless Irish. Derry was captured and renamed Londonderry. Before long, King James' soldiers had confiscated six counties of Ulster—more than half-a-million acres. All of the land was given to English settlers or to absentee landlords in England. They were under stern orders to permit only English or Scottish Protestant tenants to work the expropriated holdings. The rightful Irish owners, now pauperized, were herded to unproductive bog land to fend for themselves.

But as bad as the times were for the Irish Catholics, the worst was yet to come. In 1649, Cromwell the Cruel, among the most bloodthirsty despots to rule England, landed in Ireland. His atrocities began at once, indiscriminately slaughtering Irish fighters, noncombatant civilians, even children. The following year, Kilkenny, by that time a hub of Irish resistance, was forced

93

into surrender. In time, even the bog lands to which the farmers had been driven, were seized by Britain and handed over to English and Scottish Protestant landlords. The usurpers were now solidly entrenched. Ireland had suffered a grievous wound from which she has not recovered to this day.

The plantations were productive enough, but the hard-working tenant farmers were compelled to ship cereal grains and livestock, as "rental fees," to the landlords in England. There was, however, one crop they were permitted to keep—the potato. The Irish farmer ate potatoes three times a day, year in and year out. In good years—that is, under ideal conditions—he managed to harvest sixty barrels of potatoes a year; a barely adequate food supply for a family of five or six. But during such crop failures as occurred in 1822 and 1831, the hapless farm families suffered terrible privation. In the dread potato famine of 1845-1850, hundreds of thousands died of starvation and 2 million others fled to other countries, mostly to the sanctuary of the United States.

Nonetheless, despite their adversities, rural Irish families found the time and occasion, somehow, for laughter. Gathered in a semicircle before the hearth, savoring the warm and fragrant glow of a peat fire in the fireplace, they would grin at the master-serf relationship with such stories as the comical "Andy's Postal Problem"; or recount the adventure of that lovable spalpeen[1] of Limerick, whose blarney was so delightfully illustrated in the tale, "That Good Old Limestone Broth"; or the joys of partying in each other's homes, as in the heartwarming poem, "The Donovans," all of which have been selected for this chapter.

It was that sense of Irish brotherhood which the English could never understand, and the Irish sense of humor, which the English understood even less, that has kept Ireland alive through war, famine, pestilence, and natural disasters of all kinds.

In the United States, however, ninety per cent of the Irish immigrants, nearly all of whom were from rural areas, turned their backs on farming and remained in the cities. They could hardly be blamed, considering their dreadful experience on the land back home. But there were a number of practical and more pressing reasons why they chose the cities. First, most immigrant farmers had raised little else but potatoes, and lacked the knowledge to manage a multicrop farm with its additional necessities of fowl and livestock. Second, even the poorest land cost more than most immigrants could afford. There was land available in the Middle West, and a number of

---

[1]The word spalpeen, used in this context, refers not to a rascal but to an itinerant farm worker. A farmer, unable to feed his family on the poor bit of land allotted to him, became a spalpeen—the original meaning of the word. He would walk barefoot to "Dubh-linn," pay his passage to England, then wearily tread the countryside as far north as Scotland, searching for work. He would help one farmer for a few days or a week before moving on to the next farm. His wife and children usually went begging for potatoes or whatever other scraps they could get while he was away. When the harvesting was done, the traveling farmer, or spalpeen, would return home with enough money to pay the rent to his absentee landlord. The *praties* (potatoes) they had planted in the spring were dug and stored for the winter. Then the family hoped and prayed for good health and gave thanks to the Creator that they had survived the year—unlike some who had perished for want of food and shelter.

Irish aid societies urged the newcomers to the United States to form Irish settlements in rural areas. Many such settlements were indeed started by those whose love for the soil was based not only on their need for food but also for inspiration and solace. But the average immigrant-farmer did not even have the few dollars it required to move to the Middle West, let alone settle there.

In any case, isolating himself on a farm was not what the Irishman had hoped for in America. The United States, for him, presented excitingly new opportunities. He would not, he felt, find many chances to realize the American dream on some lonely farm. Moreover, the Irish man and woman had always been gregarious, and preferred to live near their neighbors, their parochial school, the Church. This was rarely possible in many rural communities where anti-Irish, anti-Catholic sentiment was strong. So he stayed in the city.

Many decades have now passed since the Irish immigrants sought a better life in America. Some of their grandchildren and great grandchildren have returned to the farms (or never left), but now they operate the lands under corporate names. They have long since become an integral and respected part of American life. And they have bequeathed a tint of green to the red, white, and blue American standard. An old Irish saying tells us: "The Irish changed America, and America changed the Irish." They would not have it any other way.

The droll stories and poems in this chapter will not tell you how to hive a swarm of bees, how to swing a scythe, or how to grow potatoes. You may learn how to hitch your wagon to a star, but not to a horse. And yet you will know from their humor that the Irish knew how to do these things.

—H.D.S.

*

"Gettin' Borned"

When once a chick busts through a egg
　　He gives three little squeals,
Then works out backwards through a hole
　　By kickin' with his heels.

Or maybe he'll keep peckin' 'round,
　　With now and then some cursin',
Until his head pokes through and then
　　Comes all his little person.

Or like as not he'll puff his chest,
　　A grunt and then some kickin'—
He's standin' there out in the air,
　　A promissory chicken.

—Anthony Euwer (1877-1945)

*

Item in the Dublin Observer, April, 1896

The extraordinary sensitivity of some devout churchgoers was illustrated by little Rosemary when she recently visited a farm near Belfast. The farm, operated by the Church of England, contained the usual assortment of domestic animals. First off, the girl wanted to see a horse. Together with her friend, Helen, the Protestant girl who had invited her, they went to the corral where two horses were kept. One of them approached the children who were now standing at the fence.

"Oh, I'd love to pet this beeyootiful horsie!" squealed Rosemary in delight.

"No, no, you mustn't touch that one," cried Helen. "He'll kick you!"

"For goodness sake," exclaimed Rosemary, drawing back in alarm, "how could a horse know I'm Catholic?"

*

"You Irish farmers have nothing to worry about," said the American who was visiting his relatives in Eire. "You have your own cow, milk, butter, cheese, chickens, eggs, meat, fruit, nuts, and vegetables. With all that to eat and a cozy place to sleep, what more could you want?"

"Cousin Joe," suggested the farmer, "you come back to Ireland a few months from now and you'll see the fattest, healthiest, Irish farmer you ever saw—and the nakedest!"

*

Farms in Ireland are not always profitable. Such a one was McNichols's place in County Down. Discussing the hard times with the local priest, he revealed that he was heavily in debt.

The puzzled cleric, new to the area, said at length: "How in the world do you manage to keep your ownership of this little farm?"

McNichols shrugged and pointed to a young hired man who was working in the potato patch. "Father, you see that lad? That's O'Farrell. Well he works for me, but I can't afford to pay him. In two more years, he gets the farm. Then I go to work for him till I get it back. Then he goes to work for me again. Then I...."

*

Many long years before you were born, when the boats were running between Glasgow and Paisley, a traveler—a very simple rustic from Louth—asked the boatman if he would let him work his passage from Paisley to Glasgow.

"That I will," agreed the boatman, who considered himself a bit of a wag, "but you'll have to lead the horse."

"As good as done," said the Louth man. He took the towline, tied the end to the horse, and then led it along the bank pulling the boat in the customary manner of those days.

When they arrived at Glasgow, the poor traveler sank to the turf in weariness. "Do ye call that workin' me passage now?" he demanded with justifiable indignation. "Bedad, and I might as well have walked it!"

*

Some of us are too prone to measure another man's corn by our own bushel, as this nineteenth-century exchange of dialogue illustrates.

A nearsighted gentleman was peering through his thick-lensed spectacles at a small sign posted above a shop. But the lettering was too small for his poor vision.

"My good man," he asked an old farmer who chanced to pass by, "can you tell me what that sign says up there?"

"Sure and I'm in the same boat, sor," replied the old-timer apologetically. "It was mighty little schoolin' I had meself whin I was a boy!"

*

The Irish have seldom been intimidated by rank, privilege, or wealth—at least not for long. The poorest Irishman, so 'tis said, will bridle at what he considers an affront to his dignity. All this profound philosophy naturally leads to a classic and ancient anecdote, revived for a new generation of readers:

A country lad, driving his wagon peacefully along the bank of the Shannon, was startled to hear a frantic cry for help. There, in the water, he perceived a drowning man struggling and flailing about. It was clear that the man could not swim. So, our hero jumped down from his wagon, leaped into the river, and brought the half-dead man safely to shore.

"You have saved my life," said the stranger. "Permit me to reward you." He reached into his gold-filled purse and handed his rescuer a sixpence.

"Sir," replied the country boy, looking the man straight in the eye, "I'm afraid you've overpaid me!"

*

Fahey, the farmer, was known as the most precise man in all of County Clare. Whoever spoke to him had to mean exactly what he said—or he would be quickly set to rights.

A city-bred man happened to walk by and observed Fahey at work with a pick and shovel.

"I see you're digging out a hole," said the stranger.

"You are wrong, sir," snapped Fahey. "I am digging out the *dirt* and *leaving* the hole!"

*

The farmer's wife was beginning to worry about her husband. He had hitched up the mule to the wagon and gone to town to purchase some supplies, and he should have returned an hour ago. Aware that his fiery Irish temper and profane tongue could bring him trouble, her concern mounted as another half-hour slipped by. But a few minutes later, her fears were stilled. There he was, pulling up at the front door.

"What took you so long?" she asked.

"I got slowed down on my way back home," he explained with a rueful smile. "I picked up Father Haloran and, from there on, that mule of ours didn't understand a damn thing I said!"

*

A wealthy American had just moved to Ireland, where he planned to breed fine horses. But whatever knowledge he may have had about the animals in the United States—and that was scanty enough—apparently did not suffice in the Emerald Isle. Soon, he was complaining that his horses were listless. He had tried every medicine he had heard of: condition powder, vitamin tablets, and a very long list of other medicines and tonics. But to no avail—the horses would not improve.

A stable boy whose sympathies were aroused by the tale of woe, comprehended the problem at once.

"Sor," he modestly suggested, "did you iver thry corn?"

*

A salesman, representing a farm implement manufacturing company, heard that Mr. Hennessy did not own a tractor. Here was a prospective customer, and he hurried to Hennessy's bit of land. He arrived in time to see the farmer plowing his field, with a bull dragging an old-fashioned plow.

"Don't you have a horse for your plow?" asked the amazed salesman.

"I do," replied Hennessy, "but I prefer the bull."

"But why not get a tractor, suggested the salesman eagerly. "It would do do twice the work of a horse and three times the work of that bull."

"I have a tractor," said Hennessy doggedly, "but I'm not about to use it."

"Why not?"

"Because," rasped the farmer, "this bull is going to learn the hard way, that life ain't all romance!"

*

Some people are born with brains, some without them, and there are others who wouldn't know what to do with them if they had them. One of the latter was Raymond, the incurable optimist of Roscommon. He was meandering through a meadow one bright and sunny day when he came upon a man running for his life. Behind him was a snorting bull. Luckily for the intended victim, he managed to reach a tree and scramble up into the safety of the branches, a bull's whisker from physical contact with his pursuer.

The scene was so funny to simple-minded Raymond that he burst into hilarious laughter, which was not at all to the bull's liking. The animal turned to the source of the raucous mirth, pawed the ground, and, with nostrils flaring, it charged. Taken by surprise, Raymond, who had suddenly lost his sense of humor, attempted to dodge the oncoming bull. Alas, he was too late. As he presented his backside to the beast and made for a nearby fence, the bull caught the fleeing Raymond and sent him on a brief journey into the heights. He came down with a thump on the other side of the fence.

"Faith," muttered Raymond to himself, "there's a little bit o' good in everything. If I hadn't had my laugh when I did, I wouldn't have had it a'tall!"[2]

*

This little anecdote will also be found in the humorous folklore of other cultures. The Irish version, however, appears to be the oldest of all the West European variants.

A rustic by the name of O'Casey was trudging along a country road with a heavy bundle slung across his shoulder. Before long, a farmer, driving his wagon to town, caught up with the man and offered him a ride.

"Thankee kindly, sor," acknowledged the weary O'Casey, lifting himself up to the seat beside the farmer. He settled back and, with a sigh, transferred his heavy load to his other shoulder.

"Why don't you put that bundle in the back of the wagon?" asked the surprised driver.

"I'm not the sort who'd be afther takin' advantage," said O'Casey humbly. "The poor horse has enough to do to drag me. I'll carry the bundle meself!"[3]

*

The rain was coming down in torrents when a young farmer arrived at the greengrocer's to deliver his products of the field.

"Come in, lad, and warm yerself by the fire," said the greengrocer sympathetically. "Ye be very wet indade."

"Aye, that I am!" agreed the farmer. "And if ye can belave the curosity iv it, I'm also very dhry!"[4]

*

From *The Irish Farmer's Dictionary:*

ABSENTEE LANDLORD: A landowner who squeezes the last drop of moisture from another's potato, but who performs that function at a safe distance from the potato-owner's shillelagh.

---

[2]*Dublin University Press* (October 1791)
[3]*"The Merry Farmer of Kildare"* (As related by "Zozimus.") Not dated. See Biographical Index of Authors, p. 399.
[4]*Tales of Old Ireland* (Dublin 1881), Robert Gallagher, translation from the Gaelic.

JACKASS: An animal with a fine voice but no ear. This may come as a surprise to those who view the donkey's ears as a splendid acoutrement, but their length does not imply perfection, any more than a long nose indicates beauty in an Irishman. However, the donkey's resemblance to an *English*man lies in its willingness to eat and reluctance to labor for its eatments.

SPALPEEN: One who "moves in mysterious ways," usually with other people's property; i.e—

Spring beckons! All things to call respond;
The trees are leaving and cashiers abscond.

—Patrick Ireland

*

In the Church of St. Mary, near Athlone, Padraic was receiving a severe lecture from the priest. "Ye should not have stolen that goose, me son," admonished the priest. "It was sinful."

"Father, it's repintin' I am," said Padraic humbly, lowering his head in shame. "Would ye be afther acceptin' the goose as a prisint from me?"

"Of coorse not," snapped the priest. "Ye'll have to return it to its legal owner. You stole it—it's not yours to give to me."

"But, Father, I did thry," protested Padraic, "but he refused to take it back."

"Well, if the owner refused yer kind offer, kape it fer yerself."

"Heaven be praised!" Padraic replied happily. "Me conscience is now clear!"

After dinner, that evening, the good priest went to feed his flock of geese. One was missing.

*

Through the centuries, the Irish have refused to bend a knee to the inevitable tragedy of their lives. They turned it into a song, a poem, or a joke. There were many stock jokes told over and over again by the rural Irish. The Irish farmer liked to quip that his house was so small "you can put your hand down the chimney and open the door from the inside." And he loved to tell of the two weary farmers, traveling to town on foot, who realized they still had ten miles to go. "Take heart," said one, " 'tis ownly five miles apiece!"

These jokes, some of which are more than a hundred years old, brought a little laughter into the otherwise drab existence of old Ireland's farm families. Some of the jokes remained popular for years and then faded from memory. A few regained their popularity for short periods, only to fade again. But the droll folk tales, anecdotes, and poems that farmers enjoyed relating to each other as they sat before the fireplace after a hard day's work have been passed on from one generation to another, and have still not lost their appeal. The stories that follow are representative of the humorous rural tales of eighteenth- and nineteenth-century Ireland, as are the rollicking poems.

"The Christian Pipe"

A witty peasant named Larry Hogan, passing the hut of the widow Mrs. Rooney and her niece, Oonah, stopped by to get a light for his pipe. "It went out with the fright," he explained to them without the trace of a smile on his good-natured face.

"Well, I've heerd iv quare things, Larry Hogan," said Oonah, laughing and showing her white teeth, "but I niver heerd so quare a thing as a pipe goin' out with fright."

"Now don't laugh so, Oonah," objected Larry. "Ha-ha indade! Afther all, now, a pipe is like a Christian in many ways, so why could it not be frightened? Consider this: it is made iv clay like a Christian, and has the spark iv life in it, and while the breath is in it, the spark is alive. But whin the breath is out iv it, the spark dies and grows cowld like a Christian."

"Sure, and some Christians isn't pleasant companions, just like your pipe," Oonah again laughed, wrinkling her nose at the smell of the tobacco.

"Faith, that may be," agreed Larry Hogan with a grin. "And I must admit that smokin' is the most improvinist thing in the world." He relit his pipe and squatted himself on a three-legged stool beside the widow's peat fire. "Yes (puff) improvinist, like a puff (puff), and the tibakky turns to ashes (puff) like his poor perishable body. As the song says—

"Tibakky is an Indian weed,
Alive at morn and dead at eve;
It lives but an hour,
Is cut down like a flower—
Think o' that when you're smokin' tibakky.

"A pipe it larns us all this thing:
'Tis fair without and foul within,
Just like a sowl begrimed with sin—
Think o' that when you're smokin' tibakky."
                              —Anonymous (circa 1890)

*

"That Good Old Limestone Broth"[5]

My father went about the country, once upon a time, in the idle season, seeing if he might make a penny at all by cutting hair, or setting razors and penknives, or any other job that would fall his way. Well and good. He was walking alone in the mountains of Kerry one day, without a hai'p'ny in his pocket, and knowing there was but little love for a County Limerick man in the place where he was. Evening was drawing nigh, he was half perished with hunger, and he didn't know well what to do with himself till morning.

---

[5]Gerald Griffin of Limerick, *The Blarneyin' Barber,* published about 1839, a year before Griffin's death.

Very good. He went along the wild road and he soon sees a farmhouse at a little distance away—a snug-looking place with the smoke curling up out of the chimney, and all tokens of good living inside. Well, some people would live where a fox would starve. Now my father wouldn't beg, and he hadn't the money to buy a thing, so what does he do? He takes up a couple o' the big limestones that were lying on the road in his two hands, and away with him to the house.

"Lord save all here!" says he, walking in the door.

"And you kindly," says they.

"I'm come to you," says he, looking at the limestones, "to know would you let me make a little limestone broth over your fire, until I make my dinner."

"Limestone broth, is it?" says they. "Faith, and what's that?"

"Broth made o' limestone," says he. "What else would it be?"

"We niver heerd of sich a thing," says they.

"Why, then, you may hear of it now," says he, "and see it, too, should you gi' me a pot and a couple of quarts o' soft wather."

"You can have it, and welcome," says they.

So they put down the pot and the wather, and my father wint over and tuk a chair hard by the plisint fire for himself, and put his two limestones to boil, and kep' stirrin' them round like stirabout.

Very good—well, by-and-by, whin the wather began to boil— " 'Tis thickening finely," says my father. "Now if it had a grain of salt at all, 'twould be a great improvement to it."

"Raich down the saltbox, Nell," says the man o' the house to his wife. So she did.

"Oh, that's the very thing, just!" says my father, shaking some of it into the pot. He stirred it again awhile, looking sober as a ministher. By-and-by, he takes the spoon he had been stirring with, and tastes the salted stone-wather.

"It is very good now," says he, "although it wants something yit."

"What is it?" says they.

"Oyeh," says he, "Maybe 'tis only my fancy."

"If it's anything we can give you," says they, "sure you're welcome to it."

" 'Tis very good as it is," says he, "but whin I'm at home I find it gives it a fine flavor just to boil a little knuckle o' bacon or mutton trotters, or anything else that way, along with it."

"Raich hither that bone o' sheep's head we had at dinner yesterday, Nell," says the man of the house.

"Oh, don't mind it," says my father. "Let it be as it is."

"Sure, if it improves it, you may as well," says they.

"Then so be it," says my father, putting it down into the pot. After boiling it a good piece longer, he says again, " 'Tis as fine a limestone broth as iver was tasted, and if a man had a few *praties* he couldn't desire a better dinner."

So they gave him the potatoes and he made a good dinner of them and the broth, not forgetting the bone which he polished equal to chiney before he let it go. The people themselves tasted it, and thought it as good as any mutton stirabout in the world.

The limestone rocks? Faith, they never did boil down soft. Why do you ask?

—Gerald Griffin (1803-40)

*

"Andy's Postal Problem"

"Ride into town and see if there's a letter for me at the post office," said the squire to his servant, Andy.

"Yes, sir," replied Andy, getting astride his hack and trotting away. On arriving at the postmaster's shop (for that person carried on a brisk trade in gunpowder, groceries, gimlets, broadcloth, and linen drapery), Andy presented himself at the counter.

"I want a letther, sir, if you plaze," he said.

"Who do you want it for?" asked the postmaster in a tone which Andy considered an aggression upon the sacredness of private life.

"What's that to you? The directions I got was to get a letther here—and that's the directions."

"Who gave you those directions?"

"The masther."

"And who's your master?"

"What consarn is that o' yours?"

"See here, if you don't tell me his name, how can I give you a letter? Your master must be as great a goose as yourself to send such a messenger."

"Bad luck to your impidince," says Andy. "Is it Squire Egan you dar' to say goose to!"

"Oh, Squire Egan's your master, then?" ventured the postmaster.

"Yes, and have you anything to say agin it?"

"Only that I never saw you before."

"Faith, then, you'll never see me agin if I have my own consint."

"I won't give you any letter for the squire unless I know you're his servant. Is there anyone in the town who knows you?"

"Plenty," said Andy. "It's not everyone is as ignorant as you."

Just at this moment, a person to whom Andy was known entered the place and vouched to the postmaster that he might give Andy the squire's letter. "Have you one for me, too?" he inquired.

"Yes, sir," said the postmaster, producing one. "That will be fourpence."

The gentleman paid the fourpence postage and left the shop with his letter.

"Here's a letter for the squire," said the postmaster. "You've to pay me elevenpence postage."

"To the divil with you!" exclaimed Andy. "Didn't I see you give Mr. Durfy a letther for fourpence this minute, and a bigger letther than this? And now you want me to pay elevenpence for this scrap of thing! Do you think I'm a fool?"

"I'm sure of it!"

Determined to give no more than fourpence, Andy waited for above half-an-hour while the postmaster served many others. But at last he left when he found it impossible to get common justice for his master.

The squire, in the meantime, was getting impatient for his return, and when Andy made his appearance, he asked if there was a letter for him.

"There is, sir, but I haven't got it," said Andy. "He wouldn't give it to me."

"Who wouldn't give it to you?" asked the squire.

"That ould chate beyant in the town—wanting to charge double for it."

"Maybe it's a double letter. Why the devil didn't you pay what he asked for?"

"Arrah, sir, why would I let you be chated? It's not a double letther at all—not above half the size o' one Mr. Durfy got before my face for four-pence. Yes, he was sellin' them before my own face for fourpence apiece."

"Go back, you fool, and get my letter! And if you are longer than an hour I'll have you ducked in the horse pond!"

Andy vanished and made a second visit to the post office. When he arrived, two other persons were getting letters, and the postmaster was selecting the mail for each from a large parcel that lay before him on the counter. At the same time, many shop customers were waiting to be served.

"I'm come for that letther," said Andy.

"I'll attend to you by-and-by."

"The masther's in a hurry."

"Let him wait till his hurry is over."

"He'll murther me if I'm not back soon."

"I'm glad to hear it."

While the postmaster went on with provoking answers to these appeals for dispatch, Andy's eye caught the heap of letters which lay on the counter. So, while certain weighing of soap and tobacco was going forward, he contrived to become possessed of two letters from the heap. Having effected that, he waited patiently enough till it was the great man's pleasure to give him the missive directed to his master.

Then did Andy bestride his hack and, in triumph at his trick on the postmaster, rattled along on the road homeward as fast as the horse could carry him. He came into the squire's presence, his face beaming with delight, and an air of self-satisfied superiority in his manner...all quite unaccountable to his master. Andy then pulled forth his hand from the bottom of his pocket and, holding three letters over his head, he cried, "Look at that!" He slapped them down under his broad fist on the table before the squire.

"Well," Andy crowed, "if he did make me pay elevenpence, by gor, I brought your honor the worth o' your money anyhow!"

"But they're not mine!" cried the horrified squire.

"Oyez," affirmed Andy with a certitude that brooked no argument, "you paid for them!"

—Samuel Lover

*

After the harvesting of their crops, and the long, drab winter was upon them, farm families would relieve the monotony by inviting their neighbors to a party. And, oh! what parties they were! In this recollection of old Ireland gatherings, drinking is mentioned only once, and then in passing ("She'll never let you rest till your glass is brimming o'er again"). The theme here focuses on the country hospitality and the expression of brotherhood for which the Irish are so famous. In his song-poem, *The Donovans,* author Fahy has captured that blend of conviviality and affection.

"The Donovans"[6]

If you would like to see the height of hospitality,
The cream of kindly welcome and the core of cordiality;
Joys of old times are you wishing to recall again?—
Then come down to Donovans, and there you'll meet them all again!

(Chorus)
Cead mille failte they'll give you down at Donovans,
As cheery as the springtime and Irish as the *ceanabhan;*
The wish of my heart is—if ever I had a one—
That every luck in life may linger with the Donovans.

Soon as you lift the latch, little ones are meeting you;
Soon as you're 'neath the thatch, kindly looks are greeting you;
Scarce have you time to be holding out the fist to them—
Down by the fireside you're sitting in the midst of them!

There sits the gray old man, so *flaitheamhail* and so handsome,
There sit his sturdy sons, well worth a monarch's ransom;
Songs the night long you may hear your heart's desire of them,
Tales of old times they will tell you till you tire of them.

There bustles round the room the *lawhee*-est of *vanithees,*
Fresh as in her young bloom and trying all she can to please;
In vain to maintain you won't have a *deorin* more again—
She'll never let you rest till your glass is brimming o'er again.

There smiles the *cailin deas*—oh! where on earth's the peer of her?
The modest grace, the sweet face, the humor and the cheer of her?
Eyes like the skies, but when twin stars beam above in them—
Oh! proud may be the boy that's to light the lamp of love in them.

Then when you rise to go, 'tis "Ah then, now, sit down again!"
"Isn't it the haste you're in?" and "Won't you come round soon again?"
Your *cothamor* and hat you had better put astray from them—
The hardest job in life is to tear yourself away from them!
—Francis Arthur Fahy

---

[6]*The Donovans,* written in 1885 and published in 1887, was signed "Dreoilin" (the wren), *nom de plume* used by Francis Arthur Fahy, a number of whose other works appear in this volume. Definitions for the several Gaelic words and terms used in this poem will be found in the Glossary section of this book.

There is a popular misconception that only city folks are conceited or dazzled by their own possessions. But their country cousins occasionally suffer from the same affliction—bad cess to the disease! Here, in this famous folk-poem, an indignant poet voices his scorn for the woman who owned three cows at a time of famine in Ireland, and who permitted her wealth to go to her head.

"The Woman of Three Cows"[7]

O Woman of Three Cows, *arrah!* don't let your tongue thus rattle!
Oh, don't be saucy, don't be stiff because you may have cattle;
I have seen—and here's my hand to you, I only say what's true—
A many a one with twice your stock not half so proud as you.

Good luck to you, don't scorn the poor, and don't be their despiser;
For worldly wealth soon melts away and cheats the very miser;
And death soon strips the proudest wreath from haughty human brows;
So don't be stiff and don't be proud, Good Woman of Three Cows.

See where Momonia's heroes lie, proud Owen More's descendants—
'Tis they that won the glorious name and had the grand attendants!
If *they* were forced to bow to Fate, as every mortal bows,
Can *you* be proud, can *you* be stiff, my Woman of Three Cows?

The brave sons of the Lord of Clare, they left the land to mourning;
Mavrone! for they were banished, with no hope of their returning;
Who knows in what abodes of want those youths were driven to house?
Yet *you* can give yourself those airs, O Woman of Three Cows!

Oh, think of Donnell of the Ships, the chief whom nothing daunted—
See how he fell in distant Spain, unchronicled, unchanted!
He sleeps, the great O'Sullivan, where thunder cannot rouse—
Then ask yourself, should *you* be proud, good Woman of Three Cows!

O'Ruark, Maguire, those souls of fire, whose names are shrined in story—
Think how their high achievements once made Erin's greatest glory;
Yet now their bones lie mouldering under weeds and cypress boughs,
And so, for all your pride, will you, O Woman of Three Cows!

The O'Carrolls also, famed when fame was only for the boldest,
Rest in forgotten sepulchres with Erin's best and oldest;
Yet who so great as they of yore in battle or carouse?
Just think of that, and hide your head, good Woman of Three Cows!

Your neighbor's poor, and you, it seems, are big with vain ideas,
Because, forsooth, you've got three cows, one more, I see, than she has;
That tongue of yours wags more at times than charity allows—
But if you're strong, be merciful, great Woman of Three Cows!

---

[7]James Clarence Mangan, translated from the Old Irish.

(Now there you go! you still, of course, keep up your scornful bearing,
And I'm too poor to hinder you—but, by the cloak I'm wearing,
If I had but *four* cows myself, even though you were my spouse,
I'd thrash you well, to cure your pride, my Woman of Three Cows!)

—James Clarence Mangan (1803-49)

*

James Clarence Mangan, whose contribution, The Woman of Three
Cows, *is presented above, was pre-eminent among the early Irish poets, and
was noted for the warmth of his lines, despite their heroics. This warmth
seems to be a major attribute of Irish writers, whether they live in Ireland or
elsewhere. An Irish-American, born in the year of Mangan's death, was
James Whitcomb Riley, whose homespun humor, although expressed dif-
ferently than Mangan's, was just as intimate. The difference lies in
Mangan's historical phrases, in contrast to the "country" simplicity that
earned Riley his sobriquet, "the Hoosier poet."*
Here is Riley at his nostalgic, "down-home" best:

"The Old Backhouse of Fond Memory"

When memory keeps me company and moves to smiles or tears,
A weather-beaten object looms through the mist of years.
Behind the house and barn it stood, a hundred yards or more,
And hurrying feet a path had made, straight to its swinging door.
Its architecture was a type of simple classic art,
But in the tragedy of life it played a leading part.
And oft the passing traveler drove slow, and heaved a sigh,
To see the modest hired girl slip out with glances shy.

We had our posey garden that the women loved so well,
I loved it, too, but better still I loved the stronger smell
That filled the evening breezes so full of homely cheer,
And told the night-o'ertaken tramp that human life was near.
On lazy August afternoons, it made a little bower
Delightful, where my grandsire sat and whiled away an hour.
For there the morning glory its very eaves entwined,
And berry bushes reddened in the steaming soil behind.

All day fat spiders spun their webs to catch the buzzing flies
That flitted to and from the house, where Ma was baking pies.
And once a swarm of hornets bold had built a palace there
And stung my unsuspecting aunt—I must not tell you where.
Then father took a flaming pole—that was a happy day—
He nearly burned the building up, but the hornets left to stay.

When summer bloom began to fade and winter to carouse,
We banked the little building with a heap of hemlock boughs.
But when the crust was on the snow and the sullen skies were gray,
In sooth the building was no place where one could wish to stay.
We did our duties promptly, there one purpose swayed the mind;
We tarried not, nor lingered long on what we left behind.

The torture of that icy seat would make a Spartan sob,
For needs must scrape the goose-flesh with a lacerating cob,
That from a frost-encrusted nail, was suspended by a string—
For father was a frugal man and wasted not a thing.

When grandpa had to "go out back" and make his morning call,
We'd bundle up the dear old man with a muffler and a shawl,
I knew the hole on which he sat—'twas padded all around,
And once I dared to sit there—'twas all too wide I found.
My loins were all too little, and I jack-knifed there to stay,
They had to come and get me out, or I'd have passed away.
Then father said ambition was a thing that boys should shun,
And I just used the children's hole till childhood days were done.

And still I marvel at the craft that cut those holes so true,
The baby hole, and the slender hole that fitted Sister Sue.
That dear old country landmark! I've tramped around a bit,
And in the lap of luxury my lot has been to sit.
Before I die I'll eat the fruit of trees I robbed of yore,
Then seek the shanty where my name is carved upon the door.
I ween the old familiar smell will soothe my jaded soul,
I'm now a man, but none the less, I'll try the children's hole.

—James Whitcomb Riley (1849-1916)

Chapter Six
Sports and Athletes
Introduction

The old established lace-curtain Irish enjoyed the bounty of a burgeoning industrial expansion during the last quarter of the nineteenth century, but for most Irish-Americans it was no easy existence. Living in shanty towns and sleazy tenements, they worked hard and long, drank, and had many children in the best Catholic tradition, went to mass regularly, and sent ship's passage money back to Ireland so that other family members could join them. They were turbulent, combative, and proud, those earthy Hibernians who, regrettably, had not yet had time to develop a literature through which they could articulate their American experience. Nevertheless, we can speculate about some aspects of their more carefree hours by the heroes they cheered and the unique characters they produced: especially in the field of sports.

"The reason why the Irish dominated professional boxing, for example, was mainly economic," suggested former heavyweight boxing champion Gene Tunney. "The prize ring offered an Irishman immediate money he could not otherwise earn. It presented a rare opportunity to improve his lot, to make things easier for his family. We seldom find an Irish youth in the professional ring today because the financial urgency is gone," concluded Tunney. "His primary interest now is to acquire an education, and if he has a superior talent for sports he uses it with the hope that it will lead to a scholarship at a college."

Fighting, it is clear, had always been a pleasant pastime for the Irish, and it was with wondrous joy that they discovered they could get paid for doing what came naturally. They did not enter professional boxing: they erupted. The first Irish-American heavyweight champion was "Yankee" Sullivan, who lost his title in 1853 to another Irishman, John "Old Smoke" Morrissey, a great "broth of a bhoy," in a bare-knuckles bout that lasted thirty-seven rounds. Morrissey was succeeded in 1858 by yet another transplanted son of Erin, John Heenan, who offered to fight all contenders "wid me lef' han' tied behin' me back."

It was John L. Sullivan, "The Boston Strong Boy," who brought a measure of respectability to professional boxing. John L., as he was always called, found prizefighting to be nothing more than mean, eye-gouging, knee-to-groin, part-wrestling, street brawling. But when he left, he had created a modern sport and made his name an enduring legend, much as his grandfather had done as the champion shillelagh fighter of Ireland in the days before the potato famine.

In 1882, the great John L. defeated Paddy Ryan for the bare-knuckles title. Thereafter, the new champion fought under the Marquis of Queensberry rules, taking on all comers, but repeatedly returning to bare-knuckles fighting to defend his crown. After 1889, however, he had eliminated all contenders for the London prize ring title. Almost single-handedly, he had changed the course of professional boxing.

When John L. Sullivan unsuccessfully defended his crown against James J. "Gentleman Jim" Corbett in 1892, he had already fallen victim to the "curse of the Irish." He had been drunk the night before the fight, and when his fellow Irishman, Corbett, knocked him out after twenty-one rounds, consensus had it that John Barleycorn was the real winner of the Queensberry title. Sullivan subsequently "took the pledge" and lectured on the evils of drink, but "Gentleman Jim" was never forgiven by his countrymen for bringing down "The Boston Strong Boy," the Irish patron saint of fisticuffs.

The sports pages have been filled with accounts of other Irish-American fighters: Jake Kilrain, Mike McTigue, Terry McGovern, Tom Sharkey, Packy McFarland, Tommy Gibbons, Mike Gibbons, Billy Conn, Jack Dempsey (who is also part Indian and Jewish), Gene Tunney, Tommy Burns, Jack Sharkey, Jim Braddock, and in our own time, The Quarry brothers, Jerry and Mike.

At the turn of the century, the rising educational levels of the Irish were especially felt in college sports. The rough and tumble of football was particularly appealing to young Irish-Americans who prided themselves on what they considered their genetic heritage of brains, brawn, and speed. And they did indeed make gridiron giants of such schools as Notre Dame, Fordham, St. Mary's of California, Georgetown, Holy Cross, and Villanova, to name a few.

It would seem, however, that the sports-loving Irish reserved a special place in their hearts for professional baseball. The roster of famous ballplayers and managers sounds like a *Who's Who* of Dublin. There was the immortal John J. McGraw, who became manager of the New York Giants in 1902 at the age of twenty-seven, and won ten National League pennants. Cornelius McGillicuddy, better known as Connie Mack, managed the Philadelphia Athletics to eight flags and participated in baseball until his death in 1956 at the age of ninety-three. Other big-league managers included Joe McCarthy, Hugh Jennings, Pat Moran, Joe Cronin, and Steve O'Neal. McCarthy won seven World Series.

No recount of Irish ballplayer "greats" would be complete without mention of the Delahanty brothers of Cleveland, five of whom played in the major leagues. A sixth brother was hit by a pitched ball and was forced to retire from the game just as he was about to be signed for the big time. The eldest of the Delahantys, Big Ed, was honored with a plaque in Baseball's

Hall of Fame in Cooperstown, New York. Other Irishmen who are represented in the Hall of Fame include catcher Roger Bresnahan, the "Duke of
Tralee," who was battery mate of Christy Mathewson and later a manager;
Mickey Cochran, another of the game's great catchers; Hugh Duffy, who
batted .438 in 1894; Michael J. "King" Kelly, who inspired the popular
song, "Slide, Kelly, Slide" (he led his league in batting in 1886, but his
greatest claim to fame was as a base runner); "Iron Man" Joseph
McGinnity, the pitcher; Connie Mack, another great catcher until he became an equally great manager; and outfielder Jim O'Rourke.

"You don't have to be Irish to be a great baseball player, but it helps,"
observed Charles A. Comiskey at a Saint Patrick's Day festival. Comiskey,
the son of an Irish immigrant, started as a rookie on third base for Milwau-
kee at the early age of seventeen. After a long career as an outstanding ballplayer, he helped organize the American League and served as president of
the Chicago White Sox from its organization in 1900 until his death in 1931.
"What we need in baseball," concluded Comiskey, "is a little bit more
malarkey, a little more blarney, and a lot more Irish laughter. And why
not? Hell, we already have the talent!"

Yes, the Irish did indeed have the talent, the malarkey, the blarney, and
the Irish laughter to help make American sports among the most exciting
and entertaining in the world. Some of that laughter has been captured in
this chapter. As Comiskey might have said: "Read on, MacDuff!"

—H.D.S.

"The Old School Tie-Up"

Eliot Cass was from Boston, Mass.
Spike Jones from New Haven, Conn.
They headed the show at Boggs & Co.
    A business they carried on.
From Tues. to Fri. they saw eye to eye
    And peace would, in fact, prevail.
But beginning with Sat. things were not like that
For Cass was from Harvard—and getting fat—
While slenderer Jones was from Yale.

Through Oct. and Nov., Spike Jones would rove
    With the football team each week,
He was glad to confer on Wed. or Thur.,
    But on Sun. he refused to speak.
He explained on Mon. to everyone
    Each play—for an hour apiece—
And all the stenogs who worked for Boggs
Got terribly bored with the chorus of frogs
    Right up to the first of Dec.

From Jan. through Mar. Cass wandered far
    For hockey and basketball,
While Apr. and May found Jones away
    Where the Eli batteries call.

A rift in the blue is the Eli crew
  But June brings Cass to his dreams,
And if Harvard led in the track, it's said
That all of the bookkeeping girls see red
  As he talks of the Crimson Teams.

One day in Aug. it was like a morgue
  In the office of Boggs & Co.
For the son of Jones, in solemn tones,
  Said Harvard was where he'd go.
Jones hated to pass the relentless Cass
  Whose cracks were becoming stale,
But 'twas Cass who wept on the first of Sept.
When he learned the secret his son had kept.
  That *he* was going to Yale.

Now from Tues. to Fri. any passer-by
  Finds Cass and Jones the same,
But see those two harps* on that Sat. P.M.
  When they go to that One Big Game.
For old Eli, Jones utters awful groans
  When the Harvard passes fail,
But we must confide he is satisfied
For Eliot sits on the Harvard side
  And yells like hell for Yale.

              —Laurence McKinney (1891-)

*

Old-time students of Irish fisticuffs ("fight fans" to the low-brows) may recall the time that Terry Maguire, the diminutive champ of the Emerald Isle, received his comeuppance from Beerbelly Tommy.

According to indisputably impeachable witnesses, Jerry, a scrappy broth of a lad, decidedly under the influence of Irish joy juice, objected violently when Tommy, the barkeep, refused to serve him any more drinks.

"G'wan home," growled Tommy, "you've had enough."

"Home, is it?" yelled the inebriated young fellow. "I'll have yez know I'm the featherweight champion of all Ireland!"

"Be ye now?" replied Tommy, his voice grim. "Well, one more peep out iv you, me lad, and out you go—feathers and all!"

*

There are many stories about the "Mighty Casey," hero of the epic poem, *Casey at the Bat*, the original of which is offered at the end of this chapter. But here is one lesser known tale that illustrates his superhuman speed.

**Harp:* A slang term meaning "Irishman" or "Irishwoman," current in the Northeast United States, from Maine to Maryland, during the first three decades of the twentieth century. It was often used by Irish-Americans themselves to denote newly-arrived emigrants from Ireland, as a synonym for "greenhorn."

A bunch of the boys were whooping it up at the corner *poteen* palace. The stories were flying faster than feet at an Irish reel when Dooley spoke up. Spaketh he:

"I recall seein' Casey when he was the star of the Mudville Nine. You all know what a hitter he was, but did you know he was the fastest man in baseball who ever lived? Fast? Listen, I remember the time Mudville was playing Centerville, and Casey, first time up at bat, slammed out a homer. Well, you ain't gonna believe this, but ol' Casey he reached first base before anybody could hear the crack of the bat on the ball. Then, when he rounded second, the second baseman said something that made him mad, so he slapped the third baseman in the catcher's mouth!"

＊

Casey Stengel, famous baseball player and manager, is quoted here in view of his adoption by the New York Hibernian Society as "Unofficial Irishman of the Year." He was persuaded, against his better judgment, to attend a performance of George Abbott's musical production, *Damn Yankees,* which was an adaptation of Douglas Wallop's sprightly (and wishful-thinking) novel, *The Year the Yankees Lost the Pennant.*

After the show, critic George Jean Nathan asked him how he liked Abbott's play.

"George," declared Casey, drawing himself up in his most haughty manner, "I ain't gonna comment about a guy which made $100,000 writin' how my club lost!"

＊

Sunday—and again her husband was riveted to the chair, watching a football game on TV. "It's like this every week," she muttered angrily.

"Wally," she complained when he rushed into the kitchen for another beer during a timeout, "you love football more than you love me."

"That I do, *macushla,*" he replied thoughtfully, "but, faith, I love you more than baseball!"

＊

The score was 34-33, with a minute left to play in an intramural basketball game between the engineering and medical facilities at McGill University. The engineers grabbed the ball and "froze" it with some deft pass work. Then the whistle sounded— and they learned *they* were the team with 33!

＊

A couple of rooters were so engrossed in this, the last half of the ninth inning of the World Series game, that they wouldn't even consider the thought of marching back to the refreshment stand for hot dogs, and there wasn't a vendor in sight. But both were hungry. They finally bribed a kid nearby to go for them.

"Here's a dollar-and-a-half, kid," they told him. "Get us each one, and buy one for yourself, too."

The kid came back with a dollar change. "Sorry," he explained, "but they only had *my* hot dog left!"[1]

*

The football game between Holy Cross and Yale was in full swing. The score was tied. The spectators were yelling wildly, and the players were grimly determined that their side would win.

About the middle of the third quarter, time was called at the request of the Yale center.

"Look here," he said, walking up to the referee, "I don't like to complain, but every time we get tangled up in a scrimmage play, that big Irish center bites me."

"Well, in that case," snapped the referee impatiently, "my advice is that you play him only on Fridays!"

*

We don't know whether sportswriter Dan O'Herlihy invented this one, but it's too good to pass up. Malarkey or not, here it is:

Stan Musial, former champion batter of the National League, was aptly described by Joe Garagiola, catcher on a rival team, but close friend of Musial's during the off-season:

"Stan," brooded Garagiola, "comes sauntering up to the plate and asks me how my family's making out. Before I can answer him, he's on third base."

*

Pat O'Brien's fame as the actor who portrayed the life of football coach Knute Rockne, remains a hallmark of sports-film lore. But Rockne was no match for tough-talking Father Healy, coach of St. Joseph's football team. The players would rise to heights of competitive derring-do whenever they heard the good Father yell:

"Wham 'em, jam 'em, bam 'em, slam 'em—in th' name iv th' gintle Jazus!"

*

In Belfast, they still tell about the hurling* match that took place between an all-Catholic team and an all-Protestant team. A limey attended that game, according to the sports columnists of the day, and, when the Catho-

---

[1]From *The New Hibernian,* August 1932.
*An outdoor ball and stick game similar to field hockey. The national pastime of Ireland, it has been played in the United States by Irish immigrants and their descendants since long before the formation of the Gaelic Athletic Association in 1914.

lics made a skillful play, he applauded. But when the Protestants in their turn scored, he again joined in the applause and shouting.

At this point, an Irishman jabbed him in the ribs.

"My God, man," demanded the appalled son of Erin, "have you no religion at all!?"

*

Voice from Fordham U.'s alumni boxes: "Go to it, fellas! Win or tie, we're behind you all the way!"

*

In seventeen years as a stellar pitcher in the American League, "Lefty" Gomez of the Yankees didn't exactly knock down the fences with his bat. In fact, he averaged about four scratch singles a season. One day, he closed his eyes, took a hefty swing and, to everybody's amazement, including his own, smacked a solid triple to left center. Poised on third, the triumphant "Lefty" boasted to Coach Art Fletcher, "Hey, Art, I think I can steal home."

"Faith, laddie," begged Fletcher, shuddering, "it's taken you four months to get this far—don't blow it!"

*

John O'Sullivan, who made "O'Sullivan's Heels" a household word, liked to boast that he was never at a loss for an answer, no matter how difficult the question. But pride goeth before a fall, as he learned when his precocious ten-year-old grandson, Michael, propounded a riddle.

"Gran'pa, if two women finish off a bottle of whiskey while watchin' a ball game, what inning is it, an' how many guys are on base?"

O'Sullivan gave the problem his long and deliberate consideration and then shook his head. "I don't know, Michael. I give up."

"It's the last of the fifth, and the bags are loaded!"

*

A minor crisis of sorts occurred when John F. Kennedy visited Ireland. While there, he was awarded honorary degrees by the two leading universities, Trinity and National. Trinity is an old-line Protestant school, and National is the seat of Catholic culture. Naturally, they are bitter rivals.

"Having a degree from each could present a few problems," said Kennedy, "especially if I should ever return to Ireland on the day of the annual Trinity-National rugby game.

"However, I have solved the dilemma," he announced. "I will cheer for Trinity and pray for National."

*

William O'Dwyer, on Senator Joe McCarthy: "The nearest he ever came to participating in an athletic event was when his colleagues in the Senate nominated him to receive an Olympic gold medal for jumping to conclusions."

＊

Six-foot-four, 238-pound Larry Quinn, the strong-man football player, was ribbed so much about his long hair that he decided to have it trimmed a little, but not more than an inch or two. One Saturday morning, he visited his barber.

"Don't take off too much," he warned as he sat down in the chair.

The barber shrugged. "Okay, if that's what you want," he said, eyeing the athlete's shoulder-length tresses. "I suppose if I did cut your hair real short nobody would recognize you."

"Yeah," agreed the giant tackle, "and nobody would recognize *you* either!"

＊

It has been said of William Russell Grace, the shipping tycoon, that he spent more time on the golf links than he did in his office. Obviously, he loved the game with a passion.

"Tell me something, Dad," inquired his son, Joseph, one day. "How can you play so much golf and still conduct your business?"

"There's no conflict at all," explained William cheerfully. "I make it a point never to play at the office!"

＊

Voice from the Dean's office: "We here at Loyola are straining every effort to develop a college that the football team can be proud of!"

＊

At a fashionable bar—one of those places where the whiskey costs a dollar a shot plus two dollars for the "atmosphere"—a drunk wandered in and, wide-eyed, gazed at the wall decorations of mounted fish and game. Fascinated by them, he carefully walked from one to the other, mumbling as he went. Suddenly, he came upon the main exhibit: an enormous stuffed tarpon. Swaying precariously, he stared at it for a full minute and then turned to the bartender. "Mister," he shouted indignantly, "the guy who caught that fish is a damn liar!"

＊

According to columnist Joe Fales of the *Detroit Free Press*, the athletic director of the University of Nebraska, Bob Devaney, had this wry comment:

"You've heard of the Rambling Wreck from Georgia Tech? I'm the Total Loss from Holy Cross!"

*

If there was any one sport that claimed city-bred Gavin's enthusiasm, it was fishing. He read in the Sunday papers one lazy weekend that the fish were really jumping in the streams of northern Wisconsin. The next Sunday found him there, hoping for a good catch of pike, pickerel, and muskies. But to no avail. Nary a bite did he get. He was sitting disconsolately on a rock at the riverbank, fishing pole in hand, when a young country boy came by.

"How many fish didja catch?" asked the lad.

"None yet," sighed Gavin.

"How long you been here?"

"About an hour."

"Heck, that ain't bad, mister," said the boy reassuringly. "There was a feller fished here for two weeks and he didn't get any more than you got in only an hour!"

*

Writing in *Hockey News*, Ken McKenzie reported that Jacques Plante, National League goalkeeper, had invited a friend and his son to dinner.

"Seated around the table," wrote McKenzie, "were the father, the son, and the goalie host!"

*

Old man Quigley, a seasoned fisherman, found his new neighbor on the bank of the Shannon making a stab at the art of angling. It was plain that he was a novice. The newcomer fished for more than an hour, doing practically everything wrong. Nevertheless, from the sheer operation of the law of averages, the beginner finally got a bite. Feverishly, he grabbed his reel and drew the fish in, until, at last, some miracle having saved his line, he brought his small catch all the way up to the tip of the pole.

"Now what should I do?" he cried, overcome with excitement. "What should I do?"

"Seems to me, lad," replied old man Quigley, "there's not much you *can* do except climb up the pole and git 'im!"

*

From Grandma's Irish Wisdom Book: "It's getting so, these days, that the only men who chase a little ball around the golf links are those who are too old to chase anything else!"

*

At Fordham University, they've solved the vexing controversy over academics versus sports. Their football team has one squad for defense, one for offense, and one to attend classes. Sundays, the varsity team attends mass for everybody.

*

"Pop" Moriarty, football coach at a small Catholic college in the hinterlands of Minnesota, had seen his charges trampled eight Saturday afternoons in a row, the last time by a humiliating score of 55 to 0. He called them to a meeting on the following Monday.

"Next week, we'll be having our last game of the season," he began bitterly. "But, we might as well forget all the trick plays I tried to teach you dimwits. We're going back to basics. Now, for lesson number one: this object I am holding in my hand is called a football. Do you understand that? I'll spell it for you: f-o-o-t-b-a-..."

He was interrupted by an urgent cry from the back row: "Hey Pop, not so fast!"

*

The Washington Redskins had just finished one of the toughest football games of the season. Later that evening, they were relaxing over a beer or two and discussing their reasons for leaving college to play professionally.

"I went to Georgetown University, but it was calculus that threw me. It got so bad I didn't even know what the professor was talking about."

"What knocked me out was trigonometry," confessed the second man. "At least you got to your senior year. I had to leave Holy Cross while I was still a junior."

The third player took a long drink of beer and stared moodily into space. "You guys think you had it tough, do you?" he said after a long silence. "You should have attended Notre Dame. God, did you ever run into a subject called long division?"

*

Crusher Connolly, the Roscommon wrestler, was bemoaning his ill luck, the clear evidence of which was a scratched face and the imprint of molars on his left hand.

"Molly, my new girl, did this to me," he moaned piteously. "And to think, that was the only match I ever had that wasn't fixed!"

*

This little anecdote is over thirty years old, and still going strong. No doubt, it will still be doing yeoman service for another thirty.

Horse-owner and fancier Sissie O'Bryan came back from the Kentucky Derby with a tale about an old Louisville hostelry that traditionally named one of its rooms for the winner of the big annual racing classic. There was a Zev room, a Gallant Fox room, a Whirlaway room, and so forth. After the 1964 Derby, however, the management was reluctantly compelled to abandon the idea. Winner that year was Assault.

*

The most believable golf story of the year appeared on the sports pages of a Daytona Beach newspaper recently. It read:

> "At this point, the gallery deserted
> the defending champion to watch Miss Kathleen
> Moore, whose shorts were dropping on
> the green with astonishing regularity."

*

O.K. Kelly and Johnie O'Keefe, both rival automobile dealers, and also confirmed rivals at the Lehigh Country Club in Allentown, Pennsylvania, fought so consistently that they finally agreed not to talk to each other at all during a golf match. The outcome of this anecdote, however, depends on which one tells it. In this case, Kelly's version is presented.

After their pact of silence, they began their game. All went smoothly and silently until the sixteenth hole, when Kelly walked ahead to a ball on the edge of the green while his opponent, O'Keefe, climbed into a sand trap to play out. O'Keefe took one swing, then another, and another, finally topping a shot clear across the green and into a trap on the other side. Then he whanged the ball back into trap number one.

As he wearily recrossed the green, Kelly broke the long silence.

"Can I say just one word?"

"Well," snarled O'Keefe, "what is it?"

"I don't want to ruin your day," replied Kelly, "but you're playing with my ball!"

*

In view of the nation's bicentennial celebration, it would be unseemly to omit the following anecdote.

History records that in 1916 a young lieutenant, just graduated from West Point, was summoned from his post at Fort Sam Houston to coach the football team of a nearby school named St. Mary's. The coach, one Dwight D. Eisenhower, found the spirit of the school willing, but the material sparse. Desperately seeking reinforcements for the skimpy squad of eighteen, he suddenly spotted a husky specimen crossing the campus.

"You there," he called, striding toward the young fellow, "what's your name?"

"Brian Murphy."

"Well, why the heck aren't you out to play football for your Alma Mater?"

"Lieutenant," the husky specimen replied, "I'll have you know I'm the principal of this school!"

*

"Golf," observed columnist Dan O'Herlihy, "is a game in which a ball measuring one-and-a-half inches in diameter is placed on another ball eight thousand miles in diameter. The object of the game is to hit the smaller one, not the larger."

*

Fishing is simplicity itself. All you have to do is get there yesterday when the fish were biting. It explains the reason why so many Irish outdoorsmen prefer hunting. One of them was Rory Mullins, the writer. A proud father, Mullins decided to teach his little son the fundamentals of duck hunting. He took the boy along to show him how it was done—and to display his expertise.

They were safely hidden in their blind for a half-hour or so when a solitary duck flew overhead.

"Down you go," chuckled Rory, blasting away.

The duck flew serenely on.

"Son," said the quick-thinking Rory, "you are witnessing a miracle. "There flies a dead duck!"

*

Joe McNulty, Cultural Attaché of the Irish Republic in Washington, D.C., tells about the first time he took his wife on a hunting trip in the Maine woods. They were in good rabbit territory, and other hunters were about, so McNulty cautioned his wife about the necessity of extreme care when firing her rifle. He and his missus were separated by some twenty yards or so when he heard a shot. Running to his wife's side, he found her smiling broadly and pointing to the bushes.

"I must have hit something," she announced triumphantly. "Just listen to that language!"

*

Another McNulty anecdote, containing the usual maximum of malarkey and the minimum of fact:

He and a few other members of the Irish embassy had been in the north-woods for a week, and each night a huge grizzly bear played havoc at their campsite. They finally decided to track down the animal and teach him the futility of fooling around with a bunch of Irishmen. With some difficulty they talked their faithful cook, old Mose, into accompanying them.

"All right, Mistah McNulty, I'll go," Mose conceded reluctantly, "but i dat b'ar gits anywhar near an' you looks round an' don' see nobody—dat' me!"

*

Haggerty had a miserable run of luck at the track and was down to hi last ten dollars when, just before the last race, he happily caught sight of hi parish priest anointing one of the horses entered in the event.

"With the Holy Father blessin' the craiture," reasoned Haggerty, "how kin I lose?" So he put the whole ten on the nose to win.

There were eight horses in the race, and Haggerty's choice finished eighth. A few days later, he encountered the reverend gentleman on the street.

"Father, it's been lettin' me down you have, that's what!" he grumbled. "I bet on a horse because ye stop to bless it and begorra, it finishes last!"

"You should have more faith than that," the priest told him sadly. "I wasn't blessing that horse, my boy...I was giving him the last rites!"

*

Years ago, Jimmy Dykes, the famous baseball player and manager, enjoyed telling this story on himself.

When he first joined the A's back in 1918, he struck out four times in his first game. On his next turn, Connie Mack used a pinch hitter. Jimmy sulked on the bench, but the understanding Connie soothed him.

"I suppose you know why I took you out," said Mack.

"Why?" asked Jimmy in a harsh voice.

"Because the American League record for striking out is five times in one game," explained Mack, "and I didn't want you to tie it in your very first big league game!"

*

Another old-timer in the annals of baseball is the tale of woe about Babe Ruth and his money problem. According to sportswriter Dan O'Herlihy, it was one of the worst years of the Great Depression when the mighty Babe was asked to submit to the first salary cut of his career. To say that he demurred is an understatement. He insisted on his customary eighty-thousand-dollar contract.

"But, Babe," protested an official of the Yankee ball club, "these are trying times. That's more money than Hoover got last year for being President of the United States."

"I know," persisted the Babe, "but I had a better year than Hoover!"

*

Casey at the Bat[2]

The outlook wasn't brilliant for the Mudville nine
    that day;
The score stood four to two with but one inning more
    to play,

---

[2]Of the hundreds of versions of this epic ballad, only two can be attributed to the actual author, Ernest ᵀ Thayer: the original, which was published in the Sunday edition of the *San Francisco Examiner*, June 3, 1888, and his authorized revision of 1895, which contained only minor corrections of punctuation and the changing of two or three words. Published above is the original, with Thayer's own correction of three commas.

And then when Cooney died at first and Barrows did
    the same,
A sickly silence fell upon the patrons of the game.

A straggling few got up to go in deep despair. The rest
Clung to that hope which springs eternal in the human
    breast;
They thought, "If only Casey could but get a whack
    at that—
We'd put up even money now, with Casey at the bat."

But Flynn preceded Casey, as did also Jimmy Blake,
And the former was a lulu* and the latter was a cake;†
So upon that stricken multitude grim melancholy sat,
For there seemed but little chance of Casey getting to
    the bat.

But Flynn let drive a single, to the wonderment of all,
And Blake, the much despised, tore the cover off the ball;
And when the dust had lifted, and the men saw what had
    occurred,
There was Johnnie safe at second and Flynn a-hugging
    third.

Then from five thousand throats and more there rose a
    lusty yell;
It rumbled through the valley, it rattled in the dell;
It pounded on the mountain and recoiled upon the flat,
For Casey, mighty Casey, was advancing to the bat.

There was ease in Casey's manner as he stepped into
    his place;
There was pride in Casey's bearing, and a smile on
    Casey's face.
And when, responding to the cheers, he lightly doffed
    his hat,
No stranger in the crowd could doubt 'twas Casey at
    the bat.

Ten thousand eyes were on him as he rubbed his hands
    with dirt;
Five thousand tongues applauded when he wiped them on
    his shirt.
Then while the writhing pitcher ground the ball into
    his hip,
Defiance flashed in Casey's eye, a sneer curled Casey's
    lip.

---

*Something extraordinary. Used here in a derisive sense.
†A slang word of the day meaning a dude, dandy, or homosexual. As used here,
however, it denotes a handsome, conceited ball player, vain about his appearance,
but a weak player.

And now the leather-covered sphere came hurtling through
    the air,
And Casey stood a-watching it in haughty grandeur there.
Close by the sturdy batsman the ball unheeded sped—
"That ain't my style," said Casey, "Strike one!" the
    umpire said.

From the benches, black with people, there went up a
    muffled roar,
Like the beating of the storm-waves on a stern and distant shore.
"Kill him! Kill the umpire!" shouted someone on the
    stand;
And it's likely they'd have killed him had not Casey
    raised his hand.

With a smile of Christian charity great Casey's
    visage shone;
He stilled the rising tumult; he bade the game go on;
He signalled to the pitcher, and once more the spheroid
    flew;
But Casey still ignored it, and the umpire said, "Strike
    two!"

"Fraud! cried the maddened thousands, and echo answered
    "Fraud!"
But one scornful look from Casey and the audience was
    awed.
They saw his face grown stern and cold, they saw his muscles
    strain,
And they knew that Casey wouldn't let that ball go by
    again.

The sneer is gone from Casey's lip, his teeth are clenched
    in hate;
He pounds with cruel violence his bat upon the plate.
And now the pitcher holds the ball, and now he lets it go,
And now the air is shattered by the force of Casey's blow.

Oh, somewhere in this favored land the sun is shining
    bright;
The band is playing somewhere, and somewhere hearts are
    light,
And somewhere men are laughing, and somewhere children
    shout;
But there is no joy in Mudville—mighty Casey has struck
    out.

—Ernest L. Thayer (1863-1940)

Chapter Seven
Those Lace-Curtain Irish
Introduction

The Irish-American community of the nineteenth century presented a single face to Americans of other origins, but this surface unity masked a growing diversity and stratification. The term "lace-curtain" probably originated in the late 1850s or early 1860s (no one knows precisely when), but it did not become popular until the 1890s, to denominate those more affluent Irish in the United States who could afford lace curtains on their windows.[1] There is no hard and fast rule that exactly defines the term. The late Fred Allen, himself an Irish-American, offered his own definition: "Lace-curtain Irish have fruit on the table when no one's sick!"

However, it is not wealth alone that symbolizes the lace-curtain set. In tandem with financial achievement is an extraordinary degree of social awareness—a deliberate effort to maintain a level of gentility that sets them apart (and above) the "masses." In that context, the masses, at the turn of the present century, were understood to be the "shanty Irish" who, forty years earlier, smoked clay pipes and kept pigs in what was to become New York's Central Park. Or the term might allude to the shanty Irish who dwelt in the slums of New York, Chicago, or Boston.

The irony lies in the fact that many a lace-curtain Irish family can trace its roots in America to a great-grandfather and great-grandmother who *both* smoked clay pipes, lived in makeshift shanties, and kept a pig; or to raffish-mannered rowdies who inhabited the city slums. Naturally, that description did not apply to all Irish of the day, but it did for most, resulting in painful embarrassment to the first lace-curtain generation of the nineteenth century. To separate themselves from their fellow Irishmen of lesser status, the lace-curtain Irish embarked upon a determined drive for ultra respectability. With each successive generation they became more pious, more genteel, more sober, more fiercely dedicated in their attempt to place a wide distance in time and circumstance between themselves and the "quaint" Irish men

---

[1]"Lace-curtain," although two distinct words, are hyphenated when used to denote the wealthy, "Social Register" Irish-Americans.

and women who were their forebears. Some were so successful that when most working-class Irishmen could at last afford lace curtains after World War I, the term "cut-glass Irish" was coined to denote those who now considered themselves a few degrees more refined than the old line lace-curtain crowd. The expression, however, never attained the popularity its sponsors had hoped for.

As we have seen, the affluent "Social Register" Irish Catholics of America, or the F.I.F. (First Irish Families) as they term themselves, owe their financial and class status to desperately poor ancestors, many of whom fled Ireland's great potato famine of the 1840s. Huddled together in city ghettos, their hopes for decent employment stultified by the ever-present "No Irish Need Apply" notices, they were forced to accept the most humble or the most dangerous work, and for outrageously low wages.

In the face of these obstacles, how was it possible, then, for the Irish immigrants of yesteryear to trod the long and stony road from poverty to lace-curtain respectability in such areas as Chicago's Beverly community, or *le comfort bourgeois* of New York's Park Avenue? A number of reasons are evident. By nature, the Irish have always been fighters. For them, the necessity to improve their lot was a challenge—a battle to be won. By tradition, they were highly political and knew where to pinpoint the sources of power, and how to use that political power when they themselves attained it. They recognized the fact, far better than other immigrant nationalities who had not suffered as they had in Ireland, that without political representation of their own, the Irish could not achieve the economic and social gains that America had to offer. Moreover, and this is more important than many realize, their inherent and often irresistible gift of Irish blarney helped to open doors that otherwise might have been closed to them. But their most telling advantage was that, unlike other competing immigrant groups, they spoke the language of their new homeland. Indeed, their accented English, commonly known as the Irish brogue, far from being a hindrance to their advancement, was a charming asset, and many an Irishman cheerfully cultivated it throughout his life in the United States.

Technically speaking, a lace-curtain joke is a story or quip which is told by First Irish Family members to others of their class, and which revolves around some facet of their personality or life style. But the Irish, being what they are, were never sticklers for technicalities. The humorous anecdotes and taut retorts were (and still are) just as often directed *against* the F.I.F., not only by themselves but also by their less fortunate kinsmen. The jokes frequently involve the servant-employer relationship of the past, as personified by the lovable but feisty Irish maid, Rosie Haggerty, some of whose mirthful antics have been selected for this chapter. Other stories poke good-natured fun at the newly rich—the parvenu who is under the mistaken impression that wealth alone, without social position, is the key that will magically open the portals to America's "Irishtocracy."

In the jokes that follow, we make no such class distinctions. If the subject of the anecdote is wealthy, and refined enough to daintily elevate his pinkie when sipping a cup of tea, then for the purposes of humor he is considered lace-curtain. But there is no question as to the *bona fides* of such giants as Robert J. Cuddihy, the publishing genius of *Literary Digest* fame, or

Michael Cudahy, who began his career as a fourteen-year-old butcher boy, and later revolutionized the meat-packing industry by developing the process for summer curing of meat under refrigeration. Here, too, is the engineering wizard, Thomas E. Murray, who started as a street lamplighter and, thanks to his inventive talents, ultimately controlled seven giant industrial corporations, to say nothing of a 50 million dollar bank account. They, and a number of others in the rarefied stratosphere of America's First Irish Families who are not usually associated with humor, are quoted in the following pages. Included are such other stalwarts as James Butler, the kitchen helper who built the first chain grocery empire in the United States; the Buckleys of Boston and New York; the Kellys of Philadelphia, known locally for their construction company, and nationally for their Princess Grace of Monaco; and the Kennedys, who gave us Cutty Sark Scotch whiskey and a president of the United States.

These lace-curtain tycoons appear to be rather somber characters when viewed through the morose-colored glasses of *Wall Street Journal* editors, but they seem to be anything but awe-inspiring when their quirks, mishaps, and escapades are subjected to the broad leveling process of humor. And what makes it so appealing is that it is all in fun, as a host of smiling Irish men and women now demonstrate.

—H.D.S.

> Is that Misther Reilly, can annywan tell?
> Is that Misther Reilly that owns the hotel?
> Well, if that's Misther Reilly they speak of so highly,
> 'Pon me sowl, Reilly, yer doin' quite well!*
>
> —Anonymous

*

The distinguishing characteristic of the lace-curtain Irish is that they live the life of Reilly. But the question is: How did Reilly get so rich in the first place? Well, here's the answer:

Way back in 1911, a cub reporter named George Delahanty, of the old *New York Journal,* was sent to get a personal interview with the immensely wealthy Reilly whom everybody talked about. The young fellow's editor wanted a human interest story on how Reilly had accumulated his riches.

"Wel-l-l, 'tis a long sthory, it is," said the old man. "And while I'm afther tellin' it, we moight as well be savin' the candle," whereupon he leaned over and blew it out.

"Never mind the story," said the reporter. "I understand!"

*

In other words, "I'll see!"

"Is Mrs. Moore at home?" asked the lady caller at the Beacon Hill mansion.

---

*Thought to be the original of the phrase, "leading the life of Reilly," meaning to enjoy a good life without heed to the cost.

"Physically speaking, madam, that may be the case," replied the butler. "Indeed, as an abstract question, the fact cannot be denied. But, in relation to your desire to see her, I cannot say definitely until I have ascertained Mrs. Moore's wishes in the matter. Pray be seated until I have received advice from above."

*

Mrs. Rafferty had just hit the jackpot in the Irish Sweepstakes. In keeping with her new station in life, she decided to call in one of those specialists to redecorate her home—a man whose snobbish manner was fortified with a tongue that could clip a hedge. Almost immediately they fell into an argument.

"Are you sayin' me taste ain't fancy enough fer the likes o' you?" demanded Mrs. Rafferty.

"Madam," said the interior decorator haughtily, "I was not criticizing your taste. All I said was that your house looked like it was furnished in Early Salvation Army."

*

Suffering from profound melancholia, a male patient visited the office of the eminent Park Avenue physician, Dr. John A. Flynn. After a careful examination, Dr. Flynn made his diagnosis.

"My friend, you are suffering from unnecessary depression. What you need is some light entertainment. Go and see the famous clown, Emmet Kelly. He's bound to make you laugh, and that will be better for you than any drugs I might prescribe."

"See *Kelly*?" groaned the patient. "My God, Doc, I *am* Kelly!"

*

In the days of the "robber barons," when steel tycoons and railroad magnates were bamboozling the public under the precept of *caveat emptor*—"let the buyer beware"—a father and son were discussing the old Irish adage, "Integrity and wisdom are the keys to success." The son, rather cynical in the aftermath of news headlines about industrial price-fixing, bribery, and other commercial shenanigans, expressed his doubts that the proverb applied to business practices.

"I'm sorry you are so disillusioned," said the father, "but let me give you an example. When I speak of integrity, I mean that when you promise that you will deliver merchandise on a certain day and at a certain price, then you should live up to that promise even if it bankrupts you."

"Well, if that's integrity, it's pretty extreme," observed the son. "But what is wisdom?"

"Don't make such damfool promises!"

*

Friends and Acquaintances

An acquaintance," according to Patrick Ireland, "is a person whom we know well enough to borrow from, but not well enough to lend to. However, when we refer to a lace-curtain Irishman as a friend, always bear in mind that *he* may consider *you* an acquaintance!"

*

A cut-glass Irishman, who is 1.5 per cent higher on the Irish totem pole than a lace-curtain Irishman, can usually be identified at a bank. The lace-curtain Irishman who seeks a loan is usually required to furnish adequate collateral. The cut-glass Irishman disdains this arrangement. "Sir," he declares to the loan manager, "my word of honor is worth its weight in gold!"

*

The well-known but eccentric physician of the 1920s, Dennis Kirby, is recalled in this short but delightful remembrance.

A talkative lady patient of the lace-curtain set, came to Dr. Kirby's office and babbled endlessly about her symptoms. For half an hour or more he listened in stony silence, unable to get a word in, even while brandishing a scalpel under her nose. Finally his Irish temper rose to the exploding point.

"Madam," he barked, stopping her tiresome chatter, "put out your tongue."

The lady complied.

"Now keep it there," snarled Dr. Kirby, "till I finish talking!"

*

Oliver Pollock, the barrel-chested Irish immigrant who raised $300,000 for the American Revolution, most of it from his own pocket, also carved out a trading empire in the West and Deep South. He was eminently fair to the Indians, unlike the general practice of the day. Nevertheless, after he had bankrolled an expedition against the British in Florida, a curious tale arose concerning his trading practices. It was said, and utterly without foundation, of course, that he concluded the first treaty that white men ever signed with the Seminole Indians. Pollack's Treaty stated:

"The Seminole Indians shall keep their lands for as long as the sun shines, the rivers run, and the grass grows—or 90 days, whichever comes first."

*

In response to a telephone call from an irate citizen in the fashionable Silk Stocking district of Manhattan, a police officer knocked on the door of apartment 3-B, and was admitted by an elegantly-attired little old lady.

"Officer, it's demandin', I am, that ye take yer shillelagh to thim shanty

Irish nixt door," she began, before he could utter a word. "Ivry night, fer the past two weeks, they've been poundin' on me wall an' yellin' at me till three o'clock in the mornin'."

"I don't blame you for being upset, madam," said the policeman sympathetically. "I'll certainly put a stop to those shenanigans right away. Why, with all that noise, I don't suppose you get a wink of sleep."

"Faith, it isn't that a'tall," explained the sweet old lady tearfully, "but with all the yellin' an' poundin' goin' on, I can't enjoy me piano playin'!"

*

When an Irish family comes into a substantial amount of money, and they prepare to live the good life of the lace-curtain gentry, everyone, it seems, has designs on their purse-strings. First, the newly-rich decide to build a house in a high-class neighborhood, so they call in an architect—one who simultaneously drafts a plan of their house and plans a draft of their money. Then they decide to furnish their house with antiques, but economically. So they visit an auctioneer who proclaims with a hammer that he has picked their pocket with his tongue.

—Patrick Ireland

*

The late showman, Ed Sullivan, who possessed a wealth of charm even in his Celtic gloom, was a sharp and canny character—but not when it involved the stock market. This failing no doubt helped contribute to the wide disparity between his finances and that of Bill Walsh, his very wealthy stockbroker.

Ed Sullivan was reading the *Wall Street Journal* one morning when an item caught his eye. He immediately called his broker.

"Bill, I see where Bonded Irish Whiskey is down to ten cents a share. I think it's due for a rise. Shall I buy?"

"I'll check it out and call you back," promised Bill. As good as his word, he phoned Sullivan a half-hour later. "It's hot all right," he assured his client. "Ten cents a share."

"Buy five thousand shares for my account," said Ed eagerly.

Bill Walsh pocketed his commission, kept his eye on Bonded Irish Whiskey quotations, and, a few days later, called Sullivan again.

"You sure were right about that stock, Ed. It just climbed to a dollar."

"Buy another five thousand shares for me!" ordered Sullivan promptly.

On the following Thursday, the broker called once more. "Listen, Ed, that stock is bouncing off the ceiling. It's now *two* dollars a share!"

Jubilantly, Ed yelled into the phone, "Buy me ten thousand shares this time!"

Every few days thereafter, Bill Walsh phoned Ed Sullivan, announcing new and dizzying heights for his stock, with Sullivan buying additional blocks of ten thousand, and Walsh, of course, pocketing his hefty commissions for each transaction.

But the day of reckoning finally came, alas, when Bill telephoned the last exciting price rise.

"That stock of yours just went through the roof!" he shouted. *"Five dollars a share!"*

"Sell my shares!" ordered Sullivan.

There was a deep silence at the other end of the line, and then, in a small voice, Walsh quavered, "Sell! To whom?"

*

"Will the Irish never change?" sighed Mrs. Gloria Astor. "In the old days, the Irish immigrants came to America in steerage. Now, with the 'troubles' starting all over again, they're flying over in the baggage compartment!"

*

Mrs. Margaret Ryan—dowager of the *Boston* Ryans, if you please—was a hypochondriac of the first order. She would scurry off to Dr. Dugan's office at the first symptoms of her many imaginary illnesses. The good doctor, let it be said, was anything but pleased with this silly woman's constant complaints. But, one does not argue too much with a wealthy patient.

The day came, however, when Mrs. Ryan really did suffer an injury. A small splinter went into the tip of her forefinger, and though she quickly extracted it, the tiny wound caused her great anxiety. Shrieking for her chauffeur, she threw herself into the family Rolls Royce and, within moments, the limousine was racing against time for medical aid.

Dr. Dugan procured a magnifying glass and examined his patient's finger. Then he summoned his nurse.

"Miss Flynn," he commanded, an urgent note in his voice, "bring me the iodine—quickly!—before it heals itself!"

*

During the height of the recent recession, O. B. Ryan, the Wall Street stockbrocker, was bemoaning his losses at the Stock Exchange.

"Were you a bull or a bear?" asked a sympathetic friend.

"Neither," sighed Ryan. "Just a plain old-fashioned jackass!"

*

When her personal maid married and went to live with her new husband, Lady Plushbottom placed an advertisement in the papers for a new girl. The ad stipulated that the applicant must be experienced and British. The first to apply for the job was Rosie Haggerty, with a brogue as broad as the Shannon.

"Are you sure you're English?" asked Lady Plushbottom suspiciously.

"Faith, and that I am, mum," Rosie assured her prospective employer.

"Where were you born?"

"In Ireland, an' plaze Yer Ladyship."

"How then can you be an Englishwoman?"

"Saints presarve us, mum," replied Rosie, "sposen I was born in a stable, that's no rason I should be a horse!"

*

From the humorous folklore of Irish-Americana come these further adventures of saucy Rosie Haggerty, whose philosophy was: "I've niver met annywan betther than I, and damn few as good!"

Lady Plushbottom, having just taken her Saturday night "bawth," reached for a towel and then drew back, shuddering.

"Rosie," she yelled from the top of the stairs, "come up here this very instant!"

Dutifully, Rosie went upstairs, first taking a snifter of brandy and kissing the butler.

"Yes, mum, an' what would yer problem be this time?"

"It's this towel," snapped Lady Plushbottom. "It—it—well—it positively stinks!"

"I don't smell a blessed thing," said Rosie from six feet away.

"Well, it does. It smells of—of—dead fish!"

"Faith, mum, I don't see how that can be," objected Rosie. "I washed it with me very own hands." She hesitated a moment, and then her eyes lit up. "Beggin' Yer Ladyship's pardon," she exclaimed, "but are ye sure ye haven't used this towel wanst before?"

*

Madam Buff-Orpington, the wealthy society lady, was carefully explaining the correct procedure for serving meals. She ended her little lecture with a stern admonition to Rosie, lately of Lady Plushbottom employment, but now her own new maid.

"Now, Rosie, don't ever forget that you must always serve from the left and take the plates from the right."

"I won't forget, mum," answered Rosie. "But, faith, I didn't know you were that superstitious!"

*

Having more or less voluntarily left the employ of Lady Plushbottom and Madame Buff-Orpington, Rosie the maid found a position with the Kelly clan of Philadelphia. Rosie arrived only a few hours before they were to have a big party for their daughter, Grace, and Prince Rainier. Mrs. Kelly now had the additional problem of breaking in a new maid.

"Above all," she cautioned, winding up her instructions about proper dress, "don't wear any jewelry."

"Jewelry, is it? Sure and I don't have any," Rosie assured her, "but it's thankin' ye I am for the warnin'!"

*

A chuckle from the past is revived with this brief exchange between John W. (Bet-a-Million) Gates and a lecturer named Brady.

The incident occurred at a meeting of the Ancient Order of Hibernians. Brady, who happened to be the visiting lecturer, droned on and on, endlessly, in the same monotonous voice, until the bored audience, one by one, departed the lecture hall. Only one man, John W. Gates himself, was left, sitting uncomfortably in the first row.

"Sir," said the appreciative bore when he had concluded his very long speech, "I want to thank you for remaining after everyone else walked out."

"Don't thank me," replied Gates sourly. "I'm the next speaker!"

*

A legend of doubtful authenticity has it that Joseph Kennedy once entered the fashionable Gentlemen's Shamrock Grille on Wall Street and joined a group of financiers. He beckoned to a waiter and ordered a double scotch.

"When Kennedy drinks," he declared loudly, "everybody drinks!"

Naturally, everyone at the table ordered scotch.

Kennedy finished his drink, again summoned the waiter, and then slapped two dollars upon the table.

"When Kennedy pays," he asserted, "everyone pays!"

*

Despite the similarity in their names, the very affluent Cudahy and Cuddihy families are not one and the same—although there have been a few intermarriages. But the variant spelling of their names is not the only difference between the families. According to insiders, the Cudahys are spendthrifts, while the Cuddihys, it is said, are penny pinchers. To prove the assertion the following tidbit is offered by a Cudahy.

Soon after Anne Cudahy married Frank Cuddihy, she suggested that he move from his unprepossessing little office to a more pretentious place of business, as befitting an important industrialist and financier.

"I can't afford it," he quickly complained, thinking of the additional rent such a move would entail.

"Well," said Anne, "you should think of keeping up appearances."

"I don't have to keep up appearances," Frank protested. "Look at Bernard Baruch. He was far richer than I am, but a park bench served as his office. In fact, it was practically his home."

"Yes, and if he was as careful about money as you are," Anne agreed calmly, "it was probably his *real* home!"

*

"That Mr. Greeley sure is absent-minded," complained Pegeen, the downstairs maid. "I swear, he'd leave his head if it were loose."

"And that's the truth," agreed Rosie the upstairs maid. "Ownly yestiddy I heard the man say he was goin' to Arizona for his lungs."

*

We journey back in time—about half a century—to discuss multimillionaire Thomas Fortune Ryan (his mother's maiden name was Fortune). He started out in life as the son of a poor tailor. Orphaned at the age of fourteen, he parlayed his Celtic charm and money-making abilities into a fortune far in excess of 100 million dollars at a time when income taxes were nonexistent or negligible. His power was immense. He was the undisputed czar of the Tobacco Trust and owned or was the principal stockholder in a network of railroads, city transit companies, electric power utilities, life insurance firms, and diamond mines.

But, like many successful Irish-Americans, he was also a charitable man. Ryan contributed heavily to the Democratic Party and to the Catholic Church, giving the Church, all told, some 20 million dollars. He was especially generous to New York's Church of St. Jean Baptiste. Of course, these acts of charity may have been motivated by more personal reasons: a seat in the high councils of the Democratic Party, for example; or a reserved front-row seat in Roman Catholic heaven. But he did offer financial assistance to other worthwhile endeavors. One instance is found in the following anecdote:

For many years, Thomas Fortune Ryan made up the deficit for the New York Philharmonic Society. Like most classical music organizations, the Philharmonic was always on the brink of financial disaster, and, as is usually the case, it made only feeble attempts to raise enough additional money when it knew that a rich donor was waiting in the wings, checkbook in hand.

But, in 1924, Ryan's patience snapped. He called a meeting of the Philharmonic's directors and made known his displeasure.

"It seems to me that others should share some of the responsibility for making up the annual deficit," he declared. "From now on, I will expect you to raise half of the deficit from other donors, and I'll give the remaining half."

The offer was, indeed, a generous one and the directors, though worried, agreed. But their concern was short-lived. A week later, the chairman called the philanthropist with the news that half the money had been raised.

"You promised to make up the rest, so that our deficit would be wiped out," the chairman reminded him.

"That I did," agreed Ryan, "and you will receive my check in the morning. But, as a matter of curiosity, would you mind telling me who gave you all that money?"

"Of course not, sir," replied the chairman. "The money was given to us by Ida, your wife."

*

Mrs. Beatrix Fairfax (formerly "Beaumont" Bessie before she got lucky and married real good) was standing in line with her French poodle, waiting her turn to buy the latest model Rolls Royce. Nearby was old Cassidy, the handyman employed by the Fifth Avenue auto dealership. As he was washing the display window, Cassidy came a little too close, and the little poodle sniffed suspiciously at his leg. He drew back.

"Don't be afraid," said Mrs. Fairfax comfortingly. "Henri doesn't bite."

"Faith, mum, I'm not afraid he'll bite," retorted Cassidy. "But when he lifted his leg I thought he was about to kick me!"

*

Millionaire Vincent Cannon, who had a towel named in his honor, was the chief of nine different corporations, the driving force behind several national charities, sparkplug of church activities, and the power behind most of the important political decisions of New York. He was a busy man indeed!

But the day came when all of those weighty responsibilities threatened his mental stability. He awoke one morning, and, his body bent sideways, he proclaimed to the world that he was the Leaning Tower of Pisa. A few days later, he conceived the notion that he was Saint John. But, when he finally proclaimed himself as the Saviour, his family prevailed upon him to visit a psychiatrist.

"Well, well," welled the doctor, "so you think you are the Christ?"

"No, not anymore," said Cannon. "That was *last* week!"

"Oh, I wasn't aware of your change of status," said the psychiatrist, smiling tolerantly. "Suppose you tell me all about it...and start at the beginning."

"All right," agreed Cannon. "In the beginning I created the heavens and the earth...."

*

The late Dwight Morrow, who was very absent-minded, was deeply engrossed in a book while on a train. The conductor approached and asked for his ticket. Frantically, Morrow searched for it.

"Never mind, Mr. Morrow," said the conductor, recognizing the famous man. "When you find it, just mail it to the company. I'm certain you have it."

"I know I have it!" exploded Mr. Morrow. "But what I want to know is, where the hell am I going?"

*

There is an erroneous impression that only the poor are frustrated by the pomposity and often downright foolishness of United States government agencies. But the rich have their problems, too. Take the case of the Mannings, who made their millions in steel.

Mrs. Winifred Manning, so the neighbors related, viewed her dandelion-strewn lawn in front of her Hyannisport mansion and gave a despairing sigh. Even her chief gardener was unable to cope with the weeds. As a last resort, she wrote to the Department of Agriculture in Washington, D.C., telling them how much she loved her lawn and flowers, and begging for advice on how to rid the place of the unwanted dandelions.

Back came a reply from the D of A, with the practical suggestion that only a government bureaucrat could offer:

"You must learn to love dandelions, too!"[1]

＊

Al Smith, who aspired to become the first Irish-Catholic president of the United States was fond of recounting his first meeting with Will Rogers, among the wittiest men in recent history. Smith had invited the comedian and his wife to dinner, but they were unavoidably detained and arrived late.

"I shore hope you folks ain't already et," said Rogers, shaking Smith's hand.

"Will," hissed his mortified wife, "how many times have I told you to say 'have eaten'!"

"Wal," drawled Rogers with his inimitable grin, "I know a lot of fellers who say 'have eaten' who ain't et!"

＊

The Buckley family is at the center of the F.I.F.'s—the First Irish Families—who comprise America's Irishtocracy. But they, too, have their problems—especially when it comes to hiring new maids.

Having had little luck at finding a local girl, the Buckleys became interested in a red-cheeked country girl from the northern part of Finland. She had just arrived in the United States, and they decided to offer her employment.

"Can you cook?" asked Mrs. Buckley.

"No," said the girl. "I can't cook at all. My mother did the cooking."

"Well," ventured Mrs. Buckley, "can you do the housework?"

"No," said the girl, "I don't know how. My oldest sister always did the housework."

"I see. Then perhaps we could let you take care of the children."

"No, I couldn't do that. My grandmother always took care of the children."

"Can you do the sewing?"

"No," said the girl, "my aunt always did the sewing."

"For heaven's sake, what can you do?" cried Mrs. Buckley.

"Oh, there's one thing I do quite well," volunteered the girl cheerfully. "I'm very good at milking reindeer!"

＊

A Chicago matron was seated next to the austere dowager, Mrs. Constance Mackay, at a recent tea party in Boston. During their crisp exchange of mutual introductions, Mrs. Mackay advanced a bit of information that brought a glint to the eye of the Chicago lady.

"In Boston," asserted the haughty Mrs. Mackay, "we place all our emphasis on breeding."

"You don't say!" replied the Chicago matron, feigning surprise. "Where I come from we, too, think it's a lot of fun, but we do manage to have a great many outside interests!"

*

"I have often been asked how I started up the ladder to becoming so affluent," said Harry McGrath, the wealthy publisher. "The truth is that I have a good head for figures.

"It all started when, in a dream one night, I saw a huge sign with a big number six painted on it. Later on, in that same dream, I came to another sign with a tremendous nine on it. Well, that was all the hint I needed. The very next morning, I arose bright and early and went to see a bookie. Adding the six and nine together, I won a fortune by betting on the total—number fourteen!"

*

It takes determination and a bit of resourcefulness to make that long climb to the top, as Jim Moran learned soon after he arrived here from Galway. Today, Jim is the senior partner of the Wall Street firm that bears his name, but he remembers his initial encounter with an especially resistant client.

Moran had just gotten his New York insurance license, and was now ready to tackle his first prospective customer—none other than the immensely wealthy Frederick Ryan. Into Ryan's Park Avenue retreat strode the brash young Irishman, his native brogue still very pronounced.

"Faith, sor, yer a harrd man to see," commented Moran.

"Young fellow," griped Ryan, "the only reason I'm seeing you now is that I'm sick of you hanging around here."

"Sure, and it's sorry I am that me prisince makes ye ill, Misther Ryan—a foine name ye have: it makes me proud to know ye—and I hope yer health is improvin' by the minute."

"So, you're proud to know me, are you? Well, young man, that Irish blarney of yours won't work with me; I'm an old hand at it myself. If you want to know the truth, I've already refused to see six insurance men today."

"Ah, and how well I'm aware iv it, sor," declared the bold son of Erin, his brogue as thick as Irish pudding. "I'm all six iv them!"

When the industrial financier, Bradley Murray, visited Ireland some years ago, he was invited to tea by the Prime Minister, Eamon de Valera. In almost no time at all, Murray found himself in a hideously embarrassing predicament. At the table, he was astonished to see de Valera take his cup and pour most of the tea into a deep saucer. The Prime Minister then added a bit of cream and a little sugar.

But let Bradley Murray tell the rest of the story in his own words:

"I was that disconcerted I'm afraid I lost my head. I panicked. As a house guest of the Prime Minister of Ireland, common courtesy, I felt at the moment, made it obligatory that I do as he did. So I hastily poured my own tea into a saucer and, likewise, added a little cream and sugar.

"But I was frozen with horror when de Valera leaned over and placed his saucer on the floor for the cat!"

＊

Mrs. Abigail O'Dwyer of the Cape Cod O'Dwyers was tooling down the turnpike doing ninety or more, when the growl of a siren sounded right behind her. Dutifully, she pulled her Rolls Royce over to the side of the highway and waited, a haughty look on her aristocratic features.

"Madame," the officer began, his voice ominously low key. "do you know how fast you were going?"

"Certainly!"

"I'm afraid I must ask you to follow me to the station house."

"I'll do no such thing! You can't arrest me, young man. I'll have you know I come from one of the best families in New England!"

"My dear lady," replied the officer, his lips drawn in a tight, white line, "I'm arresting you for speeding, not breeding!"

＊

Padraic had just arrived in the United States from County Meath and obtained a position as gardener for the fashionable Rockefeller family. Innocently unaware of the prejudice of class distinction, he applied for membership in the most exclusive church in all of upstate New York, simply because it was near to his place of work and his living quarters. The priest attempted to put him off with all sorts of evasive excuses until Padraic became aware of the fact that he simply was not wanted.

"Why not go home and sleep on it for a few days?" suggested the priest, not too unkindly. "I'm sure the Lord will tell you what do do."

A week later, Padraic returned.

"Well, my son, did the Lord send you a message?" asked the priest.

"That he did, Father," replied Padraic. "He said, 'Sure, an' 'tis meself that's been thryin' to get into that same churrch for twinty years, an' they've still to let me in!' "

＊

Freudian slips occur in the best of lace-curtain families. As proof positive that such psychological mistakes respect neither rank nor privilege, we present this naughty anecdote:

One of the hobbies enjoyed by William Grace, founder of the Grace Line of vessels, was gardening. True enough, he employed several gardeners, but he enjoyed working among the plants and trees on his estate.

One day, as he was raking the fallen pine needles in front of his mansion, a gorgeous, titian-haired young lady came up the flagstone walk and approached him. Her figure was absolutely breathtaking, and she wore a tight-fitting sweater to accent her twin charms.

"Good morning," she said. "I'm the new secretary. Your office sent me here to get some papers."

"Ah yes, Miss, I'd forgotten," he crooned, his eyes darting to her sweater. "Please do come inside. But walk carefully so you don't slip on the pine nipples!"

*

When her daughters were very small girls, Mrs. Dwight Morrow invited the financier, J. P. Morgan, to tea. The little girls were to be brought in, introduced, and then quickly ushered out. Mrs. Morrow's greatest fear was that Anne (later to become Mrs. Lindbergh), the most outspoken of the family, might comment audibly about Morgan's celebrated and conspicuous nose.

"Anne," cautioned Mrs. Morrow, "I will expect you to conduct yourself like a real little lady and make no comment of any kind about Mr. Morgan's nose. I realize it is rather large, but it would be very impolite to mention it. Do you understand, my dear?"

"Yes, Mama," replied Anne like a good girl.

When the dreaded moment came and the children were brought in, Mrs. Morrow held her breath as she saw Anne's gaze fix unfalteringly upon the financier's proboscis and remain there. But, to her vast relief, her daughters were models of propriety. The girls simply curtsied and were sent on their way.

With a sigh of thanks to the Creator, Mrs. Morrow poured a cup of tea and handed it to her famous guest.

"And now, Mr. Morgan," she murmured, "will you have cream or lemon in your nose?"

*

Feeney, the self-made Brooklyn contractor, was very rich, having accumulated his wealth by getting up early every morning, working hard, and winning the Irish Sweepstakes. He also married a Delahanty—one of the Hartford Delahantys; that is, the ones who are not in jail very often.

Well, the Feeney-Delahanty union produced a scion who wanted to enter Georgetown University, but he had no desire to spend four years at the institution. Two years, he thought, was long enough for a smart young fellow like himself. His father was of a like opinion, so the old man went to see Georgetown's chancellor in his son's behalf.

"Sor," began Mr. Feeney with a degree of politeness that was ordinarily conspicuous by its absence, "afther I make a big donation to yer little college—and a big wan 'twill be indade if me foine son is enrolled—I'd like him to be grajiatin' in two years instid iv th' usual four."

"Sorry, but it takes four years to complete the course," said the chancellor, making an effort to curb his normally acid tongue.

"Well," suggested Papa Feeney as he meaningfully patted his wallet, "can't ye give him a shorter course than th' reg'lar wan?"

"Oh, yes, he can take a shorter course," agreed the chancellor, his voice now grim. "It all depends on what you want to make of him. When God wants to make an oak tree he takes a hundred years, but he takes only ninety days to make a peanut!"

*

"Father Goose" Rhymes for Lace-Curtain Kids

As I was playing on the green
A little book it chanced I seen.
Carlyle's *Essay on Burns* was the edition;
I left it laying in the same position.

———————

Teach not thy parent's mother to extract
    The embryo juices of the bird by suction.
The good lady can that feat enact
    Quite irrespective of thy kind instruction.

———————

I'm glad the sky is painted blue;
    And the earth painted Irish green;
And such a lot of nice fresh air
    All sandwiched in between.

—Patrick Ireland

Chapter Eight

Barmaids, Bar Stools, and Bibulous Banter

Introduction

"The curse of the Irish," a term applied to the Irishman's affinity for hard liquor, has long been caricatured by the stage Paddy and other humorists.[1] Mark Twain, for example, observed, "Give an Irishman lager for a month and he's a dead man. An Irishman is lined with copper, and the beer corrodes it. But whiskey polishes the copper and is the saving of him." Saving indeed! John Maguire, a Dublin journalist who toured the United States after the Civil War, wrote, "Were I asked to say what I believed to be the most serious obstacle to the advancement of the Irish in America, I would unhesitatingly answer—drink!"

The situation has improved during the past few decades, yet a number of authoritative studies show that the Irish, in proportion to the general population in the United States, still suffer the highest rate of problem drinkers. Strangely enough, there were few allusions to alcohol addiction in Ireland prior to the seventeenth century. In fact, convivial libations were associated with Saint Patrick in song and story, as some of the examples in this chapter illustrate. In the earliest times, faction fighting among Celtic tribal kings was often (if not usually) stimulated by the cup that cheers. However, there is ample evidence to believe that heavy drinking took a noticeable rise among the viciously persecuted Irish who lived under the penal code.[2]

In America, the Irish immigrant continued his drinking. The Shamrock Society of New York, as far back as 1817, warned its members of the "dire consequences" of alcohol addiction. In 1820, temperance groups were formed among the Irish work gangs along the Erie Canal. A gentle Capuchin friar, Father Theobald Mathew, came to the United States from

---

[1]The masculine gender is always used when alluding to "The curse of the Irish." It is the Irish*man* who drinks excessively, seldom his colleen. This was true in yesteryear's Ireland as it is today in the United States.

[2]It is small wonder that the Irishman of the eighteenth and nineteenth centuries

Ireland in 1849 and soon won national recognition as the "Apostle of Temperance." administering "the pledge" to tens of thousands of Irish-Americans. More than one hundred Hibernian temperance societies were established by the time he returned to Ireland.

Today, many Irishmen, still drink—joyously, without guilt, but with a kind of triumphant zest that seems to be absent in the folklore of other cultures. A gregarious people, their grog shops, such as exist in the Irish sections of Boston or along New York's Third Avenue, are often social centers where men of the immediate neighborhood gather for good conversation in the evening, after work. There, too, they tell and retell the jokes and humorous anecdotes that induced Irish laughter down through the centuries.

The droll stories and poems in this chapter were selected to cover a long period of time, from the day of Saint Patrick to last night's donnybrook at Tim's Tavern. But their primary function is to entertain, for " 'tis a dark day indeed when a cloud obscures an Irishman's smile."

——H.D.S.

*

turned to *poteen* as a source of forgetfulness and solace. The Draconian laws of the new penal code, added to earlier codes after the subjugation of Ireland by the British in 1691, compounded his miseries. By that time, more than a third of the Irish people had died in the wars, plagues, and famines of the preceding thirty years. Natural deaths and a substantial decrease in births had further reduced their numbers. The ancient Irish aristocracy of scholars and scientists had been almost wiped out by the enemy. Farmers and small property owners had lost their lands; a once relatively prosperous people were now beggars in their own country. But the British did not stop there. The laws of the penal code deprived the Irish people of any semblance of civil rights they might have had in the past. They were mercilessly exploited and were subject to hanging or sold into slavery to Jamaica plantation owners as punishment for the most trivial offenses. Under the penal code, an Irish Catholic was forbidden to vote, serve on a jury, own a horse valued at more than five guineas, enter a university, become a lawyer, or work for the government. All Irish Catholics were compelled to pay tithes for the support of the Anglican Church. No Catholic Church could have a spire. Irish Catholics were forbidden to marry Protestants or buy land from Protestants. The very few Irish who still clung to a bit of land could retain it only by forsaking the Catholic religion and joining the Anglican Church. When an Irish Catholic died, his estate was divided equally among his sons, but if the eldest became a Protestant, he received all of it, disinheriting the other sons. Priests were subject to arrest and deportation. The Irish language was forbidden and schools were abolished. The repressive penal code continued for the next 125 years. During that time, the Irishman sought escape from his degradation and humiliation by bolstering his damaged ego through the use of whiskey, in addition to his periodic rebellions against his oppressors.

"Ode to a Street Light"

The last lamp of the alley is burning alone,
All its brilliant companions are shivered and gone;
No lamp of her kindred, no burner is nigh,
To rival her glimmer, or light to supply.

I'll not leave thee, thou lone one, to vanish in smoke,
As the bright ones are shattered, thou too shalt be broke;
Thus kindly I scatter thy globe o'er the street,
Where the watch in his rambles thy fragments shall meet.

Then home will I stagger as well as I may,
By the light of my nose, sure, I'll find out the way;
When thy blaze is extinguished, thy brilliancy gone,
Oh! my beak shall illumine the alley alone!

—William Maginn

＊

Here's one that your great-great-grandpappy laughed at:

The Civil War was raging furiously. In Virginia, General Ulysses S. Grant reared back on his trusted steed and shouted triumphantly to his company of men: "We have taken Atlanta! We have taken Savannah! We have taken Charlestown! We have taken Richmond! What remains now for us to take?"

"General," shouted Corporal McGinty, "let's take a drink!"

＊

As usual, it was a festive Saturday night at Tommy's Tipperary Tavern.

The air, thick with cigar, cigarette, and pipe smoke, was that heavy with the added effluvium of stale beer and whiskey you couldn't even smell an Englishman if he were standing next to you—may the seven saints of Sullivan County prevent us from making the test!

Dudley McGonnicle had already downed a quart of Monaghan's Mountain Dew and was swearing by all that's holy that he could drink another quart if he'd a mind to. Up spoke Jamie Maloney, the jealous one.

"Faith, Dudley, I've drunk as much as you, I have. And I could drink another quart, too."

"I can drink *two* more quarts," yelled Dudley, his professional pride stung to the quick—and the man had a sensitive quick indeed.

"Ten dollars says you can't," wagered Jamie, as bold as you please. "And the loser pays for the whiskey."

The bets were laid down and tavern-owner Tommy poured the drinks, filling up one glass and then another—and another—and another.

The first wagered quart was now swishing at high tide in Dudley's kidneys as Tommy opened the second bottle. His eyes were glassy, his vision blurred, his tongue thick. But, he bravely proceeded to down the rest of the mountain dew. Jamie, though as astounded as anyone else in the place, reluctantly admitted defeat, paid the bet, and was even magnanimous enough to carry Dudley home.

But once in the privacy of his room, strange and awful things occurred in Dudley McGonnicle's internal plumbing system. He clutched at his midsection in agony and rolled around the floor as the pain grew more and more intense. His time had come: he was sure of it! And so young, too! A pity!

"Oh, swate Jazus, save me in this, me hour iv nade," he moaned, lifting his eyes to the ceiling and hoping the Saviour could see through plaster. "Help me get rid iv that last quart—I can handle th' first two meself!"

*

"Oh, Eamon," wailed Peggy as her husband staggered in at midnight, "all that drinkin' will drive you to your grave."

"Will it now?" grinned Eamon, reeling as he made for the couch. "And isn't that better than walkin'?"

*

The Syracuse Society for Strict and Steady Sobriety was celebrating National Beware of Booze Week. Invited as guest speaker was Mamie Malone. Mamie, who secretly enjoyed an occasional nip after her three kids had been put to bed, had never addressed a group before, but she was flattered at the invitation and promptly accepted. On the podium, she was somewhat nervous, but she began bravely enough.

"From my own experience, I can assure you that motherhood exerts a strong barrier against the use of alcoholic beverages," she declared in an even voice. "Personally, I make it a rule never to drink—at least not in front of the children. And when they aren't around..." here Mamie faltered... "well, it isn't necessary!"

*

An Independence Day word of caution: He who goes forth with a fifth on the Fourth may not come forth on the fifth![3]

*

Old man Costigan reeled into Dinty's Bar and pleaded for a drink "on the cuff."

"Well," said kindhearted Dinty, "yer credit's in disgrace in ivry bar in the city iv Greater New York, but I'll do it this wan time. See that ye pay fer it next Sat'day."

---

[3]Patrick Ireland, Address to the Saint Patrick's Day Parade Committee (New York, 1976).

Saturday arrived and old man Costigan paid for the drink in full. A few days later, broke again, he prevailed upon Dinty to advance another drink, promising to pay for it on a specified date. Sure enough, he appeared on the agreed-upon day and promptly paid the amount due. On the following Wednesday, he again approached the bartender.

"Me mouth's as dry as an owld miser' heart," he whined. "Could ye be advancin' me another dhrink? I'll pay ye back next Choosd'y."

"I'll not be advancin' ye a penny's worth!" snapped Dinty. "Do ye take me fer a blitherin' fool, Misther Costigan? Ye decayved me wance an' ye decayved me twice't, but ye won't be decayvin' me a third time!"

*

"Faith, Padraic," exclaimed the priest who had set himself up as the conscience of Ballyhooley, "do me eyes and sharp nose tell me you have just left that den iv iniquity—the inn?"

"Sure, Father," agreed Padraic, smiling and gently reeling, "and would ye have me spending *all* me time there?"

*

"The Test"

> He is not drunk who, from the floor
> Can rise again and drink some more;
> But he is drunk who prostrate lies
> And cannot drink, and cannot rise.

—Eugene Field

*

The seedy panhandler sidled up to multimillionaire Joseph P. Kennedy, father of the late President of the United States.

"Mister," he whined in piteous tones, "couldja spare five dollars fer a respeckable, hard-woikin' fambly man?"

"Don't kid me," growled Kennedy. "You just want the money for a bottle."

"Well, yeah," confessed the bum. "I need a few heavy snorts."

"For five dollars?"

"Sure," replied the panhandler. "Ya expeck me ta eat on a empty stomach?"

*

Strains of "Sweet Adeline" could be heard issuing from the staggering figure as he made his unsteady way home to his door. After some fumbling with the key, he managed to open it and weaved inside, his breath reeking with the fumes of fermented barleycorn. He was greeted by the silent presence of his wife, her mouth drawn in a tight, determined line.

"Happy three-o'clock in th' mornin' to ye, me darlin'!" he shouted.

"By all th' saints, I've had enough," she snarled. "If iver I see or even hear iv ye takin' wan more dhrink I'll be divorcin' ye, Catholic er not!"

"Aye, *macushla*," he exclaimed joyously, "I'll dhrink to that!"

*

Immortalia from Dennis Duffy: "The best way for an Irishman to hold his liquor is in a frosted glass, twixt thumb and forefinger."

*

If you have never enjoyed a mellow evening at the Tam O'Shanter in the City of Brotherly Love, you haven't experienced that certain glow of pure Irish conviviality. One typical Saturday evening, not too long ago, a son of Erin flung wide the portals of the Tam O'Shanter emporium, weaved his way to the bar, and called out, "Happy New Year! Drinks for everybody—on me! Who cares if it's only June 5th?"

The patrons grinned good-naturedly, and one of them raised his glass aloft in an appreciative toast: "To the most important thing in your life, sir—your health."

"Now hold on!" interrupted the bartender. "Health isn't the most important thing of life to a good Irishman. It's his job that counts most. Without it he'd be drinkin' sarsaparilla!"

*

A Belfast man of intemperate habits was describing the horrors of delerium tremens to his clergyman. In vivid terms, he told of the monsters who had visited him after some of his drinking bouts—devils of all shapes and sizes. "But, of course, sir," he concluded, "I know they're all imaginary."

"Imaginary, is it!" retorted the outraged clergyman. "I'm not so sure of that. You say you've seen devils, but isn't it strange that you never saw angels?"

*

The evening was still young, but Matthew had already absorbed a snootful. Reeling along Forty-seventh Street, he came upon a theater where the Ballet Russe was appearing. Squinting his eyes, he viewed the pictures on the signboards and took special note of the scantily clad ballerinas. Pulling his pint bottle from his coat pocket, he took another swig, took another look at the signboard, took another drink, another look—and then brought a ticket.

Inside, he watched the ballet, utterly amazed as the star ballerina danced on her toes for a full twenty minutes without coming down once. Unable to stand the suspense a moment longer, he nudged the mink-swathed dowager sitting in the seat next to his.

"Beggin' yer pardon, shweetie, but thish ish ridiclish," he asserted. "If 'twas a taller gurrl they wanted, why didn't they shay sho an' hire one?"

*

The grand opening of the Essex Cocktail Lounge in Chicago was given a hearty sendoff by Mark Sullivan, who wrote in his newspaper column: "They have the nicest tables I was ever under!"

*

Old farmer John was returning home from town with a fat hen under his arm. As usual, he had spent the better part of the afternoon at Willie's Whiskey Wagon, and his rubbery legs advertised his tippling to all. On the way, who should he run into but his neighbor, Hattie McCormick, chairlady of the Women's Christian Temperance Union. She took one look at his crimson nose and bleary eyes, and stopped short.

"What are you doing with that pig?" she snapped.

"Is it mad ye are, Hattie?" he exclaimed. "That's not a pig."

"Howld yer tongue, John," she retorted. "I was talkin' to the chicken!"

*

She had only been married for two months, but the young bride had already returned home to mother. "It's his awful drinking," she explained tearfully.

"If you knew he drank, why did you marry the man?" demanded the girl's mother.

"But, Mama, I didn't know he drank," wept the bride, "until one night he came home sober!"

*

After an especially hard day at the mill, Pat decided to have a short beer before going home. Well, one led to another—you know how it is.

Later that evening—much later—he was staggering and stumbling homeward, when he passed a pet shop. Suddenly, it occurred to him that it might be a good idea to bring his wife a little gift to forestall the scolding she was sure to give him for being so late. Deciding to buy her a goldfish, he entered the shop.

Inside the pet store, he happened to come upon a cage with a large, multicolored parrot inside. He put in his hand to pet it.

"Hello, hello," squawked the parrot.

Startled, Pat hastily withdrew his hand, stepped back, and tipped his hat.

"Beggin' yer pardon, shir," he mumbled, embarrassed. "Faith, I thought ye was a burrd!"

*

No durance vile could be more pathetic than that suffered by O'Leary, the drunk, who was found wandering agonizedly around and around on the sidewalk outside the fence which encloses Gramercy Park.

The police nabbed him as he was beating upon the bars and screaming, "Let me out! Let me out!"

*

Sandy MacTavish and his wife, who recently arrived in New York from Edinborough, moved next door to the O'Sullivans.

"Weel, Maggie," ventured Sandy, "I think I'll go and pay my respects to the neighbors."

Maggie busied herself around the house until her husband returned some time later. "What kind of a mon is our neighbor?" she asked.

"He's a guid mon, that O'Sullivan," replied Sandy, "a guid mon and verra lib'ral with his liquor. But you know that Irish whiskey, Maggie. Verra bad quality it is. It was that bad, I nearly left some!"

*

"I see you're drinking coffee, Judge," remarked a friend to Richard O'Connor of the Massachusetts Circuit Court. "Why don't you try something cooling in this hot weather? Did you ever try gin and tonic?"

"No," said Judge O'Connor dryly, "but I've tried several fellows who have!"

*

With no intention to downgrade as noble a firm of auctioneers as Farrell and Brady of Boston, we herewith relate the following incident.

By way of explanation, when called to a home in preparation for an auction, Farrell and Brady usually took an inventory of the goods to be sold; Brady calling out the items, and Farrell listing them on the sales sheet.

One day, they were scheduled to conduct an auction at the Vanderbilt residence, but Brady was ill, so Farrell went without his partner. In Brady's place, he took with him a young assistant named (no kidding!) Righteous O'Rourke.

The taking of the inventory progressed in an orderly manner through many large items, with Righteous calling them aloud and Farrell listing them in detail. First, there was a mahogany dining room set, then a crystal chandelier, then other large items of household furnishings, all of which Farrell listed as they were called. At last came the individual items of miscellany.

"One quart Irish whiskey, full!" sang out Righteous O'Rourke. The list then continued until Righteous called out again, "One quart whiskey, half full!" A number of other items were called, and Righteous once more called, "One whiskey bottle, empty!"

Farrell had been busy writing down the inventory, but he stopped short and raised his head when Righteous finally called—

"Two revolving Oriental rugs!"

*

Suffering from one of his daily hangovers, W. C. Fields sank heavily into a chair at Donovan's Reef, his usual place of refreshment.

"Let me bring you an Alka-Seltzer," suggested the sympathetic waiter.

"Ye gods, no!" moaned Fields. "I couldn't stand the noise!"

*

A question of perspective was raised in the case of the drunk who passed out after imbibing too much at a Saint Patrick's Day celebration. His drinking buddies, as a prank, rubbed some Limburger cheese on his mustache. Then they awakened him.

"My God, ain't it awful?" gasped the drunk.

"Ain't *what* awful?" they asked, grinning.

"The world," he moaned. "The whole world stinks!"

*

In 1963, during his last visit to the United States, firebrand Brendan Behan,[4] the Irish author, dropped in at Eddie Condon's jazz emporium in New York's Greenwich Village. Drink in hand, as usual, Behan was declaiming on the merits and virtues of Ireland for all to hear. Suddenly he was interrupted by an equally inspired Englishman, also visiting this country, who lifted his voice in sodden song:

> "Kathleen Mavourneen, the gry dawn
> is bryking,
> The 'orn o' the 'unter is 'eard on
> the 'ill."

Behan extended a friendly hand to a traditional foe. "Not to be makin' fun iv your manner o' spakin'," he grinned, "but, sure, tis indade funny how you limeys drop your haitches!"

*

[4]Brendan Behan (1923-64) is remembered as an exceptionally skilled Irish dramatist. A notoriously outspoken and uninhibited man, he joined the Irish Republican Army in 1937 and was twice imprisoned for political offenses. His first play, *The Quare Fellow* (1956), a somewhat somber drama of prison life, was followed by *The Hostage*, a wild and joyous farce set in a brothel. His last book (1962) was *Brendan Behan: An Irish Sketchbook.*

Here are two jokes in one anecdote, published in deference to economy-minded readers.

Haloran, the habitual hypochondriac, was at the doctor's office—again!

"Well, what is it this time?" grumped the busy physician.

"Same as last time," complained Haloran. "It's me cough."

"Frankly," observed the good doctor, listening closely while the patient gave a reasonable demonstration, "you are coughing more easily now."

"And why shouldn't I now?" demanded Haloran crossly. "Was it not meself that practiced all night?"

"Then tell me," persisted the doctor, scrutinizing Haloran's rum-blossom nose and bleary eyes, "do you drink excessively?"

"No, I sildim go over a quart a day—but ownly to quiet me nerves."

"Ridiculous!" snorted the doctor. "Nobody's nerves are that noisy!"

*

Have you ever wondered why and how the feud got started between the Martins and the Coys? No? Well, read on anyway—in case your children ever ask.

Martin had been out fox hunting and, in the excitement of the chase, found himself in strange territory. Soon, he came to a ramshackle house in the woods. But, before he could approach within fifteen feet of the place, a man came out of the door, holding a shotgun.

"Name's Coy," the stranger announced laconically. He held out a large jug. "Have a drink."

"No, thankee," said Martin politely. "I better be a-gettin' home."

Coy lifted his gun and aimed it dead-center at Martin's forehead. "Drink!" he commanded grimly.

Martin took a long pull on the jug, swallowed, coughed, strangled, got red in the face, and shook. "Godamighty," he gasped when he could finally open his throat, "that thar stuff's turble!"

"Ain't it, though?" affirmed Coy grinning. "Now *you* hold the gun on *me* while *I* take a snort!"

*

The following classic of eighteenth and early nineteenth-century Irish humor represents the "tavern tale" under English suppression, much as the "speakeasy" anecdotes of the United States flourished during Prohibition. The difference is one of style: American tavern tales, at the time of the prohibition of alcoholic beverages, were centered mainly on poor quality of product, the difficulty of obtaining good whiskey, and corruption. Few of the anecdotes survived because of their contemporary nature. Irish "tavern tales," however, are as appealing today as they were a century or more ago, when they were first told, because, generally speaking, they revolve around the human factor, the reaction of people to restrictions that are universally recognized. In the tale that follows, we feel quick empathy with the naive, good-natured Peter and his cautious, determined wife, Ellish. And we also

recognize the scalawag in that free-loading character, Condy, and his ef-
forts to "con" Peter and Ellish out of free poteen *at their* shebeen *house*
(the place where poteen *is sold). And now for the story.*

A Pox on Credit[5]

It was a great day in the morning for them when Peter and his wife,
Ellish, who understood *poteen*, decided to open a *shebeen* house. They took
a small house at the crossroads where, in the course of time, they gathered
many customers. Peter's wife was an excellent manager, and he himself a
pleasant, good-humored man, full of whim and inoffensive mirth. His
powers of amusement were of a high order, considering his near poverty
and his want of an education. These qualities contributed, in a great degree,
to bring both the young and the old to his house during the long winter
nights to hear the fine racy humor with which he related his frequent
adventures and battles with excisemen.* In the summer evenings, he usually
engaged a piper or fiddler, and held a dance, which not only made him
popular but increased his business.

In this mode of life, the greatest source of anxiety to Peter and Ellish was
the difficulty of not offending their friends by refusing to give credit. Many
plans were, with great skill and forethought, devised to obviate this evil; but
all failed. A short board was first procured, on which they and a more
learned neighbor wrote with chalk:

NO CREDIT GIVEN—BARRIN' A THRIFLE TO PETHER'S FRIENDS

Within a week after this ultimatum had been posted, the number of
"Pether's friends" increased so rapidly that neither he nor Ellish knew the
half of them. Every scamp in the parish was hand in glove with him: the
drinking tribe became desperately attached to him and Ellish. Peter was
naturally kindhearted, and found that his firmest resolutions too often gave
way before the open flattery with which he was assailed. He then changed
his hand and left Ellish to bear the brunt of their blarney. Whenever any
person or persons were seen approaching the house, Peter, if he had reason
to expect an attack upon his indulgence, prepared himself for a retreat,
immediately slipping into bed behind the drinking quarters, and lay there in
order to escape the freeloaders. In the meantime, they entered:

"God save all here! Ellish, *agra machree,* how are you?"

"God save you kindly! Faith, I'm middlin', thank you, Condy; how is
yourself, an' all at home?"

---

[5]From William Carleton's *Humorous Folk Tales of Old Ireland* (Manchester: Crofton & Sons, circa 1963). English definitions for Gaelic words and phrases will be
found in the Glossary section of this book, or you can take them in through the
pores, as James Stephens said of the French language.

*Tax collectors. In this context, the excise man would correspond to the American
revenue officer, or "revenooer" of the Ozarks. *Poteen* is illegally distilled liquor on
which no tax has been paid.

Condy turned to the men who had accompanied him to Peter and Ellish's illegal tavern. "Go way wid yez, boys, down to the other room till I spake to Ellish here about the affairs o' the nation." He returned his attention to Ellish. "Do you know thim that came in with me?"

"Why, I can't say I do. Who are they, Condy?"

"They're relatives on my in-laws' side. They've come to this neighborhood till the 'sizes—bad luck to them—goes over; for, you see, they're in a little bit of throuble."

"The Lord grant them safe out of it, poor boys!"

"I brought them up here to treat them, poor fellows; an' Ellish, *avourneen,* you must credit me for whatsoever we may have. The thruth is, you see, that when we left home none of us had any notion of dhrinkin', or I'd a put a something in my pocket. But, sowl, Ellish, how's your little Dan? Sure I don't think there's a finer child in Europe of his age, there isn't."

"Indeed, he's a good child, Condy. But, Condy, *avick,* about givin' credit—by thim five crasses, if I could give it to anyone in the parish, it ud be to yourself. It was only last night that I made a promise against doin' sich a thing for man or mortual. We're almost broken an' harrish'd out o' home an' business by it. Atween ourselves, Condy, that's what ails Pether—him with a smotherin' about the heart. He jist laid himself down on the bed for awhile to see if it would go off him—God be praised for all His marcies!"

"But you know I'm safe, Ellish!"

"I know you are, *avourneen,* as the bank itself; an' you'd have the credit, but for the promise I made to poor sick Pether last night on my knees. If you were fed from the same breast with me, I couldn't, nor wouldn't, break my promise. I wouldn't have the sin of it on me for the wealth o' the three kingdoms."

"Bedad, you're a quare woman, Ellish, but I know you're a dacent woman still."

Condy then left her and joined his friends in the little room that was appropriated for drinking, where, with a great deal of mirth, he related the failure of the plan they had formed for outwitting Peter and Ellish.

"Boys," said he, "she's too many for us! St. Pether himself would not be a match for her. Faith, she's a cute one! I palavered at the rate of a fox, an' she paid me back in my own coin, with dacent intherest—but no whiskey! Well, now for a try at Pether. Jist sit where yez are, till I come back."

He then left them enjoying the intended confrontation, and went back to Ellish.

"Well, Ellish, I'm sure if anyone had tuck their oath that you'd refuse my father's son such a thrifle, I wouldn't believe them. But bad as you thrated us, sure we must see how poor Pether is."

As he spoke, and before Ellish had time to prevent him, Condy pressed into the room where Peter lay.

"Why, Pether, is it in bed you are, at this hour o' the day?"

"Eh? What's that—who's that? Oh!"

"What's asthray with you, man alive?"

"Troth, Condy, I don't know rightly. I went out, wantin' my coat about a week ago, an' got cowld in the small o' the back."

"Is your *heart* safe? You have no smotherin' or anything about *it?*"

"No, thank goodness; it's all about my back an' my hinches."

"Faith, Pether, I've found you out: Ellish is afther tellin' me that it was a smotherin' on the heart; but it's a pain in the small o' your back. Oh, you born decayver! You've no pain at all, a'tall, have you?"

"Why, thin, all sorts o' fortune to you, Condy—ha, ha, ha—there's no escapin' you." They entered the kitchen and he turned to his wife. "Ellish, I suppose we must give him the liquor to kape our saycrit from leakin' out."

"Now, Pether," said the wife, "sure it's no use axin me to give it, afther the promise I made last night. Give it yourself. Ez for me, I'll have no hand in it."

Peter accordingly furnished them with the liquor and got a promise that Condy would certainly pay him at mass on the following Sunday, which was only three days distant. The boys in the back room were exuberant over Condy's success: they drank, laughed, and sang until pint after pint followed in rapid succession.

Every additional inroad upon the keg brought a fresh groan from Ellish; and even Peter himself began to look blank as their potations deepened. When the night was far advanced, they departed, after having first overwhelmed Ellish with professions of the warmest friendship, promising that, in the future, she exclusively would reap whatever benefit was to be derived from their patronage.

But Condy forgot to perform on his promise. The next Sunday passed, but Peter was not paid, nor was Condy seen at mass, or in the vicinity of the *shebeen* house, for many a month afterwards—an instance of ingratitude which greatly mortified Peter, who now realized he had been taken in. He therefore resolved to cut short all hopes from his patrons of obtaining credit in the future.

In about a week after Condy's hoax, Peter got up a board, presenting a more vigorous refusal of credit than he had on the former sign. His friends, who were more in number than he could possibly have imagined, on this occasion were altogether wiped out. The new declaration, boldly lettered in chalk, read:

> NOTICE TO THE PUBLIC, *and to Pether*
> *Connell's friends in parthicular*—Divil
> the morsal of credit will be got
> ·or given in this house, while there is
> stick or stone of it together, barrin'
> them that axes it *has the ready money.*

> Pether x Connell, his mark
> Ellish x Connell, her mark

—William Carleton (1794-1869)

*

"Whiskey and Wather"

It's all mighty fine what taytotallers say,
  "That ye're not to go dhrinking of sperits,
But to keep to pump wather, and gruel, and tay"—
  Faith, ye'd soon have a face like a ferret's.
I don't care one sthraw what such swaddlers may think,
  (Ye'll find them in every quarther),
The wholesomest liquor in life you can dhrink,
  I'll be bail, now, is whiskey and wather.

Don't go dhrinking of brandy, or Hollands, or Shrub,
  Or gin—thim's all docthored, dipind on it—
Or ye'll soon have a nose that ye niver can rub,
  For the blossoms ye'll grow at the ind iv it;
But the *raal potheen* it's a babby may take
  Before its long clothes are cut shorther;
In as much as would swim ye there's divil an ache,
  Av* it's not mixed with *too much* could wather.

Do ye like thim small dhrinks? Dhrink away by all manes—
  I wanst thried ginger beer to my sorrow—
Ye'll be tuck jist as I was, with all sorts of pains,
  And ye'll see what ye're like on the morrow.
Ye'll find ye can't ate—no, nor walk—for the wind;
  Ye'll have cheeks jist the color of morthar;
Av ye call in the docthor he'll jist recommind
  A hot tumbler iv whiskey and wather.

Av the colic ye get, or the cramps in yer legs,
  Don't go scalding yerself with hot bottles:
(Though thim's betther, they tell me, than hot flannel bags),
  And take no docthor's stuff down yer throttles;
But just tell the misthress to hate the tin pot—
  (Maybe one for tay ye'll have bought her)—
And keep dosing yerself off and on, hot and hot,
  Till ye're aisy—with whiskey and wather.

Av ye go to a fair, as it maybe ye might,
  And ye meet with some thrifling disasther,
Such as having the head iv ye broken outright,
  Iv coorse ye'll be wanting a plasther.
Don't sind for a surgeon, thim's niver no use—
  Sure their thrade is to cut and to quarther—
They'd be dealing with ye as ye'd dale with a goose;
  Thry a poultice iv whiskey and wather.

---

*Av, in Irish brogue, means "if," *Iv*, in brogue, corresponds to "of," in proper English. However, depending upon their geographic area, some Irish writers reverse the meanings, and others sometimes use *av* and *iv* interchangeably.

Av ye can't sleep at night, an' ye rowl in yer bed
   (And that's mighty disthressin'—no doubt iv it),
Till ye don't know the front from the back iv yer head,
   The best thing ye can do is—rowl out iv it.
Av ye've left out the fire and can't get a light,
   Feel yer way to the crock till ye've caught her
(In the dark it's ye are, so remimber, hould tight),
   Take a pull—an' thin dhrink some could wather.

Av ye meet with misfortune, beyant yer controwl,
   Av disease gets a hould iv the *praities,*
Or the slip iv a pig gets the masles, poor sowl;
   No matther how sarious yer case is—
Don't go walking about with yer hands crossed behind,
   And a face like a cow's—only shorther—
Sure the best way to keep up yer sperits, ye'll find
   Is to keep to hot whiskey and wather.

It's in more ways than thim ye'll find whiskey yer frind,
   Sure it's not only jist while ye dhrink it—
It has vartues on which ye can always depind—
   And perhaps, too, when laste ye would think it.
One fine summer's day it was coorting I wint,
   To make love to Dame Flanagan's daughter—
And I won her—and got the ould woman's consint:
   Sure I did it with whiskey and wather.

In the Liffey I tumbled, one could winther's day,
   And, bedad, it was coulder than plisint,
Out they fished me, and stretched me full length on the quay,
   But the divil a docthor was prisint,
When a blessed ould woman of eighty came by
   (There's no doubt expariance had taught her),
And—in jist a pig's whisper—I tell ye no lie—
   Fetched me to, with hot whiskey and wather.

It's the loveliest liquor ye iver can take,
   And no matther how often ye take it;
The great thing is niver to mix it too wake;
   And see now—it's this way ye make it:
Take three lumps iv sugar—it's jist how ye feel—
   About whiskey, not less than wan quarther;
No limon—the laste taste in life of the peel,
   And be sure you put screeching hot wather.

It'll make ye all over, as warm as a toast,
   And yer heart jist as light as a feather;
Sure it's mate, dhrink and washing, ana lodging almost,
   And the great-coat itself, in could weather.
Oh! long life to the man that invinted *potheen*—
   Sure the Pope ought to make him a marthyr—

If myself was this moment Victoria, our queen,
    I'd dhrink nothing but whiskey and wather!

—Anonymous[6]

*

"Whiskey, Drink Divine!"

Whiskey, drink divine!
    Why should drivellers bore us
With the praise of wine
    While we've thee before us?
Were it not a shame
    Whilst we gaily fling thee
To our lips of flame,
    If we could not sing thee?

Greek and Roman sung
    Chian and Falernian—
Shall no harp be strung
    to thy praise, Hibernian?
Yes! let Erin's sons,
    Generous, brave and frisky,
Tell the world at once
    They owe it to their whiskey.

Bright as beauty's eye,
    When no sorrow veils it;
Sweet as beauty's sigh,
    When young love inhales it.
Come, then, to my lips,
    Come, thou rich in blisses!
Every drop I sip
    Seems a shower of kisses.

Send it gaily round—
    Life would be no pleasure,
If we had not found
    This enchanting treasure.
And when tyrant Death's
    Arrow shall transfix ye,
Let your latest breaths
    Be Whiskey! Whiskey! Whiskey!

—Joseph O'Leary (circa 1790-1854)

---

[6]Taken from a song book published in Dublin, where it is attributed in a vague way to "Zozimus." (See "Zozimus" in Biographical Index of Authors.)

*

"The Monks of the Screw"[7]

When St. Patrick this order established,
   He called us the "Monks of the Screw,"
Good rules he revealed to our abbott
   To guide us in what we should do.
But first he replenished our fountain
   With liquor, the best from on high;
And he said, on the word of a saint,
   That the fountain should never run dry.

Each year, when your octaves approach,
   In full chapter convened let me find you;
And when to the convent you come
   Leave your favorite temptation behind you.
And be not a glass in your convent
   (Unless on a festival) found;
And, this rule to enforce, I ordain it
   One festival all the year round.

My brethren, be chaste—till you're tempted;
   While sober, be grave and discreet;
And humble your bodies with fasting,
   As oft as you've nothing to eat.
Yet, in honor of fasting, one lean face
   Among you I'd always require;
If the abbott should please, he may wear it,
   If not, let it come to the prior.

Come, let each other take his·chalice, my brethren,
   And with due devotion, prepare,
With hands and with voices uplifted,
   Our hymns to conclude with a prayer.
May this chapter oft joyously meet,
   And this gladsome libation renew,
To the saint, and the founder, and abbott,
   And prior, and Monks of the Screw.

—John Philpot Curran (1750-1817)

*

---

[7]Curran, the author, in the latter part of the eighteenth century, belonged to a small convivial society in Dublin known as The Monks of the Screw, whose membership included some of the most famous Irishmen of the time. Curran was "prior" (actually an officer in a monastic order, sometimes just below an abbot in rank). On that account, he called his residence at Rathfarnham "The Priory"—to the high indignation of the *real* priors and the *real* priory in the area.

"St. Patrick of Ireland, My Dear!"

A fig for St. Denis of France—
He's a trumpery fellow to brag on;
A fig for St. George and his lance,
   Which spitted a heathenish dragon;
And the saints of the Welshman or Scot
   Are a couple of pitiful pipers;
Both of whom may just travel to pot,
   Compared with that patron of swipers,[8]
   St. Patrick of Ireland, my dear!

He came to the Emerald Isle
   On a lump of a paving stone mounted;
The steamboat he beat by a mile,
   Which mighty good sailing was counted.
Says he, "The salt water, I think
   Has made me most fishily thirsty;
So bring me a flagon of drink
   To keep down the mulligrubs,[9] burst ye—
   Of drink that is fit for a saint."

The flagon he lifted in sport
   (Believe me, I tell you no fable),
A gallon he drank from the quart,
   And then placed it full on the table.
"A miracle!" everyone said,
   And they all took a haul at the stingo;
They were capital hands at the trade,
   And drank till they fell; yet, by jingo,
   The pot still frothed over the brim.

You've heard, I suppose, long ago,
   How the snakes, in a manner most antic,
He marched to the County Mayo,
   And trundled them into th' Atlantic.
Hence, not to use water for drink,
   The people of Ireland determine;
With mighty good reason, I think,
   Since St. Patrick has filled it with vermin,
And vipers and other such stuff.

---

[8] A drinker of malt liquor. From *swipes,* an informal English word meaning malt liquors in general but usually referring to beer, ale and stout.
[9] Colic; ill-temper.

Oh, he was an elegant blade
As you'd meet from Fairhead to Kilcrumper;
And though under the sod he is laid,
    Yet here goes his health in a bumper!
I wish he was here, that my glass
    He might by art magic replenish!
But since he is not—why, alas!
    My ditty must come to a finish,
        Because all the liquor is out.

—William Maginn

Chapter Nine
Masters of Malarkey and Lesser Liars
Introduction

The Irish are truly endowed with the gift of gab: they love to elaborate and embellish. But this does not mean they are addicted to falsehood. An old Irish saying has it that a liar is a lawyer with a patently guilty client. Since most Irishmen are clients rather than lawyers, and since at least forty per cent of those clients are innocent, or nearly so, it stands to reason that the Irish, by and large, are as honest and truthful as the traffic will allow. Even the backbiting, or malicious gossip, with which Irish washerwomen were once associated, is not necessarily lying. In fact, the rumormongers were more than likely to be males, if we are to believe the Irish dictionaries, which define backbiting as meaning "to speak of a man as you find him when he cannot find you."

The Irish classicists of literature tell us that only the bigots do not like a cheerful liar. According to these men of letters, a bigot is a man or woman who is obstinately and zealously attached to an opinion that differs from yours. The Irish politician, however, may be guilty of a little malarkey now and then, but he is not really a liar. He is just a careless orator who has wrestled with his conscience and lost the match. What he says is involuntary—an act of God, as in getting caught with your chicken in his pot. Not too surprisingly, say the Celtic sages, a politician is much better company than a compulsive teller of the truth. There are only two things worse than a truth-teller, we are reminded—*two* truth-tellers.

Malarkey has been defined as a bit of truth, a bit of exaggeration, and two bits of class. It is a form of expression invented by a Pterodactyl, that is, a prehistoric native of Ireland. The name is pronounced by the Irish as Terry Dactyl or Peter O'Dactyl, as the man pronouncing it may chance to have heard it spoken by his peers or seen it in print.

Some malarkey surfaces as an April fool joke. In Irish folklore, the April fool is the March fool with another month added to his folly. He seldom deserves to be included in the same company with a master of malarkey who carefully deliberates before uttering a sentence—deliberation, in this sense, meaning the act of examining one's bread to determine which side it is buttered on. Conversely, malarkey can be a vehicle for a verbal joy ride, just for the fun of it, as in "The Mad, Mad Malarkey of Brian O'Linn," the last offering in this chapter, illustrating the difference between a lie and malarkey.

It has been rumored, no doubt by the British who have always been jealous of the Irish, that the fairy folk of Ireland are nothing more than a concoction of the Gaelic mind; a myth, a national Irish lie. Not so! A fairy is a real, or almost real creature that inhabits the streams, bogs, meadows, and forests of Ireland. It is nocturnal in its habits, and somewhat addicted to dancing and the theft of children. Some of the more knowledgeable fairies steal young girls away. These fairy folk are believed, by some poorly-informed naturalists, to be extinct: this despite the fact that a clergyman of the Church of England saw three near Kilkenny while passing through a park after dining and drinking with the lord of the manor. The sight greatly staggered him, and he was so affected that he converted to Catholicism. He now spends his time watching statues weep and bleed.

To say that leprechauns and other fairy folk are a figment of the Irish imagination, and that the sons and daughters of Erin lie in their teeth about their existence, is a canard that must be dealt with. Accordingly, we offer one more example of indisputable proof that the wee people are alive and well on the "ould sod." On February 2nd, 1976, a troop of fairies visited a wood near Galway and carried off the daughter of a *poteen* distiller. This abduction was witnessed by Rory McCarrion, son of a wealthy landowner. The youth disappeared about the same time, but afterward returned, having been in pursuit of the fairies. Rory averred that so great was the fairies' power of transformation that he saw one change itself into two opposing armies and fight a battle with terrible ensuing slaughter, and that the next day, after it had resumed its original shape and gone away, there were seven hundred bodies of the slain which the villagers had to bury. Rory McCarrion, whose veracity cannot be questioned, did not say whether any of the wounded recovered. We close this entire episode of the existence of fairies with the reminder that, in the time of Henry III, of England, a law was passed which prescribed the death penalty for "Kyllynge, wowndynge, or mamynge" a fairy; proof positive that fairies did indeed exist, and that Henry was a rotten speller.

The tradition of malarkey, from the heretofore mentioned Pterodactyls to the modern Irish-Americans, has not faltered. During the Civil War, for example, a soldier of the all-Irish "Fighting Sixty-ninth" Regiment, approached General Thomas Meagher, a hero of the Irish Revolution of 1848.

"Gin'ril, sor," began the buck private, "would ye be afther grantin' me a furlough? Me wife's that sick, an' she's nadin' me to look afther the children."

"Now that's a quare wan, indade," replied General Meagher. "The chaplain towled me, ownly this mornin', that he has a letther from your wife, askin' us not to send you home. She says that ivry time you go home on lave, you're afther gettin' dhrunk, and that you bate her an' frighten the children."

The soldier scrutinized his commanding officer's face for a long moment before he answered. "Faith, Gin'ril, an' the two most splindid liars in the army are right here in this room," he snapped. "I was niver married in me life!"

The Irishman's great sense of humor also helped carry him through World War I. In that conflict, a bit of malarkey found its way into print with this story: Paddy was carrying a fellow Irish soldier to a first-aid station. The fallen man, it seems, had suffered a grievous leg wound. Unknown to Paddy, however, a stray cannonball took the injured man's head off while he was being transported. When they reached the station, and the corpse was dumped onto a mattress, a medic pointed out that the body lacked a head.

"Why, the deceivin' crayture!" exploded Paddy. "He towld me it was ownly his leg that was botherin' him."

Whether the Irish are prone to innocent malarkey or whether they like a tall tale or two, refuge of sorts will be found in the old Irish adage, "If ye can't fight 'em, jine 'em." You are therefore invited to "jine 'em" in the following pages—Celtic wit at its hyperbolic best.

—H.D.S.

> If you your lips would save from slips,
>   Five things observe with care;
> Of whom you speak, to whom you speak,
>   And how, and when, and where.[1]
> —Francis X. Riordan (1862-1902)

＊

An old reprobate, the worst liar in town, was strolling down the street when he came upon Sister Agatha of Holy Conception Church.

"Wh-why," she stammered in surprise, "Father O'Malley told me you passed away!"

"Passed away, did I?" he laughed. "Faith, Sister, I'm alive and well, as you can see for yourself."

"You *appear* so," she replied hesitantly, "but you must admit, Father O'Malley has a better reputation than you for the truth!"

＊

Back before Ireland gained its independence, an Englishman and an Irishman happened to be journeying through a dense forest. As the first day wore on, they stopped to rest for a while, but, to their great distress, their horses ran off. Problem after problem arose. They became hopelessly lost and wandered about in a pitiable condition until, on the following day, they came upon a miserable hovel which was deserted—except for one lone and wretched little chicken.

The chicken's mortal existence ended, finding its valhalla in a soup pot, preparatory to being served for supper. But, when it was placed before them on the table, the Irishman concluded that it was far too small for both himself and the Englishman. After some serious thought on the subject, he proposed that they save the chicken until the next morning, and that the one

---

[1] Translated from the Old Irish, 1889.

who had the most pleasant dream during the night would have the chicken. The Englishman readily agreed.

In the morning, the Englishman related his dream:

"It was exquisitely beautiful," he began. "A band of angels drew me up into heaven in a pearly white basket, and I heard the most gorgeous music imaginable, and all the while I felt happier than I had ever felt before in my entire life."

"Sure, and that was a beautiful drame," agreed the Irishman. "Indade it was! And I want ye to know that 'twas meself that saw ye bein' lifted up into heaven in that pearly white basket, and 'twas meself that heard all that gorgeous music the angels was singin' an' playin' for ye, an' 'twas meself that could see by the smile on your face, how happy ye were. An', by me troth, ye looked so happy I was that sure ye wouldn't be afther comin' back—so 'twas meself that got up an' ate the chicken!"

*

Teen-aged Mollie was a nice enough girl but, to her father's annoyance, she was something of a gossip. One morning, at breakfast, she startled her father with a bit of neighborhood news.

"Daddy, those new people who just moved in next door are secret drinkers," she revealed.

Mollie's father glared. "Young lady," he snapped, "how many times must I tell you not to repeat rumors, and stick to the facts."

"But, Daddy," Mollie protested, "it's a fact that rumors are flying!"

*

Gallegher and Donovan, both in their late forties, were exchanging pleasantries during their lunch break at the mill.

"How do you always manage to look so fit at your age?" asked Gallegher, surveying his coworkers' powerful chest, shoulders, and legs.

"It's exercise that does it," explained Donovan. "Every morning, instead of taking the bus to work, I just run alongside it until we get to the mill. It not only keeps me in a good physical condition, but it saves me thirty-five cents, too."

Gallegher was just about to congratulate Donovan when he caught the grin on his friend's face. It spurred him to some quick and creative thinking.

"I'm way ahead of you," said Gallegher. "I save two dollars and eighty cents a day."

"How?"

"I run alongside a taxi!"

*

A British dandy decided to have some fun with an Irish laborer. The Hibernian, it seemed to the Britisher, was a slow-witted lout, and fair game for what he considered his brilliant wit.

"Here, you bog-trotter," said the Englishman, grinning broadly, "tell me the biggest lie you ever heard in your life and I'll treat you to a whiskey."

"By me sowl," retorted the Irishman promptly, "yer honor's a gintle-min!"

❉

"How did I ever leave the Church and become a Moslem?" you ask. Well, it's a long story, but I'll make it brief."

Settling back in his gold-brocaded chair and lighting a Corona-Corona cigar-cigar, Pat O'Malley continued his reminiscence.

"I wasn't always this rich, you know. My parents farmed a piece of Texas land where the soil was so poor you couldn't raise your voice on it, let alone crops. Then, one day, while digging up a few miserable-looking carrots in that awful ground, my daddy struck oil. He dropped dead with a heart attack—right there on the spot, poor man. But I kept on drilling new wells, and that's when I became a Moslem....They made me an honorary Arab!"

❉

This bit of malarkey concerns movie star Peter O'Toole, and how he got into the British Royal Navy before embarking on his film career.

Peter was actually too young to be accepted by the Navy, so he resorted to a slight falsehood: he told the recruiting officer that he descended from a long line of Irish sailors and wanted to devote his life to the sea. The dubious recruiter felt that a test question might be in order:

"Imagine that you are an officer. It is your job to get a heavy barrel over a thirty-foot wall. But all you have are two lengths of rope, each only ten feet long. Now, how would you get that barrel over the wall?"

"Nothing to it, sir," replied O'Toole promptly. "I'd just summon the chief petty officer and I'd say, 'Mr. Chief Petty Officer, get that barrel over that wall!' "

❉

Comedienne Patsy Kelly, recalling her childhood:

"We were so poor, on Thanksgiving we had to stuff our turkey with newspapers!"

❉

The wealthy McDonnell clan of New York and Boston were not always the influential bankers and financiers they are today. Like many other Irishmen, they began their experience in the United States as refugees from a homeland ravaged by the terrible potato famine of the 1840s. Yet, such is the Irish sense of humor, in retrospect, of course, that the descendants of those who fled those inhospitable shores can today find humor in the tragedy of pre-Republic Ireland. The following brief quip is an example, as are many of the anecdotes in later chapters.

"My great, great grandparents were so poor," reminisced Pegeen McDonnell, "that they and their nine children all lived together in a three-room cottage."

"For heaven's sake!" gasped Pegeen's neighbor, Mrs. Buckley. "How did they ever manage?"

"Oh, they got along," was the breezy reply. "They took in roomers!"

•

"Back in the old days in Ireland," said the guest speaker at the annual banquet held by the New York police department, "my grandparents were so poor they had trouble deciding whether to wash with a cake of soap or eat it!"

•

Fatty Flanagan, possessor of a jelly belly and a jolly sense of humor, waddled into the doctor's office and faced the glowering physician.

"Obviously, you haven't been following my orders," said the medical man testily. "I told you to exercise and get rid of some of that excessive weight."

"But I did!" protested the irrepressible Flanagan. "In fact, I just finished twenty push-ups—at the rate of one a day."

The flippant reply evoked no smile of appreciation on the doctor's stern countenance. "I hate to say this," he went on, "but unless you have a significant reduction in weight you'll wind up as chief guest of honor at your own wake. Come back in two weeks for another checkup."

Exactly fourteen days later, Flanagan returned to the doctor's office. "Well, Doc, I have some good news this time," he said, smiling happily. "I lost one hundred twenty pounds."

The physician glanced at his patient's unchanged, billowing beltline. "Impossible!" he snapped in utter disbelief.

"But it's true," insisted Flanagan with a straight face. "My wife left me!"

•

The old-timer was fishing by the side of a stream, patiently waiting for a nibble. A youngster, ambling along the bank, stopped to watch him.

"How many you caught?" asked the kid.

"Wal, sonny," drawled the ancient mariner, "if I ketch this one I'm after, and two more, I'll have three!"

•

"Faith, you young wans don't know the maynin' iv poverty," scolded Grandpa. "Whin I first came to this counthry from dear owld Limerick—

the ownly spot in Ireland that's wurrth mentionin' in dacint society if ye ask me—all we could afford was a dingy flat in the owld part iv town. The walls were that thin ye could hear the neighbors in the next flat complainin' ivery day.

"And what were they complainin' about? The thin walls!"

*

For the first time in their long married life, Mrs. Reardon persuaded her husband to take her fishing with him. Mr. Reardon was silently doing his best to make a catch, but his wife kept chattering away, asking all the questions she could think of, despite his repeated warnings that she was "scaring" the fish away.

"Oh, look at that!" exclaimed Mrs. Reardon all of a sudden. She pointed to a strip of oily water seeming to cross the lake like a broad smooth street. "What's that streak over there?"

"Where?" muttered hubby, endeavoring to bait a hook.

"Right over there. What is it?"

"That, my dear," he snarled as the hook caught his finger, "is where the road went across the ice last winter!"

*

"Uncle" Joe Cannon, the Speaker of the House of Representatives of a few decades ago, was telling then-Governor Al Smith about a fish he had nearly caught in Chesapeake Bay. His description of the event, to put it conservatively, was lurid.

"About the size of a whale, wasn't it?" observed Smith, grinning.

"A whale!" echoed "Uncle" Joe defensively. "Listen, Al, I was *baitin'* with whales!"

*

Stirred by the patriotic fervor that swept the country upon the United States' entry into World War II, O'Keefe, age forty-one, tried to enlist in the Army. But the recruiting officer could not accept anyone over thirty-eight, even though he could see that this man would make a fine soldier.

"Listen, fella," counseled the sergeant, "are you really sure of your age? Let me give you a tip," he added, winking. "You can go on home and think it over. Then come back tomorrow and tell me your correct age."

O'Keefe smiled broadly and returned the knowing wink. Sure enough, he returned the next morning, bright and early.

"Well, how old are you now?" asked the sergeant.

"I'm thirty-eight," answered O'Keefe promptly. "It's me owld mother who's forty-one!"

Mike was so fat he couldn't turn around in the supermarket without knocking all the canned goods off the shelves. Nevertheless, Sally, his best girl, still loved him.

One evening, after having unaccountably disappeared for almost a week, Mike showed up at her house with a valid excuse. "I've been in the hospital," he explained. "I had my tonsils taken out."

Sally surveyed her boyfriend from head to foot, remembering that he had had a tonsilectomy several years earlier.

"Mike," she finally murmured, "I hate to sound critical, and I really don't know how much a tonsil weighs, but isn't that an extreme way to lose weight?"

*

"Diamond" Jim Brady was recalling the hard times he had known as a young fellow.

"I remember one summer that was especially rough," reminisced "Diamond" Jim. "I was working as a pitchman in a carnival, selling some kind of snake oil or other. But I couldn't sell that particular crowd of country bumpkins a single bottle. I became so disgusted that I finally yelled, 'You pikers are not only too cheap, but even too suspicious to offer me fifty cents for a dollar.'

" 'I'll buy a dollar for only fifty cents,' one of the rustics spoke up.

" 'All right,' I agreed, 'hand over the fifty cents.'

" 'I ain't takin' no chances,' yelled the rube. 'Take it out of the buck and hand me the change!' "

*

A white-haired grandfather, with his little granddaughter in tow, happened to pass by a sidewalk café.

"Oh, that must be fun, eating outdoors like that," cried the little girl, clapping her hands.

"Indade it is, darling'. I know all about it," said the grandfather. "Back in Ireland, whin I was a wee lad, we enjoyed open-air dinin' all the time."

"You mean in one of these outside places?"

"No, not a bit iv it. Y'see, we lived in a cottage with a straw-thatched roof. There was a hole in that roof, little darlin', an' it was right over the dinner table."

"But, Grandpa, what did you do when it rained?" asked the child solemnly.

"We kept right on eatin'," grinned the old-timer, squeezing his granddaughter's hand. "But believe me, darlin', we had to keep the spoons flyin' to finish our soup!"

*

Faith, now don't be afther tellin' me you niver heard iv a talkin' horse! And you an Irishman? For shame!

Francis Xavier was the fastest horse in County Cork—until he was two years old. After that, he gradually lost his speed. By the time he was four, he was an also-ran whose only view of other horses in a race was their behinds. Finally, when Francis Xavier had not won a single race for a whole year, his owner gave him an ultimatum.

"Now see here, you sorry excuse for a racehorse," fumed the man, "if you don't win tomorrow's race you'll be up at daybreak every morning from now on, pulling a plow on my farm."

But the stern stuff of which champions are made was not in Francis Xavier. He not only was running last—*waaay* last—but he got lost halfway around the track and wandered into somebody's rose garden, where he started to nibble daintily on the flowers. His humiliated jockey was screaming imprecations:

"Ye spalpeen! Ye lazy, stupid bag o' bones! Git back on that race track," he yelled, applying the whip to the horse's rump.

"Faith, lad," protested Francis Xavier, "take it aisy with that whip. I have to get up at five tomorrow mornin'!"

*

When Callahan's daughter informed him that she had fallen in love with an Orangeman, he was outraged. The girl tearfully protested that love has nothing to do with politics or religion.

"I am not talkin' about that," he stormed. "An orangey's not our intelleckshul ayqual, thassall. The ownly difference betwixt wan o' thim and a chimpanzee is that a chimp can peel his own banana."

"Oh, Papa, that's not what my young man says," insisted the girl. "He towld me he had to hire one hundred Dubliners to paint his house—wan man to howld the brush while the other ninety-nine turned the house."

"B'Jazus, that's a durrty Protestant lie!" roared the indignant Papa Callahan. "I heard it t'other way round. If he's so superior, why isn't he here explainin' his own case?"

"Because he's in the hospital with forty-eight noles in his head," murmured the daughter ruefully. "He's learnin' to eat with a fork!"

*

It was a balmy summer day in July, and two hobos, bumming their way across the country, were relaxing on the fringe of a railroad yard somewhere in the boondocks of Pennsylvania. They had been lucky in their scrounging for food that morning, and now they sat before a small fire, enjoying the fragrance of a mulligan stew that was simmering in a tomato can over the flames.

"Ah, this is the life iv Reilly," said one of the bums contentedly. "I'd not be changin' places with a rich man for a million dollars."

"Oh, yeah?" snorted the other derisively. "Suppose he had five million?"

"No, not even for five million."

"How about ten million?"

"Nope, not ten million, either."

"Well, how about twenty million?"

"Hmmm, that puts a little different light on the matter," replied the contented bum, giving the matter his serious consideration. "Now you're talkin' *money!*"

*

According to the society page in the *Boston Globe,* the lace-curtain McDonnell family had entered their bloodhound in a fancy dog show, where it won first prize. The fact was duly noted and read aloud by Joe the bartender at the Wubble Dhiskey Bar. The Irish malarkey at once rose to new and blazing heights.

"Some bloodhound!" snorted Joe derisively. "It really should be working for the Fire Department. The only thing that mutt could locate is a hydrant."

"Yeah," laughed one of the elbow-benders. "I heard that old man McDonnell once cut his finger and the bloodhound fainted."

"Considering the size of the McDonnell family," chimed in another imbiber, "they should have bought a dachshund, so all their kids could pet him at the same time."

"I remember the time Mary, my sister, worked as a maid at the McDonnell mansion," recalled another, a grin spreading across his Celtic face. "Mrs. McDonnell yelled down to my sister, who was in the kitchen, 'Mary, I don't want Fido in the house—it's full of fleas,' So Mary, being a dutiful maid, turned to the dog and hollered, 'Fido, don't go in the house—it's full of fleas!' "

"Well, you're lucky," growled an old-timer down at the other end of the bar. "I did some carpentry work for that family once, and, when I was through with the job, Mrs. McDonnell herself brought some lunch down to me in the kitchen. I thought it was mighty nice of her, until I noticed that damn dog starin' at me like he'd enjoy takin' a piece out of my leg. So I asked her, 'Mrs. McDonnell, beggin' your pardon, but why is your dog starin' at me like that?' And she said, 'Probably because you're eatin' out of his plate!' "

*

Finnegan had announced his intention to open a new tavern in the neighborhood. He was busily engaged in setting up the bar and installing the equipment, when Meehan and Moore, representing competing breweries, descended upon him. Each of the salesmen was determined to sell his own brand of beer, and equally determined to downgrade the quality of the other's. Old man Finnegan listened attentively, his shrewd, wrinkled face betraying nothing of his thoughts.

"Our reputation for making the very best beer on the market is well known," said Meehan by way of openers. "In fact, it took us ten years just to develop our secret formula."

"Yeah," growled competitor Moore, "that's how long it took them to steal it from us."

Finnegan rubbed his bewhiskered chin. "An' how much did it cost your company to divilip your beer, may I be askin'?" he said, addressing Meehan.

"Over a hundred thousand dollars."

Moore brushed aside the figure with a disdainful jeer. "He means a hundred thousand for development and five million for false advertising. Believe me, Mr. Finnegan, our beer tastes better than his: I oughtta know—I drink it myself everyday."

"That's because it's in his contract," Meehan argued. "The only endorsement his beer ever got was from his company president's mother. Anyway, he never guarantees delivery—his company trucks were designed by the same guy who created the Edsel. They have to borrow *our* trucks!"

Moore thought about his firm's ancient vehicles and prudently changed the subject. "Look, Mr. Finnegan," he began bravely, "you don't have to give me your business just because I'm a veteran with five Purple Hearts. I realize it isn't actually any of your concern if my gray-haired old mother, my sick wife, and my skinny little children starve. Go ahead and give this liar, Meehan, the order. I just hope you don't mind seeing a grown man cry."

"Faith, lad," said Finnegan, his voice oozing sympathy. "I wouldn't draym iv...."

"Wait a minute!" interrupted Meehan. "That man lies even when he's telling the truth. Gray-haired old mother? Wife and children? Believe me, sir, the man's an orphan and a bachelor!"

"My dear Mr. Finnegan," Moore hastily broke in, "you don't have to make up your mind right now. I can wait until this evening."

"Sure, an' what's th' matther with tomorrow?"

"Tomorrow, I check into St. Vincent's Hospital for my cancer operation," confided Moore in doleful accents. "It's terminal."

"*Cancer,* is it?" Finnegan exclaimed. "Why, that's turble! Maybe it's *you* yerself should be gettin' the order, ye poor, sufferin' man."

"Sir," Meehan cried, aghast that his competitor would steal his best sales pitch, "I don't want you to think I'm hinting or anything, but when did you say your birthday was?"

Old man Finnegan eyed them both for a long, silent moment. Then, with studied casualness, he asked, "Are ye both devout, churchgoin' Roman Catholics?"

"Certainly! Absolutely!" they answered in unison.

"An' do ye hear mass in Latin, with yer prayer books open, an' abide by the 'postle's Creed?"

"Oh, of course!" cried Meehan.

"Always!" exclaimed Moore.

"In that case, the divil take ye both!" snapped Finnegan. "I don't mind liars and I don't mind domn liars. I don't even mind domn *Irish* liars! But whin a couple iv domn Irish liars cannot be afther recognizin' a Protestant Ulsterman whin they see wan, they don't desarve his business." He pointed to the door. "Out with ye," he ordered in a voice that prohibited any and all backtalk, "an' the sole iv me shoe to ye both!"

Outside, on the sidewalk, Meehan turned sadly to Moore. "After all that lying I did, how could I tell Finnegan the real truth...that I'm an Orange-man, too?''

"No, and I didn't dare tell him I was really born in Belfast. He'd never have believed us.''

Meehan shrugged. "We have to give the old boy credit, though," he said reflectively, his voice tinged with reluctant admiration. "At least he wasn't afraid to confess our religion openly.''

Watching Meehan and Moore from the window, Finnegan chuckled softly to himself, as he bustled about inside his tavern.

"May th' sivin saints iv th' Repooblic iv Ireland fergive me," he said, crossing himself. "Imagine—*me,* a haythin Protestant!''

*

A gentlewoman at Miss Hogan's School for Proper Young Ladies, Dublin, waxes poetical in her diary:

Shawn Murphy told a story,
Shawn Murphy told a fib;
Shawn Murphy's old and hoary,
But that tongue of his is glib.
And when Shawn says 'tis I he kissed
And set my heart afire—
I tell you this, so you won't miss;
Shawn Murph's a blatherin' liar!''

*

"The Mad, Mad Malarkey of Brian O'Linn''

Brian O'Linn was a gentleman born,
His hair it was long and his beard unshorn,
His teeth were out and his eyes far in—
"I'm a wonderful beauty," says Brian O'Linn!

Brian O'Linn was hard up for a coat,
He borrowed the skin of a neighboring goat,
He buckled the horns right under his chin—
"They'll answer for pistols," says Brian O'Linn!

Brian O'Linn had no breeches to wear,
He got him a sheepskin to make him a pair,
With the fleshy side out and the woolly side in—
"They are pleasant and cool," says Brian O'Linn!

Brian O'Linn had no hat to his head,
He stuck on a pot that was under the shed,
He murdered a cod for the sake of his fin—
"'Twill pass for a feather," says Brian O'Linn!

Brian O'Linn had no shirt to his back,
He went to a neighbor and borrowed a sack,
He puckered the meal-bag under his chin—
"They'll take it for ruffles," says Brian O'Linn!

Brian O'Linn had no shoes at all.
He bought an old pair at a cobbler's stall,
The uppers were broke and the soles were thin—
"They'll do me for dancing," says Brian O'Linn!

Brian O'Linn had no watch for to wear,
He bought a fine turnip and scooped it out fair,
He slipped a live cricket right under the skin—
"They'll think it is ticking," says Brian O'Linn!

Brian O'Linn was in want of a broach,
He stuck a brass pin in a big cockroach,
The breast of his shirt he fixed it straight in—
"They'll think it's a diamond," says Brian O'Linn!

Brian O'Linn went a-courting one night,
He set both the mother and daughter to fight—
"Stop, stop," he exclaimed, "if you have but the tin,*
I'll marry you both," says Brian O'Linn!

Brian O'Linn went to bring his wife home,
He had but one horse that was all skin and bone—
"I'll put her behind me, as nate as a pin,
And her mother before me," says Brian O'Linn!

Brian O'Linn and his wife and wife's mother,
They all crossed over the bridge together,
The bridge broke down and they all tumbled in—
"We'll go home by water," says Brian O'Linn!

—Anonymous[2]

---

*Mettle; courage.
[2]Collected by Paul J. McCall (Dublin), *The Humor of Ireland* (London: Walter Scott, Ltd., 1894).

Chapter Ten
Spalpeens, Scalawags, and Blatherskites
Introduction

Spalpeens and scalawags (see Glossary), being closely related, are sometimes called "spalawags," a term disliked by both, tending, as it does, to becloud their cherished individualities. The spalpeen, let it be known, is lacking a proper respect for civic and social mores; the scalawag is a spalpeen with a diploma. It is a sad commentary on our institutions, but both may be depended upon to end their mortal existence with an inspiring epitaph—an inscription on their tombstone showing that virtues acquired by death have a retroactive effect. Following is a touching example:

> Here lies the bones of good Paul Platt,
> Wise, pious, humble and all that,
> Who showed us life as all should live it;
> Let that be said—and God forgive it!

The word "blatherskite," meaning a chatterbox, owes its origin to, of course, Dublin University Professor Daniel Blatherskite (1715-92), who disputed the contention that the heart is the seat of human emotions. He theorized that the sentiments and emotions reside in the stomach, and that love, for example, evolves from food by the chemical action of the gastric juices. The exact process by which corned beef and cabbage become a feeling—tender or otherwise—or a lettuce and tomato sandwich—with or without mayonnaise—is transmuted into a sentimental sigh, has been expounded in Professor Blatherskite's two volumes, *The Essential Identity of the Affections and Certain Intestinal Gases Freed in Digestion,* and *Love as a Product of Alimentary Maceration.* Regrettably, Professor Blatherskite fell into disrepute and oblivion when he aroused the ire of the Church. He boldly published his opinion that the Protestant is more remote from the Catholic than is the Hebrew, the latter being a Jewish male, as distinguished from the Shebrew, an altogether superior creation. For this belief, the professor was excommunicated by the Church of Rome—an act which left Blatherskite unmoved, he being a Presbyterian.

Politically, spalpeens, scalawags, and blatherskites are often impartial, unable to adopt either of two conflicting issues. In the Emerald Isle, they reside on both sides of the Ulster-Republic line, an imaginary boundary

172

between north and south Ireland, separating the foul claims of one from the sweet claims of the other. The aroma of the respective claims depends upon the direction of the wind and which side of the boundary you happen to be smelling from. Additionally, they are also to be found in all English-speaking legislative bodies where it is customary to mention the members as honorable: i.e., "The honorable gentleman from Killarney is a scurvy cur!"

It is interesting to note that, despite the subject matter contained in the following pages, the work "damn" is absent. The reason for this deliberate omission is that its precise definition is unknown to Irish writers and humorists who abhor the idea of using words they do not understand. Miss Moonyeen Monaghan, of County Mayo, eminent Gaelic scholar and popular lady of the evening, believes that "damn" expresses an emotion of sublime spiritual delight, because it so frequently occurs in combination with the word *jod,* or *god,* meaning "joy."

And joy be with *you* as you read the shamrock-green selections in this chapter.

—H.D.S.

"The Scalawag's Golden Rule"[1]

My brethren, be chaste—till you're tempted;
While sober be grave and discreet;
And humble your bodies with fasting—
Whenever you've nothing to eat!

*

O'Shaughnessy the shopkeeper purchased a tub of freshly made butter from Mrs. Quinn, who owned three cows. He weighed it carefully, and then turned to the woman, his face grim.

"Mrs. Quinn, you told me the butter weighs nine pounds. My scales show it to weigh only seven. 'Tis sorry I am to say this, but you cheated me."

"Chated ye, did I, ye spalpeen?" cried Mrs. Quinn in a furious voice. "I'll have ye know I weighed that butther aginst the nine pounds iv soap ye sowld me last week!"

—Anonymous (circa 1840)

*

Pat Rooney, Sr., vaudeville star and entertainer *par excellence* of a few decades ago, was a close and long-time friend of Jimmy Walker, erstwhile mayor of New York City. But even they had their occasional differences. There was the time, for example, when Rooney, who had imbibed a few more than was compatible with total sobriety, decided to "go calling." The object of his first visit was his old pal, Walker, who had just acquired a very valuable Chinese rug. It was of an intricate and exquisite pattern with pale gold and blue dragons, and the mayor was understandably quite proud of it.

---

[1]From *The Monks of the Screw.* See Chapter Eight, p. 156, for complete text.

Walker displayed the Oriental masterpiece to Rooney, who was indeed impressed. Even in his state of middling inebriety, he could see that it was priceless. His praise was lavish. He gaped, whistled appreciatively through his teeth, made a sweeping gesture of approval—and in so doing upset a bottle of red ink....

Uh-huh, right on the rug!

Conservatively speaking, Jimmy was irked.

Pat Rooney knew it. He made profuse apologies and then left, promising to make suitable amends.

"Don' you worry 'bout a shing, ol' boy, ol' boy, ol' boy," he said comfortingly. "Nobody'sh gonna shay I let my buddy Jimmy Walker down. Yesh, shir! I'll fixsh ev'thing up!"

Pat was a man of his word.

The very next day Jimmy received his compensation: a brand new bottle of red ink!

*

"How's that new refrigerator you bought from Cheap Clancy's?" asked Cynthia's neighbor.

"It broke down two days after it was delivered," sighed Cynthia.

"But I thought you said it came with a twenty-year guarantee!"

"It did," moaned the unhappy Cynthia. 'When I complained to Clancy he told me the only thing that was guaranteed was the guarantee. I had to take my chances on the refrigerator, but the guarantee was printed on parchment and, with the proper care, would last a lifetime!"

*

Let me tell ye about three robbers: two Ulstermen and a proud risidint iv Dublin. They had just robbed a gintlemin iv four guineas and were now in hot dispute about the difficult task iv dividin' th' loot in equal parts. It was plain as th' nose on yer face they were not edicated like you an' me.

Well, sor, afther sivril unsuccessful efforts by the two Ulstermen, the Dubliner settled the business wance an' fer all.

"Permit me to do the dividin', he said, promptly suitin' his word. "There's two fer you, an' here's two fer me. Even-steven!"[2]

*

A special, front-row seat in Paradise has now been set aside by the Authorities up there for the used car salesman who finally became so devout he no longer cheated on Sundays.[3]

*

[2]*Tales of Old Dublin,* 1909.
[3]Pat Hennessy, *Auto Times,* November 1974.

Much has been said of the luck of the Irish, but more often than not, it's a question of "damned if you do and damned if you don't." For example:

If an Irishman chases money, he's money-mad; if he keeps it, he's a capitalist. If he spends it, he's a playboy; if he saves it, he's a miser. If he doesn't get it, he's a ne'er-do-well; if he doesn't try to get it, he lacks ambition. If he gets it without working for it, he's a parasite; and if he accumulates it after a lifetime of hard work, people call him a fool who never got anything out of life.

Of course, he can always dismiss all that name-calling from his mind and relax over an after-dinner brandy; but if he does, he's a damn drunk!"

*

Clancey, a professional bank robber, had just punished his little son. Now, he regretted having struck the boy.

"Tommy," he said with fatherly concern, "I didn't spank you for taking the jam, you understand. I spanked you for leaving your fingerprints!"

*

The telephone rang and Mr. Dooley picked up the receiver. "Yeah?"

"Mr. Dooley?"

"Talkin'."

"This is Mr. Anderson of the Internal Revenue Service."

"Whaddya want?"

"I'm afraid, Mr. Dooley, that the I.R.S. finds it necessary to question your tax return; namely, item 4a, where you claim depreciation on your wife."

*

In response to the insistent, not to say churlish, demands of his wife, Robert hied himself to the Church of the Ascension and Similar Miracles. There, he confessed that he had stolen some beef from his employer, the Cuddihy Packing Company, to make an Irish stew.

"My son, you will have to make a novena," said the priest sternly. "Do you know what a novena is?"

"I'm not sure, Father," Robert answered hesitantly. "But, if you'll supply the vegetables, I know where we can get the meat."

*

Every Sunday, after leaving church, the nice old lady would give twenty-five cents to a panhandler who regularly stationed himself just outside the door. It so happened that the lady went to see her children in another city, and did not return from her vacation for a whole month.

On her first Sunday back home, as she left the church, she was greeted by the indignant beggar.

"Lady," he said reproachfully, "you owe me a dollar!"

*

Addressing the graduating class of Holy Cross College, a self-styled, self-made millionaire began and ended his speech with the declaration, "And all my success in life is due to one quality—pluck, pluck, pluck!"

"We understand that, sir," called an eager student from the front row of the auditorium, "but how, where, and whom do we pluck?"

*

Never let it be said that Chicago's Mayor Richard Daley had no sense of humor. During the 1976 Democratic Convention, he and Adlai Stevenson, Jr. had just finished lunch and, as they were about to leave the restaurant, Daley left a dollar tip on the table. Stevenson, however, noticed a young lad eyeing the money intended for the waiter.

"Richard," said Stevenson in a low voice, "that boy is about to steal your dollar tip."

"Aw, let 'im alone," murmured Daley. "We all had to start small!"

*

Have you ever wondered how it was that Michael Cudahy rose to become the biggest meat processor and packer in the United States? Here is the inside story:

When Cudahy was a small retailer with only one little butcher shop in Chicago, he had many customers whose accounts were in bad standing. One day, he put a sign in his window:

THIS STORE WILL SOON CLOSE BECAUSE OF BAD
DEBTS. NAMES AND AMOUNTS WILL BE POSTED HERE.

Cudahy's business is now worldwide.[4]

*

A new method of collection was practiced in Schenectady by a banker who called up one of his debtors and demanded payment of a long overdue note.

"Sorry, but I can't pay you at the moment," was the answer, as usual.

"Oh, yes, you will," retorted the diabolically ingenious banker, "or I'll tell all your other creditors you've paid me!"[5]

*

[4]*New Hibernia*, 1973.
[5]*Catholic Digest*, December 1971.

Not all the denizens of the Tobacco Road region of Georgia are as indigent as the Lester family. Witness the sad case of Jack Mulhall, the old-time movie star whose Studebaker became bogged down in the sticky clay of an unpaved rural road. He had no alternative but to pay a Georgia cracker ten dollars to pull him out with a team of mules.

"Seems to me," observed Mulhall as he got back into his car, "that you'd be pulling people out of this stuff day and night."

"Nope," drawled the mule driver, "at night's when me an' maw tote the water fer these yere roads!"[6]

*

"That old saying about two heads being better than one is true," averred O. B. Brian, the Las Vegas gambler, as he jingled some coins in his pocket. "And I've got the quarter to prove it!"

*

It is not proper to tattle on Irishmen like this, but, anyway, this is what happened to Haloran.

Returning from a visit to Lourdes, he opened his suitcase for the customs inspector.

"Sir," asked the inspector, "what's in all these bottles?"

"Lourdes water," explained Haloran.

The inspector cast a suspicious eye on the bottles, uncorked one, and sniffed it. He did the same with another, and then another.

"Water, is it?" snapped the customs agent. "These bottles contain nothing but pure whiskey."

"Well, as I live and breathe!" exclaimed Haloran ecstatically. "A blessed miracle!"

*

Kevin O'Shea, the nineteenth-century Irish-American horticulturist, was a neighbor of Mark Twain. One day, they met at the racetrack.

"I'm broke," confessed O'Shea, smiling sheepishly. "Would you do me a favor and buy me a railroad ticket back to town?"

"Well, Kevin, I'm pretty broke myself," replied Twain. "But I'll tell you what to do. You get under my seat and I'll hide you with my legs."

It was agreed. Twain then went to the cashier's window and bought *two* tickets. When the train was under way and the supposed stowaway was snug under the seat, the conductor came by and Twain gave him both tickets.

Puzzled, the conductor glanced around and then asked, "Where is the other passenger?"

"That's my neighbor's ticket," said Twain, tapping his forehead significantly, and speaking in a loud voice. "He's a little eccentric and likes to ride under the seat!"

---

[6]*Gonzaga Clarion,* 1948.

*

It has been said of the late and great Irish composer, Victor Herbert, that although he had a violent temper he was also a very compassionate man. On one occasion, in a fit of anger, he threw his wife out of the kitchen window and immediately stuck his own head out after her, exclaiming, "Good God, I forgot the violets!"

*

This contribution was born in Dublin, smuggled into Belfast, transported to New Bedford and thence to New York, where it was seized upon by the professional comedians who "originated" the joke for television and nightclubs.

Mulvaney, a stranger in town, needed a new wristwatch, so he dropped by a jewelry store. As he entered the shop, he was amused by the sign on the window announcing the name of the proprietor: A. SWINDLER.

After he had made his purchase, Mulvaney, grinning, offered a suggestion to the store owner.

"Sir, don't you think that your full name on the window would make a better impression than just using your first initial? Good God, A. SWINDLER!"

"No," said the jeweler, "it would be worse. My first name is Adam!"

*

Into the exclusive Park Avenue Bakery Shoppe, the most famous in all New York, came a customer with an order for a huge cake to be baked in the shape of a shamrock. Across the top layer of frosting, the name of Saint Patrick was to be inscribed with various colors and flavors of confection. Directly underneath the name was to be a cross. The rim of the cake was to be festooned with flying angels, and the sides decorated with tiny rosettes in pink, red, green, violet, and gold. He specified that it must be ready by Saint Patrick's Day.

The evening before the deadline, the customer visited the bake shop and found that the elaborate and complex cake was finished and completely decorated.

"Oh, this is all wrong!" he cried, flying into a rage. "The cross is too big, and not green enough. The angels should have their wings spread wider, and the rosettes should be more delicately tinted. The whole thing will have to be done over, and you'll have to finish it by tomorrow—without fail! Do you hear? *Without fail!*"

He created such a fuss that the apologetic manager assured him that he and his staff would make every effort to please him. "We'll make it over," the manager said. "You may be sure that this natural mistake will be rectified and we'll have everything ready for you by tomorrow."

The following day, the customer returned and found the cake now decorated perfectly, down to the minutest detail. "That's fine," he said, much mollified. He drew out his wallet and paid for the cake.

"Now, sir," inquired the manager respectfully, "where shall the cake be sent, or do you wish to take it with you?"

"Oh, that's all right," said the customer with an airy wave of his hand, "I'll eat it here."

*

"Presence of Mind"
(An Irish Lullabye)

When with my little daughter Blanche,
    I climbed the Alps, last summer,
I saw a dreadful avalanche
    About to overcome her;
And, as it swept her down the slope,
    I vaguely wondered whether
I should be wise to cut the rope
    That held us twain together.

I must confess I'm glad I did,
But still I miss the child—poor kid!

—Harry Graham (1898-1965)

*

"Nell Flaherty's Drake'"

My name is Nell, quite candid I tell;
    That I live near Coote Hill I will never deny;
I had a fine drake, the truth for to spake,
    That my grandmother left me before she did die;
He was wholesome and sound, he would weigh twenty pound,
    The universe round I would rove for his sake;
Bad cess to the robber—be he drunk or sober—
    That murdered Nell Flaherty's beautiful drake.

His neck it was green—most rare to be seen,
    He was fit for a queen of the highest degree;
His body was white—and would you delight—
    He was plump, fat and heavy, and brisk as a bee.
The dear little fellow, his legs they were yellow,
    He would fly like a swallow and dive like a hake;

'Many versions of this ballad were published in the ballad-slips of nineteenth century Ireland. The variants were nearly always obscene.

But some wicked savage, to grease his white cabbage,
  Has murdered Nell Flaherty's beautiful drake.

May his pig never grunt, may his cat never hunt,
  May a ghost ever haunt him at dead of the night;
May his hen never lay, may his ass never bray,
  May his goat fly away like an old paper kite.
That the flies and the fleas may the wretch ever tease,
  And the piercing north breeze make him shiver and shake;
May a lump of a stick raise bumps fast and thick
  On the monster that murdered Nell Flaherty's drake.

May his cradle ne'er rock, may his box have no lock,
  May his wife have no frock for to cover her back;
May his cock never crow, may his bellows ne'er blow,
  And his pipe and his pot may be evermore lack.
May his duck never quack, may his goose turn black,
  And pull down his turf with her long yellow beak;
May the plague grip the scamp, and his villainy stamp
  On the monster that murdered Nell Flaherty's drake.

May his pipe never smoke, may his teapot be broke,
  And to add to the joke, may his kettle ne'er boil;
May he keep to the bed till the hour that he's dead,
  May he always be fed hogwash and boiled oil.
May he swell with the gout, may his grinders fall out,
  May he roll, howl and shout with the horrid toothache;
May the temples wear horns and the toes many corns,
  Of the monster that murdered Nell Flaherty's drake.

May his spade never dig, may his sow never pig,
  May each hair in his wig be well thrashed with a flail;
May his door have no latch, may his house have no thatch,
  May his turkey not hatch, may the rats eat his meal.
May every old fairy, from Cork to Dunleary,
  Dip him snug and airy in river or lake,
Where the eel and the trout may feed on the snout
  Of the monster that murdered Nell Flaherty's drake.

May his dog yelp and howl with the hunger and cold,
  May his wife always scold till his brains go astray;
May the curse of each hag that e'er carried a bag
  Alight on the vag* till his hair turns gray.
May the monkeys afright him, and the mad dogs still bite him,
  And everyone slight him, asleep or awake;
May the weasels still gnaw him, and jackdaws still claw him—
  The monster that murdered Nell Flaherty's drake.

*Vagrant.

The only good news that I have to infuse
   Is that old Peter Hughes and blind Peter McCrake,
And big-nosed Bob Manson, and buck-toothed Ned Hanson,
   Each man had a grandson of my lovely drake.
My treasure had dozens of nephews and cousins,
   And one I must get or my heart it will break;
To keep my mind aisy, or else I'll run crazy—
   This ends the whole song of my beautiful drake.

—Anonymous

Chapter Eleven

Shinbones and Shillelaghs

Introduction

It seems to be a traditional American custom to use qualifying adjectives when referring to specific nationalities. There are, for example, the "phlegmatic Germans," the "inscrutable Chinese," the "singing Italians," and the "canny Scots," among others. Of such descriptive terms, probably the most frequently heard is the "fighting Irish"—and with good reason. Apparently, the Irishman's combative nature finds a ready and cheerful outlet in physical confrontations, whether in peace or war. The perceptive G. K. Chesterton, in "The Ballad of the White Horse," wrote:

> For the great Gaels of Ireland
> Are the men that God made mad,
> For all their wars are merry,
> And all their songs are sad.

In 1899, returning home to Boston from the Spanish-American War, Captain Dennis O'Hare remarked, "It wasn't much of a war, but it was the only one we had." For the Irish, however, the comment is not necessarily confined to national conflicts. An old Irish ditty sums it up:

> "Whenever there's Kellys there's trouble," said Burke.
> "Wherever fighting's the game,
> Or a spice of danger in grown men's work"—
> Said Kelly, "You'll find my name!"

One would think that this propensity for fighting would mark the Irish as a rather truculent people. Surprisingly enough, however, the opposite is true. In fact, they are usually described as loving and sociable. The problems arise when these qualities occasionally get a little out of hand. "But that's the way we are," explained James Joyce. Kipling sensed that quirk in the Irishman's disposition when he wrote:

> For where there are Irish there's loving and fighting,
> And when we stop either, it's Ireland no more.

182

Prior to the turn of the twentieth century, the phrase "fighting Irish" was used in a pejorative sense; a term of disdain. It was employed by the medieval English as an expression of contempt for the Irish whom they regarded as wild and barbaric. The phrase also stemmed from the notoriety which the eighteenth-century Irish obtained as a result of their faction fighting. But let it be said that in pre-Republic Ireland the fighting was conducted with shillelaghs and other cudgels called *kippeens* and black-thorns; never with guns. The joy was in the combat, not in killing.

In the United States, where the population was still predominantly of English ancestry and still harboring its anti-Irish prejudices, the "fighting Irish" were often blamed for street violence which had, in fact, been committed by native hoodlums. However, the phrase gradually began to lose its insulting connotations after the Civil War and the Spanish-American War, when Irish soldiers fought with such outstanding distinction. But it was not until the demeaning "comic Irishman" of the stage and cartoon had run its course, in the first decade of this present century, that Irish-Americans could refer to themselves *with pride* as the "fighting Irish."

The old stigma, it is said, has died, been properly waked, and buried. If true (and we are merely advancing an opinion, not championing it), the wrong is ended but the malady lingers on. After all, no one else but a "fighting Irishman" would swagger up to a bar and, for no discernible reason under God's blue sky, challenge a score of brawny strangers with the defiant proclamation, "I can lick any man in the house!"

Shades of old Shannon's shillelaghs, but it brings back fond memories!

—H.D.S.

*

My fist landed with a heavy punch,
I swang a mighty clout;
And then *he* threw a roundhouse punch
The spalpeen knocked me out!

–Patrick Ireland

*

An altercation between McCarthy and Cavanagh resulted in McCarthy being felled by a brick wielded by the aforesaid Cavanagh. Damage to the brick was minimal, but the fallen combatant suffered a fractured skull that called for the immediate attendance of a priest. Father Flaherty quickly arrived at the scene of conflict.

"McCarthy, I shall pray for you," said Father Flaherty, "but first I want you to forgive Cavanagh for the deed."

"All right, Father," whispered McCarthy in a scarcely audible voice, "pray for me everlastin' sowl—I forgive Cavanagh."

But, as the good father reverently bowed his head, McCarthy suddenly raised himself on one elbow and snarled:

"But if I live through this, ye'd betther be prayin' fer that shanty Irishman, Cavanagh!"

＊

From the Old West of the mid-nineteenth century comes this descriptive shortie:

Lord Fairfax, traveling the frontiers of America, stopped at the ranch of a friend—another ex-British lord. As he turned into the front yard, he was met by ranch foreman Big Jim Hennessy.

"Is your mahstuh at home?" inquired Lord Fairfax in his upper-crust royal accent.

"Me master, is it?" snapped Big Jim, looking Fairfax straight in the eye. "The son-of-a-bitch ain't been born yit!"

＊

An Irishman, accused of demolishing a tavern one riotous Saturday night, was hauled into court by a couple of unsympathetic policemen.

"May it plase yer honor," averred the son of Erin, "thim scalawags arristed the wrong man, they did. Faith, sor, me reputation's spotless."

"Have you anyone here who can vouch for your character?" asked the judge.

"Indade I have, yer honor. These two fine officers will spake up fer me character."

"What?" exclaimed one of the policemen indignantly. "Why, we don't even know the man!"

"There ye have it now!" cried the Irishman exultantly. "I've spint the greater part o' me life right here in this neighborhood, and, faith, the police don't even know me!"

＊

Four stalwart sons of Erin, recently arrived in the United States, decided to enjoy a few sociable drinks after their day's labors. Before the evening was spent, however, a disputation arose among them. The cause of the argument has been lost to posterity: suffice it to point out that valid reasons are not always necessary when a good time is had by all. The archives of Boston, however, bear testimony to the events that followed; namely, they were collared by a dozen policemen despite their protests, which included physical damage to the minions of the law. At public expense, they were carted off to facilities provided by a benevolent city for the convenience of nonpaying guests. In court the next morning, the bruised and battered quartet stood before the bar of justice, a little awed, but far from contrite.

"It appears that you imbibed rather freely last night," observed the judge, "and that you visited a number of taverns during that spree. What did you drink at the first place?"

"We each had four bottles of beer, two of ale, and one of stout," replied the self-appointed spokesman.

"And what did you have in the second place?"

"Three Irish whiskeys and two brandies."

"And the next?"

"Two more Irish whiskeys and two glasses of rum."

"Next?"

"A fight!"

*

Brock McCarthy had a party and all the b'ys were there.

"McCarthy," yelled neighbor O'Rourke, making himself heard over the gaiety at the joy juice barrel, "where's McGinnis, the landlord?"

"I invited him," yelled McCarthy, "but th' scalawag couldn't get anny police perteckshun!"

*

Riley and Meaghan got into a shillelagh contest, and Meaghan came off second best in the little encounter. He went to a pharmacy to get something for his aching body. The druggist sold him a bottle of Sloane's Liniment. That evening, a friend dropped by to visit the vanquished warrior.

"Faith, an' 'tis black and blue ye are," sympathized the friend. "What are you taking fer yer bruises an' aches?"

"I'm usin' Sloane's Liniment," explained Riley.

"But, Riley, that stuff's no good fer bruises!"

"No good, is it?" retorted Riley, offended. "Let me tell you something, me good friend—if it's good enough fer Sloane, sure it's good enough fer me!"

*

An Irishman and a Scot, who had just met in the local Belfast tavern that very evening, were weaving their way home when they noticed a large placard in a shop window with the words *Butter! Butter! Butter!* printed on it.

The Scot gazed owlishly at the sign and then asked: "Those peculiar strokes after the words—I wonder what they mean!"

"Och, ye ignorint Scotsman!" cried the Irishman. "That's *Irish* butther they're sellin', is it not?"

"That it is."

"Well, those strokes are meant to *prove* the butther is Irish—those strokes are shillelaghs!"

*

A sergeant cannot always be blamed for his rough treatment of rookie soldiers. There is the incident concerning Sergeant Rooney of the Irish

Grenadier Regiment, who was training a squad of recruits on a rifle range. At a hundred yards, he gave the order: "Fire!"

After the smoke had cleared away, the target was revealed to be smooth and untouched. Sergeant Rooney ordered his men to move up to fifty yards. Again the firing order was given—and still the target was untouched. They moved up to twenty-five yards—with the same results. Ordering the troops into closed ranks, Rooney, crimson-faced and seemingly about to burst a blood vessel, bellowed:

"All right, ye blind, ham-strung, blitherin', blatherin' ijits; *fix bayonets an' charge!*"

*

Those who believe in conducting their business affairs on a strictly cash basis, have, as their shining example, the small son of a mountaineer who was accosted by a revenuer.

"Who are you," asked the officer, "a Martin or a Coy?"

"I'm a Martin," replied the boy.

"Where's your pappy?"

"Pappy's up at the still."

"I'll give you a dollar if you take me up there."

"All right, gimme the dollar."

"Oh no you don't," smiled the officer. "I'll give it to you when we get back."

"No sir, mister revenooer, I gotta have it now," insisted the lad. "You ain't *a-comin'* back!"

*

Mr. Milquetoast borrowed a small sum from "Muscles" Malone, the toughest, brawniest Irishman on the Atlantic seaboard. Unfortunately, Milquetoast was unable to repay the loan on the stipulated date, so, knees shaking, he went to see the burly, quick-tempered Malone to explain his inability to pay.

"Now, don't you go worryin' about that loan," said "Muscles." "I'll not be afther askin' ye fer the money a'tall a'tall."

"Wh-what?" gasped the astonished Mr. Milquetoast.

"Sure, an' I would niver be botherin' the likes iv a gintlemin."

"But if you never ask a gentleman for money," persisted Milquetoast, "then how do you get it if he doesn't pay?"

"Faith, that's no trouble," grinned the Irishman, flexing his bulging biceps. "Afther awhile I decide he is no gintlemin, and *then* I knock his head off!"

*

Maggie, the cleaning woman, arrived for work just as her employer, Dr. Johnson, was ushering a young patient out of the clinic.

"That's the Murphy boy, is it not?" asked Maggie. "One iv the *rich* Murphys?"

"Yes," said the doctor.

"Then ye'll be afther gettin' a fine fee fer medicatin' the lad?"

"Why, yes!" he answered, surprised at her unexpected audacity.

"Well, Docthor," said Maggie eagerly, "it's hopin' I am ye'll not be fergettin' it was me very own boy what threw the brick at him!"

*

Open the windrow and let the shunsine in!

On the subject of proofreading, some authors are a menace to their publishers, while others suffer from legitimate grievances. One of those who deserves sympathy was the late Sean O'Faolain, the gifted Irish author. After having corrected more than one hundred fifty galleys of printed material, and, later, all the final page proofs where the same error had occurred, O'Faolain wrote to his publisher:

"In all the proof that has reached me, windrow has been spelled window. If, in the bound book, windrow still appears as window, then neither rain nor hail nor gloom of night nor fleets of riot squads will prevent me from assassinating the man who is responsible. If the coward hides so that I cannot find him, I shall step into your offices, sir, and take a shillelagh to you, Irish style!"

*

The accused stood before the bar of justice, returning Judge Moran's glare with a defiant one of his own.

"Your Honor," stated the defendant, "I hit that man because nobody except my wife can call me a harp and get away with it."

"I don't blame you one bit," declared Judge Moran. "And as for you," he added, facing the plaintiff, "I fine you ten dollars for calling this mick a harp!"

*

A certain well-known movie star—we'll call him Bob to avoid the libel laws—was reputed to have had an aff—well it seems that he had been indis—

Anyway, one day Hollywood Hannah (as she was called in less elegant circles) learned that her boyfriend had been seen at Malibu Beach with another girl who was described as "younger and prettier" than she. Hannah didn't like that. In fact, she was mad as hell. She showed up at the great Bob's studio with a pint of gin in her purse and another pint swishing around in her innards. Loudly—*very* loudly—she demanded to see the big star, *in person!* The nickname that she invented for him on the spot left no doubt that her feelings for him were not as affectionate as they had been of yore.

Far down at the other end of the movie lot, Bob heard her. He could have heard her had he been atop the Statue of Liberty. With somewhat undue haste, he took what is sometimes called "a powder" and at other times "a fast disappearing act.'' You might say he got the hell out of there, were you so inclined.

Hannah, meanwhile, made her way to his dressing room, only to find that it was empty.

She was hurt. And when a red-haired Irish lass is hurt, she proceeds with reckless abandon. If Reckless Abandon happens to be out of town on business, she goes it alone. Especially when she is fortified with the cup that sneers.

The gin bottle did all right on the picture frames and lighter pieces of furniture, but it wouldn't stand up under a real test. Undaunted, however, she dropped the bottle gently against the full-length mirror where Bob was accustomed to admire himself, and then grimly deposited herself in a chair to await further developments—and the arrival of her absent ex-boyfriend.

In the meantime, studio officials were running about in circles, trying to think of something, anything, to rid the premises of her presence. One of them called an assistant to the assistant director to get a car from the Transportation Department. Then, several of the more hardy among them bearded the lioness in Bob's den. After a brief thirty-minute struggle, they had the harried and hapless Hannah on her back. The gin bottle, applied to her noble brow, was the deciding factor.

They looked about for the assistant-assistant director from whom they had requested a car. He was still there, standing in the doorway. The panting official, who was lying on the floor and holding Hannah's head between his legs in an interesting scissor-hold, yelled:

"Where the hell's the car?"

But the assistant-assistant director was smart. He knew his picture business. He answered:

"Yuh never give me no requisition!"

"Well, dammit, get one, and then get the car!" screamed the executive-turned-wrestler. "And then drive her out of here!"

"B-but where will I take her?"

And from somewhere between the official's knees came Hannah's muffled voice:

"To McGinty's Bar, sweetie. The sonofabitch busted my last bottle!"

*

Tiny Timothy O'Toole entered into a free-swinging difference of opinion with Big Red Riordan and, as a result, came out second best. Lips puffed and his jaw aching, he went to his dentist for repairs.

"Hmmm," hmmd the dentist, "I see you lost two teeth."

"Not a bit of it," retorted Timothy. "I've got 'em right here in me pocket!"

The Saga of Long Mat
and Black Michael[1]

Part One
The Faction Fight

Carrala Valley, in the heart of the Connemara Highlands, hides in a triangle of mountains. Carrala Village lies in the corner of the mountains near Loch Ina, and Aughavanna in the corner nearest Kylemore. Aughavanna is destroyed now: if you were to look for it you would see only a cluster of walls grown over by ferns and nettles. But, in those remote times before the Great Famine, when no English was spoken in the valley, there was no place more renowned for wild fun and fighting; and when its men were to be at a fair, every able-bodied man in the countryside took his *kippeen* from its place in the chimney, and went out to do battle with a glad heart.

Long Mat Murnane was the King of Aughavanna. There was no grander sight than Mat smashing his way through a forest of *kippeens,* with his enemies staggering back to the right and left of him; there was no sweeter sound than his voice, clear as a bell, full of triumph and gladness, shouting, "Hurroo! Whoop! Aughavanna forever!" Where his *kippeen* flickered in the air, his followers charged after; and the enemy rushed to meet him, for it was an honor to take a broken head from him.

But Carrala Fair was the black day for him. That day, Carrala swarmed with men—fishers from the near coast, dwellers in lonely huts by the black

[1]Similar versions, originally told in Old Irish (Gaelic) and "Middle Irish" (Irish-English), have been handed down from generation to generation in the oral tradition of folklore. This tale, also titled *Their Last Race,* was translated in about 1885, and seems to be the first *published* variant in modern *English*-Irish (as opposed to *Irish*-English). The legendary characters, Black Michael and Mat Murnane, were probably ancient Celtic kings, ruling over what later may have been counties. The periodic wars conducted by these regional kings were not recorded in written form but remembered in the folk tales of the survivors and other witnesses. The greater-than-life exploits of the principal characters assumed heroic proportions with each telling, and the tales, as is common in folklore, grew to become epics of valor. However, the stories are not necessarily mythical, each having some substance in original fact.

189

lakes, or in tiny ragged villages under the shadow of the mountains, or in cabins on the hillsides—every little town for miles, by river or seashore or mountain-built, was emptied. The fame of the Aughavanna men was their ruin, for they were known to fight so well that everyone was dying to fight them.

The Joyces sided against the men of Aughavanna. Black Michael Joyce had a farm in the third corner of the valley, just where the road through the bog from Aughavanna (the road with the cross by it) meets the highroad to Leenane, so his kin mustered in force. Now Black Michael, "Meehul Dhu," was Long Mat's rival. Though smaller, he was near as deadly in a fight, and in dancing no man could touch him, for it was said he could jump a yard into the air and kick himself behind with his heels in doing it.

The business of the fair had been hurried so as to leave the more time for pleasure, and by five of the afternoon every man was mad for the battle. Why you could scarcely have moved in Callanan's Field out beyond the churchyard at the end of the village, it was so packed with men—more than five hundred were there, and you could not have heard yourself speak, for they were jumping and dancing, tossing their *caubeens,* and shouting themselves hoarse and deaf: "Hurroo for Carrala!" "Whoop for Aughavanna!" Around them a mob of women, old men, and children looked on breathlessly. It was dull weather, and the mists had crept halfway down the dark mountain walls, as if to have a nearer look at the fight.

As the chapel clock struck five, Long Mat Murnane gave the signal. Down the village he came, rejoicing in his strength, out between the two last houses, past the churchyard and into Callanan's Field. He looked every inch a king; his *kippeen* was ready, his frieze coat* was off (with his left hand he trailed it behind him, holding it by the sleeve), while with a great voice he shouted—in Irish, "Where's the Carrala man that dare touch my coat? Where's the cowardly scoundrel that dare look crooked at it?"

•In a moment, Black Michael Joyce was trailing his own coat behind him. He rushed forward with a mighty cry: "Where's the face of a trembling Aughavanna man?" In a moment, their *kippeens* clashed; in another, hundreds of *kippeens* crashed together, and the grandest fight ever fought in Connemara raged over Callanan's Field. After the first roar of defiance, the men had to keep their breath for the hitting, so the shout of triumph and the groan as one fell were the only sounds that broke the music of the *kippeens* clashing and clicking on one another, or striking home with a thud.

Never was Long Mat nobler. He rushed through the enemy, ravaging, shattering their ranks and their heads. No man could withstand him. Red Callanan of Carrala went down before him. He knocked the five senses out of Dan O'Shaughran of Earrennamore, who herded many pigs by the sedgy banks of the Owen Erriff. He hollowed the left eye out of Larry Mulcahy, who lived on the Devil's Mother Mountain....

---

*"Frieze" pertains to the material, a heavy, napped woollen cloth, used in the manufacture of coats for the nobility and other persons of means. It was often embroidered and otherwise decorated. As a legendary "King" or leader, Long Mat would have worn a frieze coat.

Yes, and he killed Black Michael Joyce by a beautiful swooping blow on the side of the head: who would have dreamt that Black Michael had so thin a skull?

For near an hour Mat triumphed; then, suddenly, he went down underfoot. At first, he was missed only by those nearest him, and they took it for granted that he was up again and fighting. But, when the Aughavanna men found themselves outnumbered and driven back to the village, a great fear came on them, for they knew that all Ireland could not outnumber them if Mat was to the fore. Then disaster and rout took them, and they were forced backwards up the street, struggling desperately, till hardly a man of them could stand.

And when the victors were shouting themselves dumb, and drinking themselves blind, the beaten men looked for their leader. Long Mat was prone. His forehead was smashed, his face had been trampled into the mud—he had done with fighting. His death was untimely, yet he fell as he would have chosen—in a friendly battle. For when a man falls under the hand of an enemy (as of anyone who differs from him in creed or politics), revenge and black blood live after him. But he who takes his death from the kindly hand of a friend leaves behind him no ill will, but only gentle regret for the mishap.

Part Two

The Last Race Between Long Mat and Black Michael

When the dead had been duly waked for two days and nights, the burying day came. All the morning, Long Mat Murnane's coffin lay on four chairs by his cabin, with a kneeling ring of disheveled women *keening* round it. Every soul in Aughavanna and their kith and kin had gathered to do him honor.

And when the Angelus bell rang across the valley from the chapel, the mourners fell into ranks, and the coffin was lifted on the rough hearse. The motley funeral—a line of carts with a mob of peasants behind, a few riding, but most of them on foot—moved slowly toward Carrala. The women were crying bitterly, *keening* like an Atlantic gale. The men looked as sober as if they had never heard of a wake, and spoke sadly of the dead man, and of what a pity it was that he could not see his funeral.

The Joyces too had waited, as was the custom, for the Angelus bell, and now Black Michael's funeral was moving slowly toward Carrala along the other side of the bog. Before long, either party could hear the *keening* of the other, for you know the roads grow nearer as they converge on Carrala. Before long, each of the two parties began to fear that the other would be there first.

There is no knowing how it happened, but the funerals began to go quicker, keeping abreast; then still quicker, till the women had to break into a trot to keep up; then still quicker, till the donkeys were galloping, and till everyone raced at full speed, and the rival parties broke into a wild shout of "Aughavanna *abu*!" "Meehul Dhu forever!"

For the dead men were racing—feet foremost—to the grave. They were rivals even in death. Never did the world see such a race. Never was there such whooping and shouting. Where the roads meet in Callanan's Field, the hearses were abreast; neck to neck, they dashed across the trampled fighting place, while the coffins jogged and jolted as if the two dead men were struggling to get out and lead the rush. Neck to neck, they reached the churchyard, and the hearses jammed in the gate. Behind them, the carts crashed into one another, and the mourners shouted as if they were mad.

But the quick wit of the Aughavanna men triumphed, for they seized their long coffin and dragged it in...

192

And Long Mat Murnane won his last race.

The shout they gave then deafened the echo up in the mountains, so that it has never been the same since. The victors wrung one another's hands. They hugged one another.

"It's himself would be proud," they cried, "if he hadn't been dead!"

—Frank Mathew (1865-?)

*

"The Gathering of the Mahonys"

Jerry Mahony, arrah, my jewel, come let us be off
    to the fair,
For the Donovans all in their glory most certainly mean
    to be there;
Say they: "The whole Mahony faction we'll banish 'em out
    clear and clane."
But it never was yet in their breeches their bullaboo words
    to maintain.

There's Darby to head us, and Barney, as civil a man
    as yet spoke,
'Twould make your mouth water to see him just giving a
    bit of a stroke.
There's Corney, the bandy-legged tailor, a boy of the
    true sort of stuff,
Who'd fight though the red blood was flowing like buttermilk
    out of his buff.

There's broken-nosed Bat from the mountain—last week
    he burst out of jail—
And Murty, the beautiful Tory, who'd scorn in a row to
    turn tail.
Bloody Bill will be there like a darling—and Jerry—och!
    let him alone,
For giving his blackthorn* a flourish, or lifting a
    lump of a stone!

And Tim, who'd served in the Militia, has his bayonet
    stuck on a pole;
Foxy Dick has his scythe in good order—a neat sort of tool
    on the whole.
A cudgel, I see, is your weapon, and never I knew it to
    fail,
But I think that a man is more handy who fights, as I do,
    with a flail.

---

*A shillelagh.

We muster a hundred shillelaghs, all handled by iligant
   men,
Who battered the Donovans often, and now we'll do ıt
   again.
Today we will teach them some manners, and show that, in
   spite of their talk,
We still, like our fathers before us, are surely the cocks
   of the walk.

After cutting out work for the sexton by smashing a dozen
   or so,
We'll quit in the utmost of splendor, and down to Peg
   Slattery's go;
In gallons we'll wash down the battle, and drink to the
   next merry day,
When mustering again in a body, we shall all go leathering
   away.

—William Maginn

*

"Lanigan's Ball—
And the Dire Consequences That Ensued
When McCarthy Kicked a Hole in
Miss Halloran's Hoop-skirt"

In the town of Athy one Jeremy Lanigan
   Battered away till he hadn't a pound;
His father he died and made him a man again,
   Left him a house and ten acres of ground!
He gave a grand party to friends and relations
   Who wouldn't forget him if he went to the wall;
And if you'll just listen, I'll make your eyes glisten
   With the rows and the ructions of Lanigan's ball.

Myself, to be sure, got free invitations
   For all the nice boys and girls I'd ask,
And in less than a minute the friends and relations
   Were dancing as merry as bees round a cask.
Miss Kitty O'Hara, the nice little milliner,
   Tipped me the wink for to give her a call,
And soon I arrived with Timothy Glenniher
   Just in time for Lanigan's ball.

There was lashins of punch and wine for the ladies,
   Potatoes and cakes and bacon and tay;
The Nolans, the Dolans and all the O'Gradys
   Were courting the girls and dancing away.
Songs they sung as plenty as water

From *The Harp That Once Through Tara's Ould Hall*
To *Sweet Nelly Gray* and *The Ratcatcher's Daughter,*
   All singing together at Lanigan's ball.

They were starting all sorts of nonsensical dances,
   Turning around in a nate whirligig;
But Julia and I soon scatthered their fancies
And tipped them the twist of a rale Irish jig.
Och! *mavrone!* 'twas then she got glad o' me;
   We danced till we thought the old ceilin' would fall
(For I spent a whole fortnight in Doolan's Academy
   Learning a step for Lanigan's ball).

The boys were all merry, the girls were all hearty,
   Dancin' around in couples and groups,
When an accident happened—young Terence McCarthy
   He dhruv his right foot through Miss Halloran's hoops.
The crayture she fainted, and cried "Millia murther!"
   She called for her friends and gathered them all;
Ned Carmody swore he'd not stir a step further,
   But have satisfaction at Lanigan's ball.

In the midst of the row Miss Kerrigan fainted—
   Her cheeks all the while were as red as the rose—
And some of the ladies declared she was painted,
   She took a small drop too I suppose.
Her lover, Ned Morgan, so pow'rful and able,
   When he saw his dear colleen stretched out by the wall,
He tore the left leg from under the table
   And smashed all the china at Lanigan's ball.

Oh, boys, but then was the ructions—
   Myself got a lick from big Phelim McHugh,
But I soon replied to his kind introductions
   And kicked up a terrible hullabaloo.
Old Casey the piper was near being strangled,
   They squeezed up his pipes, his bellows and all;
The girls in their ribbons they all got entangled,
   And that put an end to Lanigan's ball.

—Zozimus

*

"Notes to a Tourist"

And if ever ye ride in Ireland,
   The jest may yet be said:
There is the land of broken hearts,
   And the land of broken heads.

—G. K. Chesterton (1874-1916)

Chapter Twelve
Passin's, Wakes, and Rayqueems

Introduction

Some of the selections in this chapter are old Irish classics of humor; others are newer Irish-American variants. But whatever their origins, it would seem at first glace that the Celtic people are prone to take death rather lightly. That, of course, is not true: philosophically, perhaps, but not lightly! The Irishman's calm acceptance of his mortality has been conditioned by centuries of tradition and custom. From the time of Ireland's dark years of famines and miseries, the Irishman has faced the inevitability of his appointment with Death, that grim gentleman who became such a familiar visitor with the first wave of invaders of the hapless country.

The Irishman's religion certainly contributed to his stoicism. He easily accepted Christianity's doctrines of evil and original sin, for they presented an understandable reason for his hard life and its termination on earth. Man's weaknesses and man's death were not idle, alien beliefs imposed on him by others, nor were they considered as biblical rhetoric to be believed or disbelieved. They were, instead, realities; the most compatible truths of his religion. They conditioned his thinking about all the intimate concerns of his daily life.

In addition to his religion, environment played an important role in the Irishman's view of death. His was a captive society in which he lived on the edge of poverty. His homeland, in the international halls of power, was an obscure, underdeveloped island where the forces of nature raged unimpeded by human barriers. This was not a strong, vital, urban world with the resources to cope with nature and affirm human strengths. This was life on the land, hard and lonely.

Under those conditions, it was small wonder that a pervasive feeling of melancholy, of impending doom, was a common frame of mind. Death, in a religious sense, not only brought surcease and reward, but it presented rare opportunities for social gathering—among the few pleasantries afforded the rural Irish, and therefore all the more cherished. The Irish wake, that national institution, was one of the social customs that accommodated and reflected the needs of the people. The "kitchen racket," the dance in which neighbors young and old foregathered in the main room of the cottage, became a permanent feature of country life. Paradoxically enough, in the midst of poverty, hospitality and openhandedness were enshrined as virtues. Only in this way could they beat back the loneliness of the land, deny the darkness of their common lot, and laugh in the face of death itself.

The newer Irish-American "death jokes" which are presented in the following pages may be more exuberant, more impertinent than the traditional classic humor of old Ireland, although not, perhaps, as clever or thoughtful. However, both express the same undercurrent of feeling: a love of life and a philosophical acceptance of man's mortality. It is the thought behind the Irish quip, "I know I can't take it with me, but I won't be needing it, either!"

The charge that some Irish-Americans may be disrespectful in the presence of the departed, may have some substance in fact, if we are to believe this cheery account of the wake in which the former governor of New York, Al Smith, was the lamented guest of honor. Jim Farley, one of the most astute political managers of recent times, sidled up to Margaret Riordan, one of Al's numerous nieces, and asked her to dance. It soon became apparent that Jim had imbibed too frequently and too well. Unsteadily, he guided her across the floor, his legs rubbery, bumping into other "mourners," and repeatedly stepping on the young lady's feet.

"I beg your pardon," apologized Jim. "I'm a little stiff from polo."

"I don't care where you're from," snapped Margaret. "You're lousing up our wake!"

In another vein, we have this macabre report from the *University of Dublin Press*, May 1926:

Until recent times in the United States and in Ireland, the law of supply and demand governed both the quick and the dead, without favoritism. The dearly beloved was tenderly laid to rest to await the coming of the grave-robber; that is, one who supplies young doctors with the product which old doctors supply to undertakers. Few of these body-snatchers were ever arrested, the persons most affected having never preferred charges in a duly constituted court of law. In 1923, however, at the Dublin College of Medicine, a student tattooed the picture of a harp upon the *gluteus maximus* of a departed member of the Irish Republican Army, an act which so enraged the populace that a law was passed which frowned on such shenanigans. To the credit of both the United States and Ireland, the enactment of the "Ghoul Law" has had a salutary affect upon artistically inclined medical students, and body-snatchers have been much more careful.

Nearly all of the jokes in this category have always been told for their entertainment value: they had no other purpose than to amuse. A few, however, ended with a moral. The *Grandpa Hennessy Recollections*[1] of the nineteenth century were intended to make one think, as this example suggests:

"Manny years ago," began Grandpa Hennessy, beginning still another of his questionable remembrances of his younger days, "I fought a dool with Donnelly iv Donegal—the selfsame wretch who went to Americky and made a killin' in the ile business.

" 'Donnelly,' says I when I had the spalpeen in me power, 'ask for your life.'

" 'I'd rather die first,' says he.

" 'In that case, you coward, I'm lettin' you live,' says I. " 'If a man's life is not worth the askin', then nayther is it worth the takin'!' "

The wise men tell us that it isn't nice to laugh at the misfortunes of other people, but you will doubtless be forgiven if you just smile a little at the anecdotes and poems that follow.

—H.D.S.

"Cold, Cold Paddy"

The night that Paddy Murphy died
I never shall forget!
The mourners all got pie-eyed,
And they're not sober yet.

There is one thing they did that night
That filled me full of fear—
They took the ice right off the corpse
And stuck it in the beer.

That's how they showed their respect
for Paddy Murphy,
That's how they showed their honor
and their fight,
That's how they showed their respect
for Paddy Murphy—
They drank his health in ice-cold beer
that night!

—Anonymous (circa 1890)

*

A Longford man, well past the age of fourscore and ten, had accumulated a moderate fortune. Now he was about to die. He called in the parish priest and the family lawyer to make his last will and testament. In the presence of his wife, a grasping, covetous old harridan, the preliminaries of the will were concluded, and it became necessary to inquire about the debts owed the estate.

---

[1]William Corcoran, Dublin: McHugh and Stevens, Ltd., *circa* 1900.

"Now then," said the lawyer, clearing his throat, "state explicitly the amount owed you by your friends."

"Timothy Cassidy," replied the old man, "owes me fifty pounds. John Casey owes me thirty-seven pounds."

"Good!" exclaimed the prospective widow. "Rational to the last!"

"Luke Bryan owes me forty pounds," resumed the old man.

"Ah, rational to the last!" put in the eager old crone.

"To Michael Lafferty I owe sixty pounds."

"Oh," moaned the woman, "hear the poor man rave!"

＊

Pat was crossing the Commons in the fair city of Boston, when a large and very impressive funeral passed before him. He stopped to stare, wondering what important person had earned this tribute.

"Sir," he asked an aged man standing beside him, "who's funeral is this?"

"I can't say fer sartin," answered the old-timer, "but I'm afther thinkin' it's the man's in the coffin!"

＊

When a canny Scotsman and a stubborn Irishman enter into an agreement, "'tis sometimes enough to thry th' patience iv a saint." So it was with Angus MacTavish and John Brady. They were inseparable, those two: not so much because of friendship, but better to keep a sharp eye on each other.

In their younger days, they had solemnly vowed that whichever of them survived, the other would automatically inherit the money left by the deceased. Now they were both hanging on precariously to the thread of life, each grimly determined to collect the other's money.

The inevitable day finally arrived when Angus came down to breakfast only to find that John, who was usually first at the table, was not at his accustomed place. He hurried to his companion's bedroom. There was John Brady, pale as a ghost, scarcely breathing.

"Ye look turr'ble," said MacTavish, heroically suppressing a pleased smile. "Would ye like a leetle breakfast?"

"A pooched aig an' a wee spot o' tay," replied Brady weakly.

When MacTavish returned with the egg and tea, Brady was too weak to eat.

"Listen to me," said MacTavish anxiously, "do ye ken our agreement?"

"What agreement?" whispered Brady, obviously sinking fast.

"The money!" MacTavish fairly hissed. "Who iver dies furrst leaves all his money to th' ither!"

Brady was now gasping for air, the death rattle making ominous noises in his throat. Frantically, MacTavish shook the dying Irishman. "Tell me, quick—where is it? Hurry, mon, before it's too late!"

"Sure an' it's sorry I am to confess it, but I had the divil's own time savin' a chit iv the money," declared Brady, his voice now scarcely audible. "I spint ivry penny on women, an' double whuskies—er, wubble dhiskeys—

I mane wibble dhuskies...O Angus, me ould an' thrusted friend, I'm broke!"

"Why, ye ondacint, blackhearted shanty Irishman!" MacTavish screamed, almost incoherent. He rose from his chair beside Brady's bed and danced about in a cold fury, yelling curses, his face getting bluer and bluer by the minute. All of a sudden, he clutched at his heart, gasped, and then pitched to the floor, as dead as a politician's promise.

And John Brady—bad cess to th' decaivin' ould rogue—leaped from his bed, shouting the glad tidings to the world:

"It wurrked! It wurrked! Got that ould skinflint at last!"

*

"I must say, this job has its advantages," declared an old-hand social director at St. Mary's College. "At Donovan's wake last month, I allotted each member of the faculty just two ounces of liquor per half hour, and not a drop more. It worked beautifully, too. I drank everything that was left!"

*

No book about the Irish would be complete without a bit of science fiction. Accordingly, the following offering:

Andy Muldoon, janitor at St. Thomas Aquinas High School in the Bronx, passed away while still a comparatively young man. To the surprise and chagrin of his priest, to say nothing of his family, he left strict instructions that he was not to be buried. Instead, his body was to be frozen so that he could be restored to life one hundred years later. His last will and testament was a no-nonsense document which also stipulated that his tiny bank account of two hundred dollars and his one share of U. S. Steel stocks, valued at five hundred dollars, was to remain intact in his name. No lawyer could break his ironclad will, and his last wishes were carried out to the letter. Andy was confident, as he closed his eyes for the last time, that the science of the future would be sufficient to breathe new life into his body.

Sure enough, a century later, at the Eezie-Freezie Coolatorium in Coldbutte, Montana, Andy Muldoon was thawed out. After consuming a hearty breakfast—the poor man hadn't eaten a blessed morsel in 104 years—the reawakened old-timer called his bank.

"How's my savings account?" he asked. "I was supposed to check with you in 100 years, but I slept late—it's now 104."

"Well, Mr. Muldoon, including your interest, and your interest on your interest, and your interest on your interest on your interest, and so on—compounded daily for 35,310 days—your original $200 is now $852,785."

"Aha! Just as I planned!" cried Andy. "Tell me, how about my U. S. Steel stock?"

"Your one share is now worth $998,000."

"The saints and the Coolatorium preserve us!" marveled the happy man. "I'm rich!"

Muldoon was just about to ask another question when the telephone operator broke into the conversation.

"I'm sorry, sir," she purred, "but your time is up. That will be $12,500 for the next three minutes."

*

The Dublin Players Company
presents

"Alive, Alive-O"

-Distinguished cast of characters-
Tricia ... Rhonda Corner
Waiter .... Chuck Roast
Scene: *A table at the Shamrock Restaurant*

Tricia: Waiter—oh, waiter! Come quick! My husband just dropped dead!
Waiter: Hey, chef! There's something wrong again with the cockles and mussels!

*

The sad experience of dying by inches arose *after* old man Doheny passed on in his sleep, not *before,* as might be expected. It seems that his grandson, who had been quite fond of the old-timer, went to the local newspaper and consulted with the advertising manager.

"How much is an announcement in the obituary column?" he asked.

"Two dollars an inch," said the ad man.

"Two dollars an inch!" gasped the young fellow. "Is it mad ye are? Why, me ould grandfather was six-feet-four!"

*

To a small and loving child, the death of a favorite pet can be as calamitous as the death of a family member is to an adult. Witness:

It was Easter on Boston's south side, and little Timmie, age six, was ecstatic. His daddy had bought him a bunny rabbit—a furry little ball of white fluff, all warm and cuddly. The child's joy was boundless and he promptly named it Hockaday O'Flanigan.

For hours on end, Timmie played with his Easter bunny, brushing, feeding, and petting it, the boy's devotion for the little creature flowing freely from his Irish heart.

Then disaster struck. Timmie arose early one day, as usual, and what should he behold but Hockaday O'Flanigan lying cold and stiff in a corner of the room. His little friend had gone to bunny heaven.

Timmie's grief welled up from his very soul. Tears splashed down his cheeks and he cried as only a boy of six can cry—one who is not old enough to comprehend the cruel vagaries of life but old enough to realize that a loved one has departed forever. He wept for hours on end. He refused to eat. He was inconsolable.

Timmie's daddy knew he would have to do something to divert his son's attention from the shattering loss. He called him to his side, and placed an arm around the lad's shoulder.

"Timmie, you must remember that Hockaday is now in a happy place called Paradise.... I'll tell you what we'll do. First, I'll build him a little coffin, and you can help me. Then, we'll dig a grave together, right in the garden by the prettiest flowers. After that, we'll hold a wake and you can invite all your friends in, and I'll bring ice cream, cookies, lemonade, and lots of other good things. Next, I'll give party hats to everyone, and we'll have the funeral, and everybody can sing songs."

Timmie was all ears and he began to smile. Encouraged, the father continued: "I'll get my old fiddle out and we'll both sing together like we do on your birthday. And then I'll take you to a movie."

Timmie clapped his hands in glee, his laughing face giving clear evidence of his newly-found pleasure.

Suddenly, they heard a squeak and the soft shuffling of feet. They turned around and there, to their amazement, was Hockaday, as alive and frisky as ever.

Timmie looked at the rabbit, looked at his father, and then back again at the rabbit.

"Daddy," he said after an agonizing silence, "let's kill 'im!"

*

A Dublin attorney died in poverty, and many barristers of the city subscribed to a fund for his funeral. Toler, later Lord Chief Justice of Orbury, was approached for the donation of a shilling.

"What?" he cried. "Only a shilling to bury an attorney? Here's a guinea—go and bury twenty of them!"

*

The late Gavin Meighan, founder of the New England hardware company that bears his name, had long been infamous for his frequent lapses into bankruptcy. Unknown at this time, however, was his macabre sense of humor. After he died, this note was found among his effects:

> I hereby name the following six bankers to be my pallbearers. Since they have carried me for so long during my lifetime, they might as well finish the job.

*

Ascending the mountain road between Dublin and Glencullen with a sympathetic English friend, Michael Collins,[2] the patriot, happened to meet a funeral procession. The mourners recognized him at once and broke into vociferous hurrahs.

---

[2]Gen. Michael Collins. (See *Sinn Fein* in the Glossary.)

The astonished Englishman, accustomed to the solemn decorum of English funerals, was hardly prepared for this outburst of Celtic enthusiasm, considering the occasion.

"My word!" the Briton exclaimed. "Isn't it rather odd to hear a political hurrah at a funeral?"

Collins just smiled and shrugged, but a member of the bereaved's family chanced to overhear the amazed question.

"Sir," he declared with a certitude that permitted no denial, "I can assure you that, if it were at all possible, the corpse would have cheered too!"

*

Of all the worthless, miserable imitations of a human being, old man Murphy was the worst. Small wonder, then, that everyone was silent at his wake. Even kindhearted Father Healy could not think of a good word to say about him. Finally, however, the gentle priest smiled as a sudden remembrance came to his mind. He approached the coffin and looked down on the late Mr. Murphy.

"A toast to ye, Murph me b'y, no matther where ye are at th' prisint time," he announced, holding his glass high. "Whativer annywan ilse may say, ye sure could peel *praties* rale good!"

*

McNulty's body was found floating in the Hudson River. There was no water in his lungs, a huge anchor was tied to his ankles, a rope was twisted around his neck, there was a bullet in his skull, and poison in his system. The coroner's autopsy also showed that McNulty had once suffered from a bad heart.

Unable to arrive at a precise cause of death, they wrote their official determination:

"An act of God under very suspicious circumstances."

*

At Finnegan's wake, John and Mark appreciatively downed another shot of good Irish whiskey, and complimented their host—or what remained of him—for his excellent taste in potables.

"Sure and it's too bad Finnegan's not here to jine us in sperrit as well as in body," observed Mark. "The way he drove a car, 'tis no wonder a'tall he died in a collision."

"Spakin' iv collisions," said John, pouring another shot, "av ye had yer choice twixt wan or t'other, which would ye rather be in—a collison or an explosion?"

"Go on with ye fer that foolish question!" retorted Mark. "A collision, iv coorse!"

"But why, man?"

"Because, me friend, if ye're in a collision, there ye be," explained Mark, "but if ye're in an explosion, where are ye?"

*

Mark Twain, being a celebrity, turned the famous erroneous announcement of his death into a well-known quip. More difficult, however, was the situation of an obscure man named Joe Kirby, a Hartford bricklayer, whose death was mistakenly noted in the obituary column of the *Hartford Courier*. The "corpse" hastened to the editor's office to protest.

"I'm awfully sorry, Mr. Kirby," apologized the editor, "but it's too late now to do much about it. The best I can do for you is to put you in the 'Birth Notices' column tomorrow morning, and give you a fresh start!"

*

It was on a Tuesday, bad cess to that day, when Murphy fell from a high scaffold and lost his life. Now, at the construction site, the new foreman was puzzling over the formal papers which had to be filled out, explaining the details of the casualty. At last he managed to complete all of the task except for one more unfilled line which seemed to stump him.

Finally, licking his pencil point, he applied himself firmly to the section headed "Remarks," and wrote—

"He didn't make none!"

*

Old man Lundigan was at death's door. His family physician had been unable to help or even to diagnose his case. At last, despite the old codger's insistence that he didn't need anybody's help, his sons and daughters called in a team of specialists. When the specialists had gone, the old man's family trooped into the sickroom and asked what the high-priced doctors had said.

"I told you I was right!" cried old Lundigan triumphantly. "Them big doctors used a lot of fancy la-de-da words I couldn't understand, but they said everything would be all right."

"They said that!" gasped a member of the family. "What did they say, exactly?"

"They said," explained Lundigan, "no use worryin' or arguin' about it. The autopsy will give us the answer!"

*

Father O'Haloran, of Saint Theresa's in Detroit, was chagrined by the fact that one of his parishioners, a friend and golfing companion, invariably beat him at the game.

"Don't take it too hard," counseled the golfing friend. "Remember, you win in the end. It's you who'll be burying me one of these days."

"Yes," grumped Father O'Haloran, "but even then it'll be your hole!"

*

Among the interested tourists visiting the battlefield of Bunker Hill was Mary, lately of Galway. She listened to every word the guide was saying, eager to learn everything she could about her newly-adopted homeland.

"And this is Bunker Hill monument," announced the guide, "where Warren fell."

"Is it now?" clucked Mary sympathetically as she looked up at the lofty shaft. "Oh, the poor man! Killed him, did it?"

*

Up in Danbury, the financial dispute between Clancey and a Scot has long since been resolved. This is what happened:

Clancey, Proprietor of CLANCEY'S SLUMBER PARLOR—FUNERALS WHILE-U-WAIT, had negotiated a price of four hundred dollars with a fellow named MacDonald for the disposition of his wife's remains. The haggling had been intense, with MacDonald arguing about the cost of every single item involved, no matter how trivial. Both were worn out when the price was at last agreed upon.

After the funeral services, MacDonald lingered in the cemetery after the mourners had gone to make sure the gravediggers did the work he had paid for. His eyes narrowed, and he walked over to Clancey, who was preparing to leave.

"How much are those two gravediggers being paid?" he asked.

"Thirty dollars each," said Clancey. "Why?"

"Thirty dollars each!" screamed MacDonald, shattering the peacefulness of the sanctuary. "That's too damn much for such light soil!"

"That's the Union's minimum wage. I couldn't reduce the price even if I wanted to."

"Well, I won't pay it!"

"Sir," declared Clancey in a grim, determined voice, "whether it's light sandy soil, rich loamy soil, or gravel and rock, those men get thirty dollars each, and the total for your wife's burial remains four hundred dollars—or *up she comes!*"

"I'll pay it!" screeched MacDonald.

*

Editor Mike O'Farrell, of *Hibernia Today,* derived a great deal of pleasure in telling of his favorite typographical errors, and other "boners" that frequently appear in newspapers. Among his favorite recollections was the major goof that occurred one Friday in the old *New York World,* when the obituary column and the Marine and Shipping News column were transposed—and both on the same page.

As a result, a number of respected and deceased citizens were listed under the disconcerting heading: *Passes Through Hell Gate Today.*

*

Looking down at the sick man, the doctor decided to tell him the awful truth.

"Frank, I believe you'd want to know the facts. You have only a few more hours to live. Is there anyone you would like to see?"

Frank's lips moved, and the doctor leaned over his patient to hear the feeble answer.

"Yes, there is," came the faint whisper.

"Who is it, Frank? Just tell me and I'll get him."

Making a last superhuman effort, Frank wheezed:

"Anither docthor!"

*

Horace Greeley, the famous newspaper publisher of the past century, had a passion for brevity in his correspondence. But he met his match one day when he sent a notice to a Mr. James Feeney that his subscription had expired.

Back came the note with a terse message from Mrs. Feeney: "So's Jim!"

*

A physician and his lawyer friend were discussing their respective professions as they made their way around the golf greens.

"Not that I'm casting any aspersions on your medical ability," said the lawyer a bit maliciously, "but it is rumored that a patient you were treating for sclerosis of the liver died of a heart attack."

"That's a damn lie!" the doctor exploded, outraged at this slur against his professional skill. "When I treat someone for sclerosis of the liver, he *dies* of sclerosis of the liver!"[3]

*

When George M. Cohan, the famed entertainer, lay dying, reporters were on the spot for the story. One of them, Dan Fahey, who worked for the *New York Journal,* was notorious for his enormous expense accounts.

After Cohan's death, Fahey's expense account, carefully itemized but out of all just proportions, was handed to Jerry Donovan, the *Journal's* city editor at that time. Donovan looked it over and handed it back.

"Fahey," he sighed resignedly, "if this is Cohan's will, it's worth a story."

*

Who says our senior citizens do not have high opinions of themselves, or that they lose their ability to do a bit o' blarneyin' when they choose? Read on.

---

[3] *Catholic Digest, 1971.*

Tears of sorrow coursed down the wrinkled cheeks of devoted old John as he sat beside the bed where his wife of sixty years lay, only minutes away from her journey to the Beyond.

Now she was trying to say something. He leaned forward to better hear her last words.

"Johnny, me darlin'," she whispered, "ye've been a good husband iver since we were married. Niver a man was there ez fine ez you. Sure you were the best."

"Tha's all right, Maggie," he sobbed, "you deserved me!"

*

An anonymous sage once stated that doctors fall into three classifications: expensive, exorbitant, and outrageous. But whoever originated that observation probably stands sponsor for this little anecdote.

"Doctor," asked the nurse, "do you remember that elderly patient who stopped visiting your office last year because he said your fees were too high?"

"Yes, he bought some medical books and decided to be his own physician," affirmed the doctor. "Why?"

"Well, he died the other day."

"I'm not surprised. What was the cause of death?"

"A misprint!"[4]

*

Although this tale is old enough to have earned the respect of the folklorists, there are a few people still alive who will remember the last will and testament of O'Connor of Cork. O'Connor was a well-to-do old gentleman who realized that his last hours were upon him. He therefore sent for his lifelong friend, attorney Tom Toohey, and the dying man began his list of bequests.

"Put down 50 pounds for masses up at the Church for the repose iv me soul."

Toohey scratched away with his quill pen, and then asked, "What next?"

"Put down 200 pounds for the Little Sisters iv the Poor."

"All right, I've written it down. What next?"

"Put down 250 pounds for the Cork Orphan Asylum."

"It's done."

"Put down 1,000 pounds for me brother, Padraic. He don't nade it, but it makes no difference. I can't carry it with me."

So the work went on, slowly, the dying man bringing himself up with an effort to the task, and Mr. Toohey stopping now and then to draw his finger across his nose and sniff sympathetically. Finally, old Mr. O'Connor said, "I'm thinkin' that's all I have."

Toohey added up all the figures, looked at the balance, compared it with

⁴From *Erin Go Bragh and Other Irish Jests*, Alec Brodie. Advance Publishers, Ltd., London, 1920.

the figures in O'Connor's bankbook, and shook his head.

"No, old friend, you still have 10 pounds left."

O'Connor lay absorbed in thought for a few moments and then, in a surprisingly strong voice, he ordered: "Put down that 10 pounds to spind with the b'ys at me funeral."

Toohey began to write, then he paused and asked softly, "O'Connor, shall I put it down to spend going *to* the funeral or coming back?"

Old man O'Connor lay very quietly while he thought of the problem. Then, in a faint but quite cheerful voice, he gave his answer:

"Put down the 10 pounds goin' *to* the funeral. At laste I'll be with me own money an' me own friends. An' spare me just wan or two shillin''s out iv the tin pounds for a wee dhrap o' whiskey on me pale an' waitin' lips!"

*

A man had two sons. The elder was virtuous and dutiful, the younger wicked and crafty. When the father was about to die, he called them before him and said: "I have only two things of value—my herd of cows and my blessing. How shall I allot them?"

"Give to me," said the younger son, "thy blessing, for it may reform me. The cows I would be sure to sell and squander the money."

The elder son, disguising his joy, said that he would try to be content with the cows and a pious mind.

It was arranged and the man died. Then the wicked younger son went before the magistrate and said: "Behold, my brother has defrauded me of my lawful heritage. He is so bad that our father, as is well known, denied him his blessing; is it likely that he gave him the cows?"

So, the elder son was compelled to give up the herd and was soundly bastinadoed for his rapacity.

—Ambrose Bierce

Mrs. Murphy, in widow's weeds was weeping upon a grave.

"Console yourself," said a sympathetic stranger. "Heaven's mercies are infinite. There is another man somewhere, besides your husband, with whom you can still be happy."

"There was," sobbed Mrs. Murphy, "there was. This is his grave."

*

Of Popery and Sweeney's Soul

It so happened that the tombstone of old Sweeney, the apothecary, bearing the Popish phrase "Pray for the soul of Dennis Sweeney," stood provokingly close to the pathway leading to the door of the Church of England. Every Sunday, when the departed Sweeney's son, the attorney, attended divine services as by law then established, his Church-of-Englandism was much scandalized by having this damaging (and damnable) proof of his apostasy staring him in the face. Not that he cared a fig about it: he was one of those callous-hearted individuals who could have planted a vegetable garden on his mother's grave. He simply did not like the evidence to remain there in the sight of other people. So he asked Rory O'More how the nuisance could be abated.

Rory, after hearing the attorney's complaint, said he thought he could rectify the objectionable passage on the tombstone.

After breakfast, he asked his friend, De Lacey, would he go with him to see "the churches," as the old burial place in the neighborhood was called, where the ruins of some monastic buildings stood. De Lacey assented, and together they went to the cemetery. There, on one side of the path, stood a rather conspicuous tombstone with this inscription:

Pray for the soul of

Dennis Sweeney

who departed, etc.

"Do you see that?" asked Rory.

"Indade I do," replied De Lacey.

"Well, me own father cut the same tombstone—and a nate bit o' work it is. See the cross on it, and cut so deep that the divil wouldn't get it out— God fergive me fer sayin' divil in the prisince o' the cross."

"It's deep enough, indade," said De Lacey.

"Aye, and so I towld that durrty brat, Sweeney—the 'turny, I mane— when he axed me about it. What do you think he wants me to do?" said Rory indignantly. "He wants me to alther it."

"Why?" asked De Lacey.

"I axed him that same question and he said, 'Because I'm ashamed iv it,' says he. 'It's ownly Popery.'

" 'Well,' says I, 'if it's Popery, sure it's your father's doin'—and anny shame there is in it, it is to him, not to you, so you nade not care about it. If your father did wish people to pray fer his sowl, I think it's very bad iv you to wish to prevint it.'

" 'It can do him no good,' says he.

" 'It can do him no harm, annyhow,' says I.

"He couldn't get around that very well, and made no answer about the good or the harm iv it, and said he didn't want to argue the point with me, but that he wanted it althered; and as me own father had done the job, he thought I was the man to alther it.

" 'And how do you want it changed?' says I.

" 'Take out *Pray for the sowl*,' says he. 'That's nothing but Popery.'

" 'My father always cut the *sowl* very deep,' says I, 'and to take it out is impossible. But if it's only the Popery you object to, I can alther it if you like, so that you will have nothin' to say agin it.'

" 'You won't charge me much?' says he.

" 'Not a shillin',' says I. 'I'm not a mason by thrade, and I'll do the job for love.'

" 'But how do you mane to do it?' says he.

" 'Never mind,' says I. 'Go your way. I'll do the job complate, and next Sunday, when you go to church, you'll see the divil a bit o' Popery will be on the same tombstone.' "

De Lacey had listened attentively without interruption of any kind. Now he asked, "And how do you mane to effect the altheration, Rory?"

"As aisy as kiss hand," said Rory. "Jist amuse yourself with lookin' into the churches: there's some writings in owld Irish and quare carvins round the windows and doors, and a mighty cur'ous owld stone cross up there beyant. Or, if you like, sit down over there with your book and you can read while I work."

After a brief lapse of time, Rory completed his task and sought his friend to show him how thoroughly he had neutralized the Popery that had so much distressed Sweeney.

"How could you have done it so soon?" asked De Lacey.

"I won't tell you...You must see it for yourself," said Rory. "It was simple—four letters did it."

Over the objectionable request, Rory had carved the word *Don't* so that the inscription now read:

Don't
Pray for the soul of
DENNIS SWEENEY

—Anonymous (circa 1830-40)

✱

"The Widow's Lament"

Ochone, *acushla mavourneen!* ah, why thus did ye die?
   (I won't keep ye waitin' a minit: just wait till
     I wipe my eye);
And is it gone ye are, darlint—the kindest, the fondest,
     the best?
   (Don't forget the half-crown for the clerk—ye'll find it
     below in the chest.)
And to leave me alone in the world—O *whirra, ochone, ochone!*
   (Is that Misther Moore in the car?—I thought I was goin'
     alone);
Why am I alive this minit? Why don't I die on the floor?
   (I'll take your hand up the step, an' thank ye, Misther Moore!)

An' are ye gone at last from your weepin', desolate wife?
   (Not a dhrop, Misther Moore, I thank ye—well, the laste
     little dhrop in life!)
'Twas ye had the generous heart, an' 'twas ye had the noble mind,
   (Good mornin', Mrs. O'Flanagan! Is Tim in the car behind?)

Oh, that I lived till this minit, such bitther sorrow to taste,
   (I'm not goin' to fall, Misther Moore! Take your arm from
     around my waist.)
'Twas the like of you there wasn't in Ballaghaslatthery town,
   (There's Mary Mullaly, the hussy, an' she wearin' her
     laylock gown!)

I'll throw her into the river; I'll never come back no more;
   ('Twon't be takin' ye out of the way to lave me at home,
     Misther Moore?)

It's me should have gone that could bear it, now that I'm young
    and sthrong,
    (He was sixty-nine come Christmas; I wondhered he lasted
      so long!)

Oh, what's the world at all when him that I love isn't in it?
    (If 'twas any one else but yourself, I'd lave the car this
      minit!)
There's nothin' but sorrow *forninst* me, wheresoever I roam,
    (*Musha!* why d'ye talk like that—can't ye wait till we're
      goin' home?)

                                         —Anonymous[5]

*

Epigram on a stern security guard:
    What a pity Hell's gates are not kept by O'Flynn—
    The surly old dog would let nobody in!

                                         —Patrick Ireland

*

"Elegy on Mrs. Mary Blaize"
    Good people all, with one accord,
      Lament for Madam Blaize,
    Who never wanted a good word—
      From those who spoke her praise.

    The needy seldom passed her door,
      And always found her kind;
    She freely lent to all the poor—
      Who left a pledge behind.

    She strove the neighborhood to please,
      With manners wondrous winning;
    And never followed wicked ways—
      Unless when she was sinning.

    At church, in silks and satins new,
      With hoop of monstrous size;
    She never slumbered in her pew—
      But when she shut her eyes.

---

[5]*"The Widow's Lament"* is believed to have been written in Dublin, some time between 1880 and 1885. It appeared in an Irish-American paper in 1893. In 1894 it was
published by Walter Scott, Ltd. of London. Attempts to identify the author have
proved futile. A few scholars attribute the poem to Lady Dufferin (see Biographical
Index), but her work was far more exquisite than this.

Her love was sought, I do aver,
  By twenty beaux and more;
The king himself has followed her—
  When she has walked before.

But now her wealth and finery fled,
  Her hangers-on cut short all;
The doctors found, when she was dead—
  Her last disorder mortal.

Let us lament in sorrow sore,
  For Kent Street well may say
That had she lived a twelvemonth more—
  She'd not have died today.

—Oliver Goldsmith (1728-74)

Chapter Thirteen

For Heaven's Sake

Introduction

The reality of a literal Heaven and Hell has been accepted by the people of rural Ireland ever since the establishment of Christianity in that country, some 1,500 years ago. One suspects that this belief is shared by much of the urban population as well. Yet, although there can be little doubt that the Afterworld inspires awe and probably trepidation among many of the believers, it also evokes some of Ireland's funniest humor. The reason is not too difficult to fathom. For centuries, the Irish have lived in intimate association with widespread death, a consequence of invasions, pestilence, and famine. It was almost inevitable that wistful thoughts of immortality should arise.

However, everlasting life on earth ran counter to Christian teachings. But eternal life *after* death was a solemn promise made by the Church itself, an authority that was not easy to reject. That promise embodied a duality of reward and punishment: the devout went to Heaven and the unworthy went to Hell.

Over the long centuries, a sense of familiarity with both Satan and the minions of Heaven slowly evolved, a familiarity nurtured by the frequence of their visits. And, as with all other types of Irish folk humor, the "familiar" became a legitimate target for homespun jokes, and, later, for the most sophisticated of wit and humor. One example is this philosophical view of life without end, by Patrick Ireland:

"Immortality"

> A toy which people cry for,
> And on their knees apply for,
> Dispute, contend and lie for,
> and if allowed
> would be right proud
> Eternally to die for.

Irish-American humor differs from that of the Emerald Isle in that it is often more trenchant, more contemporary, and certainly more irreverent.

Consider the following dialogue, popular in San Francisco at the turn of the century:

PARISHIONER: Is there really a Heaven, Father?

PRIEST: Indade there is, me son.

PARISHIONER: But how do you *know?*

PRIEST: Sure and didn't the Pope say so his very own self?

PARISHIONER: Yes, but how can *he* be so sure?

PRIEST: Faith, sor, would ye be afther questionin' the Pope?

PARISHIONER: Oh, no, Father! I wouldn't dream of it!

PRIEST: Well, then, there ye be! There's a Heaven!

Exactly what and where is this place called Heaven? In the United States, it is said, "Ireland must be Heaven 'cause me mother came from there." This geographical and somewhat personal observation does not satisfy those who are already in Ireland, or whose mother came from Toronto. Here, then, is the official explanation according to Saint John the Barleycorn, not to be confused with the better known Saint John who won fame for communing with grasshoppers and baptizing Important People.

Heaven is where all the devout, dead Irish Catholics live. As a reward for having experienced an earthly life of abstinence, penance, and acceptance of guilt for Original Sin, the good Catholic is presented with wings, a harp, and a decent apartment looking down on Galway Bay. The poor Protestant, however, not being acceptable in Heaven, must suffer throughout eternity in Hell, where he has nothing to comfort him but wine, whiskey, and wild women. This inequitable division of punishment often makes a Catholic weep.

It is Saint Peter's duty to guard the Pearly Gates, his primary function being to refuse admittance to undesirables and thus preserve neighborhood values. The Gates are located at the southeast corner of the Kingdom, situated precisely 934-1/4 miles above Cincinnati. The northeast corner is known as Oblivion, where authors renew acquaintance with their works.

As a surprise to no one, there is a healthy degree of imbibing going on Up There, with the preference running slightly to nectar. Nectar is a drink served at banquets of the Olympian gods, as opposed to whiskey, which is preferred by Irish Catholics. The secret of nectar's preparation is lost, but the *poteen* distillers of Ireland believe that they know its chief ingredient. When an Irish angel feels the urge to down a few nectars—usually when the whiskey keg is dry—he waits until after dark to sneak into the Greek Orthodox quarter of Heaven. There, across the tracks from Heaven proper, which is 98.3 per cent Irish, he joins other patrons at the Mt. Olympus Bar and Grill, in some joyous singing:[1]

---

[1] Irish Catholics and Irish Protestants share a common virtue: they love their mothers (one each, as of this writing). The Catholics, who are all tenors, sing such sentimental songs as "Mother Machree," although it is well known that the original Mother Machree was a toothless, profane old harridan who pushed a cart through the streets, crying, "Cockels—*dammit!*—mussels—*dammit!*—alive, alive-o *dammit!*" Irish Protestants, on the other hand, are all baritones, and notoriously poor singers who like such songs as "When You Were Eight and I Was Eight, and We Were Sweet Sixteen." They are very good at arithmetic.

Juno drank a cup of nectar,
But the draught did not affect her.
Juno drank a cup of rye—
Then she bade herself good-bye.[2]

Those who take their own lives are not permitted entry into Heaven, according to Saint Patrick. But we can only hope that the Creator, in his infinite compassion, made an exception in the case of the late lamented Rory McCord. Rory, in collaboration with a female genius named Maggie Sweeney, was writing a serialized story for the *Irish Weekly,* of Dublin. They wrote not jointly, but alternately, with Rory supplying the chapter for one week, and Maggie for the next, and so on, world without end, they hoped. Unfortunately, they quarreled over whose turn it was to buy the week's supply of Guinness Stout—and on Monday morning when Rory read the paper to prepare himself for his task, he found his work cut out for him in a way to surprise and pain him. Maggie Sweeney had embarked every character of the narrative on a ship and sunk them all in the deepest part of the Irish Sea. Maggie later became a nun, thus assuring herself of a front-row seat in Heaven, while poor Rory McCord's post mortem whereabouts must forever be shrouded in uncertainty.

According to the Celtic sages of old, death is God's way of effecting an involuntary change of environment. The new locations are Heaven, as we have noted, and Hell. Hell, or Hades, is where the Devil presides over deceased felons, assorted spalpeens, white slavers, and Congressmen. This is the abode of Cerberus, watchdog of Hades, whose duty it is to guard the entrance—against whom or what is not clear, no one ever having tried to steal the entrance or sneak past it. Cerberus, not an Irish terrier according to the aforementioned Saint John the Barleycorn, is known to have had three heads. Some Irish bards have credited him with having as many as a hundred. Professor MacIntosh Appel, of the Belfast Home for Dublin Refugees, has averaged all the estimates and arrived at a figure of twenty-seven—a judgment that would be entirely conclusive if Professor Appel had known [a] something about dogs, and [b] something about arithmetic.

When we speak of Satan we refer to one of the Creator's lamentable mistakes, a fact that is conceded by devout Irish Catholics who agree that while the Pope is infallible, God is not. Satan, having been instated as an archangel, made himself multifariously objectionable and was finally dispossessed by the Great Landlord in the Sky.

The selections that follow represent the newer witticims of Irish-Americans as well as the folk classics of old Ireland. But whether they emanated from the United States or from the Emerald Isle, each belongs to the same people, and is joyously colored green.

—H.D.S.

---

[2]Attributed to Saint John the Barleycorn, but who made the attibution has not come down to us.

"No Marriages in Heaven"

> Cries Celia to a reverend dean,
> "What reason can be given,
> Since marriage is a holy thing,
> That there are none in heaven?"
>
> "There are no women," he replied.
> She quick returns the jest:
> "Women there are, but I'm afraid
> They cannot find a priest!"

＊

In Belfast, a man was hanged by the neck until he was dead. The year was 1913.

"Whence do you come?" Saint Peter asked when the man presented himself at the gate of heaven.

"From Belfast," replied the applicant.

"Enter, my son, enter; you bring joyous tidings."

When the man had vanished inside, Saint Peter took his memorandum tablet and made the following entry:

"February 2, 1913. Ulster settled by the Christians."[3]

＊

For over a thousand years, the fence between Heaven and Hell had needed mending, and Saint Patrick, chief fence-fixer for the Paradise Development Corporation, was in a perfect dither. It seems that the Hell side of the fence needed more repairs than the Heaven side. Exasperated to the point of Christian endurance, he finally confronted Satan with an ultimatum:

"Now see here, Sate owld b'y, you mend that fence at wance, or I'll sue!"

"Sue me, will you now, Pat?" replied the Devil with a confident grin.

"Well, go ahead then. But considerin' your neighborhood, where would you be findin' a lawyer?"

＊

It was a beautiful, sunny afternoon and Malone was alone in the mountains, on a fishing trip. Spotting a likely trout stream, he wandered too close to the edge of a cliff. He slipped off, but managed to grab the root of a small tree. Clinging to his precarious hold, just a few feet from the rim, and with the vast chasm yawning below, he raised his eyes to Heaven and prayed loud and mightily:

"Oh, dear Lord, help me! Help me or I will fall to my death!"

---

[3]If the reader happens to be an Irish Protestant, the scene may be shifted to Dublin for his or her spiritual convenience.

"All right, my son, I will help you," responded an eerie, faraway Voice from beyond a cloud. "But first I must ask you a question. Do you have perfect faith in me?"

"Oh yes, Lord, I do, I do!"

"Very well, my son," the Voice said reassuringly, "just let go of the tree root."

Malone, clutching the root in a viselike grip, looked down the length of the huge precipice, and then up into the blue skies. "Listen," he yelled, "is there anyone else up there who can help?"

*

"Well, whaddya know—the doctors were right for a change!" declared the newly-arrived angel as Saint Peter handed him a harp. "They said I'd be out of the hospital in a week!"

*

After the death of John McCormack, the eminent singer, he was said to have ascended to Heaven. There, he bustled about and made a general nuisance of himself by demanding that he be entrusted with some major responsibilities. Wearily, the higher powers finally acquiesced and sent Saint Peter to offer him a position befitting his lofty attainments during his earthly existence.

"John, I have good news for you," began Saint Peter. "I have been authorized by the Boss—all three of Him, in fact—to tell you that you will be permitted to train a celestial choir to replace the old one. It seems that it's gone a little stale."

"Now that's more like it, Pete!" enthused McCormack. "First, I'll need ten thousand sopranos; next ten thousand contraltos; then, ten thousand basses. And hurry—hurry! You're holding up the works!"

"All right," agreed Saint Peter, awed by the mighty order. "But won't you also be needing ten thousand tenors?"

McCormack fixed him with a scornful glare: *"I'll* sing tenor!"

*

My Father, the Jug!

Hark to the tale of how *two* persons were delivered from Purgatory for only one modest fee.

Mr. Darby M'Keown once had a most ardent attachment to a certain Biddy Finn, and, at last, through the intervention of Father Curtain, agreed to marry her.

Darby's consent to the arrangements was not altogether the result of the good Father's eloquence, nor was it quite owing to Biddy's black eyes and pretty lips—but, rather, to the soul-persuading powers of some fourteen tumblers of strong drink which he consumed at Biddy's father's house one cold evening in November. After that, he betook himself to the road homeward, where....But we must give the story in his own words:

"Whether it was the prospect of happiness before me, or the *poteen*," quoth Darby, "I niver felt a step iv the road home that night, though 'twas ivery foot of five miles. When I came to a stile I'd give a whoop, and over it; then I'd run a hundred yards or two, flourish my stick, cry out, 'Who'll say a word against Biddy Finn?' and then over anither fence, flying. Well, I reached home at last, and wet enough I was, but I didn't care about that. I opened the door and struck a light; there was the least taste of kindling on the hearth, and I put some dry sticks into it, and some turf, and knelt down and began blowing it up.

" 'Troth,' says I to myself, 'if I wor married, it isn't this way I'd be on my knees like a nagur, but when I'd come home there'd be a fine fire a'blazin' fornint me, and a clean table out before it, and a beautiful cup o' tay waiting for me—and somebody I won't mention sitting there looking at me, smilin'.'

"Suddenly, I heard a gruff voice from near the chimney: 'Don't be making a fool of yourself, Darby M'Keown!'

"I jumped to my feet and cried out, 'Who's that?' But there was no answer, and, at last, after going around in the kitchen, I began to think it was only my own voice I'd heard. So I knelt down again and set to blowing away at the fire.

" 'And it's yourself Biddy,' says I, 'that would be an ornament to a dacent cabin, and a purtier leg and foot...'

" 'Be the light that shines, you're making me sick, Darby M'Keown!' said the voice again.

" 'The heavens be about us!' says I. 'What's that, and who are you at all?'...For somehow I thought I knew that voice.

" 'I'm your father,' says the voice.

" 'My father!' says I. 'Holy Joseph, is it the truth you're telling me?'

" 'The divil a word o' lie in it,' says the voice. 'Take me down and give me an air o' the fire, for the night's cowld.'

" 'And where are you, Father?' says I. 'Av it's plasing to ye.'

" 'I'm on the dhresser,' says he. 'Don't you see me?'

" 'Sorra bit o' me. Where now?'

" '*Arrah,* on the second shelf, next to the rowling pin. Don't you see the green jug?—That's me.'

" 'Oh, the saints in Heaven be above us!' says I. 'And you a green jug?'

" 'I am,' says he, 'and sure I might be worse. Tim Healey's mother is only a cullender, and she died two years before me.'

" 'Oh, Father darlin', I hoped you were in glory,' says I, 'and you only a jug all this time.'

" 'Never fret about it,' says my father. 'It's ownly the transmogrification of sowls, and we'll be all right by-and-by. Take me down, I say, and put me near the fire.'

"So I up and took him down and wiped him with a clean cloth, and put him on the hearth before the blaze.

" 'Darby,' says he, 'I'm famished with the drouth. Since you took to coortin', there's nothing ever goes into my mouth. Haven't you a taste of something in the house?'

"It warn't long till I heated some wather and took down the bottle of whiskey and some sugar, and made a rousing jug-full, as strong as need be.

" 'Are you satisfied, Father?' says I.

" 'That I am,' says he. 'You're a dutiful son—and here's your health, and don't be thinking of Biddy Finn.'

"With that, my father began to explain how there was never any rest or quietness for a man after he married—less so if his wife was fond of talking, and that he never could take his dhrop of drink in comfort afterward.

" 'May I never,' says he, 'but I'd rather be a green jug, as I am now, than alive again with your mother. Sure it's not here you'd be sitting tonight,' says he, 'discoorsing with me, av you were married; divil a bit. Fill me,' says my father, 'and I'll tell you more.'

"And sure enough I did and he did, and we talked away till near daylight; and then the first thing I did was to take the ould mare out iv the stable and set off to Father Curtain, and towled him all about it, and how my father wouldn't give his consent.

" 'We'll not mind the marriage,' says his riverence, 'but go back and bring me your father—the jug, I mane—and we'll try to get him out of trouble—for it's trouble he's in, or he wouldn't be that way. Give me the two-pound-ten you had for the wedding,' says the priest. 'It will be better spent getting your father out of Purgatory than sending you into it.'

"And that is how my father, the green whiskey jug, and myself were rescued from Purgatory. And when Father Curtain sobers up, sure he'll vouch for every word I've said."

—Anonymous, from the Old Irish

*

The High Cost of Getting the Hell Out of Purgatory

Have you heard of the way Mickey Free's father—rest his soul wherever he is—came to his end? Well, you needn't mind the particulars: he was murdered in Ballinsloe one night, and a very agreeable wake was had by all, excepting the deceased. After he was put away, Mickey thought it was all over, but somehow, though he paid Father Roach fifteen shillings, and made him mighty drunk, he always gave the bereaved son a black look whenever they met.

One day, however, Mickey was coming home from Athlone market when Father Roach overtook him.

"Mickey," said he in a cold voice, "if you ownly knew what I know, you'd be thremblin' in your skin this very minute."

"Know what?" asked Mickey.

"I saw your father last night."

"The saints be merciful to us! Did ye now?"

"I did," said Father Roach.

"Tear-an'-ages!" said Mickey. "Did he tell you what he did with the corduroys he bought at the fair?"

"Mickey, you are a cowld-hearted crayture," said the priest, "and I'll not lose time with you." With that, he started to leave, but Mickey took hold of his arm.

"Father, darlint," said he, "God pardon me, but them britches is standin' twixt me and my night's rest. Tell me all about my father."

"The poor sowl is in a melancholy state."

"Whereabouts is he?" inquired Mickey.

"In Purgathory," said the priest, "but he won't be there long."

"Well, that's a comfort, anyhow."

"I'm glad you think so, but there's more of the other opinion."

"What other opinion?"

"That Hell's worse."

"Murther!" exclaimed Mickey Free. "Is that it?"

"Aye, that's it."

Mickey was so frightened he could not speak a word for some time. Finally, he said: "Father, how long will it be before they send him to you-know-where?"

"It will not be long now," said Father Roach. "They're tired with him entirely; they've had no peace night or day. Mickey, your father is a mighty hard man. Sure it's a great disgrace to a dacent family."

"Troth, it is," agreed Mickey, "but my father always liked low company. Could nothing be done for him now?"

"That depends upon yourself, my boy, and may God pardon you for it, too."

"It depends upon *me*?"

"Troth, no less," answered the priest. "How many masses was said for your father's sowl? How many *aves*? How many *paters*? Answer me!"

"Divil a wan knows! Maybe twenty."

"Twenty? *Twenty*, you say? No, not a wan!"

"And why not?" asked Mickey crossly. "Why would *you* not be helping a poor crayture out of throuble when it wouldn't cost you but a handful of prayers?"

"Mickey," said the priest in a solemn tone, "you're worse than a haythen, but ye couldn't be other; ye never could come to yer duties."

"Well, Father," said Mickey, looking very peninent, "how many masses would get him out?"

"Now you're talking like a sensible man! I've hopes for you, Mickey. Now let me see," Father Roach said, counting on his fingers and adding up numbers to himself for five minutes. "I have a batch of sowls coming out of Purgathory on Chuesday this week, and if you were to make great exertions, perhaps your father would come with them; that is, if they make no objections."

"And why would they?" demanded Mickey, indignantly defending his father's reputation. "He was always the hoith of company, and if singing's allowed in them parts . . ."

"God forgive you," interrupted Father Roach with a sigh, "but you're in a benighted state."

"Well, how'll we get him out?" asked Mickey, bringing the problem into focus.

"Two masses in the morning, fasting," said Father Roach half aloud, "—that's two. And two in the afternoon—that's four. And two at vespers is six. Six masses a day for nine days is close to sixty masses—let's say sixty. They'll cost you—mind, Mickey, and don't be telling it again: it's only for yourself I'd make them so cheap—a matter of three pounds."

"*Three pounds?*" shouted Mickey. "Begorra, ye might as well ax me to give you the rock of Cashel!"

"I'm sorry for you, my son," said Father Roach, gathering himself to leave, "and the day will come when the neglect of vour poor father will be a poor stroke agin yourself."

"Wait a bit, Your Reverence," said Mickey hastily. "Would forty shillings get him out?"

"Of coorse not."

"Maybe," suggested Mickey, "if you said that his son was a poor boy that lived by his industhry, and times was bad...?"

"Not the least use."

Mickey's private thought was that they were hardhearted indeed, but aloud he said, "All right, I'll give you the money, but I can't afford it all at wanst. I'll pay five shillings a week. Will that do?"

"I'll make my endayvors," promised Father Roach, "and I'll spake to them to trate him kindly in the mayntime."

"Long life to Your Reverence, and do. Here now, here's five to begin with. *Musha,* but I never thought I'd be spending my loose change like this."

Father Roach put the money into the pocket of his leather breeches, said something in Latin for God's benefit, bid Mickey good morning, and went off.

Mickey thereafter worked late and early to pay the five shillings a week—for three weeks. Then he brought four and fourpence; then, it came down to one and tenpence halfpenny; then ninepence; and, at last, he had nothing at all to bring.

"Mickey Free," said the priest, "you must stir yourself. Your father is mighty displeased at the way you've been doing of late. If you'd kept your word, he'd be near out by this time."

"Troth," said Mickey, "it's a very expensive place."

"Of coorse it is," agreed Father Roach, "and that's becase all the quality land is there. But, Mickey, my man, with a little exertion your father's business is done. What are you jingling in your pocket there?"

"It's ten shillings, Your Reverence. I have to buy seed potatoes."

"Hand it here, my son. Isn't it better your father be enjoying himself in Paradise, than you were to have all the potatoes in Ireland?"

"And how do you know he is so near out?"

"How do I know, is it? Didn't I see him?"

"See him! Tear-an'-ages, was you down there again?"

"I was," said the priest. "I was down there for three-quarters of an hour yesterday evening, getting Luke Kennedy's mother out—daycent people the Kennedys—never spared expense."

"And you saw my father?"

"That I did. He had an owld flannel waistcoat on, and a pipe sticking out of the waistcoat's pocket."

"That's him. Did he speak to you?"

"He did," affirmed Father Roach. "He spoke very hard about the way he was treated down there, complaining that they was always jibing and jeering him about drinking and fighting, and the coorse he led up here, and that how quare it was that for the matter of ownly ten shillings he was to be kept there so long."

Mickey took the ten shillings out of his pocket, counted it deliberately and painfully, and then handed it over to the priest. "Well, we must do our best," he sighed. "You think this'll get him out of Purgathory surely?"

"I know it will, an' I'll tell you why I am sure. When Luke's mother was leaving the place, your father saw the door open and he made a rush at it. Begorra, before it was shut he got his head and one shoulder outside of it, so that, you see, a trifle more will do the trick."

Without warning, Mickey made a sudden lunge and snatched back the money he had just given the priest. "Faith, Your Reverence, you've lightened my heart this morning," he said, returning the ten shillings to his own pocket.

"What do you mean?" asked the startled and angry priest.

"Just this," announced Mickey. "I know my own father. If it was him you saw, and he got his head and a shoulder outside the door, then, by the powers, the divil, a jail, or jailor from Hell to Connaught'd hold him!"

—Anonymous, from the Old Irish

*

"Irish Astronomy"

(A Celtic legend, touching on the Constellation of O'Ryan, ignorantly and falsely spelled "Orion.")

O'Ryan was a man of might
    Whin Ireland was a nation,
But poachin' was his chief delight
    And constant occupation.
He had an ould militia gun,
    And sartin sure his aim was;
He gave the keepers many a run,
    And didn't mind the game laws.

St. Pathrick wanst was passin' by
    O'Ryan's little houldin',
And as the Saint felt wake and dhry,
    He thought he'd enther bould in;
"O'Ryan," says the Saint, "*avick!*
    To praich at Thurles I'm goin';
So let me have a rasher, quick,
    And a dhrop of Innishowen."

"No rasher will I cook for you
 While betther is to spare, sir;
But here's a jug of mountain dew,
 And there's a rattlin' hare, sir."
St. Pathrick he looked mighty sweet,
 And says he, "Good luck attind you,
And whin you're in your windin' sheet
 It's up to heaven I'll sind you."

O'Ryan gave his pipe a whiff—
 "Thim tidin's is thransportin',
But may I ax your saintship if
 There's any kind of sportin'?"
St. Pathrick said, "A Lion's there,
 Two Bears, a Bull and Cancer"—
"Bedad," says Mick, "the huntin's rare,
 St. Pathrick, I'm your man, sir!"

So, to conclude my song aright,
 For fear I'd tire your patience,
You'll see O'Ryan any night
 Amid the constellations.
And Venus follows in his thrack,
 Till Mars grows jealous raally,
But, faith, he fears the Irish knack
 Of handling the—shillaly.

     —Charles Graham Halpine (1829-68)

    *

When Adam ivry blessed day
 woke up in Paradise,
He'd thank the Lord and then he'd say,
 "This place, indade, is nice."

But Eve, from Eden's lovely bliss
 Thransported him fer life.
The more me thoughts remain on this,
 The more I bate me wife.

     —Patrick Ireland

Chapter Fourteen

Steeple People

Introduction

Ireland is the land of faith, Catholicism's only English-speaking nation, and the most devoutly Catholic country in the modern world. It has produced more priests and nuns per capita than any other country on earth. Its religion (Ireland is almost 95 per cent Catholic), has played a vital role in the nation's political history, with the Catholics fighting Protestant ascendancy, tooth, nail, and shillelagh.

When we speak of Ireland's religion, we must begin with Saint Patrick: ex-slave, shepherd, scholar, and one of the most successful missionaries in history. Patrick was born in 385,[1] in Britain. Captured when barely sixteen by Irish marauders, he was enslaved and assigned work as a herdsman on the slopes of Slemish, near Ballymena, Antrim County, or of Croagh-patrick (and probably both). Six years later, in response to a "Voice," he escaped, to wander throughout Europe, eventually entering the monastery at Lérins where he was ordained.

He had not yet reached age thirty when he returned to his native Britain where he again heard the "Voice," this time in a vision, calling him to return to Ireland and Christianize its people. Accordingly, in 419, to prepare himself for his mission, he retraced his steps to the continent where, for the next twelve years, he studied at Auxere.

In the year 431, Saint Palladius, the first missionary bishop sent to Ireland, died, and Patrick was consecrated as his successor in 432. In the spring of that year he journeyed to Tara and gained his first major converts. There, he boldly defied the entrenched pagan priests by kindling the Easter fire on Slane, a nearby hill. This challenge to paganism, in the face of what could have resulted in his death by the pagan leaders, eventually had an opposite effect. Initial indignation in the court of the high king gave way to admiration and respect for this courageous and dedicated man. Tara became Patrick's headquarters and, with a band of followers, he

---

[1] Many, though not all, of the dates associated with Saint Patrick and the events surrounding his ministry are approximate, varying, on the average, from one to four years.

successively converted Meath, Leitrim, Cavan, and West Ireland. In 444, with the approval of Pope Leo I, Patrick established his archiepiscopal see at Armagh.

Saint Patrick's mission was most successful: Ireland was almost entirely Christian by the time of his death. He understood and wisely preserved the country's social structure, converting the people tribe by tribe. He introduced the Roman alphabet, and, at his insistence, the traditional laws of Ireland were codified and the harsher ones mitigated, particularly those that dealt with slavery and taxation of the poor. In 457 he retired to Saul, where, four years later, he died. He was buried in Downpatrick, which was a great European shrine until its destruction by the English government in 1539.

Saint Patrick is remembered by the Irish as the architect of the Catholic Church in Ireland, and also for his engaging personality. He was a man of warmth and deep understanding of the people's strengths as well as their frailties. He could, and would, share a drink with them, and convert them the next day. He possessed a lively sense of humor and enjoyed a good joke as well as any of his followers. Small wonder, then, that a body of humorous literature has been created about him, for he is recalled with earthy affection as well as reverence.

The next ten centuries following the death of Saint Patrick saw the land of the shamrock at its zenith, despite the incursion of the Norsemen who eventually left, and, two hundred years later, the Normans, who were gradually absorbed by the native population, to become "more Irish than the Irish." During those thousand years, the monastery became the center of Ireland's cultural as well as religious life. Several of its monasteries served as universities, and such was their fame that they drew the elite of students from England and the continent, many of them leaving Ireland as missionaries. One of them was Saint Columba who, in 563, became the Saint Patrick of Scotland.

The "troubles" began when Henry II of England became ruler of Ireland. For the first three centuries, the Church was only slightly affected. But in the fourteenth century, a dark omen of what was to befall the Irish people occurred: the Statutes of Kilkenny were invoked, prohibiting priests within the Pale from entering English Catholic churches.[2] Then, 150 years later, came the Reformation, which resulted in the formation of the various Protestant faiths. Among them was the Church of England, established by Henry VIII. He dissolved the Irish monasteries, expropriated their lands, and declared himself head of the Anglican Church in Ireland. But the Irish balked. Centuries of pent-up Gaelic anger exploded. It was no longer Englishman versus Irishman; it was now Protestant versus Catholic.

Events were to take another turn for the worse. Irishmen were excluded from any participation in civic affairs by the penal codes. Scottish Presbyterian settlers were planted by the British in Ulster and took root there. Thus, two permanent and sharply antagonistic communities were established on Irish soil.

---

[2] The Pale designated the area which included Dublin and its environs, in which the English could enforce their edicts by military power.

But it was the actions of two English queens that helped solidify the opposing religious factions. Queen Mary, oldest daughter of Henry VII, who detested her father, turned England back to Catholicism. "Bloody Mary," as she was called, began a reign of such devastating terror against the Protestants, burning so many of them at the stake, that she engendered in the British people a consummate hatred for all things Catholic. When Elizabeth, Mary's half-sister and daughter of Henry VIII and Anne Boleyn, ascended the throne, destiny intervened to widen the breach between Protestant England and Catholic Ireland. Spain sent its ill-fated armada against England, and Pope Pius V excommunicated Elizabeth. Patriotism was running high among the English at the defeat of Catholic Spain's fleet, and the Pope's action against Elizabeth combined to enflame their fervor. In Ireland, the two events deepened the loyalty of the Catholic populace to their Church. "Irish history, till then fluid, ran into a mold where it hardened for three hundred years," said the British historian, Trevelyan. "The native population conceived a novel enthusiasm for the Roman religion, which they identified with a passionate hatred of the English."

Thus a stand was taken by the Gaels; one that was not to be resolved for centuries: an agonizingly long period which saw their people humbled and impoverished, their lands confiscated and untold thousands of their people slain. But through it all, the oppressed Catholic population never wavered in their fealty to the Church.

The Irish Catholic immigrants to America found themselves in a strange land whose people viewed them with curiosity, and some fear. These new arrivals, for the most part, were ordinary country people who had lived in the circumscribed routines of farm and village, for whom a ten-mile trip was a long journey. They never realized there was anything unique about their religious affiliation or their devotion. Going to church and partaking of the sacraments was as natural and expected a part of life as milking the cow or gathering the hay. Only later, in America, did this become distinctive, a fact to reflect upon and boast about, a source of national chauvinism. Ironically, they fled from persecution in 95 per cent Catholic Ireland to find sanctuary in predominantly Protestant America. A further irony is that the United States, settled mainly by dissenters, was itself a product of the Reformation.

In the United States, however, antagonism between Catholics and Protestants was based more on economics and politics, rather than on religious differences alone. It resulted from a double-pronged fear: fear of Catholic competition for jobs, and fear of Catholic numbers at the polling booths. Moreover, discrimination in pre-Republic Ireland was a policy of State; in America it was expressly forbidden by the Bill of Rights. So it was that, despite early bigotry and ignorant fears, Irish Catholism flourished; not only because of the unswerving allegiance of its followers, but also because of the dedication of the cadre who led them: prelates who fought for the betterment of their flocks and, in so doing, for the betterment of all Americans.

Considering the historic Catholic versus Protestant controversies of the past, and, regrettably, still rife in the Irish Republic-Ulster violence, it comes as somewhat of a surprise that the best of Irish humor contains few interfaith jokes. This is especially true of the classic humorous anecdotes and poems of the pre-Yeats centuries in Ireland; but that should not prove too startling, since many of the authors were Protestants.

"God always writes straight, but in crooked lines," cautioned Saint Augustine. Irish-American humorists seem to have taken the admonition to heart; their humor is more trenchant and satirical than that of their counterparts in the Emerald Isle. Patrick Ireland, for example, tells us that "...a good Catholic is one who believes that the Bible is a divinely inspired book admirably suited to the spiritual needs of Protestants, and those who follow the teachings of the Church insofar as they do not overly interfere with the simple pleasures of life."

"A cardinal," we learned *sotto voce* from the late Bing Crosby, "is an ecclesiastical dignitary who is one point holier than a bishop." And Keith Preston warns of the dangers of mixed marriages with this poem:

> A Protestant married a devout Catholic wife,
> And she led him a *cat*achism and *dog*ma life.

Ambrose Bierce gave his fellow Irish-Americans this definition to end all definitions: "Confession is the acknowledgment made to a priest of a sinful act committed by a friend, neighbor, or acquaintance, and to which you reacted with righteous indignation. Mortal sins are those made by Satan who entered your subconsciousness without your prior knowledge or approval, and therefore subject to lighter and more agreeable acts of penance; such as a mandatory ten-day observance of the rhythm method."

But now let us see what some of our Irish ancestors were up to, and catch a glimpse of a few contemporary shenanigans in Irish America.

—H.D.S.

"The Friar of Orders Gray"

> I am a friar of orders gray:
> As down in the valley I take my way
>   I pull not blackberry, haw,* or hip,†
>   Good store of venison does fill my script:
>   My long beadroll I merrily chant
>   Where'er I walk, no money I want;
> And why I'm so plump the reason I'll tell—
> Who leads a good life is sure to live well.
>   What baron or squire
>   Or knight of the shire
> Lives half so well as a holy friar!
>
> After supper, of Heaven I dream,
> But that is fat pullet and clouted cream.

---

*The fruit of the Old World hawthorn.
†The ripe fruit of a rose.

Myself, by denial, I mortify
With a dainty bit of warden pie; ††
I'm clothed in sackcloth for my sin:
With old sack wine I'm lined within:
A chirping bird is my matin** song,
And the vesper bell is my bowl's ding-dong.
What baron or squire
Or knight of the shire
Lives half so well as a holy friar!

—John O'Keefe (1747-1833)

*

An Irish priest emigrated to Australia, where the bishop gave him the serviceable gift of a horse. In appreciation, the young father named it after the donor, and "Saddle the Bishop," or "Feed the Bishop," and so forth, became familiar phrases in his household.

A short time later, the children of the parochial schools were ready for confirmation, and a day was announced by the diocesan to confer this sacrament of the Catholic Church upon them. The priest, who was the soul of hospitality, invited the most important officials in the district to meet the prelate at dinner after the ceremony. It was a hot day in the Australian township, and, just as the distinguished company sat down for dinner, the door slowly opened and the priest's groom poked his head into the room.

"Might I have a word with Your Reverence?" he asked in a voice loud enough for all to hear.

"Not now," replied the embarrassed priest. "I'll talk to you after dinner. Can't you see I'm with the prelate?"

The prelate, however, considerately protested that the groom be heard on the spot.

"Well, all right," agreed the father, relieved. "What is it?"

"Sir, it's such a terribly hot day," explained the groom, "I thought I'd throw a bucket of water on the bishop, but somehow he wandered into the back kitchen and—excuse me, Your Reverence—the bishop did something horrid on the floor!"

*

Father McCloud of St. Andrew's, a very poor church, was suffering even more financial difficulties than usual. His appeals to his bishop grew more frequent and more urgent. The bishop, losing patience, finally sent a curt note to the priest, scolding him for making so many heart-rending appeals which, he was sure, were exaggerated.

Not long after his rather stern letter, the bishop received a telegram from Father McCloud which called for immediate action:

"This is not an appeal; it is a report. I have no pants!"

---

††Pie made with a pear filling.
**The first of the seven canonical hours; also called "morning prayer."

*

Cardinal Richard Cushing enjoyed telling of the time, in the early days of his priesthood, when his tongue ran ahead of his mind. He had lost the sermon on which he had labored for a week, and reluctantly told his congregation:

"I hope you will excuse my carelessness, but I seem to have misplaced my sermon. However, I will just speak as the Lord commands. And next Sunday I will try to do a little better!"

*

A clergyman was making the rounds of his country parish in the south of Ireland when he met a farmer, a stranger to him.

"If ye plase, Yer Riverince, would ye mind prayin' for a wee dhrop o' rain next Sunday? Sorra thing'll grow in me little garden with this turble hate iv the weather."

"Are you from this neighborhood?" asked the Saviour's representative.

"I'm from the next county."

"The next county, is it? Then why don't you ask your own priest?"

"Faith, an' that's just it!" complained the visitor. "What's the good iv axin' him to pray fer rain with the hay standin' foot-high on his own lawn?"

*

It happened in Lowell, Massachusetts, when Cardinal Terence Cooke encountered an ex-priest who shamelessly heckled him during a speech he was making.

"Sir," Cardinal Cooke finally asked when he could no longer ignore the frequent interruptions, "would you mind telling my why you left the priesthood?"

"I have seven good reasons," snapped the heckler.

"Well, what's the first one?" the cardinal demanded.

"The first reason is that I was kicked out."

"Never mind the other six," interjected Cardinal Cooke. "They don't really matter!"

*

Hark to a considerate priest: "I like to go fishing on a Sunday—after church, of course," said Father Kelly. "But I never wear my priestly garb: I wouldn't want to take advantage of the fish."

*

The will of Stephen Girard, endowing Girard College in Philadelphia, prohibits priests and other clergymen from entering the premises.

The Irish poet, Padraic Deever, who usually wore a flowing black cape, approached the campus in his customary, somewhat priestly-looking garb, and sought to enter the gate.

"Hey, you!" the gatekeeper challenged in a rude voice. "You can't enter here."

"The hell I can't!" retorted Deever.

"I beg your pardon, sir," replied the guard in respectfully altered tones. "Pass right in."

*

"The Spalpeen's New Decalogue"

Have but one God: thy knees were sore
If bent in prayer to three or four.

Adore no images save those
The coinage of thy country shows.

Take not the Name in vain. Direct
Thy swearing unto some effect.

Thy hand from Sunday work be held—
Work not at all unless compelled.

Honor thy parents, and perchance
Their will thy fortunes may advance.

Kill not—death liberates thy foe
From persecution's constant woe.

Kiss not thy neighbor's wife. Of course
There's no objection to divorce.

To steal were folly, for 'tis plain
In cheating there is greater gain.

Bear not false witness. Shake your head
And say that you have "heard it said."

Who stays to covet ne'er will catch
An opportunity to snatch.

—Ambrose Bierce (1842-?)[1]

*

"I'm afraid I was not as modest in my youth as I should have been," commented Cardinal Richard Cushing, reminiscing about his early days as a young priest. "But I lost my conceit just a year or two after I was ordained. I was asked to speak at a fund-raising dinner for our church one evening, but because of a bad cold I was forced to cancel the engagement.

---

[1] Ambrose Bierce disappeared in Mexico in 1913, and was not seen or heard from again.

Meanwhile, John O'Connor, the committee chairman, who was also one of my parishioners, was called on to say grace at the dinner table.

" 'But is there no clergyman present?' he protested.

" 'No, not a one,' said a guest.

" 'In that case,' said Mr. O'Connor, bowing his head, 'let us thank God for this blessing!' "

*

At a social gathering one evening, an Irish priest happened to meet another man of the cloth who introduced himself as Father Cosmo Immaculato of Peru.

The Irish priest acknowledged the introduction with a wide grin.

"Pardon me for smiling, Father," he said, "but you sure have a funny name."

The visitor chuckled good-naturedly. "And what is *your* name, Father?"

"Horatio X. McGilicuddy."

Father Immaculato laughed aloud. "To me, your name is hilarious." he said when he could finally speak. "I suppose your middle initial, *X*, stands for Xavier?"

"No," confessed Father McGilicuddy, now sorry he had mentioned the subject. "Xanadu!"

*

Two clergymen were enjoying a quiet game of poker when the younger of the two broke the news that he had had a "call" to go to another parish.

"Congratulations," said the older man heartily. "How much salary will you be getting?"

"Six hundred dollars a month," was the reply.

"Say, that isn't bad!" exclaimed the other clergyman, laying down his poker hand. "I don't blame you for going. But don't you think you should be more exact in your choice of words and call a spade a spade? That isn't a 'call'—that's a 'raise'!"

*

Applying for a job as keeper at the Bronx Zoo, Patrick came to the question: What is rabies and what can you do about it?

Patrick thought for a moment or two and then wrote:

"Rabies is Jewish priests and you can't do nothing about it!"

*

Father Dennis Quillan of the Church of the Ascension, Resurrection, and Subsequent Miracles was taking a leisurely stroll down the boulevard late one evening when he was stopped by a sweet, little old lady. She was dressed in black taffeta, with a flower-bedecked straw bonnet and high button shoes. His heart immediately went out to the darling, grandmotherly lady who seemed to have stepped out of a nineteenth-century world of cameos, sachets, and lavender and old lace.

"Father, when does the next bus leave?" she asked worriedly.

"I'm sorry," replied Father Quillan gently, "but the last bus left an hour ago."

"Oh, my," sighed the dear, little old lady, "how the hell will I ever get home!"

*

The late Bishop James Pike, the famous exponent of Celtic mysticism, once found himself in London on some Church business. While there, he decided to take in the sights of the city. Strolling down Whitehall, he stopped a passer-by and politely asked, "Sir, on which side is the War Office?"

"Good heavens!" gasped the Londoner. "Ours, I hope!"

*

Father Clendenin of St. Ignatius had just finished a rousing sermon in which he exhorted his parishioners to avoid the 238 mortal sins. The next morning, he found a note in his mailbox from Dudley McGuire, one of his more attentive congregants.

"Father," wrote McGuire, "I'd sure appreciate a list of those 238 sins. I seem to be three short!"

*

When Archbishop Patrick J. Ryan of Philadelphia was a very young priest, he was stationed at a parish in St. Louis. In that city, Archbishop Kendrick presided over the diocese, but he lived in a small unpretentious house that was scarcely in keeping with his importance in the Church.

One day, a Chicago priest who was visiting St. Louis came upon the modest house assigned to the head of the local church. He gave an exclamation of surprise and turned to his companion, Father Ryan.

"Why, you should see the splendid residence we have in Chicago for *our* archbishop!"

"Yes," said Father Ryan, "but you should see the splendid *archbishop* we have in St. Louis for our residence!"

*

The Reverend Alexander Doyle of the Paulist Fathers was a clever speaker and a warm advocate of abstinence, the closure of taverns on Sunday, and a standard of morality that would ensure a glad welcome in Heaven.

Among his listeners was a young country girl new to the parish, who was deeply impressed by Father Doyle's eloquent preaching. Indeed, she was so enthused that she included a few lines about him in her next letter to her mother:

"I never get tired of hearing the sermons in the Paulist Church, mother. Father Doyle is such a lovely and forceful speaker you'd swear that every word he says is true."

*

A new priest in town sought the services of the best local physician, a man seldom seen in church. The medical treatment was prolonged, and the young cleric, worried over the accumulating expense, spoke to the doctor about the matter of his bill.

"I'll tell you what I'll do, Father," said the doctor. "I hear you're a pretty good man in the pulpit and you seem to think I'm a fair doctor. So let's make a deal. I'll do all I can to keep you out of Heaven and you do all you can to keep me out of Hell—and it won't cost either of us a dime!"

*

Shortly before his death, Cardinal Richard Cushing presided at a Church conference. During a heated debate, a member rose and began a tirade against universities and higher education in general.

"I thank God I have never been corrupted by contact with a college," the man concluded.

"Sir," asked the surprised cardinal, "do I understand correctly that you thank God for your ignorance?"

"Well, yes," shouted the man, "if that's the way you want to put it."

"All I can say then," replied the prelate calmly, "is that you have a great deal to thank God for!"

*

A young girl came to the late Father Healy of Cork, and sadly made her confession:

"Father, I fear I've committed the sin of vanity," she announced.

"What makes you think that" asked her father-confessor.

"Because every morning when I look into the mirror, I cannot help but think how beautiful I am."

"Never fear, colleen," was the reassuring reply. "That isn't a sin; it's only a mistake!"

*

Archbishop Patrick Ryan was once accosted on a street in Baltimore by a man who recognized the prelate's face, but could not quite place it.

"Now where in hell have I seen you?" he asked perplexedly.

"I don't know," replied the archbishop. "From where in Hell do you come?"

*

A recently ordained young priest on a fishing trip was delighted to learn that his guide was once hired by Cardinal Terence Cooke. They immediately began talking about him, recalling his many noble traits and characteristics.

"Yes," the guide agreed, "he was a fine man indeed—'cept for his swearin', if you'll forgive me for sayin' so, Father."

"What!" exclaimed the outraged priest. "Bishop Cooke swear? Impossible!"

"Oh, but he did, sir. Once, he hooked a fine big bass. Just as he hoisted it into the boat, the fish slipped clean off the hook. 'Sure, Your Excellency,' I said to the cardinal, 'an' that's a damn shame!' An' the cardinal he came right back an' said 'Yes, it is....'

"But that's the only time I ever heard him use such language!"

*

It is said of the late Cardinal Richard Cushing that he rode a train one day from New York to Providence with a small, meek Jesuit priest. Cardinal Cushing, in those days, was an ardent lover of good tobacco. He took out a cigar case and, with a smile, asked, "You don't mind if I smoke, do you?"

"No, Your Eminence," replied the meek, little cleric humbly, "not if you don't mind my being sick!"

*

"Dear Lord, help us to bend thy laws just enough to avoid unnecessary problems," the illustrious Father McCarthy of Cambridge used to pray—or so he claimed. But you know Father McCarthy! Anyway, here is one of his reminiscences, to be taken with twelve large grains of salt.

After church one Sunday, a young fellow of twenty or so visited him in his study. The good father had performed a marriage ceremony for the youth only recently, and recalled him as a naïve, unsophisticated, but quite likable young man.

"Top o' the mornin' to ye, Dennis. And what can I be doin' for ye this bright and cheery day?"

"Father," Dennis began, his voice troubled, "do you remember marryin' me and Annie?"

"Indade I do! And what of that?"

"Well, she just had a baby."

"Sure and that's the best news I've heard all day. But why the long face? It's rejycin' ye should be."

"I can't rejoice, Father," sighed Dennis. "Isn't a baby supposed to be born at least nine months after the wedding?"

"Indade."

"But you yourself married us only six months ago."

"Now take it aisy, me son," urged Father McCarthy, thinking rapidly. "This often happens to younger Catholics in the case iv the first child. But as sure as me name's McCarthy, all the rest will be nine-month babies!"

*

Father Donohugh was conducting services at St. Joseph's one morning during Easter week, and so beautiful was his sermon on the Resurrection that the worshipers were moved to tears; that is, all but one.

"You must have a heart of stone," sniffed a woman sitting beside the unresponsive man. "Why is it that you did not weep with the rest of us?"

"Beggin' yer pardon, ma'am," he replied, "but I belong to another parish."

*

It was a blistering hot day, exactly 6,751 years ago. Adam and his two sons, Cain and Abel, were trudging across an expanse of burning, arid desert with their meager supply of water slung in goatskins over their backs. All at once, they came upon a lush, verdant oasis—a veritable Paradise filled with fruit trees and gorgeous flowers of every description. Wearily, they sat down to rest and to admire the lovely setting.

"Boys," sighed Adam to his two sons, "this is where your mother ate us out of house and home!"

*

There are very few Negroes in Ireland, and to hear a black woman who recently arrived in the United States from Eire, speaking with a pronounced brogue is a memorable experience. Yet, it has happened.

In Georgia, Timmie O'Rourke came in from the fields, his ebony face shining with the sweat of honest toil. His aged and devout mother took one look at him and cried out in dismay:

"Timmie O'Rourke, now ain't ye ashamed iv yerself—pickin' cotton on Saint Pathrick's Day!"

*

Voice from the boob tube:
"And now, ladies and gentlemen, the makers of Miracle Whip bring you Bishop Sheen!"

*

Mrs. Brown, a Protestant, and her next-door neighbor, Mrs. McGuire, who was Catholic, made it a point to avoid all discussions bearing upon religion—an understanding which undoubtedly helped maintain their friendship. But the day inevitably came when one of them unthinkingly broke the unspoken agreement.

"Oh, Mrs. McGuire," gushed Mrs. Brown, "I heard the brilliant Norman Vincent Peale speak last night. He was wonderful—almost like the Apostle Paul."

Mrs. McGuire glared at her neighbor. "Mrs. Brown," she replied coldly, "while I find Paul appealing, I find Peale appalling!"

*

Not everyone is especially happy about the practice of tithing, as this little complaint, voiced more than one hundred years ago, aptly illustrates.

An honest Hibernian, resentful and suspicious of the clergy for taking a tenth part of the people's wherewithall, moaned:

"Aye! They would take a *twentieth* if they could!"

*

Father O'Flaherty was examining a confirmation class in the south of Ireland one day when he posed the question, "What is the sacrament of matrimony?"

Little Cathy, at the top of her class, waved her hand wildly. The priest nodded: "You may answer, young lady."

"Plaze, Yer Riverence," said Cathy, "the sacrimint iv mathrimony is a state into which sowls enter to prepare them for another and a betther wurrld!"

*

Self-esteem, to a degree, is perfectly acceptable, but it can get out of hand. At St. Mary's Church in Los Angeles, for example, a volunteer cleaning lady, one of the parishioners whose name was Mary Kelly, was alone with her mop and bucket when the telephone rang. After a number of rings, and seeing no one else around, she picked up the receiver.

"St. Mary's Church," she announced cheerfully, "Mary speaking!"

*

The late Father O'Leary, always a staunch defender of doctrine, was well known as a wit. A classic example of his merry tongue (and sharp mind) occurred during a polemical contest he once had with the Reverend Robert Moore, Protestant Bishop of Cloyne.

Prelate Moore, in a pamphlet, inveighed with great acrimony against what he called the superstitions of Popery, and particularly against the doctrine of Purgatory.

"I would remind Bishop Moore," said Father O'Leary in his reply, "that much as he dislikes Purgatory, he might go farther and fare worse!"

*

"Which is the first and most important sacrament?" asked the Sunday School teacher.

"Marriage," avowed Julie, who was preparing for her confirmation.

"No, baptism is the first and most important sacrament," the teacher corrected.

"Not in *our* family," retorted Julie in a haughty voice. "We're *respectable*!"

*

In Philadelphia, Archbishop Patrick J. Ryan numbered this anecdote among his favorites.

The official board of his church had called a meeting to seek a means of raising funds for much-needed repairs. The little church was almost falling apart, and the pastor, having been connected with the parish for twenty years, was stirred by a very real emotion. He issued a moving plea.

Great was his surprise, to say nothing of the astonishment of the members, when the most miserly member of the board rose and offered to start the repair fund with a contribution of five dollars. But, even as he was speaking, a chunk of plaster fell from the old ceiling and struck him on the head.

"Well," said the startled miser, looking heavenward, "I guess I'd better make that twenty-five dollars."

From the back of the hall came a pleading voice:

"Hit the old cheapskate again, Lord!"

*

The young novitiate was recounting her former life to one of the nuns at the convent.

"Before I gave my life to our Lord I was very foolish and vain," she said. "Worldly pleasure, and especially fancy clothes, jewelry, and perfumes were all I thought about. But, when I saw they were dragging me down to perdition, I gave them all to my sister!"

*

Kathleen had just arrived in the United States from Ireland, and immediately found work as a maid at a country estate. The girl was a devout Catholic, and was chagrined to learn that the only church of any kind in the area was a Christian Science temple. Feeling the necessity to worship, however, she at last attended services there. When she returned home she was serene, but a little puzzled.

"Well, Kathleen," asked the lady of the house, "how did you like the Christian Science services?"

"Faith, ma'am, it was mighty quare," averred the daughter of Erin. "I went in and sat down, and afther a toime a man on wan side iv the church got up and towld what Mary Baker Eddy had done for him. Next, a woman in front iv me got up and towld what Mary Baker Eddy had done for her, and it went on and on, until I could not stand it anny longer. So I got up and towld what Lydia E. Pinkham had done for *me*!"

*

The Reverend Edgar DeWitt, arguing with an Irish Catholic prelate, set forth the requirements for a good minister:

"He should get religion like a Methodist, experience it like a Baptist, be sure of it like a Lutheran, pray for it like a Presbyterian, conciliate it like a Congregationalist, glorify it like a Jew, be proud of it like an Episcopalian, and practice it like a Christian Scientist.''

"Yes, a fellow with all those qualities would indeed make a fine man of the cloth,'' agreed the Irishman, grinning. "But to be a priest, he'd need a few more requirements: he'd have to work for his religion like a Salvation Army lassie and enjoy it like a black man.''

"But,'' persisted the Protestant Reverend DeWitt, *"our* minister would have to propagate it like a Roman Catholic. Now top that one!''

*

Some time ago, during the ecumenical era of the late Pope John, a theological tempest in a teapot raged over the issue of whether the mass could be said in Latin or English, among other problems involving fundamentalism and modernism. Francis Cardinal Spellman was reluctantly dragged into the forefront of the controversy.

There is a legend that, at that time, Cardinal Spellman was awakened in the small hours of the morning by the persistent ringing of his telephone. He climbed out of bed and hastened to answer it.

"Hello,'' he mumbled sleepily.

"Ish thish Card'nal Shpellman?'' came a thick voice over the wire.

"Yes, this is Cardinal Spellman,'' he answered, dismayed.

"Card'nal Franshish Shpellman?''

"Yes, yes,'' was the impatient answer. "What is it you want?''

"Card'nal Shpellman, beggin' yer pardon, shir, I wanna know th' diffrensh between fundamentalishm and modernishm.''

"Good heavens, man!'' snapped the exasperated prelate. "That's not something I can explain to you over the telephone; and obviously you're in no condition to understand anyway. Come around to my study tomorrow and I'll be glad to answer your question.''

"But, Father,'' insisted the voice, "I can't wait until t'morra. I gotta know now.''

"Why can't you wait until tomorrow?'' Spellman demanded angrily. "Why do you have to know now?''

"Becaush,'' said the voice patiently, "t'morra I won't give a damn!''

*

A resident of Belfast was visiting Dublin, where he became embroiled in a religious argument with a Roman Catholic.

"Where was your religion before Martin Luther or Henry VIII?'' asked the Dubliner scornfully.

"Let me answer you this way,'' replied the northerner: "did you wash your face this morning?''

"I did.''

"Then tell me, where was your face before it was washed?''

*

The story is told of a worthy old priest who was noted for never giving a direct yes or no answer to a question. It was always, "that depends." His bishop, eager to meet the challenge, decided to present the elderly man with a question that would require a definite reply. He invited the priest to his quarters for dinner and, as they enjoyed an after-meal brandy, he casually asked:

"Father, is it lawful, in the eyes of the Church to baptize with soup?"

"That depends," said the priest to the astounded bishop.

"*Depends? On what,* in the name of Heaven?"

"My dear Bishop," explained the old cleric, "if it were such soup as we just had at your table, doubtless it would be wrong. But, if the baptism was done with the soup served to us poor priests, it might indeed be permissible!"

*

The eminent conductor, Malcolm Sargent, was conducting a Dublin Choral Society rehearsal of *The Messiah*. The men's section was in fine voice, but Sargent was displeased with the rendition given by the women's section of "For Unto Us a Child is Born."

"Ladies, ladies!" he implored, rapping his baton for attention. "Just a little more reverence, please, and not so much astonishment!"

*

The noted agnostic, Colonel Robert Ingersol, and Bishop John Coakley were sharing a drink one evening at a social function when Ingersol's eye fell on a beautiful globe of the world. It portrayed, in full color, the continents, the oceans, and even the constellations with startling reality.

"Say, this is just what I've been looking for!" exclaimed Ingersol delightedly. "Who made it?"

"Why, Colonel nobody made it," echoed Bishop Coakley in well-simulated innocence." "It just happened!"

*

A clergyman, catechizing the young folks of his parish, put the first question from the catechism of Heidelberg to a girl:

"What is your only consolation in life and death?"

The poor girl could manage only a flustered, embarrassed smile.

"Young lady, will you kindly answer the question?" demanded the clergyman sternly.

"Me ownly consolation, Father—fergive me fer sayin' so—is Paddy, the young shoemaker of Galway!"

*

Bishop Carpenter, as well known for his quick wit as his Christian faith, was addressing an open-air meeting in Killarney one day, when an atheist in the audience shouted for attention.

"Yes, what is it?" asked the bishop.

"Do you believe that Jonah was really swallowed by the whale?"

"When I get to Heaven I will ask Jonah," snapped the prelate.

"But suppose he isn't there?" the atheist persisted with a grin on his face.

"Then," retorted Bishop Carpenter icily, "you will have to ask him yourself!"

*

A minister of Belfast gazed out upon his congregation one Sunday morning and, in a stern voice, he began his sermon:

"Today I shall preach on the subject of liars. But first, would those of you who have read the seventeenth chapter of Mark please raise your hands."

Nearly every hand in the congregation shot upward.

"Fine!" said the preacher grimly. "You are the very people I want to talk to....There is no seventeenth chapter of Mark!"

*

A priest of Kilkenny had just preached a sermon on miracles. As he was walking homeward, he was joined by a member of his church who asked him to explain a little more clearly what a miracle meant.

"Is it a mericle you want to understand?" asked the priest. "Walk on there *forninst* me and I'll think iv how to explain it to you."

The man walked on ahead and the priest came after him, giving him a tremendous kick in the rear.

"Ow-wow-wow!" cried the man, more surprised than hurt. "Why did you do that?"

"You mane to say you felt it?" asked the priest with a satisfied smile on his face.

"Iv coorse I did!"

"Then there's your answer, lad. It would have been a meracle if you hadn't!"

*

One of the saddest announcements ever heard in a house of worship was made by the Reverend Dennis O'Hearne of Christ Church in Ulster:

"Next Saturday, the annual strawberry festival will be held," said Reverend O'Hearne. "However, because of the small collections received these past few months, prunes will be served!"

*

Here's one that made your grandparents laugh.

One Sunday (long before you were born), during high mass at noon, in the chapel of the little village of Glengariff, three ladies of the Protestant faith were obliged to take shelter from one of those heavy summer showers which so frequently occur in the south of Ireland.

The officiating priest, knowing who they were, stooped down to his attendant who was on his knees, and whispered, "Three chairs for the Protestant ladies."

The attendant, not the brightest of men, apparently misunderstood the command. He rose to his feet and, before the dumb-struck priest could stop him, he shouted to the congregation:

"Three cheers for the Protestant ladies!"

*

Mrs. McGrath had been waiting patiently for an opportunity to speak with her priest, and, now that church services were over, she was ushered into his study.

"Father, I'm worried about my little son, Frankie. He's had diarrhea for three days now, and I just don't know what to do."

"Have you taken him to a doctor?" asked the priest.

"I don't believe in doctors, Father."

"Hmm, then I suggest that you make a novena, Mrs. McGrath. Prayer always helps."

The concerned mother followed the suggestion, and on the next Sunday, after services, she again approached her priest.

"Oh, Father, my son is all better. I'm so happy you told me about prayer. It worked just fine."

But Mrs. McGrath's joy was short-lived.

"Father," she began nervously when she again saw him, "I'm afraid that my prayers were too strong. Now my Frankie can't go at all. He hasn't been to the bathroom in four days. What shall I do?"

"Nothing to worry about," responded the priest cheerily. "Just make another novena."

"But, Father," protested Mrs. McGrath in a worried voice, "novenas are *constipating!*"

*

In Edinborough for a visit, Mrs. Flaherty of New York agreed to attend a small Scottish church, merely out of curiosity and to please her local hosts. She was somewhat deaf and only hoped that the services would be loud enough for her to hear.

Inside the church, a sexton painstakingly pursued his duties, seeing that everyone had his place and was properly quiet during the sermon.

Suddenly, to his horror, he spied Mrs. Flaherty in the front row, holding an ear trumpet, and with an expectant look on her face. Appalled at the unfamiliar but foreboding sight, he hurried over to where the lady was sitting.

"Madam," he hissed in a low but grim voice, "one toot and you're oot!"

*

"To the devout Catholic," according to Patrick Ireland, "God is the Supreme Being, as distinguished from the Supreme Being of Protestants, the Supreme Being of Jews, and the Supreme Being of Mohammedans. The difference is, of course, that the God of the Catholics is more supreme than the others."

*

Patrick Gilmore, the bandmaster, famous for his rendition of Mozart's *Twelfth Mass*, once presented his favorite classic in a small North Carolina town. The reporter of the area's one newspaper who was assigned to cover the performance, evidently thought that the occasion was one that called for a very dignified write-up of the concert—particularly with reference to the stately *Twelfth Mass.*

He began his published review with the statement:

"Gilmore's band rendered with great effect Mozart's *Twelfth Massachusetts.*"

*

Tammany Hall was holding one of its numerous testimonial suppers, and Father O'Malley, who had been invited to show that God was on the side of the Democratic Party, found himself sitting next to a disbeliever.

"I hope you'll forgive me for saying so, Father," said the miscreant, opening up a conversation, "but I never go to church."

"Why not?" asked the priest.

"Frankly, sir, the reason I don't go is because there are so many hypocrites there."

"That shouldn't keep you away," retorted the good Father, smiling blandly. "There's always room for one more!"

*

"A Cheesy Debate"

> The cheese-mites asked how the cheese got there,
>   And warmly debated the matter;
> The Catholics said it came from the air,
>   And the Protestants said from the platter.

—Patrick Ireland

"Birth of the Blues"—
Biblically Speaking

> King David and King Solomon
>   Lived merry, merry lives,
> With many, many lady friends
>   And many, many wives;
> But when old age crept onwards,
>   With all its many qualms,
> King Solomon wrote the Proverbs
>   And King David wrote the Psalms.

—Patrick Ireland

*

"On a Curate's Complaint
of Hard Duty"

> I marched three miles through scorching sand,
> With zeal in heart, and notes in hand;
> I rode four more to Great St. Mary,
> Using four legs, when two were weary:
> To three fair virgins I did tie men
> In the close bands of pleasing Hymen;
> I dipped two babes in holy water,
> And purified their mother after.
> Within an hour and eke a half.
> I preached three congregations deaf;
> Where, thundering out, with lungs long-winded,
> I chopped so fast, that few there minded.
> My emblem, the laborious sun,
> Saw all these mighty labors done
> Before one race of his was run.
> All this performed by Robert Hewit;
> What mortal else could e'er go through it?

—Jonathan Swift (1667-1745)

Chapter Fifteen

Legal Beagles and
Stalwart Members of the Police Farce

Introduction

Since the time of Henry VIII (and in some instances even going back to Henry II, first ruler of Ireland), the judicial system imposed by the British upon the Irish people, saw the hapless natives, not as defendants or plaintiffs, but as targets. Cases were judged in the interests of England, or English parties to the litigation. It was inevitable, therefore, that the instinct of self-preservation would produce a long line of brilliant Irish lawyers to combat the one-sided legal system: men who were quick-thinking, clever, and glib to the point of genius. These barristers used their talents to defend their countrymen, and their country itself, against the alien judges who were, in the English view, "judicial," but in Irish eyes, seldom just.

Among the many patriot-lawyers who battled these English courts on Irish soil was John P. Curran, the nineteenth-century barrister whose bold defense of his kinsmen won him wide renown. A master of satire and irony, he used his caustic wit as an expert swordsman uses a rapier: parrying, weaving, thrusting. A selection of Curran's more humorous adventures in court is included in this chapter. But let it be remembered that the Irish people themselves became adept at artful dodging in the face of a corrupt judge's interrogations. Some of the anecdotes in the following pages, at first glance, may give the impression that the central character is little more than a rustic simpleton, helpless in the coils of the enemy. But a closer examination reveals another man—a farmer, perhaps, using his native shrewdness to outmaneuver the opposition. His outward simplicity is often his first line of defense. He resorts to that good old Irish standby—blarney!

In America, the Irish have long since gone beyond the pick and shovel. They have gravitated to the kind of employment best suited to their characteristics: physical strength, courage, a love of excitement, and an ability to get along with people. That is why more of them wield nightsticks than batons, why they prefer politics to plowing, law to medicine...*especially* law! Every state bar association, today, boasts a large roster of Irish-American lawyers, while those who reached the supreme courts of their respective states since the founding of this nation, are far too numerous to mention

244

here. Pierce Butler and William H. Brennan, to name but two, became Justices of the United States Supreme Court. In short, to quote Patrick Ireland,"law comes as easily to an Irishman as singing does to an Italian."

For the Irish, courts and cops go together like corned beef and cabbage. As early as 1815, an Irishman named John McManus served as the chief of New York City's police department; advance man for the countless officials who have risen to top positions in the police departments of cities everywhere in the United States.

Why have so many of them gravitated to police work? A number of reasons are evident. The early Irish immigrant saw the uniform as a symbol of deep respect, an attitude brought with him from Ireland. The wearer represented the authority of the government. Donning the uniform won him instant status in his community. Most important of all, a policeman enjoyed job security: a powerful inducement in a labor market that discriminated against the Irish, or offered only menial work at disgracefully low wages. A Civil Service job offered the kind of security few had known before. And as the Irish advanced politically, they also gained the influence to dispense the plums of patronage—and "a stiddy job on the police farce" was indeed a coveted plum.

The arrangement was satisfactory to all. It took an Irish cop to handle his fellow Irish immigrants, for whom a bottle in a bar and a battle in the streets were considered clean, healthy fun, and a lovely way to spend an evening. Yes, the Irishman made a good police officer. He understood his own people; he was not averse to getting into the midst of a fracas, swinging his club as though it were a shillelagh, and meanwhile enjoying himself immensely. He was strong and courageous, but, true to his Irish nature, compassionate, as well.

In modern times, the appeal of the uniform has not diminished. In the early 1840s, there were less than one hundred policemen with Irish names in New York City, representing 19 per cent of the total. By 1855, more than one thousand of New York's police officers, 26 per cent, were born in Ireland. In Chicago, at about that time, a total of 45 per cent of that city's police were Irish. Those percentages, for Americans of Irish extraction, have carried down to today in our largest metropolitan cities.

The judge and the lawyer seem to bear the brunt of Irish "legal" humor. The police officer fares rather well, and is regarded as just another fellow doing his job. But the judge is viewed as another lawyer with political connections. And, if we are to be guided by the jokes about them, both judges and lawyers are looked upon as a pack of beady-eyed spalpeens—except when a case is decided in your favor, at which time they become temporarily respectable.

Irish "legal" humor teaches us that even though lawyers may have guilty knowledge of a crime, they invariably plead their clients innocent, no one having offered them a fee to plead them guilty. Thus, all clients are innocent until proven otherwise in a court of law. Criminal lawyers abound in every community, until they are caught, at which time they stop abounding until the next time.

Judges, say the Irish humorists, abide by the "law of the land," which is the country's reward to the taxpayer; the higher his taxes, the greater the reward. This is not as unfair as it might first appear. The judge requires that he be supported at regular intervals by people of means. Without such contributions there would be no elected magistrates of his integrity and fairmindedness. It would in effect, also be a violation of the judge's consitutional right to his pursuit of happiness.

But happiness is where you find it; as in, for example, the following pages.

—H.D.S.

"Madeline at Jefferson Market Night Court"

> If it wasn't for me and the likes of me
> And what I choose to do,
> What the hell, I'd like to know,
> Would become of the likes of you?
> Instead of tryin' to "save a soul,"
> You bums would hafta shovel coal!

—Margaret McGovern (1909-)

*

The use of chocolate as a drink was a luxury in old Ireland that few of the poorer people could afford—and that meant most of the population.

One day, just before the turn of the present century, the porter of a large grocer in Dublin was brought before a magistrate on a charge of stealing chocolate, an accusation he could not deny.

"To whom did you sell it?" asked the judge.

"*Sell* it!" cried the porter, his pride sorely wounded. "Faith now, and did ye think I stole it to *sell*?"

"Then, sir, what *did* you do with the chocolate?"

"Well, since Yer Honor must know, I was afther makin' *tay* with it!"

*

At the Monmouthshire sessions, an old woman was charged with a felonv—erroneously. as it turned out.

"Madam," said the judge at the outset of the trial, "there are three counts against you."

"Faith!" she gasped in astonishment. "And why would three Counts be afther wastin' their time on wan poor Irishwoman?"

*

It had been a grand night, full of Irish cheer, but, the next morning, Mike dimly recalled that he had been arrested for carousing, fighting, striking an officer of the law, and sundry other activities unbecoming a gentleman. His wife attempted to console him.

"Never you fear, Mike," she said comfortingly. "I heard that you'll have an upright judge to thry you."

"Ah, Biddy, darlint, the divil an upright judge I want," sighed Mike. " 'Tis wan I nade that'll *lane** a little!"

*

Dennis was in court as a witness in an assault case, stemming from an altercation in Buckley's Bar on Tenth Avenue. The defendant's attorney, an aggressive, sarcastic individual, launched his questions as though firing bullets from a rifle.

"You say that my client struck the plaintiff at precisely eleven minutes past midnight, and that you had a clear view because you were only five feet three-and-one-quarter inches distant at the moment. Is that your testimony?"

"Yes, it is," affirmed Dennis.

"Now look·here," snapped the counselor, "do you expect this court to believe that after drinking whiskey for several hours in a crowded bar you would know the exact time and distance? Perhaps you had better enlighten us. How is that possible?"

It's a matter of foresight, mister lawyer," replied Dennis. "I knew that some damn fool would be asking me, so I looked at my watch and then measured the distance."

*

The Poultroon Players Company
Presents
"THE CASE OF THE FLYING BEDPAN"

Scene One:
A courtroom in Limerick

MAGISTRATE: Can you describe the man you saw assaulting the complainant?

CIVIC GUARD: Indade I can, Yer Honor. He was an insignificant-looking little crayture, about your size.

*

A young vagabond, traveling through a distant county, was caught with a sack of stolen potatoes. He was brought before a stern judge.

"Yer Honor," the prisoner complained bitterly, "I'm sorely throubled."

"Why are you troubled?" asked the judge.

"Becase I should be thried in me own county instid iv here in this strange town, so far from friends an' home."

"Calm yourself, young man," counseled the magistrate. "You may rest assured that, although you may be far from home and among strangers,

---

*Lean.

justice will be done."

"Faith, Yer Honor," moaned the culprit, "an' that's what kapes throublin' me!"

*

Nearly all of the Irish refugees from the terrible potato famine of the 1840s were hard-working men and women, eager to labor for their share of America's worldly goods.

But not Kelly! Kelly was lazy. Kelly was a wanderer. Kelly held to the theory that honest toil was a poor substitute for panhandling. It was inevitable that he would eventually find himself in the clutches of the authorities, who looked with disfavor upon his social philosophy. He was arrested and charged with vagrancy.

"What is your trade?" asked the stony-faced judge.

"Me thrade, is it?" replied Kelly, his jaunty manner at once giving offense to the judge who was not widely known for his sense of humor. "I'm a haard-wurrkin' sailor."

"You a seafaring man? I doubt very much whether you were ever at sea in your life."

"Sure now," protested Kelly, offended at this attack upon his veracity, "and would Yer Honor be thinkin' I came over from Ireland in a wagon?"

*

In the grand and glorious state of Boston, surrounded by the sprawling boondocks of Massachusetts, Paddy Flynn was in the courthouse, testifying in behalf of his friend, O'Banion. The occasion was "Naturalization Day," a biannual event of no fixed date, but usually preceding the general elections, and energetically hailed by the local "disthric laders iv the Dimmycrathic Paarty."

"Do you know Mr. O'Banion?" asked the judge.

"I do indade, Yer Honor," replied Flynn.

"And you believe he merits American citizenship?"

"If iver a man desarved it, O'Banion does."

"Then you would say that he is a good man?"

"Good, is it?" exclaimed Flynn, clearly proud of his friend. "To be sure he's a good man! I've seen him in ten fights since he came to this counthry last year, and he licked his inimies ivry time!"

*

Healy was not only driving at an excessive rate of speed but going the wrong way on a one-way street when he was stopped by a motorcycle officer.

"Just where the hell do you think you're going?" snarled the policeman. "To a fire?"

"As a matter of fact, yes," explained Healy, surprised.

"Oh izzat so!" rasped the cop. "Well, it must be out by now. All the other drivers on this street seem to be coming back!"

*

Every police department has its quota of sterling officers who are determined to rid the streets of dangerous criminals, regardless of their political connections. Here's proof:

A sweet, silver-haired old lady took a shortcut across a lawn in the park, and was caught red-footed by a stern upholder of the law.

"Didn't you see the KEEP OFF THE GRASS sign?" he demanded brusquely. "And don't give me any of that jazz about being married to a councilman. I don't care *who* you know, Mother!"

*

A girl whose face looked like it had been designed by Picasso, hurried over to a policeman and voiced a shrill complaint.

"Officer, that man is following me and keeps trying to pick me up. He must be drunk!"

The cop took a good look at her face and muttered: "Yeah, lady, he's *gotta* be!"

*

Officer Flaherty was the rawest rookie in the city police department—actually a cadet still in training. But, tonight, he was especially proud of himself. The Captain of the Night Watch had sent him to Central Park to catch the notorious Manhattan Mugger.

"Did you catch the creep?" asked the captain, seeing the rookie's pleased expression.

"Well, not really," said officer Flaherty, blushing with pardonable pride, "but I caught four of his victims!"

*

There are still a few old-timers alive in Longford who will gleefully recall the Phelan case. If memory serves us rightly, Pete Phelan became involved in a physical difference of opinion with several of the *Garda Siochana* and nearly licked them all, he did, before he was hauled away to gaol at taxpayers' expense.

In court the next morning, the magistrate asked the now-sober prisoner, "Are you guilty of assaulting five members of the Civic Guard, as charged?"

"Now how would I be knowin' that, Yer Honor?" demanded the unrepentant Phelan whose recollection of the night before was hazy at best, "I have yit to hear th' ividince agin me!"

*

An American importer of Irish linens, thinking he had been cheated by an exporter in Eire, arrived in the "Ould Counthry" to seek court action. Immediately upon arriving, he set off for the small town in which the suspected exporter conducted his business. There, he approached an old man who had just stepped, somewhat uncertainly, from a tavern door.

"Say, old man," asked the American, "do you have a criminal lawyer in this town?"

"We think so," replied the native cautiously, "but so far we've been unable to prove it on him!"

*

Chief Inspector Donnelly and Precinct Captain Gleason were discussing the department's newest rookies.

"By the way, how's my nephew Shawn getting along?" asked Inspector Donnelly.

"Great—really great!" enthused Captain Gleason. "You won't believe this, but even though he's been on the force for only a week, everyone on his beat already hates his guts!"

*

A well-known lawyer, who shall mercifully remain anonymous, had his portrait done in his favorite posture—standing with one hand in his pocket. Proudly, he hung the painting on his office wall.

That evening, when he had long since gone home, the charwomen came to the building for their regular cleaning duties. In the lawyer's office, one of them viewed the picture critically for some moments, and then turned to her coworker.

"Mamie, there's somethin' 'bout that picture that don't look jist right."

"Sure an' it's plain ez th' nose on yer face," said Mamie. "Didja iver in all yer borned days see a lawyer with his hand in his *own* pocket?"

*

**Eavesdropping at
Police Precinct #48:**

Rrrriiinnnggg!

"Police department—Sergeant Muldoon spakin'. Make it short, plaze!"

"I wanna report a missin' husband."

"Missin', is he? Can ye describe the man?"

"Well, he's four-foot-ten, very fat, bald, knock-kneed...ah, fergit it!"

*

In all of County Down there was none so compassionate as O'Shaughnessy. It was the most natural thing in the world, therefore, that when he heard of the business failure of his friend, Billy the blacksmith, he sent over a goodly supply of iron. "Now," he said to himself, "Billy will have the material with which to shoe horses and do other work."

But, as creditors will, one of them put an attachment on the supply of iron at the forge. O'Shaughnessy promptly sued in trover. Charles Ryan, the historic lawyer-orator, appeared in O'Shaughnessy's behalf, and, at his dramatic best, he pictured the cruelty of the sheriff's proceedings:

"He arrested the arm of industry as it fell toward the anvil; he put out the breath in his bellows. Like pirates in a gale at sea, his enemies swept everything by the board, leaving him, gentlemen of the jury, not so much as a horseshoe to nail upon his doorpost to keep the witches off!"

Tears welled up in Billy's eyes at this emotional description. O'Shaughnessy leaned over and whispered, "Why, what's the matter, my friend? What are you crying about?"

"Faith, Mr. O'Shaughnessy," sobbed poor Billy, "I had no idee I'd suffered so much!"

*

It was a simple case of assault, and the evidence was plain enough for anyone to see. The witnesses were all positive and accurate in their testimony. Yet, the court proceedings dragged on and on, with the jury debating for almost a week as they tried to reach a verdict. At last, annoyed by the long delay in settling this case, the judge called the members of the jury to the box.

"I hereby discharge you," he announced curtly.

The foreman of the jury felt that his personal integrity was at stake. "You can't do that," he cried.

"Oh I can't, can't I?" snapped the judge. "And why not?"

"Because you didn't hire me," said the jury foreman, pointing to the defense lawyer. "I'm working for *that* guy!"

*

For two days, Judge Andrew Kelly of Kings County had been hearing an important case involving many thousands of dollars. On the third day, while the trial was in actual progress, he happened to notice that one of the jurors was missing. He promptly stopped the proceedings.

"Mr. Foreman," he inquired, "where is the twelfth member of the jury? I see only eleven present."

"Your Honor," explained the foreman, "the missing man is Timothy O'Hare. He took the day off to march in the Saint Patrick's Day parade—but it's all right, sir: he left his verdict with me!"

*

Sullivan was on trial for stealing a gold shamrock and four shillelaghs from the Pride of Ireland Department Store in Dublin. The case went to the jury on Monday, but, as Friday drew to a close, the members of the jury were deadlocked, eleven for conviction and one for acquittal. The court was impatient.

"Well, gentlemen," said the bailiff as he entered the jury room, "shall I order the usual twelve dinners?"

"No," snapped the foreman, "make it eleven dinners and one bale of hay!"

*

"Bob, I hear you'll be on the jury tomorrow when my client's case comes up," said Shamus the shyster lawyer. "It's two hundred dollars in your pocket if you can help get us a verdict of manslaughter in the second degree."

"It won't be easy," said the juror. "I may have to do a lot of persuading to convince the other members of the jury. Make it five hundred and I'll try."

"You did a marvelous job!" cried the lawyer when they were in private. "Here's your five hundred dollars, and thank you for the successful effort."

"It was no picnic, believe me," said the juror as he accepted the payment. "In fact, I had a helluva time. All the others wanted an acquittal!"

*

Johnson and Logan, long-time neighbors, were involved in a lawsuit. the issue at stake was small, but each was determined to win. The day of the trial arrived and Johnson strode into the courtroom surrounded by a covey of witnesses for his side of the case.

A few minutes later, Logan entered. He took one startled look at Johnson and his entourage and hurried over to him.

"Johnson, are these your witnesses?"

"That they are, me fine-feathered friend."

"Then I give up right now. You win! I've used these same witnesses twice myself!"

*

Murphy and Quinlan had been friends for years, but their friendship fell upon hard times and the day came when they found themselves in court as adversaries. Both were nearly deaf, but that did not deter them in the least.

"Your Honor," explained Murphy, "Quinlan owes me for a used car I sold him, and he won't pay."

"That's a lie!" shouted Quinlan, who had cupped his hand to his ear so as to better hear every word. "I never touched the man's whiskey!"

"Cheatin' at cards, is it?" yelled Murphy, red-faced with indignation. "I don't even play cards. The man is a liar!"

The judge glared at both of the quarreling men and rapped sharply with his gavel.

"Now that'll be enough of this," he barked. "You ought to be ashamed of yourselves. She's your mother and you should both support her!"

*

It was a clear night, and silent as a graveyard, when young Private Houlihan was standing sentry duty at Fort Dix, New Jersey. Suddenly, without so much as a growl or bark, he was attacked by a huge, vicious German shepherd dog. Houlihan fell to the ground and, after suffering a number of bites, he managed to get to his knees. In desperation, as the animal made another lunge at him, he drove his bayonet into its heart.

The dog's angry owner filed charges against the sentry and sued for damages. "It was not necessary for him to kill my dog," said the owner. "That man wasn't even badly bitten."

The judge called Houlihan to the stand.

"Why didn't you just knock the dog on the head with the butt of your rifle?" asked his honor.

"For the same reason," replied Houlihan with a bit of simple but undeniable logic, "the dog didn't bite me with its tail!"

*

Standing before the bar of justice, and charged with wife-beating, Monahan tensely awaited the judge's verdict.

"Mr. Monahan," bellowed the magistrate, "I want you to know I have no sympathy for a man who beats his wife."

"Sure and I don't blame ye wan bit," interrupted the arresting officer who stood beside the culprit. "Anny man who can bate his wife don't nade sympathy!"

*

The highly nervous young lawyer stepped up to plead his first case—one that involved several men whose disputations had led to overcrowding at St. James Infirmary. The fledgling attorney laid his topcoat on the bench beside him and approached the judge.

"Is this the first time you've practiced in this court?" asked his honor, a man nicknamed by other lawyers as "The Beast of Boston."

"Y-y-yes, Your Honor," stammered the youthful attorney, scared half to death that he had already committed some breach of precedent.

The judge glared down at him for a moment or two, and then—incredibly—he smiled.

"Then get your coat," he said benignly, "and put it where you can keep an eye on it. I never did trust those bailiffs!"

*

It's hard to believe that a fledgling lawyer would scold a judge in open court and get away with it, but you may well believe it. The late Terence O'Mahundro, a lawyer widely known to his wife and two-year-old daughter as a man of truth, swore that this story was true. Rather than dishonor the word of a dead Irishman, let us be along with the tale—the way Terence would have you believe it.

Terence O'Mahundro had a younger brother, Jimmy, who was also an attorney. Jimmy was in his twenties and, although this was the first time he had ever practiced before the State Supreme Court of New York, he was anything but apprehensive. Boldly, he pleaded his client's ignorance of an offense he had indeed committed.

Sitting on the bench was Judge Robert MacArthur. He looked down at Jimmy and glowered.

"Mr. O'Mahundro," snapped the justice, "every man is supposed to know that ignorance of the law is no excuse."

"I am aware of that, Your Honor," responded Jimmy in his usual brash but articulate manner. "Every shoemaker, every tailor, every bricklayer, every illiterate laborer, is presumed to know the law; everyone, that is, but the judges of this court—and we have a Court of Appeals to correct their mistakes!"

*

The stony-faced judge read through the papers before him and his eyes widened with incredulity. He then addressed the accused:

"Mr. Fitzwilliam, are you trying to tell this court that you threw your wife out of a second-story window because of *forgetfulness*?" he demanded in an icy voice. "I've heard a lot of excuses in my time on the bench, but this one is in a class by itself."

"But it's true, Your Honor," maintained Fitzwilliam stoutly. "We used to live on the ground floor and I forgot we moved!"

*

Mrs. Hennessy entered the Fordham Road Police Precinct and approached the sergeant's desk.

"Officer," she began, "my husband's been missin' since las' Wensdy."

"What's he look like?" asked the sergeant, reaching for a pencil.

"Hmm, well, t'start with, he's got an artificial leg; he has no more hair on his head than a doorknob; an' he's got no left eye, an' no teeth, an' no tonsils, an' no appendix, an' no personality, either." Mrs. Hennessy paused. "Come to think of it," she added reflectively, "most of him was missin' before *he* was!"

*

Judge Jeffries, of Boston's Night Court, was reprimanding Pat the pickpocket who had been brought before him for the fifth time in as many months.

"You are an unmitigated scalawag," the judge concluded.

"Scalawag, is it?" retorted Pat defiantly. "Bedad. sor, I am not as big a scalawag as Your Honor..." Pat stopped to glare at the apoplectic judge, and then hurriedly added... "takes me to be!"

*

"The Party Over There"

A Man in a Hurry, whose watch was at his office, asked a Grave Person the time of day.

"I heard you ask that Party Over There the same question," said the Grave Person. "What answer did he give you?"

"He said it was about three o'clock," replied the Man in a Hurry. "But he did not look at his watch, and as the sun is nearly down I think it is later."

"The fact that the sun is nearly down," the Grave Person said, "is immaterial, but the fact that he did not consult his timepiece and make answer after due deliberation and consideration is fatal. The answer given," continued the Grave Person, consulting his own timepiece, "is of no effect, invalid, and void."

"What, then," said the Man in a Hurry eagerly, "is the time of day?"

"The question is remanded to the Party Over There for a new answer," replied the Grave Person, returning his watch to his pocket and moving away with great dignity.

He was a Judge of an Appellate Court.

—Ambrose Bierce

*

Silver-haired Mrs. Neeley had left Ireland over a half century ago, but had never been inside a courtroom in the United States. Now, however, she was on the witness stand, about to testify in a civil case. Unaware of courtroom procedure, she insisted on directing her testimony to the prosecuting attorney, making it difficult for the members of the jury to hear her quiet voice.

"Madam," the judge finally interjected in a stern voice, "please speak to the jury!"

Mrs. Neeley turned her head, smiled at the jury, and nodded in a sociable manner.

"Top o' th' mornin' to ye!" she said brightly.

*

Curran Classics (circa 1765-1815)

Soon after John Curran[1] was called to the bar, he had the misfortune to run afoul of the notorious Judge Robinson, the author of many stupid, slavish, and scurrilous political pamphlets which he usually published anonymously. His legal decisions were equally scandalous. Lord Brougham said of him: "By his demerits he raised to eminence that which he sought to disgrace."

On this occasion, when Judge Robinson had rendered an absurd and wholly unjustified verdict against his client, Curran was moved to declare, "I have never met the law as laid down by his lordship, in any book in my library."

"That may be, sir," said the judge, "but I suspect that your library is very small."

"My lord," retorted the young counsel, "I find it more instructive to study good works than to compose bad ones [an obvious allusion to Robinson's anonymously published attacks]. My books may be few, but the title pages give me the writers' names, and my shelf is not disgraced by any such rank absurdities that their authors are ashamed to own them."

"Sir," thundered the judge, "you are forgetting the respect which you owe to the dignity of the judicial character."

"Dignity!" exclaimed Curran. "My Lord, upon that point I shall cite you a case from a book of some authority." He then briefly recited the story of Strap, in *Roderick Random,* who, having stripped off his coat to fight, entrusted it to a bystander. When the battle was over, and he was well beaten, he turned to retrieve his coat, but the man had carried it off. Curran then applied the tale:

"So, my lord, when the person entrusted with the dignity of the judgment seat lays it aside for a moment to enter into a disgraceful personal contest, it is in vain that, when he is beaten in the encounter he seeks to resume it—it is in vain that he tries to shelter himself behind an authority which he has abandoned."

---

[1]John Philpot Curran, Irish statesman and orator, became the best-known trial lawyer in Dublin when he was still very young, and sat for a while in the Irish parliament. Although a Protestant, he fought for Catholic emancipation, vigorously opposed the repressive policy of the British government in Ireland, and was defense lawyer for many of the rebels at the turn of the eighteenth century. He opposed the union of Ireland with England, but refused to support acts of open rebellion; yet, surprisingly, was esteemed by even the most violent of Irish patriots. Subsequently, he sat in the privy council of the United Kingdom. His daughter, Sarah, was in love with Robert Emmet, who was captured and hanged when he came to Dublin to visit her. Their tragic love affair inspired Thomas Moore's verses beginning, "She is far from the land where her young hero sleeps," and "Oh! breathe not his name."

For all his brilliance as a trial lawyer, John Curran was also famous for his sharp and sometimes acerbic wit. His favorite targets were dolts, hypocrites, and tyrants. The many stories that have survived his death so long ago attest to his popularity of the day, and have earned him a special niche in the annals of Irish folk humor. A modest selection of those anecdotes are published here, some for the first time in 150 years.

"If you say another word, I will commit you!" shouted the angry judge.

"If your lordship does so," retorted Curran, "we shall both have the consolation of knowing that I am not the worst thing your lordship has ever committed!"

———

A simple farmer whose name was Quinn took overnight lodgings at an inn, in the city where he wished to attend a fair. He had heard many dark tales of the robbers thereabouts, and having a hundred pounds in his pocket, he took the precaution of depositing it with the landlord. On the following day, Quinn made ready to return to his farm and asked the innkeeper for the money he had placed with him for safekeeping.

"What money?" asked the proprietor innocently.

"My hundred pounds!"

"You gave me nothing at all," replied the landlord brusquely. "Bother me no more."

In his dilemma, farmer Quinn consulted John Curran.

"Have patience and do exactly as I instruct," said the counsel after Quinn had told his sad story. "First, I want you to return to the inn and speak to the landlord in a civil manner. Tell him you are now convinced you must have left your money with some other person. Then deposit another hundred pounds with him for safekeeping, but this time be sure to take a friend with you. When you have done that, come back here to me."

The farmer approached the landlord and, with the local priest as his witness to attest to the transaction, he deposited another hundred pounds "for safekeeping."

"Now what must I do?" asked the puzzled farmer when he returned to his counsel's office.

"Now, Mr. Quinn, go back and demand your hundred," advised Curran, "but see that both you and the innkeeper are alone when you ask for it."

The farmer again did as he was instructed, and the landlord, remembering that a priest had witnessed the deposit, reluctantly returned the money.

"Well, Mr. Curran," sighed farmer Quinn, "I received the second hundred, but am I to be cheated out of the first?"

"You will not be cheated at all," replied Curran, a broad grin lighting his features. "In fact, the innkeeper has just returned the *first* hundred pounds to you. Now, take your friend, the priest, with you, and ask the innkeeper for the hundred pounds your witness saw you deposit with him."

Within the hour, the farmer returned with both hundreds safely in his pocket, but Curran was so amused with his strategy that he refused to accept a fee for his "legal" services.[2]

---

[2]Variants of this anecdote are represented in the humorous folk tales of such cultures as the Scandinavian, Italian and Jewish. (See *Encyclopedia of Jewish Humor,* Henry D. Spalding (1969). Jonathan David Publishers, Inc., Middle Village, New York.)

———

Curran and his friend, Donoghue, were walking one day when they stopped to chat with another acquaintance who repeatedly pronounced the word *curiosity* as *curosity*.

"It's terrible, the way that man murders the English language," observed Donoghue when they resumed their walk.

"Oh, I wouldn't say he murders it," said Curran affably. "All he does is knock an *i* out!"

———

It is almost sacrilegious to say it, but Curran once met his match in a pert, jolly, keen-eyed son of Erin named Malolly. For the first time in his life, according to official records, the great barrister was floored by a simple rustic. Unable to recover from the exchange of repartee, the case went against him. But let us get on with the story.

Malolly was in court as a witness in a case involving a controversial horse deal. It was Curran's intention to break down the credibility of this witness by entangling him in a network of adroitly framed questions, forcing him to contradict himself. But his efforts were fruitless. Malolly's native common sense, equanimity, and good nature were not to be overturned. Finally, in a towering wrath, Curran roared as no other counsel would have dared to do in the presence of the court:

"Sirrah, you are incorrigible! The truth is not in you! I can see the villain in your face!"

"Faith, sor," replied Malolly with the utmost simplicity of truth and honesty in his voice, "me face must be moighty clane and shinin' indade, if it can reflect like that!"

———

Lord Avonmore, as a judge, had one great fault: he was apt to jump to conclusions—to take up a first impression—and it was very difficult to obliterate that initial impression. Curran, therefore, had not only to struggle against the real obstacles presented by the case itself, but also with the imaginary ones created by the hasty anticipation of the judge. This habit became so annoying to Curran that he decided to correct it—in his own whimsical manner.

The opportune evening came when they were both invited to dine at the house of a mutual friend. Curran, contrary to his usual custom, was late for dinner, and at length arrived in the most admirably effected agitation.

"Mr. Curran," grumbled Lord Avonmore, "you have kept us a full hour waiting dinner for you."

"I truly regret the inconvenience," replied the barrister, "but I have just been witness to a melancholy occurrence."

"Hmm, you seem terribly moved by it. Here, take a glass of wine."

"First let me collect myself," moaned Curran quite convincingly as he sipped his wine. "I had been detained at court—in the Court of Chancery.

Your lordship knows the chancelor sits late."

"I do, I do—but go on, please!"

"Well, my lord, I was hurrying here as fast as I could—I did not even change my clothes—I hope I shall be excused for coming in my boots."

"Poh, poh! Never mind your boots! The point—come to the point of your story!"

"Of course, my lord. I walked here—I would not even wait to get a carriage ready: it would have taken time, you know. Now, there was a market exactly in the road by which I had to pass—your lordship may perhaps recollect the market. Do you?"

"To be sure I do. Go *on*, Curran—for heaven's sake, go *on* with the story!"

"I am very glad your lordship remembers the market, for I totally forget the name of it: let me see—the name—the name..."

"What the devil difference does the name make, sir? It's the Castle Market."

"Your lordship is perfectly right; it's the Castle Market indeed. Well, I was going through that very identical Castle Market when I observed a butcher preparing to kill a calf. He had a huge knife in his hand; it was as sharp as a razor. The calf was standing beside him, and he drew the knife to plunge it into the animal. Just as he was in the act of doing so, a sweet, beautiful little boy, about four years old—the butcher's only son—the loveliest child I ever saw—suddenly ran across his path, and he killed—oh, good heavens!—he killed..."

"The child! the child!" gasped Lord Avonmore, horrified.

"No, my lord, the calf!" continued Curran in cool tones. "He killed the calf—*but I'm afraid your lordship is in the habit of anticipating!*"

———

Tom Goold, who could not bear the thought of taking second place to any man alive or dead, was describing the awful risk he had run one day while riding his horse on the North Strand, near Dublin.

"The tide rose so suddenly," he told Curran, "that I would surely have drowned had I not been the very best horseman in all of Ireland. Never, John, was a human being in such danger."

"My dear Tom," replied Curran evenly, "there was someone else who was obviously in still greater danger—a poor man was actually drowned there that very morning."

"By God, sir," bellowed Goold, "I could have drowned, too—if I chose!"

———

Irish folklorists claim that Lord Chancellor Clare's dislike of John Curran stemmed from a sarcastic retort made by the outspoken barrister soon after he had launched his career. In reply to some legal point raised by Curran, the judge snapped, "If that be law, sir, I shall have to burn my books."

"I suggest, my lord," advised Curran, "that you *read* them!"

But whether that story is true or not, witnesses of the era have attested to the truth of a later contest between the two adversaries, which occurred in the following manner:

Curran was addressing the court in a most important case, but, to his mounting anger, the lord chancellor occupied himself with giving too much of his attention to a favorite Newfoundland dog that was seated beside him at the bench. Curran's indignation rose to such a point that he abruptly ceased speaking.

"Why don't you proceed?" asked Lord Clare, raising his head.

"Sir," replied Curran, his voice choked with rage, "I thought your lordships were in consultation!"

●

"The Attorney's Winning Ways"

> He held at court a luck so high,
> The other lawyers asked him why.
> "Because," he answered, "others lack
> My skill to scratch the judge's back."

—Patrick Ireland

Chapter Sixteen
Political Bigwigs and Littlewigs
Introduction

The Irish, it is said, produce statesmen in Ireland, politicians in America. What should be added, however, is that virtually all Irish statesmen are also adroit politicians, and are equally (and providentially) distributed in both countries.

Contrary to their historic conservatism, the greatest of the Irish patriots of the past were dissenters and revolutionaries. Their motivation, like that of their American kinsmen, was freedom—and from the same oppressor. They included such heroes of Ireland as Theobald Wolfe Tone, the Presbyterian Irish freedom fighter who cheated an English hangman by taking his own life; Daniel O'Connell, the great patriot whose tongue was as sharp as a sword; Hugh O'Neill and Hugh Roe O'Donnell, sworn enemies of Queen Elizabeth, who valiantly fought her soldiers from their last stronghold in Ulster; Charles Steward Parnell, the brilliant champion of Home Rule; and Michael Collins, organizer and leader of the Irish Republican Army, which led to the creation of *Sinn Fein*, and ultimately to independence from Britain. These military and political leaders—statesmen all— were just a few of the revolutionary heroes who fought government by bullet to establish a government by ballot.

In colonial America, the revolutionary Irish not only fired their muskets at their old enemy, the British, but placed their indelible stamp upon the Declaration of Independence. At least nine known sons of Erin or first generation Irish-Americans signed that noble document. Four of them were born in Ireland: Colonel James Smith, George Taylor, Edward Rutledge, and Matthew Thornton. Five signers had Irish parents: Thomas McKean, George Read, Robert Treat Paine, Charles Carroll, and Thomas Lynch, Jr.

The section of the Declaration which itemizes the wrongs inflicted upon the colonies, was mainly written by another revolutionary Irishman, John Sullivan, a member of the Continental Congress, whose brothers included a judge, an attorney general, and a governor. As to the final draft of the Constitution itself, it was mostly the work of John Rutledge, a second-generation Irishman who was later to become Chief Justice of the United

States. Rutledge's friends included the McCarthy family, second cousins to George Washington, and frequent visitors to Mount Vernon.

The Irish, long since identified with the Democratic Party, moved into big-city machine politics shortly after the Civil War, and before long they were running most of them. Historian Edward F. Roberts, in his *Ireland in America*, aptly declared, "It is probably true that the political machine was not invented by the Irish or consciously by anyone, but it is certain that it was developed to its greatest extent and has reached its highest degree of efficiency through the peculiar genius of the Irish for political organization."

"All Irishmen are, of course, politicians," averred Bob Considine in his excellent book, *It's The Irish,* "but some earn a living at it." A number of the big-city political machines were run as personal fiefdoms by politicians who "earned a living at it"—men such as Frank Hague of Jersey City, and Richard Daley of Chicago. But none of these could compare with the notorious Tammany Hall of New York, still the most powerful political machine in the nation. It was with Tammany's initial espousal and heavy support that the Democratic party chose Irish Catholic Alfred E. Smith, four-term Governor of New York, as its candidate for the presidency. A bitter anti-Catholic campaign was waged against Smith, a firm believer in the doctrine of separation of church and state, and probably the most progressive governor New York had ever known. Republican Herbert Hoover, of course, was elected in that campaign of 1928.[1]

America's Irish Catholics were not to be represented in the White House until that long-awaited day of January 20, 1961, when John Fitzgerald Kennedy took the oath of office as the thirty-fifth President of the United States. The "No Irish Need Apply" signs were taken down forever. Irish-Americans of the Catholic faith had at last attained equality with the Protestant majority that had supplied all of the nation's chief executives since its founding, almost two centuries before.

Although Kennedy was the first Irish-American *Catholic* president, he was far from being the first man of Irish ancestry to occupy the White House. Andrew Jackson, James K. Polk, James Buchanan, Andrew Johnson, Chester A. Arthur, William McKinley, William Howard Taft, Woodrow Wilson, Grover Cleveland, Calvin Coolidge, and Harry Truman, were of Irish descent.

But it was John F. Kennedy, and he alone, who brought an awareness of an individual's worth to an electorate that had previously been conditioned to evaluate a man's merit according to his religious affiliation. With his election to the highest office in the land, the Catholic Irish—despised, derided, herded into slums, and denied all but the meanest of jobs just a little over a century ago—finally reached the ultimate and social pinnacle. For the Irish, John Fitzgerald Kennedy's election was the end of a long road.

[1] Al Smith was not the first Catholic candidate for the presidency. Charles O'Conor of New York, son of Irish immigrants, was nominated by an insurgent Democratic ticket in 1872. The regular Democratic slate was headed by Horace Greeley and B. Gratz Brown, both unacceptable to America's Irish Catholics. The Republican candidates, Ulysses S. Grant and Henry Wilson, easily won the election.

Yet, despite their centuries-old struggle for political equality, the Irish managed to retain their sense of humor. For example, when Joseph Kennedy was appointed by Franklin D. Roosevelt as the United States Ambassador to the Court of St. James, the Washington correspondent for the *Dublin Times* quipped: "A U.S. Ambassador is a man who has failed to be elected by the people, and who is appointed to high office by the Administration on condition that he leave the country." Another Irish cynic, who took a dim view of the number of elected female officials, moaned piteously, "Alas and alack! A woman's place is now in the House—and in the Senate!"

Mike Kelly, the Chicago cynic who delights in pin-pricking his kinsmen, once declared that an Irish statesman is a politician who has been successful in concealing his private life.

Here are various other levels of Irish political humor, ranging from the wistful to the winsome; sometimes crude, but never vulgar; at other times gentle. "An' divil an angel will ye be findin' in this chapter; but divil a divil, ayther!"

—H.D.S.

My Senator's a predator, a vote-gobbler is he,
   My Mayor greets payers who slip him a fee;
My Governor can't govern, his mind's in a steeple,
   The President's residence is closed to the people.

How I wish that we Irish would raise our shillaylies
   With thumps to the rumps of those rascally jailees,
And replace those disgraces, where'er they may be—
   With blatherin', blarneyin' buckos like me!

—Patrick Ireland

*

On Boston's south side, during the Kennedy-Nixon presidential campaign, Richard Nixon was making an impassioned speech on behalf of (a) himself and (b) the Republican Party. To his annoyance, he was continually interrupted by a heckler, who kept shouting, "I am a Dimmycrat!"

Finally, Nixon had to assert himself or risk losing his audience. With disarming gentleness, he inquired, "May I ask the gentleman why he is a Democrat?"

"Becaze, sor, me gran'father was a Dimmycrat, me father was a Dimmycrat an', bedad, that makes me a Dimmycrat," replied the heckler, a surprising statement from a man who had obviously just reached these shores in the very recent past.

"Well, my good man," replied Nixon, "just suppose that your grandfather had been a jackass and your father had been a jackass, what would you be?"

"Sor," bellowed the heckler, "I'd be a Raypooblican!"

*

Political opponents of John F. Kennedy often alluded to his family's wealth, sometimes hinting, and at other times stating flatly, that his father, Joseph P. Kennedy, was financing his son's presidential campaign. The younger Kennedy took the barbs with rare good humor. At a press conference in Washington, at the height of his campaign, the future president quipped:

"I have today received this telegram from my generous father:

" 'DEAR JACK, DON'T BUY A SINGLE VOTE
MORE THAN IS ABSOLUTELY NECESSARY.
I'LL BE DAMNED IF I'M GOING TO PAY
FOR A LANDSLIDE!' "

*

When Al Smith was battling it out for the Democratic presidential nomination, he was not as well known outside of New York State as he would have liked.

During the campaign, he encountered a group of people at a shopping center in Texas and introduced himself.

"I'm Al Smith," he said, shaking their hands. "I'm running for president."

"Yeah, we know," said one of the local gentry. "We were laughing about that just this morning."

*

Opponents of the Women's Liberation movement may not like, but will no doubt enjoy, this futuristic tale.

The morning of November 4th, in the year 2004, dawned cold and clear. The voting for all four major political parties was heavy, but thanks to the new computers, the tally was in by ten that morning. Lo and behold! Colleen Murphy, the Republicrat candidate for Presidentess of the United States, had won.

Emerging breathlessly from her hairdresser's, she rushed to the supermarket to get her groceries bought for the week, raced home, asked her husband for carfare, and took the very next bus for the White House.

There, in the Oval office, she immediately had two hotlines installed in the official telephone system: one to the Soviet Union and the other to her mother.

*

Al Smith, may the good Lord give him an extra set of wings, was holding forth at a press conference at Tammany Hall one day, when Westbrook Pegler, the acid-tongued columnist, called out: "Tell us all you know,

Al—it won't take but a minute."

"I'll do better than that," retorted Al. "I'll tell all we *both* know, and it won't take a second longer!"

❋

The newspaper headlines proclaimed that the United States had just increased its foreign aid by another 20 billion dollars, and that another tax increase would be required to pay for it.

"I tell ya, Vince, we gotta draw the line someplace," sighed Joe. "Charity is supposed ta begin at home."

"That's what I say," agreed Vince. "Take me, fer instance: I'd give my wife the shirt offa my back."

"Me too," affirmed Joe. "We might as well. Between our wives an' them furrin guvmints, they got everything else!"

❋

Maggie the cook, and Mary the upstairs maid, were gossiping in the kitchen of the Kennedy family's Hyannisport mansion.

"Sure, and 'tis an honor indade to be wurrkin' for the Kennedys," observed Maggie. "We must niver forgit they wanst had a prisidint in the family—the youngest wan in histhory."

"And what iv that?" sniffed Mary. "Me very own little Jamie was 'lected prisidint iv his Superman Club, and he's ownly *nine*!"

❋

When President Ford appointed Nelson Rockefeller as his vice president, Senator Edward Kennedy quipped:

"Now we have *two* vice presidents!"

❋

McGinty, pride of the Eighth Ward, staggered to the podium and, with slurred speech, pleaded for support in the forthcoming campaign for district leader.

"Vote me in fer disthric lader," he bellowed thickly, "an' I promish ye two chickensh in ivry g'rage an' proshperity aroun' ivry corner."

"B...s...!" shouted one of the listeners derisively.

"Shir, are you queshnin' my integrity?" demanded McGinty, offended.

"No, not your integrity," the listener called out, "just your sobriety, your honesty, and your veracity!"

❋

Chicago's Mayor Richard Daley, in the 1976 campaign:

"I shall pursue a course straight down the middle of the road, and let the chips fall where they may!"

*

Among the first things Gallegher learned upon arriving in the United States was to "jine the Dimmycrathic Paarty," if he ever expected to make a mark in his new homeland. Dutifully, he went to the local party headquarters, but somehow entered the building next door and found himself in the offices of the Socialist Party. There, he told the functionary in charge that he wished to sign up for membership.

"I'll have to give you a little test first," said the Socialist recruiter. "We can't allow reactionaries in our organization, you know."

"No, iv coorse not," agreed Gallegher, wondering what the word meant. "Test away."

"All right, which hand am I holding up?" he asked, extending his right hand high in the air.

"Your right," said Gallegher.

"Wrong," said the man. "That's my left."

"But av that's your left," asked Gallegher, bewildered, "then, faith, what is your other hand?"

"That," said the Socialist, "is my *extreme* left!"

*

Campaigning for a senatorial seat, James Buckley of New York was making an impassioned speech when he was interrupted by a man in the audience who apparently was not one of Buckley's more ardent admirers.

"I wouldn't vote for you if you were Saint Peter," shouted the heckler.

"If I were Saint Peter," countered Buckley, "you wouldn't be in my constituency!"

*

Miz Patricia McCallum, fighter for civil rights in the Women's Liberation movement, was jailed in New Bedford, Massachusetts, for defying a policeman's order to cease her unlawful picketing. She and an older and wiser Lady Libber were assigned adjoining cells. Before long, the older woman heard Miz McCallum sobbing in frustration and humiliation.

"There, there, dear, don't cry!" crooned the old gal consolingly. "Just put your faith in God: She'll protect you!"

*

When Chicago's Mayor James Daley was reelected—for the fifth time—various representatives of the news media were on hand to interview him. Al Doherty, a reporter from the Liberal Press of New York, no friend of the popular mayor, was able to get a work in edgewise amidst all the hubbub.

"Mr. Daley," said Doherty, his voice oozing sarcasm, "no doubt you will consult the powerful interests that control you before making your official decisions."

"Young fella," rasped Daley, "keep my wife outta this!"

*

When Jacqueline Kennedy went abroad after her husband's death, but long before she became Mrs. Onassis, she feared there would be an unnecessary fuss made over the wife of a fallen president—especially one as popular as John Fitzgerald Kennedy had been. The tragedy was still with her and her only desire now was for privacy.

"Don't worry," her sister and traveling companion assured her. "In the remote little places where we'll be stopping they don't know one American president from another. People won't bother you."

Her sister's prophecy was correct; until, that is, they arrived in the tiny Italian village of Mattarazzo. There, they received word that reservations had been made for them in the next town. This sounded ominous. When they reached the hotel on their next stop, they were greeted by the manager.

"We are proud to welcome the wife of the great President of the United States," he said, bowing low. "Will you please register, Mrs. Lincoln?"

*

This was the big night in the Fifth Ward. The two opponents, one a Democrat and the other a Republican, were scheduled to debate their qualifications for the State Legislature and, coincidentally, to prove that their adversaries were not only unfit for office but unworthy to call themselves human beings.

Reardon, a long-time resident of the district, was detained and, as a result, he arrived a little late. The debate was already in progress.

"Misther," asked Reardon of the man in the next seat, "which wan is Delahanty and which is Mulvaney?"

"I don't know," replied the man tersely. "But it doesn't make any difference—they're both damned scoundrels."

"Sure and I know that meself," retorted Reardon. "But which is the Dimmycrat and which is the Raypooblican? It's the Dimmycrat damn scoundrel I'm votin' for!"

*

In Chicago, a political hack approached the late Mayor Daley to plead for a nomination which, in Daley's fiefdom, would be equivalent to election.

"Sorry, but even I can't get you elected," reproved the mayor. "And it's all your own fault, too. Not after that newspaper story about the hotel episode in your district."

"That story is a dirty lie!" cried the politician. "Hell, my district doesn't even *have* a Hotel Episode!"

*

Columnist Pete O'Brien, as a cub reporter, once went to interview Mayor Frank ("I am the law!") Hague. The young newspaperman was curtly refused a hearing.

"I have nothing to say," growled Hague.

"Yes, I know," replied O'Brien evenly. "Now let's get down to the interview!"

*

The scene is New York. The time: the 1920s, when Babe Ruth was the King of Swat and people everywhere were singing "Sweet Rosie O'Grady" to the accompaniment of plunking ukeleles. James J. Walker, whose campaign promises had all the lasting qualities of his New Year's resolutions, had just been elected Mayor of New York. Jimmy soon appointed Grover T. Whalen as Police Commissioner and New York's "Official Greeter," a job in which the work consisted of getting the job. And therein lies a story.

Jimmy and Grover both denied the truth of this anecdote, but unfortunately for them, they were like the politician who finally admitted that he had lied—and nobody would believe him.

"Grover," said Mayor Jimmy, as they sipped an Irish whiskey at Tammany Hall, where the taxpayers picked up the tab, "I'm appointing you Commissioner of Police. Actually, all you'll have to do is shake a few hands and greet visiting dignitaries."

"How much does the job pay—at least on the surface?" asked Grover.

"Well, on the surface, about eighteen thousand dollars a year, but you can figure on a raise to twenty-five thousand dollars as soon as you've proved yourself: say in three days. And that doesn't count certain gratuities and fringe benefits."

"Where will all that money be coming from?"

"From New York City's employees."

"What?" exclaimed Grover indignantly. "Do you mean compulsory payments?"

"No, of course not," said Jimmy, unsullied virtue in his tones. "We make them pay on a voluntary basis!"

*

A British aristocrat, one Lord Pimplepater, was on the deck of the *Queen Mary,* preparing to grace the United States with his titled presence. Seated next to him in a deck chair was the late actor and comedian, Victor Moore. A radio nearby was offering the latest American election news.

"I say," interjected Lord Pimplepater, unable to conceal the snobbishness in his voice, "how unpleasant it must be for you Americans to be governed by people you'd never think of asking to dinner."

Moore's reply was prompt and chilly:

"No more unpleasant than being governed by people who wouldn't ask *you* to dinner!"

*

Another Joe Kennedy story, this one involving Al Smith, occurred in midsummer. The two above-named gentlemen were in attendance at the annual banquet to celebrate the Democratic victories at the polls. Of course, election day would not arrive for several months, but, inasmuch as there were only nine Republican voters in the region, no serious competition was envisioned.

The pleasantries of the evening were soon marred by a speaker who droned on and on, his deadly monotonous voice all but putting the audience to sleep. Bored to distraction, Joe Kennedy slipped quietly out into the hall. There, he bumped into Al Smith.

"Has that guy finished yet?" asked Al.

"Yes, long ago," replied Joe, "but the s.o.b. won't stop!"

*

According to Suds Sweeney, the sage of the saloon circuit, the reason there are so few able politicians in Washington is clear:

"All the people who know how to run the country are already employed as bartenders, barbers, and taxi drivers."

*

Robert F. Kennedy could be as witty as his older brother when the opportunity presented itself. At a Chicago campaign function where he served as the master of ceremonies, his first chore was to introduce Adlai Stevenson III.

"If there is one thing I can't stand," he began with a straight face, "it's a fellow running on his family name!"

*

The Congressional Record is not usually a fount of humorous anecdotes, but that rather austere journal was enlivened in 1976 with a report by California Senator Alan Cranston.

According to the senator, the former Postmaster General, Winton Blount, called a meeting of his top-level postal executives to determine if some way could be found to lessen the problems of mail delivery.

"I've been listening patiently for three hours," Blount finally said in exasperation, "and all I want is a simple answer to a simple question: If it is neither snow nor rain nor heat nor gloom of night that stays the couriers from the swift completion of their appointed rounds, then just what the hell *is* the trouble?"

*

Basil O'Conner, who was chief of the March of Dimes during the administration of Franklin D. Roosevelt, was on his way to the White

House one autumn day for an important conference with the president. At the entrance, he was stopped by one of those silly old socialites who abound in Washington, D.C.

"If it isn't dear Mr. O'Conner!" she gushed. "And how do you find yourself these brisk mornings?"

"Madam," replied O'Conner coldly, "I just throw back the blankets, and there I am!"

*

Senator Mike Mansfield tells the story of the two lions who escaped from the zoo in Washington, D.C., and didn't meet again for three months. One was sleek and fat, the other nothing but skin and bones.

"You certainly look well fed," said the emaciated one. "How did you ever manage?"

"Nothing to it," answered the fat one. "I've been holed up at the House Office Building, eating a congressman or two a day. So far nobody's noticed it."

*

Eamon de Valera, the Irish political leader who was born in Brooklyn, was a serious man in his later years, but in his youth he showed flashes of typical Celtic wit. Returning to Dublin from a visit to Paris some years ago, he was asked by a friend to give his impression of the French *mesdemoiselles.*

"I may safely say," replied de Valera, "that sex in Ireland is in its infancy!"

*

Back when Senator Joe McCarthy was riding the high tide of headlines, he was buttonholed by Detroit industrialist Harvey Campbell, an inveterate riddle-maker.

"Wait a minute, Joe," demanded Campbell, "I have a good question to ask you. Look, I have the face of Claudette Colbert, the torso of Ann Sheridan, and the legs of Betty Grable. Now tell me, who am I?"

"What do I care?" cried McCarthy, "Kiss me!"

*

Political blarney during a presidential campaign is an accepted method of ballyhoo, understood by all—including America's minority groups. John F. Kennedy learned all about that little truism when his campaign train stopped at an Indian reservation in South Dakota. There, he emerged to deliver a speech.

"I am appalled at the treatment given to you noble redmen and women by previous administrations, especially the Republicans. As our train pulled in, I saw many squaws washing clothes by the riverside, beating them on rocks, even as your ancestors did. I want you to know that when I am elected president I will see to it that a brand-new washing machine is installed in every teepee!"

The Indians broke out into loud cries of "Oompah! Oompah!"

Kennedy beamed at the response and continued: "And I understand that you are still obliged to dry beef for jerky. Well, I intend to equip every wigwam with a freezer!"

"Oompah! Oompah!" shouted the Indians.

The future president broke into his broadest grin and soared to a climax: "And if I am elected, I will personally see to it that your ancestral lands are restored to you, and that our treaties with your people are finally recognized and acted upon!"

"Oompah!" the Indians responded with a mighty roar that could be heard for a mile around.

Their handsome chief came forward and placed a war bonnet on Kennedy's head. Then he led the prospective Great White Father to the corrals for another gift, delivering the presentation speech in the impeccable English of a Carlyle graduate.

"The Indians of this reservation take great pleasure in presenting as a token of our esteem a silver-mounted saddle and our very best Indian pony."

As Kennedy prepared to mount the handsome animal, the Chief suddenly laid a restraining hand on his arm and cried out:

"Careful, Mr. Kennedy. Don't step in the oompah!"

*

In general, United States congressmen try to agree and disagree with a certain amount of moderation and decorum, but every once in a while, explosions during debate have led to actual blows.

Congressman Al Donohugh of Illinois did not resort to fisticuffs on the floor of the House, but he worked himself up to such a state that occupants of the Visitors' Gallery distinctly heard him mutter to himself as he stomped off the floor:

"I'm going home to dinner. If it's ready, I won't eat it. If it isn't, I'll raise holy hell!"

*

A congressman's wife sought the advice of a "Q" Street fortuneteller in Washington, D.C.

"Madam," prophesied the seeress, "prepare yourself for widowhood! Your husband is about to die a violent death."

"Oh, dear," sighed the woman. "Will I be acquitted?"

*

Joe Cannon, Speaker of the House, once characterized the Eiffel Tower as "The Empire State Building after taxes." And when nationwide scandals were rocking the Internal Revenue Bureau, and its personnel faced with prison terms, the witty congressman noted, "I'm all ready to pay the current installment on my income tax, but I don't know what jail to mail the check to."

*

Among the choice bits of gossip that spread like wildfire through the halls of Congress was the one first heard in the Senate cloakroom. As a result of the tale, Senator Bob Mahoney's wife, Mildred, never again wore a medallion her husband picked up for her on an air junket to Hong Kong.

Mildred was very proud of the unique gift for quite awhile—until one evening when a Chinese Nationalist diplomat informed her gravely that the literal translation of the Chinese characters on the medallion read:

"Licensed prostitute, City of Shanghai."

*

A not-too-reliable report in the Irish press stated that a horse had recently been elected to the British House of Lords.

"This is the first time in history," editorialized the paper, "that Parliament has seated an *entire* horse!"

*

Just before Bill O'Dwyer took office as Mayor of New York City, he found himself aboard a train with a group of mental patients being transferred to an institution for psychotics. The doctor in charge, surrounded by guards, was counting them off—"One, two, three, four"— when he stumbled into O'Dwyer.

"Who are you?" demanded the doctor, as the guards moved in.

"Sir," announced O'Dwyer proudly, drawing himself up, "you are addressing the next mayor of New York."

"Okay," snapped the doctor, "get in line! Five, six, seven, eight...."

*

The mayors of New York in days past supplied copy for every newspaper in the land. First there was John Hylan (called "Red Mike" behind his back) who escorted Queen Marie of Rumania on a tour up Fifth Avenue.

"Oh, what a perfectly marvelous avenue," exclaimed Her Majesty.

"You said a mouthful, Queenie," agreed His Honor.

Hylan seldom bothered to read the speeches that trusted "ghostwriters" prepared for him ahead of time. Addressing a Tammany audience one Saint Patrick's Day, he came to the phrase in his speech, "That reminds me of one of my favorite stories about the Protestant Irishman from Belfast who visited a Dublin whorehouse." It developed that the mayor had never heard the joke before, and when he finished reading it, he laughed so hard he broke his glasses.

The chairman of the banquet, Jimmy Walker himself, gallantly arose and read the rest of Hylan's speech for him.

The day came when Tammany Hall decided that New York needed a mayor to follow Jimmy Walker who would be a different character in every respect.

"I agree," said Jimmy. "Never follow a banjo act with another banjo act."

So the Tammany stalwarts bobbed up with John P. O'Brien, who, in his own words, was "a thousand per cent different." Mr. O'Brien quickly endeared himself to his constituents when he referred to "that scientist of scientists, Dr. Albert Weinstein," and told delighted reporters he was "a slave to litrachoor."

"I will work closely with the great governor of New York," he promised the electorate, "and I will travel every week, if necessary, to our state capital in Buffalo!"

Most memorable of all was John P. O'Brien's first interview with the press, which consisted mainly of a declaration that he would make his own decisions and take neither advice nor direction from Tammany. One reporter spoiled everything by asking: "Mr. Mayor, who is going to be your next police commissioner?"

"I don't know," answered O'Brien, scratching his head. "They haven't told me!"

*

Here, richly with ridiculous display,
The politician's corpse was laid away.
While all of his acquaintance sneered and slanged
I wept: for I had longed to see him hanged.

—Ambrose Bierce

Chapter Seventeen
Ooh, What You Said!
Introduction

If humor seems a necessary ingredient of Irish writing in general, it has avoided a theme which has not failed to engross the humorists of other countries. Lovemaking is a fundamental topic that writers in all countries have dealt with. Irish humorists have not missed this subject, but they have veered away from that small-boy curiosity in sex, that prurience which evokes a sniggering allusion in many American jokes. One might suspect the influence of religion on the strongly Catholic country of Ireland if it were not that many of the nineteenth-century Anglo-Irish writers of humor were Protestants. The jokes enjoying wide popularity in France and Italy, themselves Catholic countries, would disprove the idea that religion was a factor.

The only Irish writers who have been disposed to treat sex in a jocular way were those who lived in the United States and England, where their main literary function was to separate the fuddies from the duddies. We can infer, then, that sex, treated in this manner, is either urban or cosmopolitan in character, the product of such Centers as London, Paris, Rome, Berlin, and New York. Irish humor, generally, is remarkably chaste, and I assume this has some connection with the fact that Ireland is only now developing the highly sophisticated culture and manners of the great cities of the western world.

There are some exceptions, however miniscule though they may be. "O'Toole Tempts a Lady's Virtue" is one. The hundreds, and perhaps thousands, of limericks, are another. But one wonders if the latter were not created elsewhere than on Irish soil: certainly the original limericks were innocent of suggestive themes.

The classic writers of Irish folk humor directed their talents to other avenues than sex, hence the rarity of such anecdotes. A few examples of the rare, "naughty" humor that was popular in Ireland before the present century are published in the following pages. One of them, Grandpa Malone's story of the lady-in-waiting and the million pounds, probably the most daring in this chapter, may well be the funniest. The reason, it would seem, is in the telling rather than in the content alone.

Irish-American humor, as we shall see, is freer, though not necessarily funnier than native Irish jokes. In the United States, the Irish have veered away from the leisurely telling of longer funny stories, and have become adept at the quip, the crushing retort, and the brief joke, as though the teller was anxious to reach the punch line as quickly as possible. No doubt it is just as effective as the longer anecdote, but much of the characterization and richness of background is lost. It is the difference between the classic and the contemporary types of humor.

It was an Irish-American, James O'Brien, former president of the Chesapeake and Ohio Railroad, who said, for example, that old age is that period of life in which we compensate for the vices we still cherish, by reviling those we can no longer commit. "Passion," declared O'Brien, "is the emotion that distinguishes love without responsibility."

When confronted with the question of female beauty without thought of sex, the enlightened Irish-American responds with irrefutable logic: "Yes, but who would really be captivated if the Venus de Milo had her bloomers on?" Another comment in a similar vein was made by the late Senator Robert Kennedy at a Harvard Law School alumni banquet. "I make no accusations," declared the senator. "To accuse is to maliciously ascribe to another those actions which we have not had the temptation or opportunity to commit ourselves." He paused, a sudden afterthought bringing a wide smile to his face. "We must, however, sympathize with those accusations which grow in their bitter intensity," he concluded, "when strong drink heightens the desire but lessens the execution thereof."

Even mildly suggestive humor can sometimes evoke a cluck of disapproval in some, a chuckle of approval in others. In this chapter, I salute the "others."

—H.D.S.

> Me darlin' was swate, me darlin' was chaste,
> Faith, an' more's the pity.
> For though she was swate an' she was chaste,
> She was chased all through the city.

—Anonymous (circa 1790)

*

An elderly man, new to the neighborhood, entered Tim's Corner Tavern and ordered a glass of whiskey and two drops of water.

Tim served the drink without a word.

Then, the man ordered another whiskey and two drops of water.

Still, the bartender remained silent while he filled the order, but, after the fourth request, his curiosity got the better of him.

"Say, mister, I can understand the whiskey," he finally blurted, "but why only two drops of water?"

" 'Tis aisy enough to explain," said the old codger. "Me rason is wan iv health. I can howld me liquor but I niver could howld me wather!"

*

Voice filled with quiet desperation, yet somehow containing a tiny seed of hope that blarney still conquers all:

"Sure an' I know you're modest, me darlint, but faith, spendin' five or six hours togither with the lights off an' our clothes on is not what me sainted father would call a night iv Irish passion!"

*

There are numerous stories of the embarrassing predicaments that have ensnared public speakers at one time or another. But yesteryear's sports columnist, Phil Fitzgerald, probably experienced the worst fate of any when, with some trepidation, he finally consented to address a banquet at a nudist colony. The purpose was to help celebrate a long-distance swimming event.

Upon Fitzgerald's arrival at the extensive premises, he was greeted by large numbers of men and women in their pristine state. He was ushered into the headquarters building, where it was suggested that he might like to prepare for dinner.

Upstairs in his room, Fitzgerald, that paragon of Celtic morality, felt there was nothing he could do except face the fact that he was expected to divest himself of his clothing. In extreme mental anguish, he determined to be equal to the occasion. At last, hearing the bell peal for dinner, he marched downstairs as bare as Adam, only to discover, to his horror, that every single one of the colony's members had dressed formally in deference to the speaker!

*

It had been less than a week since Mrs. Houlihan arrived in America from County Kildare, and she was now taking her very first ride in a taxicab. It was an experience she was unlikely to forget. The cab hurtled through the streets as though pursued by a host of banshees, careening around corners on squealing tires, darting in and out of the heavy traffic with a reckless abandon that scared Mrs. Houlihan half to death. Eyes wide, lips taut, her hands clenched to suppress her fright, she called out to the driver:

"Rayjooce yer speed, ye cross-eyed orangey, or it'll be rayqueems fer both iv us!"

Scowling, the cabdriver glanced over his shoulder, muttered something inaudible but unflattering, and returned to his nefarious ways at the wheel.

"Dhriver, is it deef y'are?" screeched Mrs. Houlihan. "Be careful, I say! It's eight children I have at home!"

"Lady," the taxi driver snapped, "you got eight kids and *you* are advisin' *me* to be careful?"

*

O'Toole Tempts a Lady's Virtue

Grandpa Malone, relaxing in the glowing warmth of the peat stove, lit his pipe, took off his heavy brogans, leaned back in his chair, and began another of his tall tales.

"I'll not be afther swearin' to the truth iv this story, but I can tell ye this: the scan'lous carryin'-ons was towld to me by the main lady-in-waitin' to the Queen iv England herself—may a hundred Irishmen drink her best whiskey before she knows it's missin'! How did the likes o' me happen to know a lady-in-waitin'? Well, wan day I found her all alone an' sighin' in me cabbage garden, waitin' for a bit iv romance. She'd spied me the day before at the *shebeen* and could not get her mind off iv me; not that I blamed her, considerin' me good looks. 'Well,' says I to meself, 'I...' but that's anither story.

"Accordin' to me lady, the Queen daycided to visit Ireland, but onaisy rests the head iv a Queen in the Emerald Isle, to say nothin' iv the ace, king, and jack. So, instid, her majesty sint Kathleen, her lady-in-waitin', in her own place. Pretty, this colleen was, too, even in a cabbage garden.

"No sooner did Kathleen sittle in the Kilkinny Hotel when she caught the eye iv Timmie O'Toole, owner iv the establishment. Not knowin' her in her disguise, he set his mind to slaypin' with the grand lady, but divil the bit o' progress could he make, for all that he was a janius when it come to blarney.

"So he invited her to his private chambers for a spot o' tay—the impidince iv the man! And what he could not do with words he thried to do with tinder music. Oh, the gall iv some Irishmen! He sang her a touchin' little chune:

'In the town iv Kilkinny
    there du-wilt a fair mai-aid,
O in the town iv Kilkinny
    there du-wilt a fair mai-aid;
She had cheeks like the roses
    and hair iv the same,
And a mouth like ripe sthrawberries
    Drownded in crame.'

"But that didn't work nayther. There was only wan thing left to do, and he did it. Oh, that durrty spalpeen, that haythen!—He asked her direct!

" '*Macushla,* would ye be afther slaypin' with me fer a hundred pounds?'

"Kathleen's face got redder than Billy-be-damned, and she raised a hellabaloo that made her cup o' tay dance in the saucer.

" 'I am not yer *Macushla,* ye durrty scalawag! I am lady-in-waitin' to Her Majesty the Queen iv England, lordess iv the British Umpire and all that's in-betwixt—Britannia waives the rules. A hundred pounds indade!'

" 'Five hundred,' says O'Toole, ignorin' her maidenly objections.

" 'The toe iv me boot to ye!' says Kathleen. 'I'll have ye know I'm a Christian woman.' (And a fine and fittin' answer it was, too. Without the Christian Church I don't know what the hell the world would come to—but I'm gettin' away from me sthory)...

" 'A thousand pounds,' says O'Toole.

" 'I'll not be thradin' me vartue fer no thousand pounds,' says she.

" 'A million,' says he.

" 'A million, is it?'

" 'A million!'

" 'Wel-l-l,' says she, doin' some fast arithmetic, 'seein' as I am a poor lady-in-waitin', a million pounds would be such a comfort in me owld age...'

"But O'Toole intherrupted her by layin' tin shillin's on the table. 'Do me the honor, fair Kathleen, iv removin' yer bustle,' says he.

"Kathleen looked first at the shillin's and then at O'Toole, then at the shillin's and then at O'Toole agin.

" 'What's the maynin' iv this outhrage?' says she in a voice as cowld as an orangey's heart. 'Tin shillin's indade! Did ye think I could be got that aisy, me good man? What, pray, do ye take me fer?'

" 'It's yourself that's daycided what ye are, madam,' says Timmie O'Toole, 'Now it is ownly a matther iv hagglin'!' "

—William P. French

*

Sullivan the sinful scalawag was in church, bored and dejected, while Father Tumulty rumbled on about the Ten Commandments. Suddenly, he reached number seven, and intoned "Thou shalt not commit adultery."

All at once, Sullivan snapped to attention and brightened visibly.

"Aha," he exclaimed with satisfaction, "*that's* where I left my umbrella!"

*

Bill and his wife, Mary, were visiting New York—he for the Saint Patrick's Day parade, and she to do some shopping. He dropped in at his hotel's cocktail lounge for a drink, hoping that Mary would not spend too much money as she made the rounds of the stores. After a few more highballs, he decided to leave and asked for his check. He took one look at the bill and gasped. "I can't believe it!"

"Whatsa trouble, Mac?" asked the bartender.

"This check—it's highway robbery!" stormed Bill.

"That's what booze costs in New York," explained the bartender mildly.

"Then New York must be the most expensive place in the whole country," complained the out-of-towner. "Believe me, it's different back in Toledo. There, in my town, a man can drink as much as he wants without paying a cent, sleep in a fancy hotel for free, and wake up to find fifty dollars on the pillow."

"Aw, c'mon now," protested the bartender. "Did that ever happen to you?"

"Well, no, not to me personally," Bill confessed. "But it happens to my wife all the time!"

*

A young carpenter from Dublin, unable to find work in his native city, journeyed to London to seek employment. There, he entered the shop of a rich elderly merchant. But he had not taken two or three steps inside when he stopped short and stared at the stranger, his mouth agape. His resemblance to the merchant was fantastic.

The merchant was equally astonished. "Mister," he inquired, "where are you from?"

"From Ireland, sir. Dublin."

"Hmm. Tell me, did your mother ever visit London?"

"No," said the Irishman promptly, "but my father did!"

*

It is said of Lester Leary, the legendary lover of Limerick, that he had slept with many girls but refused to marry any of them. Fickle fate then entered his life in the person of merry Molly Malone of Monaghan. Lester, bubbling over with blarney as usual, used all his powers of persuasion to entice her to bed, but she firmly resisted his amorous advances. Stopped in his tracks at last, and so enamored of the girl was he, that he married her.

"Molly," said Lester on their wedding night, "I want you to know that I would not have made you my wife if you had gone to bed with me as all the other girls did."

"Well, experience is the best teacher," confided Molly. "That's how I lost all my other suitors."

*

Six-year-old Gracie was a precocious little girl, so her mother was not too surprised when her daughter asked, "Mommy, what does physical attraction mean?"

"You have plenty of time to think about that," said the mother, chuckling. "When you are old enough you will meet the right man. Together you will share mutual interests such as music, literature, art, and so on. In your eyes, he will be handsome, thoughtful, and kind. Do you understand?"

"I think so, Mommy," replied Gracie after a reflective pause, "but tell me, is that better than sex?"

*

"Oh, Maggie, I'm so disappointed in marriage," wept the bride of six months. "Michael hasn't touched me since my wedding night."

"Why, that's terrible!" exclaimed Maggie. "If I were you, I'd divorce him tomorrow."

"I can't," sobbed the bride. "I'm married to Jimmy."

*

On his way home from work one evening, Andy found a copy of an underground "swingers" newspaper on the subway beside him. His curiosity as well as his Irish sense of humor was aroused by the suggestive ads, obscene stories, and flagrant nudity. He thought of his very prim wife and smiled to himself.

Later, after dinner, a mischievous twinkle in his eye, he told her about the paper, and then suggested that they duplicate some of the nude scenes. "We can take our clothes off and go for a stroll, or swim at the beach, or just go to the store," he suggested, suppressing a grin.

"Now you listen to me, Andrew," she snapped (she *never* called him "Andy" when she was annoyed), "if the good Lord had intended for respectable people to run around naked, we would have been born that way!"

*

"Howl of the Wolf" Department:

"You look tired dear. Why not come up to my place where you can lie down in the bedroom?"

—Patrick Ireland

*

O'Brien could not, or would not, face the fact that modern college football is a matter of teamwork—especially at such a prestigious school as Notre Dame. He was a fast man once he had the ball, and was as artful a dodger as ever ran for a touchdown. But that wasn't enough for his ego. He had to be the *star*—the one-man team. Today, he was quarterbacking when he should have been linebacking; way out in front when he should have been running interference; or glorying in the art of the extra-long forward pass. Had he been one-tenth as clever in the classroom as he was on the gridiron, he would have been a professor. Alas, such was not the case. His coach could stand his athletic shenanigans no longer.

"O'Brien!" he yelled hoarsely. "What the hell is the matter with you? Can't you understand plain English? I told you to *carry* the ball, not pass it! Don't you know what a ball-carrier is?"

"Sure," said the unrepentant O'Brien, "a jockstrap!"

*

Hollywood film writers, it has been said, occupy a position on the social totem pole somewhere between lavatory attendants and used car salesmen. Patrick O'Herlihy, the movie scripter, tells of the time his dignity was wounded to such an extent that he finally lashed out in retaliation. The fact that he was mistaken does not detract from the story.

A famous movie star decided to produce a picture based on a very successful stage play. The so-called plot was all about a Little Girl Who Really Knew Better, and an Innocent Preacher Who Did the Best He Could. All those capital letters in the title increased the price of the play by ten thousand dollars.

The famous actress insisted that she would retain only an experienced playwright, and was delighted to learn that a writer she had never met, or even heard of, had served as a chaperone of sorts in Alaska before turning to writing. His chaperoning, so rumor had it, involved an establishment full of charming ladies.

The actress was canny. Here was her man. His name, she learned, was

O'Herlihy. She staged a big party in Beverly Hills, and the playwright was invited. For Patrick O'Herlihy, this was the *real* Hollywood! This was Big Stuff! During the festivities, the Star showered the poor guy with Attention. He was Flattered. He swelled up, and then swelled up some more, as he downed his sixth glass of champagne.

Then came a lull in what passes for conversation in Hollywood. The Star fixed the Author with her most Dazzling Smile: "I understand that you are an authority on prostitution."

O'Herlihy, his eyes a little glazed, rose unsteadily to his feet and smiled in an almost Paternal Manner. But when he spoke, it was with quiet Irish authority. No more would he be insulted like this. His Dignity, dammit, was once again being sullied.

"If you are considering going into the profession, I'd advise against it," he said, his voice surprisingly steady in view of the gallon of champagne he had quaffed. "Even if I were to give you the best street in town, you couldn't keep me in cigarettes. Good evening, my dear!"

Whereupon the intrepid O'Herlihy zigzagged toward the door, and would have made it, too, except that he fell flat on his face and was thrown out bodily through the service entrance—er—Exit!

*

Father Harrigan had just finished his breakfast coffee when his inner sanctum was invaded by a young man at whose wedding he had just officiated a month before.

"Top o' the mornin' to ye," greeted the priest. "And how is the happy bridegroom this bright and sunny day?"

" 'Tis an unhappy man you're lookin' at," replied the young fellow sadly. "Me marriage is breakin' up on the rocks iv abstinence an' religion."

"Abstinence an' religion, is it?" echoed Father Harrigan. "Sure and did ye niver hear iv th' rhythm method? A good Catholic is *supposed* to remain abstinent at sartin times iv th' month."

"It's not that a'tall," sighed the bridegroom. "Me bride is that taken with religion, she won't slape with me durin' anny week with a Sunday in it!"

*

They tell this story about Mike Hanrahan, "they" being that fine man's enemies—bad cess to 'em.

Mike, boss of his own brickmaking company, hired a new bookkeeper—a male. It was the young fellow's first job, and he was anything but experienced. That very evening, Mike had to fire him.

A mutual friend pleaded in the boy's behalf. "Give him a break, Mike. He's only a neophyte."

Mike was appalled.

"B'Jazus!" he exclaimed. "An' to think I been alone all day in a room with him!"

*

Robbi Ryan—one of those lace-curtain Ryans who regularly make the society pages—was parading down Park Avenue. Draped on his arm was Hannabelle Hogan, known in certain quarters as Hoboken Hannah. For reasons unknown, and which have nothing to do with this story, she had completely won Robbi's heart, such as it was.

As they walked down the avenue, a handsome, sportily-attired gentleman neared them from the opposite direction. His eyes met Hannah's. Hannah's eyes met his. All four eyes lit up in a mutual appreciation of the other's charms, if not instant affection.

But Robbi's eyes did not light up at all: what they did was darken with embarrassment and anger. As the stranger passed by, Robbi gave him a vicious look and then remained coldly silent as they continued their stroll.

"Aw, don't be that way, sweetie," crooned Hannah, worried lest he suffer an attack of economic thrombosis. "Why, that man was an old, old friend. He's a trouper I met years ago in the profession."

But Robbi was still steaming.

"Whose profession?" he snarled. "His or yours?"

*

Oh, but it was a sordid and shocking case that was being aired in court. The plaintiff, one Miss Dolly Farrell, indignantly claimed that she had been sexually assaulted by the defendant, known affectionately among his compatriots as "Stud" Murphy.

"Tell me this," demanded counsel for the defense as he faced the lady in the witness chair, "did you offer any resistance to this alleged assault? For instance, did you scream?"

"I did indade," replied Dolly virtuously. "I scramed at th' top o' me lungs."

"Scrame, did ye now?" cried Murphy, his voice ringing out indignantly in the courtroom. "Niver a yilp did ye give till ye rached the deliv'ry room, nine months later!"

*

A couple of professional baseball players were on the Cannonball Express, en route to their winter training quarters in Florida. Also aboard the train was a pretty lady reporter, newly arrived from Dublin, on her first sports assignment in the United States. Seated at the same table in the dining car, the two young men decided they might as well introduce themselves to the female neophyte.

"My name's Paul," said the first fellow, grinning, "but I'm not an Apostle."

"And my name's Peter," offered the other, also smiling, "but I'm not a saint."

"Sure and I'm glad to meet you," responded the girl. "My name's Mary, but I'm...aw, forget it!"

*

This truncated exposé occurred when Hollywood's Barry and Pegeen Fitzgerald were visiting Henrik van Loon at Cambridge University. He personally took them on a tour of the institution, pointing out the various sights he thought would be of interest.

"That," said van Loon, pointing to a formidable-looking female striding along before them, "is Eileen McGilicuddy. She's mistress of Ridsley Hall."

Pegeen drew her husband aside. "Barry," she whispered, "who is Ridsley Hall?"

*

Grandpa Greeley of Galway, a widower these forty-five years, decided to marry again. His eye—his good one, that is—fell upon the fair maiden, Magdalene, who was celebrating her seventeenth birthday. The slight difference in their ages made no difference to either, and Grandpa Greeley proudly announced his marital intentions to his startled children and grown grandchildren.

"Now see here, Grandpa," admonished his eldest grandson, "I don't like to be mentioning this to my own kith and kin, but do you realize that at your age all that sexual activity could bring on a heart attack? Be reasonable, Grandpa; it could even result in death."

"That it could, that it could," agreed Grandpa, shrugging. "But if the lassie dies, I'll just git me another wan!"

*

It was the beginning of a new semester at the university, and the pretty coed, recently arrived from Ireland, looked as bewildered as she no doubt felt. Holding a sheaf of papers in her hand, she approached one of the professors.

"Misther," she asked, "what do I do with me form when it is filled out?"

"That, young lady," he replied gravely, "is strictly a matter between your desires and your conscience!"

*

Anthony Brady, the industrialist, tells of the time when, many years ago, he was tormented by bedbugs at a hotel which was considered to be far above such nasty inhabitants. Upon returning home, he wrote an indignant letter to the manager of the hotel, complaining about the matter.

Brady's friends—even his own family—cautioned him about the futility of letters of complaint, so his satisfaction was understandably great when, in due course, he received an apologetic letter assuring him that such a thing would never happen again. But his elation was quashed a moment later, however, when he discovered an interoffice memo that had inadvertently been inserted with the letter, and which said tersely:

"Send this sonofabitch the bug letter!"

*

The Dublin Players Guild
presents
"THE BACK O' ME HAND TO YE!"

—Starring—

SALES CLERK..............Pat Hand
CUSTOMER..........Bertha D'Bluze

SALES CLERK: Would you be interested in this fine trunk, madam?
CUSTOMER: Faith, an' why in the wurrld would I be buyin' a thrunk, iv all things?
SALES CLERK: To put your clothes in, of course.
CUSTOMER: What! Are ye daft, young man? Me clothes, indade! And would ye have me run about nekkid?

*

The young honeymooners of New Bedford, Pat and Pauline, checked into the Hilton Hotel in Los Angeles. That was on a Saturday. On the following Tuesday, it was decided that they had better leave their hotel room and get something to eat, if they were to survive. Pat, for some strange reason, found himself too weak to get up and visit the restaurant, so Pauline went alone to purchase some sandwiches to bring back.

Returning to the hotel with the food, she got off the elevator at the wrong floor. Then unaware of her mistake, she went down the corridor until she reached what she thought was the door to her room. Finding it locked, and having no key with her, she knocked.

"Honey, oh honey," she called softly.

There was no response. She knocked again, calling somewhat more loudly, "Honey, oh honey."

But when she still received no reply, she grew apprehensive. "Honey," she yelled, "open the door!"

"Madam," a blatant male voice finally roared from within, "this is a bathroom—not a beehive!"

*

For years, old man McCall had looked forward to the time he could retire from the construction business and devote himself to small-scale farming. Then came the great day. He bought a few acres in the country, stocked it with some chickens, three cows, and a bull named Oswald. But at the end of the first year, he realized that he had an unexpected problem on his hands. So he went to a veterinarian in the nearby town.

"That bull of mine hasn't even looked at the cows," he complained. "I don't know what to do."

"Give him these vitamin pills," suggested the vet, handing him a large box. "It should arouse his romantic fervor."

It wasn't too long afterward that McCall noticed a decided improvement in intersexual camaraderie in the vicinity of the barn. In fact, to the delight of McCall and the three cows, Oswald was transformed from a nonperformer to a perpetual-motion machine.

A few weeks later, McCall's former partner paid him a visit, and listened with mounting interest as his friend related the events of the bull's improved personal life.

"What kind of vitamins did the vet prescribe?" asked the visitor. "Do you know the name?"

"No, I have no idea what they were," replied McCall, "but they have a licorice taste."

*

One of her little pupils had complained that seven-year-old Danny had been using profanity. The teacher, a strait-laced lady of the old school, called Danny aside to investigate the matter.

"Young man," she snapped, "what's this I hear about you using naughty words?"

"Who told ya that?" demanded Danny.

"A little bird told me."

"Boy, ain't that somethin'!" groaned the outraged Danny. "An' here I been feedin' the little bastards!"[1]

*

Pregnant Pauses

When Pete and Mary emigrated to this country way back in 1930, they were dirt poor, as were most of the other Irish newcomers to our shores. But Pete was an ambitious young fellow. He joined the police department, and, as an officer, he managed to accumulate a million dollars by the time he retired at age sixty-five. That is not to say that he ever robbed a bank. He was just a hard-working cop who was alert to certain opportunities, but, we repeat in his defense, he never robbed a bank. Yes, Pete was a fine broth of a man. He was also a good Catholic, and his wife, Mary, bore him twelve children—eight sons and four daughters.

But Pete and Mary, although financially secure in their old age, were sorely troubled. All of their children had been married for some time, but not one had produced a grandchild. "You are making a mockery of our religion!" he had often stormed, but his tirades had little effect on their inclinations, let alone their passions.

Then came the day when old Pete was inspired with a brilliant idea. He invited all of his children to dinner, and they came—the sons with their wives and the daughters with their husbands—all twenty-four of them.

[1] *Valley Shamrock,* Schenectady, N.Y., 1932.

When they were gathered in the huge dining room of his mansion, Pete cleared his throat and began his announcement:

"We are gathered here at this table to enjoy a family meal together. But first I want to say that I have set up a hundred thousand dollar trust fund to be given to my first grandchild. Now, we will bow our heads while I give thanks for this bountiful food the Lord has set before us."

When Pete finished the blessing, he looked up. A smile crossed his features. He and Mary were the only ones left at the table.

*

Somehow, the rumor was started at the Hartford Hibernian Club that old man Doherty was impotent. Mooney, the club's president and perennial cutup, found the slow-thinking Doherty ideally suited to his sense of biting humor.

"Say, Doherty," railed Mooney one Saturday evening, "I hear that you can still get your Irish up, but nothing else."

"Oh, yeah?" retorted Doherty, who was known for just such snappy comebacks. "Well, I'll have you know that my wife enjoyed some mighty good lovin' last night."

"So what?" observed Mooney, grinning. "Nobody suspects your wife!"

*

Back in County Donegal, around the turn of the century, they tell of the time Mike Dugan came in from the fields where he and his fellow villagers had been clearing the potato rows. His colleagues, it seems, had imparted some worrisome news to him.

"Mollie," he said to his wife, "they tell me that Mike Flynn—that disreputable *gombeenman*—has slept with every woman in this village, except one."

"I'm not a'tall surprised," answered Mollie spitefully. "I'm bettin' it's that high an' mighty Mrs. Flaherty across the road!"

*

Aside from religious matters, most priests are also quite knowledgeable about human relations. A few, however, have much to learn. We are reminded, for example, of the young priest, recently ordained, who was counseling a soon-to-be-married couple.

"Just remember," he said gravely, "that sex is not necessary for a happy marriage. People stay married for years—all their lives—without it. Why, I know one couple who are absolutely devoted to each other and never even think of sex...and they're both in their eighties!"

*

It is said of Beacon Hill Betsy that she was a lady of easy virtue—a statement no gentleman should make without substantial proof. Our only authority is the nurse who overheard an exchange of dialogue in the physician's examination room.

Miss Betsy described her ailments to the good doctor and, when she had itemized all her symptoms, he finally spoke.

"All right, just take your clothes off and lie down on this table."

"What!" exclaimed Betsy. "Without a martini first?"

*

Michael invited pretty Patricia to his apartment for dinner—and with a few naughty plans in mind. He was not the bold, brash type, however, and was wondering how to broach the subject that was uppermost in his mind, when he was struck with inspiration. Filling both their glasses with a good brandy, he raised his drink in a toast.

"Bottoms up!" he asserted. "Or any other position that appeals to you."

*

Little Miss Muffet decided to rough it
In a cabin quite old and medieval.
A blighter espied her and plied her with cider,
And now she's the forest's primevil.

Chapter Eighteen
Up the Rebels
Introduction

Strictly speaking, Irish "rebel" humor includes only those witty observations and anecdotes relating to Ireland's historic struggle for independence from British misrule. It usually bears upon a nonviolent theme, stressing the Irish revolutionary *spirit* rather than actual military confrontation. The protagonists are nearly always the English and Irish. Religion did not become a component of "rebel" humor until the establishment of the Republic of Ireland, overwhelmingly Catholic, and the creation of Ulster, two-thirds Protestant, as a separate entity within the British Commonwealth.[1]

Nevertheless, it is the current *political* struggle between the northern provinces and those to the south of Ireland that is usually emphasized in "rebel" humor; with the religious issue mentioned only incidentally. The paucity of such Catholic-Protestant jokes in this category will be noticed in the following pages which contain only three such anecdotes. Plainly, the most popular "rebel" jokes remain those in which the British are the adversaries, rather than Irish against Irish.

The funniest exceptions to the rule, however, are those which cannot always be identified as sympathetic to Ulster or to the Republic. With minor variations, they can, and often have been, repeated in Belfast or Dublin. We learn, for example, that an Irish fort is an enclosure to prevent the Irish inside from taking a shillelagh to the Irish outside. The barbed wire surrounding the fort prevents the Irish outside from mauling the Irish inside.

In Ulster, we are told, there are two kinds of calamities: a bad crop of potatoes in northern Ireland, and a good crop of potatoes in southern Ireland. In Dublin, you will learn that self-esteem is a commendable form of well-deserved respect for those living in the Irish Republic, but an erroneous appraisal for those living in Ulster. And a neutral observer; that is, an Irishman with a Catholic father and a Presbyterian mother, and living on the boundary line between the two countries, gives his opinion of the Irish Re-

---

[1]Religious humor, a separate category, will be found in the chapter titled "Steeple People."

publican Army: "The I.R.A. is a terrorist organization whose Roman Catholic members are despised by Protestants because they do not fight fair enough to suit them."

But that's the Irish! If they haven't any Englishmen to fight they'll fight each other. And when peace finally comes to all of Ireland, they'll probably get into a grand brawl with the Republic of China.

—H.D.S.

"How the Fighting Started"

> A Catholic out on his motor,
> Ran over a Protestant voter.
>   "Thank goodness," he cried,
>   "He was on the wrong side."
> So I don't blame myself one iota."
>
>   —Anonymous

✱

In Belfast, a short time ago when terrorist activity was rampant, old Mrs. Mulvaney returned home from the new First-Aid Training Class she had attended that day. At the dinner table, she told her husband all about it.

"Furrst-aid thrainin', is it?" growled Mr. Mulvaney, unimpressed. "An' do ye think ye'll iver be usin' it?"

"Faith, I used it on me way home today," cried Mrs. Mulvaney triumphantly. "There I was, walkin' acrosst the square, whin all iv a suddint I heard shots behind me. I turned around, I did, an' I see this poor man layin' in the strate. He'd been hit by the I.R.A., bad cess to thim! His head was that bloody, it was, an' his face all squished up. Oh, 'twas too awful to describe! A mess he was!

"An' at that virra moment, me furrst-aid thrainin' come to me rescue, an' I knew just what to do. I sat right down on the curb, I did, an' I put me head twixt me knees—an' that kept me from faintin'!"

✱

Ryan and Hogan, two rather impulsive young men, had just blown up a British tank in Ulster, but within fifteen minutes they were captured. The sentence: death by a firing squad.

Each of the men were tied to a post and blindfolds placed over their eyes. The British lieutenant in charge of the execution began the final count: "One, *reeady!* Two, *aim!* Three, *f...*" A shouted interruption halted the count.

"Long live the United Republic of Ireland!" yelled Ryan defiantly.

"Are ye daft, man?" gasped the outraged Hogan. "Isn't it enough throuble we're in already?"

*

The fighters in the Nationalist cause have come up with a new way to win the war. They hope to depopulate Ulster by providing cheap passage to America for any Protestant who is willing to emigrate. Best of all, the passengers only have to pay if, somehow, the plane lands.

*

It's terrible the way even little children are being drawn into the current troubles between the Catholics and Protestants in the North. One little boy in Ulster sneaked into a house where the I.R.A. was holding a meeting.

"All right, everybody," he shrilled, waving a grenade in his hand, "tell the Pope to get out of Ireland right now or I'll blow the place up!"

"But, laddie, the Pope isn't in Ireland," protested the I.R.A. leader. "You're afther makin' a big mistake."

"Misthake, is it?" yelled the tyke menacingly. "Well, there's no mistake about this choc'late bomb!"

*

IRISH PASSENGER: Steward, how soon will we be in Liverpool?

STEWARD: In about fifteen minutes, sir.

PASSENGER: Good! It is now twenty minutes to four, so I'll be able to catch the four o'clock train.

STEWARD: I'm afraid not, sir. You forget that Liverpool time is a quarter of an hour before Dublin time.

PASSENGER: Oh, holy Nellie! And I supose you call that justice to Ireland!

*

Hark to the woes of Cal Calahan of County Cork, who was arrested by a British platoon commander. Patriot Calahan, it seems, had imbibed more than was conducive to sobriety and, in his cups, climbed the village steeple. There, waving a bottle, he shouted in a stentorian voice: "Th' King iv England is a spalpeen, a scalawag, and a onsaintly scoundrel iv the furrst, second, and thurrd wathers!"

Poor Calahan was sentenced to a total of fifteen years in prison: one year for public intoxication, and fourteen years for revealing state secrets.

*

" 'Twas back in 1920 when I was a young bucko and fightin' the ondaycint Black an' Tans," reminisced old Sean O'Casey. "Our byes had capshured wan o' thim villyins afther he'd kilt wan iv ours. We stood him up forninst a wall an' give him two minutes to make his peace with the Lord.

" 'I have said me prayers, an' I have nawthin' more t'say,' sez he. 'Git on with th' execution an' the divil take ye!'

"At that p'int, pathriot that I was an' still am, bedad, I riz me v'ice an' I sez, sez I, 'If this orangey won't use his two minutes to make his peace, I'd like to say a few wurrds in behalf of *Sinn Fein!*' "

*

Among the many humorous legends which surround the nineteenth-century Irish patriot, O'Connell, this one is regarded as having some substance in fact.

Mr. Goulburn, while Secretary for Ireland, visited Killarney at the time when O'Connell, then on circuit, happened to be there. Both stopped at Finn's Hotel and chanced to get bedrooms opening off the same corridor.

It was O'Connell's habit to arise early, so, as usual, he awakened the next morning at cock-crow. Finding the hall door locked, and thereby hindered from walking outside, he commenced pacing up and down the corridor. To pass the time, he repeated aloud some of Moore's poetry, and had just uttered the lines—

"We tread the land that bore us,
The green flag flutters o'er us,
The friends we've tried are by our side—"

At that moment, Goulburn popped his nightcapped head out to see what was the matter. O'Connell instantly pointed his finger at him and finished the verse—

"And the foe we have before us!"

In went Goulburn's head in the greatest hurry!

*

During the dark days following the 1916 uprising, the editor of a small one-man journal in Londonderry was brought before the bar of justice (the "justice" depending upon which side of the bar one occupied).

"You are accused of publishing an article defending the Home Rule cause," said the magistrate sternly. "How do you plead?"

"I am innocent, Your Excellency," replied the editor bravely. "I never even saw that story until I happened to read it in my paper!"

*

During the anguished years of the potato famine, when evictions of the peasantry were common, most people confronted their problems with great courage. Many, of course, resorted to violence. But the landlords exhibited their own brand of unique fortitude.

A case in point was the absentee British landlord who demonstrated his fearless nature with this note to his Irish overseer:

"Tell the tenants that no threat to shoot *you* will terrify *me!*"

*

In the seventeenth century, when the union with England and Ireland was first in agitation, many citizens in Dublin who were firmly on the side of independence resolved "to burn every article imported from England," with one exception—
"Coal!"

*

Back before the Easter uprising of 1916, a British Army officer was escorting his Irish prisoner to jail. On their way, they passed a gallows.
"If the gallows had its due," remarked the officer grimly, "you know where you'd be right now, don't you?"
"That I do," spat the defiant patriot, straightening up in his saddle, "I'd be riding alone!"

*

John Selden (1584-1654), the erudite English scholar, jurist, and a member of Parliament, was often condemned, imprisoned, and castigated by king and church for his monumental impertinence and radical beliefs. Considering the times in which he lived, he displayed a singular gift of courage as this little memoire so well illustrates.
Charles I, troubled by the rebellions that were cropping up—civil uprisings that Selden himself had inspired through his demands for parliamentary reform—asked that gentleman, "How can I put an end to the disaffection in Ireland?"
"Remove the cause, Your Majesty," counseled Selden promptly.
"But what *is* the cause?" persisted Charles.
"You!" snapped the legislator.

*

"Grandpa," asked little Maureen, "how come our fambly never had no big heroes?"
"No heroes, did ye say?" exclaimed the oldster. "I'll have ye know, young lady, that we have been producin' heroes iver since the first iv our fambly started the Clendenin line. Yis, it all began, it did, with Matthew Clendenin, yer great, great, great grandpa."
"Ooh, tell me!" cried Maureen, sensing another of her grandfather's remarkable tales.
"Well, a long time ago—a *very* long time ago, I might say—when the French landed at Bantry Bay, yer ancisthor Matthew was posted with a musket upon wan iv the cliffs. Somehow 'r ither he wandhered a leetle out iv position and came face-to-face with an English officer.
" 'What are ye *here* for?' thundered the Britisher.
" 'Faith, sor,' answered Matthew with an impidint grin, 'it's beginnin' to look like I'm here fer a century!' "

*

Impeachable Statistics

The unfortunate "troubles" between the North and South, in Ireland, has resulted in an increase among those desiring to emigrate to the United States. The quota set by each, however, represents the total population of Ulster and the Irish Republic.

*

Then there's the terrorist who lit a bomb but was slow to let it go. He was buried. with honors. in Belfast and Dublin.

*

In Belfast, an American newspaper correspondent was writing his report of the latest violence between the forces of the North and South.

"I don't know if this will ever reach you," he wrote to his editor, "because of the Protestant censorship."

A few days later he received a note from the Belfast post office:

"Sir, the statement in your letter is not correct. We Irish Protestants *never* open letters!"

*

Whether it was a group of Protestant guerrillas or I.R.A. terrorists may never be learned, but a raid occurred one day outside of Belfast, in which several innocent passers-by were injured.

A kind old lady who had taken a first-aid course rushed over to where the injured were lying on the sidewalk. Solicitously, she bent over one of the fallen men whose head was swathed in bandages.

"I see the medics have taken care of you, lad," she said. "Were you shot in the head?"

"No ma'am," answered the victim, making an effort to keep from snarling, "I was shot in the foot and the bandages slipped up!"

*

In Ireland, it is whispered that a new technique for the fairy tale has come into existence.

The old formula began: "Once upon a time." Now it begins: "The General Headquarters of the I.R.A. communicates...."

*

During World War II, Irishmen everywhere put aside their personal and national animosities and prayed for England's victory over Hitler's Nazis,

In Ulster, they prayed, "Please, God, let the British win quickly!"

In the Republic, they prayed, "Please, God, let the dirty British win quickly!"

*

Percy and Wilburforce, two Londoners, were visiting Belfast when the train in which they were riding came to a sudden stop. The passengers began their usual complaints, but quickly lapsed into silence when they looked out the window and saw that the cause of the stop was a holdup. In a minute, the robbers were in the car where the two Englishmen were sitting.

"All right, everyone, we're takin' up a collection for a grand cause—the I.R.A.!" sang out one of the masked men. They started through the coach, taking money, jewels, and other valuables from the passengers.

In the last seats, Percy turned to Wilburforce and hurriedly produced his wallet. "Here, take this quick, Willie. It's the five pounds I've owed you for a year!"

*

The character of the natural-born revolutionary is typified by the Irishman who was cast into the waters near the beach of a remote island. Weak and exhausted after the shipwreck and his struggle with the wild waves, the castaway staggered along the sands until he encountered a native.

"What place is this?" asked the shipwrecked Irishman.

"Poontang Island," said the native.

"Is there a government here?"

"Of course."

"Then I'm against it!"

*

Eamon de Valera, the *Sinn Fein* leader and first president of the Irish Republic, was not a man to be easily dissuaded, to say nothing of being intimidated. He was once arrested at Ennis, in mid-sentence, during a fiery political speech. A year later, he was released. De Valera went right back to Ennis and resumed his speech:

"As I was saying when I was interrupted...."

*

At dinner in a restaurant one long ago day, Douglas Jerrold was forced to listen to a noisy argument between two Irishmen of opposing beliefs: one an admirer of the Prince of Orange, the other a supporter of William III. Having exhausted the political issues of the debate, they did what all good Irishmen do—they entered upon the personal phases of the question.

"*Arrah!*" exploded one of the arguers. "May all the birds iv Ireland flock togither and lave their callin'-cards on yer silly head! And as fer your King William, sor, I spit on him!"

The other, not to be outdone, leaped to his feet and proceeded to express his own opinions:

"May ye fall through the fly iv yer throusers and break yer Black-an'-Tan neck, ye thraitor! And I spit on yer dirty prince iv Orange—and anny ither orangey *galloglasses* ye may be afther mintionin'—sor!"

At this point, Jerrold, unable to endure the racket a moment longer, shouted for the waiter.

"Here, please—spittoons for two!"

*

At a meeting of the Irish Republican Army, a certain participant in the debate was shot by several of the others in attendance. The event occurred on the open floor and created a considerable stir in the little community.

An American, who happened to be in town, asked an acquaintance the reason for the shooting.

"The lad made a motion that was out of order," explained the local man.

"What!" exclaimed the American, horrified at this excess of parliamentarianism. "You mean to tell me that they shot a man in cold blood on the floor of the meeting just for making a motion that was out of order?"

"Sure now, you don't understand," drawled the informant lazily. "The motion was toward his hip pocket!"

*

A member of *Sinn Fein,* during the time of the 1916 "troubles," once made the odd remark that Scots were gentlemen but the British were not. Asked what he meant, the man explained:

"One day, a platoon of British soldiers captured me and brought me to their headquarters near Dublin. There I was interrogated by a pair of officers, one British and the other a Scotsman. They insisted that I had a store of rifles concealed behind a brick wall. I denied the accusation, of course.

" 'I give you my word of honor,' I said, 'that I have no rifles concealed in my brick wall.'

"Well, the Scottish officer was a gentleman. He accepted my word of honor and ceased questioning me. But the British officer was not a gentleman at all. He not only pulled down the brick wall but he confiscated all my rifles!"

*

An Orangeman who had acquired a comfortable living by bowing his head and bending his knee to the king of England looked down upon his less prosperous countrymen with no small degree of contempt. It so happened that he found it necessary to cross the border into the Republic. There, he came upon a Nationalist digging potatoes at the side of the road.

His voice dripping with disdain, the Orangeman jeered, "If you had only learned to flatter the king, you would not have to be digging potatoes."

"Sir," replied the Nationalist evenly, "if you had only learned to dig potatoes, you wouldn't have to be flattering the king!"

*

An Englishman and an Irishman were in the midst of a heated discussion!

"Why is it," demanded the Englishman in exasperation, "that you Irish always fight for land, land, land, while we English just fight for honor?"

"I suppose," retorted the Irishman, "that we each fight for what we most lack!"

*

An Irish member of Parliament, in the old days, who was also a theologian of note, had just finished a statement in support of his Irish Catholic constituency. Another member, opposed to his views, jumped to his feet, demanding to be heard.

"Why, I never heard of such a thing in my life!" exclaimed the opposing M.P. indignantly.

"Sir," replied the Irish member, just as heatedly, "I cannot allow your ignorance, however vast, to prejudice my knowledge, however small!"

*

Gleaned from the *San Francisco Shamrock:*

There is a unique quality inherent in Irish humor that retains its Celtic buoyancy whether it emanates from Ulster or the Republic. In witness whereof, we relate the confrontation between an American, Bill (Boom-Boom) Brady, and a terrorist.

Boom-Boom, a basketball player, was in Belfast, where his team was scheduled to play some exhibition games with the local teams. One evening, seeking a little solitude away from his teammates, he took a stroll through the city, enjoying the sights and smiling at the pretty girls.

Suddenly, on one of the city's less frequented streets, a fierce-looking man jumped out of a dark alley, brandishing a gun.

"What's your religion?" demanded the gunman.

Omigod! thought Boom-Boom. If I say I'm Catholic and he's a Protestant, he'll blow my head off! But if I say I'm Protestant and he happens to be Catholic, then I'm also as good as dead!

Suddenly, Boom-Boom was seized with an inspired idea.

"I'm Jewish!" he cried out in desperation.

"You don't say!" exclaimed the surprised terrorist. "I must be the luckiest Arab in all of Ireland!"

*

"When the Fighting's All Done"

No matter how grouchy you're feeling,
You'll find the smile more or less healing.
   It grows in a wreath
   All around your front teeth,
Thus preserving the face from congealing.

Chapter Nineteen
Irish Bulls
Introduction

The Irish bull, for the benefit of the uninitiated, refers to the anomaly, not the animal. No one knows when this unique feature of Gaelic humor began—its origins have long since been lost in the misty recesses of time. We do know, however, that the form was well established some two hundred years ago in Ireland. Probably the most famous bull-maker of his time was the Irish baronet, Sir Boyle Roche, who helped popularize the bull in the 1790s. A number of his contributions have been included in this chapter. Not all of the bulls in this modest collection are ancient, however, nor are they restricted to Ireland, as the delightful anecdote concerning Al Smith's bumbling attempt to address the inmates of Sing Sing penitentiary will attest. Other such verbal mishaps represented in this chapter are as modern as this year's fashions.

What, exactly, is an Irish bull? Consult a dozen different dictionaries and you will find as many definitions. Basically, it is a paradoxical statement that appears to make sense. In the Emerald Isle it has been defined as a horse of another color. The humorous bard, Patrick Ireland, called it "a vast idea expressed in a half-vast manner." But those are examples rather than definitions. Let us make another futile attempt: An Irish bull is a statement that twists itself into an absurdity, a contradiction in terms, an idea which starts out reasonably and ends ridiculously.

An example of the typical Irish bull is well presented in the indignant retort made by a man with a penchant for embarrassing himself as well as his friends: "No, I don't believe in abolishing capital punishment. If it was good enough for my father, it's good enough for me!" Another illustration of how a placid statement can be transformed into a roaring Irish bull was made by an exasperated mother who snapped at her little daughter: "Now see here, young lady, if you can't behave yourself I'll just leave you home the next time I take you out!" Then there is the deliberately contrived bull, exemplified by the late Brendan Behan, who offered this exercise in mental calisthenics: "I don't know why we Irish always seem to enjoy a brawl. I suppose it's because an Irishman is never at peace unless he's fighting!"

All of which proves the old Irish adage: "'Tis a pity, but due to the pull of gravity, it takes less energy to open the mouth than to close it."

—H.D.S.

"One Irishman's Thoughts on the Various Trades and Callings"

Of all the trades that men may call
　　Unpleasant and offensive,
The editor's is the worst of all,
　　For he is ever pen-sive;
His leaders lead to nothing high,
　　His columns are unstable,
And though the printers make him "pie,"
　　It does not suit his table.

The carpenter—his course is plane,
　　His bit is always near him;
He augers every hour of gain,
　　He chisels—and none jeer him;
He shaves, yet is not close, they say;
　　The public pays his board, sir;
Full of wise saws, he bores away,
　　And so he swells his hoard, sir.

St. Crispin's son—the man of shoes—
　　Has all things at control, sir;
He waxes wealthy in his views,
　　But ne'er neglects his sole, sir;
His is, indeed, a heeling trade;
　　And when it comes to casting
The toe-tal profits he has made,
　　We find his ends are lasting.

The farmer reaps a fortune plump,
　　Though harrowed, far from woe, sir;
His spade forever proves a trump,
　　His book is I've-an-hoe, sir;
However corned, he does not slip;
　　Though husky, never hoarse, sir;
And in a ploughshare partnership
　　He gets his share, of course, sir.

The sturdy Irish laborer picks
　　And climbs to fame—'tis funny!
He deals with none but regular bricks,
　　And so he pockets money;
One friend sticks to him (mortar 'tis),
　　In hodden grey, unbaffled,
He leaves below an honest name
　　When he ascends the scaffold.

I launched this skiff of rhymes upon
   The trade winds of the Muses,
Through pungent seas they've borne it on,
   The boat no rudder uses;
So masticate its meaning once,
   And judge not sternly of it—
You'll find a freight of bulls and puns,
   And very little profit.

—Charles G. Halpine (1829-68)

*

Biddy Malone was in a great fever of distress when she landed in America, direct from the "ould counthry." Her certificate of character was lost on board ship, and what would she be afther doin'?

To her great happiness and consolation, Tim Mulligan, her friend who had arrived in the United States six months earlier and was now an "American of Irish extraction," volunteered his assistance. In his own fine hand, he wrote her the following beautiful recommendation:

"This is to certify that Biddy Malone had a good character before she left Ireland, but lost it on shipboard, coming over."

*

A moment of reverent silence, please, for the coroner who was asked how he accounted for an extraordinary mortality rate in Limerick.

"I don't know," he replied, shaking his head. "There are people dying this year who never died before!"

*

The modern-day Women's Liberation movement had its counterpart in old Ireland during the 1870s. So great was its impact that one Irish business firm, with boundless liberality, published this advertisement: Ladies, without distinction of sex, will be equally served.

*

Said an editor of Killarney with commendable fair-mindedness: "I can see no earthly reason why women should not be allowed to become medical men."

*

A century ago, this vividly descriptive advertisement appeared in a paper published some one hundred miles from Dublin:
   Lost: A cameo brooch, representing
   Venus and Adonis on the Dumcondea
   road about midnight Wednesday.

*

A Kilkenny man grew overly abusive to a gentleman from Kildare, and, as a consequence, he was challenged to a duel—pistols at twenty paces.

"I accept," said the son of Kilkenny, "but I happen to be very nearsighted. Therefore, I must insist upon my right to stand ten paces nearer to you than you to me. We will then fire at exactly the same time."

*

In County Cavan some years ago, a landlord went to see Fogarty, one of his less-educated tenant farmers, about some business matter. Fogarty, however, had gone to town for the day, so the landlord left a note:

"My Dear Mr. Fogarty,
I shall be at the Shamrock Inn for the next few days. It is important that I see you. If you cannot read this note, take it to the postmaster in the village and he will read it for you."

*

A poor man of Louth offered his one and only cooking pot for sale. His children gathered around him, wide-eyed with curiosity.

"Daddy," asked his youngest daughter, "why are you sellin' the pot?"

"Ah, *macushla*," he replied in sad tones, "I'd not be afther partin' with it if I didn't nade the money to buy somethin' to put in it!"

*

Even children fall prey to the Irish bull; to wit, hereto and hereunder:

A schoolteacher of Donegal asked young Martin for the definition of an island.

"Sure, ma'am," replied Martin, "it's a place ye can't lave without a boat!"

*

Without comment from the present author, the following article is presented exactly as published in the County Cavan *Clarion,* June 8, 1909:

Ochone!—In the course of the Irish evictions from the Ponsonby estate, some Nationalists questioned one of the evicted tenants. But the only material fact elicited from the elderly man was his name, Patrick Fitzgerald.

There was no question, however, about his complaint, which he loudly proclaimed:

"Sure, and a hard thing it is to see a man turned out of a house which his father built and his grandfather was born in!"

*

"Pardon me, miss, for addressing a perfect stranger like this," began the hopeful young son of Erin with his usual dash of blarney, "but your face seems familiar to me."

"Oh, that's all right, sir," replied the colleen, smiling brightly, "it happens all the time. You see, my father and mother were first cousins, which is why I look so much alike!"

*

Ignore these modern-day claimants—O'Loghlen said it first, one hundred years ago: indelible proof that unconscious humor can be funnier than conscious wit.

In the old colony of Victoria, it was none other than Sir Bryan O'Loghlen, a member of Parliament, who gravely informed the Supreme Court that "a verbal agreement is not worth the paper it is written on."

*

During the dark and bloody days following Cromwell the Cruel's campaign of extermination, begun in 1649, in which he slaughtered thousands of Irish soldiers, priests, and civilians, including women and children, the British conscripted Irish youths to fight their fellow countrymen—a practice that continued, intermittently, for two centuries. Often, the lads would be conscripted off the streets. This little anecdote afforded a small measure of amusement to the embattled populace.

"Molly, what is all that commotion down in the street?" asked the husband.

"Oh, nothing," she answered, looking out the window. "They're only forcing some men to join the volunteers!"

*

A lad from Louth, expecting a letter from his relatives in America, went to the post office and inquired if there was any mail for him.

"What is your name, sir?" asked the clerk.

"Me name, is it?" echoed the Hibernian, chuckling. "Now there's a good wan. Sure, you'll be seeing it on the envelope!"

*

In the Court of Appeal, Londonderry lawyer Rafferty was arguing his case with impassioned earnestness. In his zeal, however, he stated a legal point which the court ruled out.

"Yer Ixcillincy," said Rafferty in a determined voice, "if it pláze the coort, it may be that I am wrong, but, faith, if I am, I have anither p'int that is ayqually conclusive!"

*

Walking down a street one day, Liam, the provident one, and his wife, Nora, passed by a shop window where a lovely silk dress was on display.

"Ah, Liam," said Nora, "do ye remimber saying I was to have a silk dress whin ye had the money to buy it?"

"Faith, Nora, did I say that?"

"Indade, ye did. And ye have the money in yer pocket to buy me the dress right now."

"That I have, darlint, but I can't buy you the dress."

"And why not?"

"Because it's best that I kape the money in me pocket *fornenst* the day when we haven't got any!"

*

McGinty, of County Monaghan, bought a pair of shiny new boots. He was quite pleased with them until he brought them home and tried them on. But, no matter how he pulled and tugged, he was unable to get his feet into them. His fingers were blistered from all the tugging and pulling when he finally realized the cause.

"Bedad," he muttered, "I'll never get them on at all until I've worn them a day or two!"

*

Irish bulls are not confined to the males; the ladies also contribute their fair share. One proud daughter of the Old Sod, a female liberationist but a chauvinistic Celt just the same, stoutly defended womankind with this reminder:

"We Irishmen, as a rule, are wonderful horsewomen, and we ride with a style that has been carried to distant lands, both far and near."

*

Luther and John, two old friends who had not seen each other in many years, chanced to meet one day. After exchanging the customary greetings, Luther inquired, "And how is that lovely wife of yours?"

"Oh, she's gone to Heaven," replied John.

"I'm sorry!" exclaimed Luther. But his answer, he hastily realized, led to a different meaning than he had intended. "I mean," he amended, "I'm glad." But that only sounded worse. "What I am trying to say," he concluded lamely, "is that I'm—well—I'm surprised!"

*

Letter from a Lovesick Swain:

"Maggie, this is the second time I've written, asking you to marry me. If you won't be my wife, then at least have the goodness to return this letter unopened!"

*

"Your money or your life!" snarled the holdup man, waving a gun in O'Rourke's face.

"Ye'd betther take me life," replied O'Rourke. "I'm savin' me money fer me ould age!"

*

"Mike," yelled his coworker, who had just seen him fall down into an abandoned mine shaft, "are ye alive? Answer me, Mike! If ye'r kilt, say so! Answer me, I say!"

"Av coorse I ain't kilt!" came back Mike's muffled voice from the depths. "Are ye daft? How can I answer when I'm unconscious?"

*

"Before I'd allow myself to be buried in a Protestant cemetery," sniffed Sister Theresa, "I'd rather be dead!"

*

'Tis said of a certain lawyer of Antrim that, having occasion to go to dinner, he left this hastily-written note pinned to his office door:

"Have gone to the Elephant and Castle, where you shall find me. If I am no longer there when you arrive, it means I shall have left and I don't know where I am!"

*

In an English act of Parliament, following the 1916 Easter rebellion in Ireland, a law was passed which called for the building of a new and larger jail to accommodate the greater number of Irish rebels.

Part One of the law stated that the new jail was to be built from the material of the old one.

Part Two of the law stated that the prisoners were to be kept in the old jail until the new jail was finished.

*

Sometimes, though not often, the Irishman's gift of blarney deserts him. And when it does, the results can be catastrophic, as though someone had substituted the Blarney stone for a millstone and draped it around his neck. Al Smith could have told you that. It happened to him—thuswise:

In the first days of his governorship of the State of New York, Al spoke to the assembled inmates of Sing Sing Prison, since renamed Ossining. Not until he had already risen to his feet did he realize that he did not know how to address this particular audience.

"My fellow citizens," he began, almost without thinking. He stopped suddenly, remembering that some of the imprisoned men had forfeited their citizenship. Embarrassed, he made another attempt: "My fellow convicts" —but that too did not seem to be the proper greeting for a governor of the great State of New York. Giving the whole thing up as hopeless, he launched headlong into his speech:

"Well, in any case, I am glad to see so many of you here!"

*

"Abstinence is a good thing," advised the confident novitiate, "but it should always be practiced in moderation."

*

Father Michael Quigley of Southampton tells of the Sunday morning when he was approached after the church services by an old lady.

"Oh, Father," she gushed, "you'll never know what your sermon meant to me. It was just like water to a drowning man!"

*

A young priest who was temporarily filling a city pulpit looked over his congregation and blessed them with a short but fervent prayer:

"May all of you be filled with fresh veal and new zigor!"

*

"I'd love to marry you, but there is something you should know first," said the bashful young lady. "In my family it's hereditary to have no children!"

*

"Hello, that you, Mrs. O'Sullivan? This is Maggie Harrigan. Listen, I'll be afther returnin' yer book on asthrology. It's thankin ye, I am, but we Aquarians just don't belave in that silly stoof!"

*

Probably the greatest number of bulls ever found in one communication was contained in a letter from an Irish baronet, Sir Boyle Roche, and written to a friend in London during the Irish rebellion of 1798. The companion bulls were italicized in the first printing of the famous letter (1832), and are presented here exactly as published, almost 150 years ago—italics and all.

My dear Oliver,

Having now a little *peace* and *quietness*, I sit down to inform you of the dreadful *bustle* and *confusion* we are in from these *active, blood-thirsty* rebels, most of whom are, thank God, *killed* and *dispersed.*

We are in a pretty mess; can get *nothing to eat* nor any *wine to drink,* except *whiskey,* and when we sit down to *dinner* we are obliged to keep *both* hands armed. Whilst I *write* this letter *I hold a sword in one hand* and *a pistol in the other.* Believe me, dear Oliver, at present there are such *goings-on* that everything is at a *stand.*

I should have answered your letter a *fortnight* ago, but I only received it *this morning.* Indeed, hardly a mail arrives *safe,* without being *robbed.* No longer than yesterday, the coach with the mails from Dublin was *robbed* near the town, but fortunately the bags had been judiciously *left behind* for fear of just such accidents, and by good luck there was nobody *in* the coach but two *outside passengers* who had *nothing* for the thieves to take.

Last Thursday an alarm was given that a gang of rebels were advancing hither, under the French *flag,* but they had no *colors,* nor any *drums* except *bagpipes.* Immediately every *man* in the place, *including women and boys,* ran out to meet them. We soon found our force *much* too *little,* and they were *far* too *near* for us to think of retreating; death was in the face; but to it we went, and by the time *half* our party was killed we began to come *all alive.*

Fortunately, the rebels had *no weapons* but *guns, cutlasses,* and *pikes,* and as we had plenty of *muskets* and *ammunition,* we put them all to the *sword. Not a soul* of them *escaped, except some* that were *drowned* in an adjoining bog, and in a very short time nothing was to be *heard* but *silence.*

Their uniforms were all of *different colors* but *mostly green.* After the action we went to rummaging about in their camp; all we found were a parcel of *empty* bottles *containing* water, and a bundle of *blank* commission-books *filled with* Irishmen's names.

Troops are now stationed everywhere *round* the country which exactly *squares* with my ideas. Nothing, however, can save us but a union with England, which would turn our barren *hills* into fertile *valleys.* I have only *leisure* to add that I am in *great haste.*

Yours truly
(Signed) Boyle Roche

P.S. If you *do not receive this* in due course, it must have miscarried in the mails. Therefore I beg you will immediately write to *let me know.*

*

Sir Boyle also once sent an amusing, equivocal invitation to an Irish nobleman of his acquaintance:

"I hope, my lord, if you ever come within a mile of my house, that you will stay there overnight."

*

On the occasion of a debate in the House of Commons about some money grant, a member declared that it was unjust to saddle posterity with a debt incurred to benefit the present. Sir Boyle rose to object.

"Why should we beggar ourselves to benefit posterity?" he demanded. "What has posterity ever done for us?"

The laughter which followed encouraged him to explain:

"Sir, by posterity I do not mean our ancestors, but those who come immediately after them."

*

Two bulls were inadvertently created by both speaker and listener in 1794, when the leather tax was being debated in the House. Mr. Vandeclure, the speaker, announced to his fellow members that "the tax on *leather* will be severely *felt* by the *barefooted* peasantry of Ireland."

Sir Boyle answered:

"This can be very easily remedied by making the leather of wood!"

*

Fearing the progress of revolutionary opinions in Ireland, Sir Boyle once drew a frightful picture of the future, warning the honorable members that the House of Commons might be invaded by Irish ruffians.

"They would cut us to mince meat," he asserted, "and throw our bleeding heads on the table, to stare us in the face."

*

Speaking again of the turbulent Irish question, Sir Boyle declared:

"The country is *overrun* by *absentee* landlords."

And, as if that were not enough for one day, he followed with:

"I tell you, the cup of old Ireland's misery is overflowing; aye, and it is not full yet!"

*

It was Sir Boyle, too, who offered his philosophy to an eager, waiting world:

"*Single* misfortunes *never come alone,* and the *greatest* of all possible misfortunes is generally followed by a *much greater.*"

*

Again, arguing for the Habeas Corpus Suspension Bill in Ireland, Sir Boyle enunciated this immortal gem of wisdom:

"It would be better, Mr. Speaker, to give up not only a part, but, if necessary, even the *whole* of our Constitution, to preserve the *remainder!*"

*

Of all the bulls made by the worthy baronet, Sir Boyle Roche, the following account is said to have reduced the members of the House to helpless laughter. Speaking of a well-known colleague's love of money, the baronet observed:

"Let not the honorable member express a contempt for money, for if there is any one office that glitters in the eyes of the honorable member, it is that of Purse-bearer. A pension, to him, is a compendium of all the cardinal virtues. All his statesmanship is comprehended in the art of taxing; and for good, better, and best, in the scale of human nature, he invariably reads pence, shillings, and pounds.

"I verily believe," Sir Boyle concluded, rising to the outer limits of oratorical splendor, "that if the honorable gentleman were an undertaker, it would be the delight of his heart to see *all mankind* seized with a common mortality so that he might have the benefit of the burial, and provide scarfs and hatbands for the *survivors!*"

Chapter Twenty
Ireland, My Sireland
Introduction

Memories! The emigrants of the eighteenth and nineteenth centuries who left Ireland forever to seek a better life in America, brought with them the remembrances of places and people and things: simple things, for they were simple country people. Vagrant thoughts winged back across the expanse of ocean to the Emerald Isle, to those long ago mornings, cutting peat in the rain, or breathing the musky fragrance of newly mown hay and gathering it in on those long summer days. Memories! Grandma churning butter by the door, and Mama making bread at the open hearth; Daddy coming home bone-weary from his toil in the fields; those cold, winter mornings, racing to school, knowing that Mrs. Corcoran would warm your hands well enough, with her cane, if you were late. Memories! Listening to the old men as they sat in a semicircle in front of the peat fire, telling each other, for the tenth time, of foreclosures by British landlords, and repeating gossip several months old. As you grew older, you returned home from country dances over dark and forbidding roads, remembering uneasily the old stories of ghosts and fairies that Grandpa himself swore he had actually seen. The *shebeen* man, and the *poteen* he made and sold. Your first kiss. Cute little Molly McGuire: a grandma by now, no doubt, and still living in the village. Memories!

There was another Ireland, of course, one of culture and letters. But village and farm was the only Ireland the country people knew, and nearly all who came to America after 1840 were country people. They knew very little more about the brilliant world of Anglo-Irish Dublin than they did of New York. O'Connell, Parnell, Tom Moore, Yeats, and Lady Gregory were just names to them. The Ireland of the sages and scholars during the early Middle Ages, when its monks and minstrels wandered to the far reaches of Christendom and made Gaelic a living language, all this was another Ireland that, for the country people, might as well have never existed.

The life of the Irish immigrants had always been simple, and much the same, whether they came to the United States in 1850 or 1750. Many important changes occurred in those hundred years, but the traditional rhythms of village life by which the people lived remained almost unchanged. Even those who ventured to live in the few larger towns of Ireland and, often the poor of Dublin itself, were unaffected by the great surface changes of that century in which most of the Irish immigrants flocked to America.

Among the memories that endured the longest, however, were the humorous stories and songs, repeated by generations of Celtic forebears. It was no accident that this humor was remembered, for it was deeply rooted in the national character. The Irish, despite their continuing struggle against poverty and oppression, never took themselves too seriously. They well understood the thin dividing line that separates self-realization from self-pity, and they guarded that line with satire and laughter. Unable to be king, the Irishman frequently became court jester, aiming his slings and arrows at king, commoner, and himself. This talent for viewing life in a comic sense, enabled the Irish to maintain a sense of proportion about their hard life. It helped them to escape the sullen pessimism that often marks the defeated and downtrodden.

The humor of the Irish immigrants, for the most part, was not expressed in the language of the classic masters, but in the provincial "mother wit" of rural farmers and villagers. Although funny enough, it was often trivial: mirthful gossip about the British; mocking a pretentious neighbor; unmasking self-interest parading as patriotism. This "people's" humor, transplanted in the United States, quickly assumed a new dimension of fierce loyalty and devotion to the land of the shamrock.

Many of the simple jokes have been anointed with sentimentality; a commendable improvement in most Irish eyes. Unfortunately, there are always a few dissidents. George Bernard Shaw, an Irishman living in London, was one. Taking issue with John Locke's beautiful tribute to Ireland, which introduces this chapter, Shaw replied:

> At last I went to Ireland,
> 'Twas raining cats and dogs:
> I found no music in the glens,
> Nor purple in the bogs.
> And as for angels' laughter in
> The smelly Liffey's tide—
> Well, my Irish daddy said it,
> But the dear old humbug lied.

Some of the tales in this chapter have obviously been modernized: the story of Prince Philip and the flying boat is one example. Mark Quinlan's idea of sending an Irish astronaut to the sun, is another. Here then is the gossip and rumors about the famous and the infamous; of the overwhelming and the underwhelming—an Irish stirabout, or porridge, of those bits of humor passed on by the grandparents and great-grandparents of today's Irish-Americans who repeat them with a tear in their eyes, although most have never been closer to Ireland than Coney Island.

—H.D.S.

> O Ireland, isn't it grand you look?
> Like a bride in her rich adornin';
> And with all the pent-up love of my heart,
> I bid you the top o' the mornin'!

—John Locke (1847-89)

*

Michael Collins, organizer of the Irish Republican Army following the Easter rebellion of 1916, was a cautious man despite his bold attempts to free his country from British rule. He took nothing for granted, as this modest vignette illustrates.

One day, in the spring of 1914, Collins and a fellow patriot were on a train passing through County Westmeath, talking and occasionally viewing the countryside. Suddenly, the colleague pointed to a flock of sheep grazing peacefully in a meadow.

"Those sheep have just been shorn," he observed.

"Well," said Collins slowly, hesitant to pass judgment without first examining all the evidence, "at least on this side!"

*

Grandfather Johnson happened to overhear a conversation in which the sphinx was mentioned.

"What is that, now?" he asked.

"The sphinx," explained one of the group, "is a monster man."

"Oh, a Munster-man!" exclaimed the old-timer, an enlightened smile spreading across his features. "I thought he was from Connaught!"

*

It is said of England's Prince Philip that he once undertook to pilot a new flying boat for his visit to Ulster. All went well as he and his Irish copilot flew across the Irish Sea. But, as they approached the rugged coast of northern Ireland, Philip decided to land the plane at the Belfast airport.

"But, Your Highness," protested the copilot cautiously, to avoid offending his royal superior, "this is a flying boat! Don't you think it would be wiser to come down on the sea?"

"Why, of course it would!" exclaimed the prince, smiling with embarrassment at his own forgetfulness.

They made a safe landing on the water, and Philip laid a friendly hand on the copilot's shoulder. "Commander," he said earnestly, "I want you to know that I greatly appreciate the tact with which you prevented me from making an incredible and stupid blunder. You may be sure that I shall recommend you for promotion."

The prince then opened the door and stepped into the sea.

*

Checking into a Dublin hotel, a tourist went sightseeing in the country-side and, before long, he became hopelessly lost. On the outskirts of an isolated village, he came to a fork in the road with two signs pointing in opposite directions. Both said DUBLIN. He approached a surly-looking, grizzled old farmer pitching hay nearby.

"Which way is it to Dublin?" he asked.

"Misther," snorted the uncooperative oldster, "if I was goin' to Dublin I'd not be startin' from here."

"But those signposts both say DUBLIN," persisted the tourist, "and they're both pointing in opposite directions. Does it make any difference which road I take?"

"No, laddie," replied the farmer, shrugging, "not to me it don't!"

*

An Irish patriot, visiting London before Ireland won its freedom in 1921, was surprised to find so many statues in the public parks and squares honoring a multitude of famous men.

"To tell the truth," the Irishman remarked dryly, "I would rather people asked why there is *not* a statue to me than why there *is*!"

*

The Honorable Mark Quinlan, member of the *Dail Eireann,* was address-ing his distinguished colleagues on the necessity of keeping abreast of the United States in scientific matters—especially the space program.

"America has sent men to the moon," he thundered. "Why shouldn't Ireland? In fact, we can outdo them by sending a man to the sun."

"The *sun!*" echoed the amazed chairman. "Surely you must know that a man would burn up long before he got there!"

"No, he wouldn't," replied Quinlan with an airy wave of his hand. "We'd send him at night!"

*

A very old folk tale of Longford tells of the two farmers who were in earnest discussion on the comparative usefulness of the sun and the moon. Translated loosely from the Old Irish, their conversation was as follows:

"Sure, and the sun is more useful," said one. "It gives a stronger light."

"Yes, but the moon is more sensible," argued the other.

"Sensible? How so?"

"Put your mind to it, man, and you'll agree with me. The sun comes out in broad daylight when even a one-eyed man can see without it. But the moon—ah!—the moon shines at night when we really need it!"

*

Michael, a proud but necessarily secret member of *Sinn Fein,* was hailed into court as a witness in a shooting. But he was not about to implicate his fellow Irish patriots for the glory of England.

"Now see here, Michael, we know you heard a gunshot and that you found a hole in the door that wasn't there before," barked the prosecutor.

"Well, av ye know it, why do ye ask?"

"Was it a bullet hole?"

"To the best iv me belafe."

"Will you swear that it was a bullet hole?"

"It *might* have been a bullet hole."

"Answer me, yes or no! Will you *swear* it was? I want the truth!"

"Now be aisy, sor. Av it's the truth yer afther, I didn't *see* the bullet doin' it!"

*

According to the older men of Munster, they can hold more liquor, pound for pound, than the men of any other region in Ireland. The statement is highly debatable, but the origin of that belief may be found in this hundred-year-old anecdote.

One mellow August evening in 1870, a farmer of Munster came to town with a wagonload of *knassters*. Having sold the potatoes, the man, who had attained a venerable old age, procured for himself a jug of mountain dew and returned to his wagon. Then, at a leisurely pace, he drove around the town, meanwhile sampling the extra strong *poteen* he had just acquired.

Soon the old farmer was diffused with energy and daring, far beyond what might be expected of a man of his many decades. Faster and faster went the horse, while he raised his voice in song, interspersed with unflattering shouts to the pedestrians who just managed to escape the flying hooves of his galloping steed. But the ancient one's adventure came to an inglorious end when he was finally stopped and arrested by the *Garda*.

He was forthwith brought before a stern-faced magistrate.

"You are charged with disturbing the peace and endangering the lives of the good citizens hereabouts," cried the outraged judge. "You should be ashamed of yourself—a man of your age, not only drunk in public like that, but setting such a bad example for the young people. What have you to say for yourself, old man?"

"Sure, Yer Honor," replied the oldster bravely, "I did not do all that dhrinkin' by mesilf, as claimed by the arresthin' offisher. I had sivril gintlemin iv my acquaintansh help me finish the jug, may it plaze Yer Honor."

"There is nothing in the record to indicate you were not alone," snapped the judge.

"It was like this, sor. That firsh dhrink made me feel like anither man. That man wanted a dhrink, too. And that made *him* feel like anither man, and *he* wanted a dhrink iv his own. And *he* felt like anither man, and *he* ..."

"Now hold on!" roared the judge. "Save that blarney for someone else. My verdict is ten days in jail or ten pounds."

"Well, av ish all the same to you, Yer Honor," said the ancient one with a delighted smile, "I'll be takin' the tin pounds—I kin use anither jug!"

*

Shevlin, the only son in his family, insulted Devlin, another only son. Devlin promptly challenged him to a duel on the field of honor.

"I'll not accept your challenge," said Shevlin coldly. "Would you have me leave your mother an orphan? Or worse yet, *mine*?"

*

Patrick O'Skinflint, a wealthy merchant of Dublin, traveled to another city in hopes of doubling his already substantial fortune. He alighted from the train and forthwith made his way to the hotel where he had made an advance reservation. But, before he could get to the door, he was immediately besieged by a crowd of beggars so thick he could hardly press his way through them. As he struggled to move ahead, he was assailed from all sides by their obstreperous prayers—all in their horrid discord and strange variety, their complaints and blessings so jumbled together as to produce a ludicrous though pathetic effect:

"Pity the blind, and may you never..."

"Tomorrow morning won't find me alive if you don't..."

"Three fatherless childhren..."

"May the Lord's grace shine on ye fer helpin' a poor..."

"... and broke his two legs..."

"... that is stone blind."

"Sure and the house fell on him and he's lyin' under it these three weeks without a bit to ate or a docthor; but you..."

"The smallpox..."

At that moment, a member of the *Garda Siochana* happened to emerge from the hotel. The rich merchant turned to him at once.

"Officer," he cried out, heavy tears coursing down his cheeks even as he clutched his purse tightly to his chest, "disperse these poor, unfortunate creatures. They're breaking my heart!"

*

If you have ever wondered why some Irishmen are considered extraordinarily shrewd and natural-born students of psychology, this story will provide the answer.

In the city of Dublin, one beautiful day in May, a blind man walked slowly in the park, tapping for attention with his cane and carrying a sign on his chest: HELP THE BLIND.

No one paid much attention to him, and he left. But, the next day, he reappeared in the lovely, flowered park, and this time he was undoubtedly doing better. Practically every passer-by put a coin in his cup, some even turning back to make their contribution.

He had changed his sign, which now read:

IT IS MAY—AND I AM BLIND!

*

Here is one of those legendary tales which sound almost too good to be true; yet, the hilarious event actually occurred in the summer of 1887, during a performance in Dublin.

An Italian company, direct from La Scala, came to play *Faust* at the Theatre Royal. Unfortunately, the actor who took the part of Mephistopheles had neglected to first try the trapdoor from which he was supposed to descend into the infernal regions. His bulk was too large for the opening and, at the supreme moment, he discovered that he could not get down above the waist. There he remained, stuck between Hades and the astonished audience.

Suddenly, a voice rang out from the gallery, shattering the tomblike silence—a voice with a brogue so thick it could be cut with a butter knife:

"Begorra!" shouted the god in the upper seats, "th' divil himsilf can't get down! Hell is too full iv Protesthants!"

*

According to reliable sources, or as reliable as one may expect of "reliable" sources, a priest of Ammergau told the following story about his bishop, in the year of our Lord 1839.

The bishop and a chaplain came to see the Passion Play. They would have preferred separate rooms, but that was not possible. They knelt down, each beside his own bed, to say their prayers that evening, but soon it crossed the chaplain's mind that it would not be seemly to make the orisons shorter than the bishop's. He glanced over his shoulder to see if his companion was about to finish.

The bishop, apparently anxious not to offend his chaplain by the shortness of his own prayers, also glanced over his shoulder and waited. The process was repeated several times. Both the supplicants were very tired and, in time, both fell asleep.

The hotel maid found them in the morning. The chaplain, still on his knees and sound asleep, looked tired and haggard. The bishop was also sleeping, a contented smile on his face, and he too was kneeling—astride a chamber pot!

*

Donald McNulty, well-known *amadan* of Galway, was fishing on the bank of a peaceful, quiet *lough*, when he grew drowsy in the afternoon sun. Taking off his shoes and making himself comfortable, he leaned back against a mossy incline and was soon fast asleep. During his slumbers, however, a stray dog made off with one of his shoes. Upon awakening, he quickly discovered the lone piece of footwear.

"Bedad," he muttered to himself, "either I am Donald McNulty or I am not Donald McNulty. If I am Donald McNulty, then I have lost a shoe. On the other hand, if I am not Donald McNulty, then, saints be praised, I have *found* a shoe!"

*

In a remote and tiny village on the banks of the Ree lived a rustic fellow named F. X. Murray. Now F. X., according to the local historians, wasn't a bad sort of fellow, but, sure, he hated to travel. In all his life he had never been a hundred yards beyond the outskirts of his village. What is more, he even boasted about it.

"Do you mean to tell me," demanded a visitor, "that you have never so much as crossed the river? Why, it's practically at your doorstep."

"Faith, and I haven't the time," explained F. X. reasonably.

"But the ferry will carry you across the *lough* in fifteen minutes," protested the visitor.

" 'Tis the truth ye've spoken," admitted F. X., "but you're afther forgettin' that it takes another fifteen minutes comin' back!"

*

A story is told of an Englishman who landed in Dublin many years ago, filled with apprehension that life had little value there and thereabouts. The Land Leaguers, he was convinced, were all bloodthirsty assassins. But it was his official duty to travel in the land—a duty he approached with fear, trembling, and similar symptoms of insecurity.

Now, there happened to be a number of towns on his route which began with the suggestive syllable *Kil*. There was Kilmartin, and so on. In his ignorance of geographical nomenclature, his affrighted senses were startled anew on hearing a fellow passenger in the railway car remark to another:

"I'm just afther bein' over to Kilpatric."

"And I," responded the other, "am afther bein' over to Kilmary."

The Englishman was aghast at this evidence of ferocity, so blatantly displayed. "What murderers these Irishmen are!" he groaned to himself. "And to think they talk of their asassinations so publicly!"

But the conversation went on.

"And where are ye goin' now?" asked assassin A.

"I'm goin' home to Kilmore," explained assassin B.

The Englishman's blood curdled.

"Kilmore, is it?" replied A, as the Englishman jumped from the train. "Ye'd better be comin' along with me to Kilnmaul!"

*

In County Cork, 'tis said, a schoolteacher by the name of O'Rourke was asked to tell the difference between a "misfortune" and a "calamity."

"You'll never be forgetting this rule I give you," laughed the teacher. "If an Orangeman should happen to fall into the Shannon, that would be a misfortune. But if anyone pulled him out, that would be a calamity!"[1]

---

[1] In Ulster the same joke is told, but the other way around.

*

In Tipperary, one day, a gentleman of small means and smaller conscience entered an ale house and ordered a bit of bacon and some bread. The waitress, a spritely lass, brought him his dinner, but instead of eating it, he voiced a complaint.

"Young lady, the bacon seems ould and the bread is turnin' green."

"Go on with ye," she retorted. "The food here is as fresh as yer manners!"

"Divil a bit iv it will I eat," stated the traveler with finality. "Take it back and bring me a pot iv ale instid."

The girl shrugged, removed his plate, and soon returned with the ale.

"That, sor, will be wan penny."

"A penny, is it? And what for?"

"For the ale, iv coorse."

"But did I not give you a plate iv bacon and some bread for the ale?"

"Well, then pay for the bacon and bread."

"Young woman, sure you're enough to thry the patience iv a saint," he muttered, rising to leave. "Pay you for the bacon and bread indade! Did I not return it to you?"

*

Your great-grandfather laughed at this joke, and it merits repeating now, a century later.

Three Mayo men were stranded one night at a lonely farmhouse. The farmer explained that two of them could sleep in the house, but that the third would have to sleep in the barn with the pig and the cow.

The first Mayo man volunteered, but he quickly returned to the farmhouse, complaining that the stench of the pig was too offensive for him. The second man then went out, but he, too, soon returned, explaining that he could stand the pig but the cow was too much for him. The third man then retired to the barn. After a few minutes, there was a knock on the farmhouse door.

Outside were the pig and the cow!

*

The age of this tale is evident in the personalities involved.

It seems that when George IV went to Ireland, one of the "pisintry," always suspicious of the monarch, said to the tollkeeper as His Majesty passed through:

"Och, now! An' his majesty niver paid the turnpike. And how is that?"

"Oh, kings niver does; we lets 'em go free," explained the tollkeeper.

"Th' hell ye say!" cried the patriotic son of Erin, reaching into his pocket. "Then here's the dirty money for ye! It shall niver be said that th' Irish are too miserly to pay the turnpike for a king!"

(There is a delightful aftermath to the above ancient story. Tom Moore, on his visit to Abbotsford, repeated the tale to Sir Walter Scott when they were comparing notes on the two royal visits:

"Now. Moore. there ye have the advantage of us." observed Scott. "There was no lack of enthusiasm in Scotland. In fact, Scottish folk would have done anything *except* pay the turnpike!")

◆

The McDonnell clan, of the F.I.F.'s, or First Irish Families, ranks among the wealthiest of the lace-curtain Irish in the United States. Like most of the F.I.F.'s, however, their origins in Ireland were humble. One of them was the late James Francis McDonnell, formerly head of the Wall Street firm, McDonnell & Company, with assets in the tens of millions. James F. McDonnell, in short, was a man accustomed to deference, and he had to go to Ireland to be "told off."

It was in the 1940s that James returned to the Emerald Isle for a nostalgic visit to Drumlish, his birthplace. The tiny hamlet of Drumlish (population 212) in County Longford, some fifty miles northwest of Dublin, boasted the one and only pub in the entire area, and a lively place it was. James entered the convivial establishment and recognized a boyhood chum.

"Paddy, as I live and breathe!" exclaimed the American, clapping the fellow on the back with a heavy hand. "I remember the sunny mornin' you came to school in your first pair of shoes."

"Do ye now?" snapped the Drumlisher, his face reddening. "And I remember you asking what they were!"

◆

Vincent Scully was not without ability and information, but his manners were eccentric and his pronunciation ridiculous because of his unfortunate, puerile lisp. Vincent was also a notoriously heavy drinker. But Francis Scully, on the other hand, was rather commonplace.

An American once asked his Irish friend, Sergeant Murphy, how he managed to distinguish between the two wonderful Scullys.

"Aisy—no throuble a'tall," replied the sergeant. "We call Vincent 'Rum-Scully' and Francis 'Num-Scully'!

◆

It is claimed by the always anonymous "reliable sources" that this old Irish folk tale is true; but just the same, don't bet your week's wages on it.

An elderly lady had an ancient maid named Ann Brady who had lived with her for many years. One day, Ann came into the parlor to seek consolation from her friend and employer.

"Oh, am I not the unfortunate woman!" she moaned. "Och, what shall I do at all at all!"

"What's the matter, Ann?" asked the old lady.

"The postman is outside," said Ann, close to tears, "and he's got a letter for me from Purgathory. I know it must be from me ould father who's been there these twinty years. I just know 'tis all about me not payin' for the masses I said I would. *Ochone!* But I am the miserable woman!"

Curious, the mistress of the house went outside and asked the postman for an explanation. "From Purgathory, indade!" she snorted.

"Purgatory?" the postman echoed blankly. "Ann Brady wrote a letter that was incorrectly addressed. It was returned in an envelope marked, 'Mrs Brady, from the Dead Letter Office'!"

*

Simple Simon of Sligo, he of slight mind and bulging biceps, was inducted into the Army. He was measured for his uniform, and then sent to the supply sergeant to receive his gear.

"How tall are you?" asked the sergeant.

The recruit scratched his head and tried to remember the measurements just told to him by the medical assistant.

"Come now, man," the sergeant snapped impatiently. "If you want a uniform, you'll have to tell me your height."

"Well," said the recruit slowly, after some deep meditation, "the man who measured me said I was—hmm—I think—er—six feet two. . . . Or else," he added hastily, "two feet six!"

*

In County Longford, Mr. Healy, the merchant, gathered his wife and three small daughters around him one day to tell them the happy news. They were all emigrating to the United States and would live out West.

"But, Daddy," cried the eldest of the daughters in a worried voice, "supposin' we're attackted by Indians?"

"Bedad, if that happens," barked the eminently respectable Mr. Healy, "I'll make 'em marry ivry wan iv ye!"

*

We travel back in time to the year 1795 when this joke was popular; the moral being that it is folly to live wholly within one's self. Just such a gentleman was Cleary, who stopped for the night at an inn. But he could get no sleep. A great storm blew, shivering the ancient timbers of the house until the very walls and foundation groaned.

A loud pounding on the door brought Cleary out of his bed with a startled bound.

"Come out! Come out!" rang the innkeeper's voice. "The house may tumble down!"

Cleary opened the door and, with obvious irritation in his tone, he snapped:

"Then let it tumble. I'm only a lodger here. Faith, it's not *my* house!"

*

The Prince of Wales once asked Hugh O'Donoghue, a member of the Irish Parliament, "What is your idea of British civilization?"

"It's a fine idea," replied O'Donoghue. "Somebody ought to start it!"

*

"Irish" Johnstone, the famed comedian of the nineteenth century, was known to be rather parsimonious—a penny pincher, in fact, of the first magnitude. On one of his professional visits to Dublin, he found comfortable (and free) lodging at the home of an acquaintance, as was his custom in whatever town he happened to be visiting.

Some weeks later, while performing in London, he chanced to mention the "great expenses" he had incurred during his stay in the Irish capital.

"Do you know what I spent?" he complained piteously.

"Not exactly," replied the other, well aware of his colleague's miserly nature, "but I'd say about a fortnight!"

*

Padraic and the Devil

In the days before modern court reporting, an elderly lawyer of County Kildare had a young servant named Padraic, who was endowed with a phenomenal memory. The old lawyer had good reason to be proud of Padraic's amazing talent. His servant was able to sit in court and, at any point in the process of a trial, he could reel off every word of testimony that had transpired before. Padraic's reputation was so great that his evidence "on the record" was accepted in any court in the county.

One day, the lawyer was in his study, contentedly smoking his *dhudeen*, when the Devil appeared.

"What do you want?" demanded the lawyer.

"I have come for Padraic," was the answer.

"Ah, so it's Padraic you'd be takin', is it? Well, my fine *Dhioul*, I can't spare him, so be off with you!"

"It can't be helped, *achora*," said the Devil impertinently. "His time is up. And he's losing his memory."

"Come now, you're a sportin' man," argued the lawyer. "I'll make a little bet with you. If Padraic's memory is failing, he's no good to me and you can take him. Test the man, and if you can fool him, he's yours. But if you can't, he stays."

"Agreed," said the Devil with a smirk, and disappeared.

Padraic was in the field, digging *knassters*, when suddenly the Devil appeared before him.

"Do you like eggs?" asked the Devil.

"Yes," answered Padraic, and the Devil disappeared in a puff of smoke.

The following years, from 1840 to 1851, were hectic ones throughout Ireland. The potato famine caused untold misery. Then the old lawyer died, and Padraic was thrown on his own. After that came a renewal of the "troubles" with England, and Padraic fought the British up and down the east and west coasts and in almost every county of his beloved Emerald Isle. He survived the many years of hunger, of wandering, and fighting, with little more than a few minor wounds. Finally, now silver-haired and bent, he settled down on a piece of land.

One day, as old Padraic was cultivating the little plot that was now his own, the Devil appeared before him.

"How?" asked the Devil.

"Fried!" said Padraic.

—Patrick Ireland

"The Native Irishman"
(By a Converted Saxon)[2]

Before I came across the sea to this delightful place,
I thought the native Irish were a funny sort of race;
I thought they bore shillelagh-sprigs and that they always said:
"Och hone, acushla, tare-an-ouns, begorra" and "bedad!"

I thought they sported crownless hats with *dhudeens* in the rim;
I thought they wore long trailing coats and knickerbockers trim;
I thought they went about the place as tight as they could get,
And that they always had a fight with everyone they met.

I thought their noses all turned up just like a crooked pin;
I thought their mouths six inches wide and always on the grin;
I thought their heads were made of steel, as hard as any nails;
I half suspected that they were possessed of little tails.

But when I came unto the land of which I heard so much,
I found that the inhabitants were not entirely such;
I found their features were not at all exactly like baboons;
I found that some wore billycocks* and some had pantaloons.

I found their teeth were quite as small as Europeans' are,
And that their ears, in point of size, were not pecul-iar.
I even saw a face or two which might be handsome called;
And by their very largest feet I was not much appalled.

I found them sober now and then; and even in the street
It seems they do not have a fight with every boy they meet.
I even found some honest men among the very poor;
And I have heard some sentences which did not end with "shure."

It seems that *praties* in their skins are not their only food,
And that they have a house or two which is not built of mud.
In fact, they're not all brutes or fools, and I suspect that when
They rule themselves they'll be as good, almost, as Englishmen!

—Anonymous

---

[2]"The Native Irishman" first appeared in a humorous periodical titled *The Man in the Moon,* which had a brief popularity in Dublin during the early 1870s. It appeared again in *Everybody's Book of Irish Wit and Humor,* second edition (Dublin: Brindley & Howe, Ltd., circa 1881).
*A round, low-crowned, soft felt hat. The "billycock" also refers to a derby.

*

"The Ould Irish Jig"

My blessing be on you, ould Erin,
    My own land of frolic and fun;
For all sorts of mirth and diversion,
    Your like is not under the sun.
Bohemia may boast of her polka,
    And Spain of her waltzes talks big;
Sure, they are all nothing but limping,
    Compared with our ould Irish jig.
        (Chorus)

Then a fig for your new-fashioned waltzes,
    Imported from Spain and from France;
And a fig for the thing called polka—
    Our own Irish jig we will dance.

I've heard how our jig came in fashion—
    And believe that the story is true:
By Adam and Eve 'twas invented,
    The reason was, partners were few.
And, though they could both dance the polka,
    Eve thought it was not over-chaste;
She preferred our ould jig to be dancing—
    And faith, I approve of her taste.

        (Then a fig—etc.)

The light-hearted daughters of Erin,
    Like the wild mountain deer they can bound,
Their feet never touch the green island,
    But music is struck from the ground.
And oft in the glens and green meadows,
    The ould jig they dance with such grace,
That even the daisies they tread on,
    Look up with delight in their face.

        (Then a fig—etc.)

An ould Irish jig, too, was danced by
    The kings and the great men of yore;
King O'Toole could himself neatly foot it
    To a tune they call "Rory O'More."
And oft in the great hall of Tara,
    Our famous King Brian Boru
Danced an ould Irish jig with his nobles,
    And played his own harp to them, too.

        (Then a fig—etc.)

And sure, when Herodias' daughter
　　Was dancing to King Herod's sight,
His heart that for years had been frozen
　　Was thawed with pure love and delight;
And more than a hundred times over,
　　I've heard Father Flanagan tell,
'Twas our own Irish jig that she footed,
　　That pleased the ould villain so well.

Then a fig for your new-fashioned waltzes,
　　Imported from Spain and from France;
And a fig for the thing called a polka—
　　Our own Irish jig we will dance!

—James McKowen (1814-

Chapter Twenty-one
Quotable Notables

Introduction

Irish humor has always resisted clear-cut analysis. The reason, in part, may be attributed to its extraordinary range, developed over centuries of emotional peaks and valleys. It embraces everything from the simple rustic retort and elemental practical joke, to the most sophisticated nuances of wit. Yet, when Americans think of the typical Irishman of humor (if, indeed, there exists such a stereotype), their thoughts turn, not to the sophisticates, but to such romanticized sons of Erin as George Michael Cohan (1878-1942), among other stage Irishmen. Cohan, during his five-decade theatrical career, epitomized the flippant, cheeky, debonair "Irish" Irishman whose blarney, song, and dance could enchant a bevy of lace-curtain dowagers at a St. Patrick's Cathedral meeting, or elicit an enthusiastic roar of approval from an audience of stevedores. Wherever Irishmen gather for a convivial evening, one can still hear the cocky, self-assured voice of Cohan's ghost, singing:

> "Haitch - i - dooble-r-i, - g - a - n spells Harrigan;
> Proud of all the Irish blood that's in me,
> Divil a man can say a wurrd agin me."

But Cohan was a man of good humor, not a humorist. Surprisingly enough, the best of Irish wit and humor stems, not from the world of show business, but from the people's men of letters: the poets, playwrights, journalists, and authors. It can be said, in fact, that no other nationality has ever produced so many humorists among their poets alone, as have the Irish. And following closely on the heels of the poets are those in the political arena. Many Americans of Irish extraction, it is true, have won fame as comics: Jackie Gleason, Arthur Godfrey, Peggy Cass, Patsy Kelly, and the late Fred Allen, to name a scant few, could make a sphinx laugh. Nevertheless, the bulk of classic Irish humor has traditonally emanated from the literary field.

Only a third of the selections in the following pages were contributed by Irish-Americans, but that is because the United States, as compared with Ireland, is a young nation and came late into the field. Regrettably, scores

323

of additional candidates who belong in this distinguished company were omitted because of the limitations of space. In any event, they will be found in anecdotal form, sporting among the other sections of this volume.

You are now invited to join such notables as William B. Yeats, George Bernard Shaw, Oliver Goldsmith, Oscar Wilde, John O'Hara, F. Scott Fitzgerald, and Eugene O'Neill. Here, too, you can enjoy the thrusts of such Irish patriots as Daniel O'Connell and Eamon de Valera. Also well represented is John F. Kennedy, without whose good-natured quips this anthology would not be complete.

In parting, please to remember that, in this chapter, you will be dealing with a very special and excellent kind of humor—more difficult because it usually lacks an introductory "build-up" and must rely on its own few words to convey a complete idea. Revere it for the rare stuff it is.

—H.D.S.

I like to quote the fragrant lines of Keats,
    And often I am caught by Shelley's tone,
And yet for clever thoughts and quaint conceits,
    Give me some little lyric of my own.
                —Mitchell D. Follansbee (1870-1941)

*

"The Irish are a fair people; they never speak well of one another."
                —Samuel Johnson (1709-84)

*

Many fascinating stories have been told about Charles Stewart Parnell, leader of the nineteenth-century Home Rule movement in Ireland. Few, however, have given due credit to the patriot's caustic wit. This tale is a memorable example.

The British government, anxious to avoid further trouble with Ireland, sent one of its most eminent and skilled statesmen to visit Parnell. Unannounced, the British nobleman entered the Irishman's office..

Parnell, busy at his desk, glanced up from a sheaf of papers he had been studying and nodded pleasantly. "Take a chair," he said.

"Sir," blustered the intruder, unaccustomed to waiting, "I'll have you know I am Lord Butf-Orpington, of the House of Lords."

"In that case," said Parnell agreeably, "take *two* chairs!"

*

"My one claim to originality among Irishmen is that I never made a speech."
                —George Moore (1852-1933)

*

Daniel O'Connell (1775-1847), known as "Liberator," was one of the foremost Irish political leaders. A successful lawyer, he gradually became involved in the Irish fight for the emancipation of Roman Catholics, and in 1823 he founded the Catholic Association, a formidable agitation society which, despite England's restrictive measures, became a great national movement. It was through his efforts that Great Britain, in 1829, finally passed the Catholic Emancipation Act. O'Connell openly supported repeal of the union of Great Britain and Ireland at a time when it was dangerous to to do so, but despite imprisonment and persecution by the British, he became the first Catholic lord mayor of Dublin since the time of James II.

The following first person anecdote was gleaned from patriot Daniel O'Connell's diary, and represents a humorous side of the Irish leader that was seldom evidenced in his long struggle against oppression.

"I remember being counsel at a special commission in Kerry against a Mr. Sullivan. Having occasion to press him somewhat hard in my speech, he jumped up in court and called me a purse-proud blockhead.

" 'Sir, you are out of order,' I said to him. 'I have no purse to be proud of. Secondly, if I am a blockhead it is better for you as I am counsel against you. However, just to save you the trouble of saying so again, I will administer a slight rebuke'—Whereupon I whacked him soundly on the backside with the judge's cane.

"On the next day, Sullivan sent a challenge by William Ponsonby of Crottoe to meet him on the field of honor for a demonstration of our respective accuracy with pistols. But very shortly he wrote me to state that since he had challenged me he had discovered that my life was inserted in a very valuable lease which he owned.

" 'Under these circumstances,' Mr. Sullivan's letter continued, 'I cannot afford to shoot you unless, as a precautionary measure, you first insure your life, naming me the beneficiary. If you do, then hi for powder and ball! I'm your man!' "

*

"I hate the sight of monkeys; they remind me so of poor relations."
—Joseph O'Leary

*

Eamon de Valera, the former *Sinn Fein* leader who became the first Prime Minister of the Republic of Ireland, and later in life accepted the less demanding office of President of the Republic, was not a man given to funny statements. A fiery orator and a skilled political debater, he could "cause an opponent's ear to crinkle with pain," as one journalist put it. However, when he chose, he could remain as silent as the grave. At such times his speech was so laconic that his brevity sometimes grew exasperating to his listeners. Even his wife, love her though he did, could get little more than the barest response from him. The following anecdote, now legendary, aptly describes the Irish statesman during those periods when he was in no mood for talk.

One Sunday morning, a year or two before he became Prime Minister of the Republic of Ireland, de Valera returned home from the Church of Our Lady of the Assumption. His wife, who had remained at home due to a bad cold, asked him whether he had enjoyed Father Kelly's sermon.

"Yes," said De Valera.

"What was it about?" she wanted to know.

"Sin."

"Well, for Heaven's sake, what did the man have to say?"

"He was against it!"[1]

*

The late Louis Briscoe, popular mayor of Dublin, was once called upon to welcome a visiting foreign dignitary.

"Your Excellency," declared Mayor Briscoe, grinning broadly, "we welcome you to Ireland in the name of our 28 million inhabitants, 23 million of whom are in the United States."

*

At a social function one evening in Dublin, the English poet, Charles Lamb, who was visiting the city, found himself pestered by a dowager named Mrs. Keneeley. Lamb, whose stutter concealed a quick, rapier-sharp mind, listened in grim silence while the woman rhapsodized endlessly about her love for her children.

"And how do *you* like babies, Mr. Lamb?" asked Mrs. Keneeley in happy conclusion.

His answer, curt and immediate—almost precipitate—put a quick end to her monologue:

"B-b-boiled!"

*

(Speaking of a colleague): "The best thing about him is that when he's drunk he's not sober."

—William Butler Yeats (1865-1939)

*

The late Brendan Behan was possessed of a cutting tongue—and he had no qualms about using it when warranted. At a party one night, the Irish author was standing in a corner, imbibing a solitary drink, and scowling at the mass of bodies that flowed like shadowy figures through the large,

---

[1] *The Irish Register,* February 1952.

dimly-lit room. He was plainly bored with them and with their idle chatter. He was approached by his hostess.

"Haven't you met any interesting people?" she asked teasingly.

"Not yet," snapped Behan. "But then, I've only been here five hours!"

*

Oliver Goldsmith (1729-74)

Goldsmith was once introduced to a successful English writer who groveled abjectly before the eminent man of letters.

"Sir," murmured the Britisher humbly, "I am simply a hack who should hardly call himself a writer in the presence of the greatest artist in all of Ireland and the English-speaking world."

Goldsmith was courteous, but later remarked: "That man had no right to make himself so small. He is not that big!"

One day, Dr. Samuel Johnson received a message from Oliver Goldsmith that his landlady had called an officer to arrest him for nonpayment of his bill. Johnson immediately sent him a guinea, and then hastened to the scene of battle. He arrived just in time to learn that Goldsmith had already broken the guinea to procure a bottle of Madeira. Now, well stimulated by the heady wine, he was berating his landlady with his entire lexicon of Irish insults. Johnson, that heavy angel of mercy, interrupted his friend's eloquence to ask if he had any means of raising money, whereupon Goldsmith produced the manuscript of a novel. Johnson pocketed it and hurried away to Newberry, the bookseller. He returned shortly with sixty pounds. This was the celebrated *Vicar of Wakefield*.

"Oliver," Johnson asked later, "why didn't you sell that manuscript yourself and pay your rent with the proceeds?"

"I didn't think of it," Goldsmith confessed.

"But if you don't write for money, then what *do* you write for?"

"My dear friend," answered Goldsmith loftily, "I can assure you that I certainly do not write for avaricious landladies. I write for—hmm—for—for...now what in hell's name *do* I write for?"

*

George Bernard Shaw (1856-1950)

"Americans adore me and will go on adoring me until I say something nice about them."

The famous exotic dancer and free spirit of a few decades ago, Isadora Duncan, wrote a fervent letter to Shaw, suggesting that, by every law of eugenics, they should become the parents of a child.

"Just think what a fortunate offspring it would be," she urged, "with your brains and my body."

"Madam," replied the great Irish playwright, "I must say that I am flattered, but I must decline your agreeable invitation. The child might not be so lucky. It might have my body and your brains!"

Shaw once received an invitation from a celebrity hunter: "Lady Tillingham-Swarthmore will be at home Thursday between four and six."

GBS returned the card. Underneath her message, he had scrawled:

"Mr. George Bernard Shaw likewise."

Vince Haloran, the editor of *Catholic Weekly,* was vacationing in England where he happened to meet George Bernard Shaw. The playwright, in his none-too-gentle manner, immediately confronted the American editor with an argument.

"Why is it that you never review my plays?" he demanded.

"Because they have little or nothing to do with Catholicism," explained the editor sharply. "From what I hear, you don't even believe in the Bible."

"Why should I?" retorted GBS. "I didn't write it!"

Shaw was in a secondhand bookstore, poring over volumes which had been considerably marked down from their original prices, when he came across a book containing his own plays. It was inscribed, moreover, to a friend, beneath whose name on the flyleaf, GBS saw the following, written in his own hand: "With the compliments of George Bernard Shaw." He promptly bought the book.

That afternoon, he sent the volume back to the early recipient with his updated inscription:

"With renewed compliments, GBS."

As the curtain came down on the first performance of *Arms and the Man,* the applauding audience began to chant, "Author! Author!" Obligingly, Shaw answered the curtain call. In the center of the stage, he smiled and bowed. But a discordant note sounded when one man in the gallery shouted, "Rotten! Rotten!"

"My friend," Shaw called out so that his voice might be heard in the nethermost region of the gallery, "I completely agree with you, but what matters our opinion against so many?"

For all his ready wit, Shaw did not always win the last word. The sharp-tongued playwright received his well-merited comeuppance one evening when he was invited to a dinner party in London. Unlike the other guests, he was served the special concoction that was always provided for him, an unyielding vegetarian, consisting of some mixed greens and salad oils.

Sir Winston Churchill, who was Shaw's neighbor at the table, took a long, hard look at his companion's plate and shook his head.

"Tell me one thing, George," said the redoubtable Winston, *sotto voce*, "have you already eaten that or are you going to?"

Another of Shaw's setbacks occurred when he replied to an invitation to lunch with Lady Randolph. He wired her his customary rude refusal:

"WHAT HAVE I DONE TO PROVOKE SUCH AN ATTACK ON MY WELL-KNOWN HABITS?"

Whereupon Lady Randolph sent another telegram:

"KNOW NOTHING OF YOUR HABITS. HOPE THEY ARE NOT AS BAD AS YOUR MANNERS."

Shavian Short Shrifts:
"Marriage is popular because it combines the maximum of temptation with the maximum of opportunity."

"He practiced the utmost economy in order to keep up the most expensive habits."

"A doctor's reputation is made by the number of eminent men who die under his care."

"I'd rather be an Irishman than an Englishman; but then, who wouldn't?"

Lilian McCarthy once asked George Bernard Shaw why he had come to live in England instead of seeking his inspiration among the Dublin poets—George Moore, Yeats, "A.E.," and others.

"Lord bless you," answered Shaw, "I'm old enough to be A.E.'s father; and George Moore had not discovered Ireland then. He was in Paris studying painting. He hadn't even discovered himself. The Ireland that you know did not exist. I could not stay there, dreaming my life away on the Irish hills. England had conquered Ireland; so there was nothing for it but to come over and conquer England, which you will notice I have done pretty thoroughly. One way or the other, my dear, we Irish will prevail!"

It would be well if all teetotalers were as gracious in their excuses as the Irish poet, George Russell, better known to his contemporaries as "A.E." When declining a drink, he would murmur:

"No thank you. You see...I was born intoxicated!"

*

Richard Brinsley Sheridan (1751-1816)

Richard Brinsley Sheridan, the playwright, wit, and spendthrift, was dunned by his tailor who rightly insisted that his customer pay at least the interest on his bill.

"Sir," Sheridan replied loftily, "it is not my interest to pay the principal, and it is not my principle to pay the interest."

Sheridan was strolling along St. James Street one day when he happened to meet two scions of nobility.

"I say, Sherry," commented one of them, "we have just been discussing which you were—a knave or a fool. What is your opinion?"

Sheridan took each of them by the arm and replied:

"You might say I am between the two!"

Whatever else may be said of the witty, hard-drinking Sheridan, he took his humor seriously. For example, Lord Lauderdale, whose bumbling efforts at humor were often funnier than his stories, declared his intention to repeat some witticism of Sheridan's.

"Please don't, my dear Lauderdale," cautioned Sheridan, a worried look on his face. "A joke in your mouth is no laughing matter!"

Michael Kelly, the singer and composer, was also the proprietor of a shop at the bottom of the Haymarket where he sold wine and copies of his music. For some time he had thought of displaying a sign to advertise his establishment, but was at a loss as to how to word it. He asked Sheridan for his suggestion. That worthy, in his cups as usual, meant well. His hastily drawn sign read:

MICHAEL KELLY—COMPOSER OF WINE AND IMPORTER OF MUSIC

During the early 1800s, when the crusading teetotaler, William Wilberforce, had reached his highest plateau of eminence, Sheridan imbibed too freely one evening and was found intoxicated in the gutter by a policeman.

"What is your name?" asked the officer.

Sheridan opened one eye, grinned through his alcoholic haze, and introduced himself:

"Wilberforce!"

*

Oscar Wilde (1854-1900)

Sir Lewis Morris was complaining to Oscar Wilde about the neglect of his poems by the press.

"It's a conspiracy of silence," he declared. "What do you think I should do?"

"Join it!" suggested Wilde.

When George Bernard Shaw, as a young man, emerged from his native Ireland and moved to England, he began writing a column for a London weekly publication. At that time, another Irishman, Oscar Wilde, was enjoying his vogue as a wit and maker of epigrams. One evening, an acquaintance of Wilde happened to read one of Shaw's characteristic articles which was signed, as usual, with the author's initials.

"Say, Wilde," asked the acquaintance, "who is this fellow, GBS?"

"He's a young Irishman named Shaw," explained Wilde. "Rather forceful, isn't he?"

"Indeed! My God, how he cuts and slashes! He doesn't seem to spare anyone he knows. If he keeps this up, he'll make himself a lot of enemies."

"Well," said Wilde reflectively, "he hasn't become important enough yet to have any enemies. But none of his friends like him."

Wilde's Wild Quotes

"Duty is what one expects from others."

"I sometimes think that God, in creating Man, somewhat overestimated His ability."

"Good taste is the excuse I've always given for leading such a bad life."

"The Niagara Falls would be more impressive if it flowed the other way."

"Don't give a woman advice. One should never give a woman anything she can't wear in the evening."

"Nothing succeeds like excess."

"Always forgive your enemies: nothing annoys them as much."

"I never travel without my diary; one should always have something sensational to read on the train."

"The public is wonderfully tolerant; it forgives everything but genius."

Wilde and Whistler

The illustrious nineteenth-century painter, James McNeil Whistler (1834-1903), had a sense of humor that could be as barbed and pointed as a fishhook. His chief rival in malicious wit was his friend, Oscar Fingall O'Flahertie, more familiarly known to us as Oscar Wilde. Throughout their lives they took inordinate delight in outwitting each other. There was one memorable quip which gave Whistler the last word: one that is still used today by modern comedians. It relates to the time the famous painter made some comment whose brilliance turned Wilde green with envy.

"Jimmy, I wish I had said that," he sighed.

"Don't worry, Oscar," retorted Whistler, "you will!"

Wilde, whose egotism even surpassed Whistler's, arrived at his friend's studio after the first performance of one of his least successful plays.

"Was the play well received?" asked Whistler.

"Oh, the play itself was a huge success," said Wilde airily, "but the audience was a total failure."

According to legend, Wilde and Whistler were never formally introduced, although they had long heard of each other. The story goes that Whistler was standing bareheaded in a hat shop one day while a clerk searched for his size hat. Suddenly the door to the shop burst open and Oscar Wilde angrily strode inside. Mistaking Whistler for a clerk, he exploded:

"See here, sir! This hat doesn't fit me!"

"Well, neither does your coat," drawled the painter, eyeing Wilde casually from head to foot. "What's more, if you'll pardon my saying so, I'll be damned if I care much for the color of your trousers!"

Whistler, after listening to a dozen previous tributes in which the goblets were held on high, heard all his favorite toasts aired before his turn arrived. At length he stood up, raised his glass aloft, and proclaimed:

"A toast, my friends, to the next drink!"

Wilde called upon Whistler one evening, only to find that his friend had been overly familiar with the cup that cheers.

"I see you've been drinking whiskey," observed Wilde fatuously.

"Sure I've been drinking whiskey!" exploded the Irish-American painter. "What the hell else would I be doing with it?"

*

Patrick Ireland

"An unnatural sex act is one you haven't the courage or imagination to perform."

"Yes, Ulster has had many obstacles to overcome of late, but its most serious problems are still January and February."

"Irishmen can say more funny things naturally than others can say purposely."

*

A thesaurus can be an invaluable tool for a writer, but its use can be overdone, especially when it breeds discontent with a choice of words in ordinary conversation.

We have, for our authority, the celebrated case of the Irish bard, Arthur Manning. The poor man simply could not leave the English language alone. He would extract a word from his verbal storehouse, drop it, substitute another, then a third, and so on, until he had constructed a veritable pyramid of synonyms. This terrible word-malady broke out on one occasion when the poet visited O'Donnell's restaurant in Washington, D.C., and gave the waiter his order:

"Bring me—fetch me—carry me—supply me—in other words (I hope you are following me) serve—when it is cooked—scorched—grilled, I should say—a large—considerable—meaty (as opposed to fatty)—chop."

*

"An extravagance is anything you buy that is of no earthly use to your wife."

—Franklin P. Adams (1881-1960)

*

For some reason unknown to most of us, the famed Irish temper has been attributed only to the males. But the ladies, too, can rise up in righteous wrath, as suggested by the following gem, circa 1932:

Peggy Ryan, the author, had been "keeping company" with Eddie Palmer, the well-known horse jockey. There was nothing in writing about their arrangement, but they had an "understanding." Imagine her chagrin when, one morning over her breakfast coffee, she read in the papers that Eddie had married a dark horse.

Irish eyes were not smiling in Peggy's house. In fact, she was floored—but she got up again. She sent a wire:

"SO YOU MARRIED SOMEONE ELSE BEHIND MY BACK! YOU MAY CONSIDER OUR ENGAGEMENT DEFINITELY AT AN END, YOU SHANTY IRISH CREEP!"

*

John McCormack (1884-1945)

For those too young to remember John McCormack, a few words of introduction are in order. Born in Athlone, Ireland, this truly great operatic tenor made his debut in London at the age of twenty-two. Two years later, having captivated England with his magnificent voice, he was brought to the United States by impressario-composer Oscar Hammerstein. Following his highly successful debut in New York, the youthful McCormack sang with the Boston and Chicago opera companies. After 1914, however, he sang principally in concert and for phonograph records. But, although he had achieved distinction in the classical field, McCormack was widely beloved for his singing of simple, sentimental ballads.

In 1936, three years before his retirement, John McCormack was prevailed upon to sing for a famed but particularly obnoxious socialite.

"My fee," said McCormack stiffly, "will be two thousand dollars."

"Two thousand dollars!" gasped the wealthy hostess who sometimes spent that much for her French poodles. "Isn't that rather high?"

"Perhaps," he replied, hoping she would refuse him, "but that is my fee."

"Very well, I suppose I'll have to pay it," she sighed. "But just remember, you are an entertainer and I must now remind you that I do not permit entertainers to mingle with my guests."

"Oh, don't you now?" exclaimed McCormack, visibly brightening. "In that case my fee will be only *one* thousand dollars!"

John McCormack had just finished a concert at Carnegie Hall in New York when a lad gained admission to the famous tenor's dressing room.

"Sir," the young fellow asked respectfully, "how can I become a great singer?"

"Why not begin with simple ballads?" McCormack suggested.

"But you were singing complicated classics when you were only ten years old," protested the aspiring vocalist.

"Yes," agreed McCormack, "but I didn't ask 'how'!"

*

Comedian Joe Cook had a speech impediment, but no one enjoyed joking about it more than Cook himself. One day, in the lobby of the old Roxy Theater in New York, he met fellow comic Fred Allen.

"F-F-Fred," he asked, "c-c-can you s-s-spare me f-f-fifteen minutes?"

"Sure," said Allen. "What is it?"

"I w-w-want to have a f-f-five m-minute c-c-c-conversation w-with you."

*

The late film star, Victor McLaglen, disclosed this "inside" story at a banquet for show business folk. Alfred Lunt and Lynn Fontanne made one movie in Hollywood, McLaglen explained, and, when they were asked to view the day's rushes (uncut scenes in the picture), Lynn saw them alone and was horrified. She raced home to her husband.

"Well?" asked Alfred. "How did the rushes turn out?"

"I was awful," cried Lynn wildly. "Terrible! Unbelievable! I can't go on with it!"

"How was I?" asked her husband.

"Oh, charming, dear; perfectly wonderful, as you always are. You'll have to do something about your makeup, though, because your lips looked a little pale. But, Alfred, as for me, I can't go on with this. My voice sounds impossible and I haven't any eyes and my face is entirely expressionless and I don't seem to know what to do with my hands and feet."

"Hmm," muttered Alfred. "Pale lips, eh?"

*

Vincent Scanlon, a prominent movie director in his day, had been at the same studio for many years. His position was almost as high as his opinion of himself, and as a mark of respect, he was allotted the best space in the studio's parking lot. He parked his car there regularly, rain or shine.

One morning, he found himself the victim of a Foul Plot, as they like to say in Hollywood. His parking space Was Occupied!

He was a Mass of Ire.

This was *lèse-majesté*.

He pushed the usurper's car out and drove his splendid Cadillac in. As an afterthought he left a note—Dignified but Scathing:

"Keep your goddam jalopy outta here!"

When he returned, a Sight met his imperial eyes.

The usurper's car was back again, in his reserved space, and the Great Director's Caddie had been pushed out. Was there no God?

An answer to his note was tucked under the windshield wiper.

"Sorry, me bucko, but I saw your last picture Saturday and I didn't think you'd be here any more!" (Signed) Errol Flynn.

*

John Barrymore (1882-1942)

Among the most illustrious of the theater's Irishtocracy were the Barrymores: Lionel, Ethel, and John. Indeed, Edna Ferber and George S. Kaufman collaborated on a play about them, titling it *The Royal Family*. Nevertheless, despite their fame, and especially in their earlier years, there were times when John, the youngest of the siblings, was not recognized. Old-timers in the movie colony still recall the day when John, then approaching the height of his fame, entered a Hollywood men's shop and selected a dozen silk shirts with cravats to match, and another dozen pairs of silk pajamas.

"Charge it," he said.

"And the name?" asked the clerk politely.

"Barrymore," said the actor, his voice cold as ice.

"And the first name?" persisted the clerk.

Barrymore's glare froze the atmosphere. "Ethel!" he snapped.

––––––––––

John Barrymore could be quite rude when he felt he was being imposed upon, a circumstance which must have happened frequently, judging by the number of squelches attributed to him. Perhaps the most famous of all the actor's snubs occurred when he was summoned to the telephone by a secretary of Harry Cohn, the authoritarian chief of Columbia Pictures.

"I am speaking for Mr. Cohn," she said. "He will expect you to attend an exclusive party he is giving tomorrow in Malibu."

"Madam," responded Barrymore in the knife-edged voice that he often used on the stage and screen, "I am speaking for John Barrymore, who has a previous engagement which he will make as soon as you hang up!"

＊

Eileen Finney, then a newly-transplanted daughter of Hibernia, currently residing in Hartford, was so enamored of Sean O' Faolain's literary works that she wrote him a letter:

"I hear that your writing yields you a retail price of $1.00 per word. I enclose $1.00, for which please send me a sample."

Much amused, the witty O'Faolain kept the dollar and sent along one word: "Thanks."

But O'Faolain had no monopoly on Irish wit. Shortly afterward, he received another letter from Miss Finney:

"Sold the 'Thanks' anecdote for $2.00. Enclosed please find 75¢ in stamps, being half the profits on the transaction, less postage and handling."

F. Scott Fitzgerald (1896-1940)

Writer F. Scott Fitzgerald and his equally eminent colleague, John O'Hara, both heavy drinkers, were chatting together one evening at Tony Pastor's emporium, when they were joined by the illustrious playwright, Eugene O'Neill.

"Pull up a chair and have a drink, Gene," said O'Hara.

"Well, John I'll sit with you for a while," agreed O'Neill, "but I've quit drinking. In fact, I've stopped smoking and gambling, too."

"I wish I could say that," replied O'Hara enviously.

"Why don't you?" put in Fitzgerald blandly. "O'Neill did!"

F. Scott Fitzgerald once received a manuscript from an aspiring dramatist. After a quick but painful perusal, Fitzgerald returned it with a short note:
"My dear Sir: I have read your play. Oh, my dear Sir!"

Here is another gem of Hollywood memorabilia involving F. Scott Fitzgerald, with the capital letters so dearly loved by movieland left intact, as God intended.

Playwright Fitzgerald was approached by a director who was wildly enthused about filming a South Seas picture. It would feature Native Maidens and the Eternal Beat of the Tom Toms. He wanted Fitzgerald to write the main scene and, naturally enough, he was Radiant with Enthusiasm and a double scotch on the rocks as he described the setting:

"An orchid-scented evening, just made for Romance, see? A silver ribbon of Moonlight over a Tropical Lagoon. On the flowered banks of the Limpid Pool, we hear the lovely strains of Native Music sifting through the palms; and over all, a breathtakingly Gorgeous Sky just lousy with goddam stars!"

O'Hara and Fitzgerald were discussing writing in general terms, when O'Hara began to grow eloquent as he described the fabulous glories of the film industry. "I write a scenario in a couple of days and get a fortune for it," he said. "You ought to try it."

"It's too baffling for me," sighed Fitzgerald ruefully. "I'll stick to writing books, magazine pieces, and for the legitimate stage."

"What's baffling about writing for the movies?" O'Hara demanded.

"Well, last year I was asked to submit something to a film company," Fitzgerald explained. "So I sent them four manuscripts—and got back nine!"

*

Basil O'Connor, who headed the March of Dimes program during the Franklin D. Roosevelt administration, was approached by a well-known industrialist. The tycoon, instead of offering a substantial contribution, said he would donate his "good name" to the cause. "I'm a self-made man," he boasted.

"That, sir," retorted O'Connor, visibly irritated, "relieves the Almighty of a great responsibility!"

*

Alfred E. Smith (1873-1944)[2]

At the 1928 Democratic National Convention, presidential candidate Al Smith was buttonholed by a timid stranger.

"Mr. Goldberg, I believe?" he murmured questioningly.

Smith stared at the man, speechless for several moments.

"Mister," he replied when he finally found his voice. "If you believe that, you'll believe anything!"

To a young, aspiring politician, Al Smith offered this advice:

"Never make people laugh. If you would succeed in life you must be as solemn as an ass. All the great monuments are built over solemn asses!"

*

"But, look, I was born here. My children were born here. What the hell do I have to do to be called an American?"

—Joseph P. Kennedy (1888-1969)

John Fitzgerald Kennedy (1917-63)

A number of biographies have been written about John F. Kennedy, all of them extolling his warm, Irish wit and his obvious enjoyment of repartee. The President's humor, sometimes ironic, often directed against himself, undoubtedly reflected his intellectual and coolly objective temperament. He seldom told standardized jokes, relying, instead, upon spontaneous witticisms.

---

[2]The son of poor Irish parents, Alfred Emanuel Smith quit parochial grammar school to help support his widowed mother. Al, as he was always called, cherished a boyhood dream of becoming a song and dance man in the tradition of George M. Cohan, but this was not his destiny. He worked as a trucker's helper and then as a fish peddler at the Fulton Fish Market in New York City. After several other menial jobs he entered politics where his gift for blarney and very real abilities caught the attention of his fellow Irish-Americans at Tammany Hall. He gained that organization's favor and won an election to the New York State Assembly, where he became Assembly speaker. After serving as Sheriff of New York and President of the New York City Board of Aldermen, he was elected Governor of New York for four successive terms (1918-26). Al Smith's reputation as a progressive, reform-minded statesman won him the Democratic nomination for President, the first Roman Catholic to receive this recognition. He was defeated by Herbert Hoover in the 1928 national election. He then retired from politics to become president of the firm that owned the Empire State Building, and served as editor of *New Outlook* magazine. Although sometimes brusque, he was known as "a man of the people," and was highly esteemed until his death at age seventy-one.

Not all of his humor was confined to penetrating observations, of course. He also enjoyed laughter for its own sake. There was the day he addressed a graduating class at Harvard, for example, and then announced he would answer questions from the podium.

"Mr. President," asked one of the students, "how did you become a war hero when you were commander of a *PT* boat?"

"I had no choice," responded Kennedy with a grin. "They sank my boat."

The martyred President could become quite garrulous on occasion and furnish the Washington press corps with columns of interesting copy. But there were other times, however, when he simply was not in the mood for talk and would maintain a strict silence on practically everything. During one of those periods when he evaded all controversial questions, he was buttonholed by a group of White House reporters.

"Mr. President," asked one newsman, "have you anything to say about Fidel Castro and our relations with Cuba?"

"No," replied Kennedy.

"Will you state your views on our current relations with the Soviet Union?"

"No," he repeated.

"How about the Middle East problem? Any opinion?"

"No."

"About your State of the Union message to Congress?"

"No."

As he turned to leave, President Kennedy suddenly paused. "And don't quote me," he added, smiling.

———

Here are some further samplings of the effervescent, flashing, Kennedy wit that are as endearing as they are enduring.

Presidential candidate John F. Kennedy, at a political rally in Muskegon, Michigan, September 1960: "I want to express my appreciation to the Governor for introducing me as the potentially greatest president in the history of this country. I think he is overstating it by a degree or two. George Washington wasn't a bad president and I do want to say a word for Thomas Jefferson. But, otherwise, I accept the compliment."

In Salem, Oregon, September 1960, Kennedy explains why Jacqueline, his wife, who was expecting a child, has not accompanied him: "Ladies and gentlemen, I would like to introduce my sister, who is representing my wife, who is otherwise committed."

Addressing a youth rally in which many children were present, in Girard, Ohio, October 1960: If we could only lower the voting age to nine, we'd sweep the state."

San Diego, California, November 1960, referring to the Republican "truth squad" that dogged his footsteps everywhere he went: "I see where the 'truth squad' has been ditched. They told the truth once and now they are not allowed to travel around anymore."

Speaking to the Democratic Women's Club, Queens, New York, Novem-

ber 1960: "I have come here to ask your help. There's an old Irish saying, 'Never send a boy to do a man's job—send a lady!' "

At the National Press Club, Washington, D.C., December 1960: "A few Catholics have criticized me because of my assurances that, as President, I would not be influenced by the Vatican. Now I can understand why Henry the Eighth set up his own church."

Addressing a farmers cooperative meeting in Grand View, Missouri, December 1960: "How can you possibly vote Republican? I know one farmer who planted corn last year, and then said to his neighbor, 'I hope I break even this time—I really need the money.' "

Presidential comment at a White House function, January 1961, honoring his new administration appointees: "The reason for this reception is my desire to see some of the names I have been reading about in the newspapers."

Kennedy, joking at a dinner given by Jacqueline at the White House, May 27, 1961, in honor of his forty-fourth birthday: "When we got into office, the one thing that surprised me most was to find that things were just as bad as we'd been saying they were."

When Arthur Hays Sulzberger, Chairman of the Board of The New York Times, *purchased a new rocking chair, he received this note from President Kennedy, dated May 1, 1961:* "You will recall what Senator Dirksen said about the rocking chair—it gives you a sense of motion without any sense of danger."

At a private dinner among friends at the White House, January 1962: "There is no city in the United States in which I get a warmer reception and less votes than Columbus, Ohio."

Replying to the suggestion that his brother, Attorney General Robert Kennedy, would make a fine president: "I have consulted Bobby about it and, to my dismay, the idea appeals to him."

Shortly after his election as President of the United States, Kennedy sent his education bill to Congress without mention of Federal aid to parochial schools. Alluding to Catholic criticism, he joked: "As you all know, some circles invented the myth that after Al Smith's defeat in 1928, he sent a one-word telegram to the Pope: 'Unpack!' After my press conference on the school bill, *I* received a one-word wire from the Pope: 'Pack!' "

Addressing the faculty and student body at the University of California at Berkeley, March 1962: "This has been a week of momentous events around the world. The long and painful struggle in Algeria came to an end. Both nuclear powers and neutrals labored in Geneva for a solution to the problem of a spiraling arms race, and also to the problems that so vex our relations with the Soviet Union. The Congress opened hearings on a trade bill, which is far more than a trade bill, but an opportunity to build a stronger and closer Atlantic community. And my wife had her first and last ride on an elephant!"

In April 1962, having just been named an honorary chief of an Indian tribe in Wisconsin, President Kennedy donned the feather headdress and proclaimed to his Indian audience: "The next time I see cowboys and Indians at the movies, I'll be with *us!*"

At the famous White House dinner honoring Nobel Prize winners: "I think this is the most extraordinary collection of talent, of human knowledge, that has ever been gathered together at the White House—with the possible exception of when Thomas Jefferson dined alone."

Speaking at a fund-raising banquet at the Mayflower Hotel in Washington, D.C., June 1962, in honor of Matthew McCloskey who had just been appointed Ambassador to Ireland: "I commend this idea of a $250 dinner. This is like the story of the award of prizes by the Moscow Cultural Center, the first prize being one week in Kiev and the second prize being *two* weeks. For $100 you get speeches; for $250 you *don't* get any speeches. You can't get bargains like that anymore!"

To Press Secretary Pierre Salinger, November 1962: "Karl Marx wrote for the *Herald Tribune,* but that is not why I canceled my subscription."

Referring to the thin-skinned sensitivity of his vice president, Lyndon B. Johnson, during a White House staff meeting, December 1962: "Writing a birthday note to Lyndon is like drafting a state document."

President Kennedy, while visiting Cork, Ireland, in June 1963, introduced his friend and traveling companion: "And now I would like to introduce to you the pastor at the church I go to. He comes from right here in Cork—Monsignor O'Mohoney. He is the pastor of a poor, humble flock in Palm Beach, Florida."

In Galway, Ireland, June 1963, the President invited his audience to the White House: "If you ever come to America, come to Washington and tell them, at the gate, that you come from Galway. The word will be out—it will be *Cead mille failte"* ["a hundred thousand welcomes," in Gaelic].

New Ross, Ireland, June 1963: "Some years ago, an Irishman from New Ross traveled to Washington. In order to let his neighbors know how well he was doing, he had his picture taken in front of the White House. On the back of the picture, he wrote, 'This is my summer home. Come and see it.' "

In Duganstown, Ireland, June 1963, at an elegant buffet prepared in President Kennedy's honor by his third cousin, Mary Ryan: "I want to thank all of those who prepared this. It was a great effort on their part. We can promise that we will come only once every ten years."

Wexford, Ireland, June 1963: "Ladies and gentlemen, I don't want to give the impression that every member of my administration in Washington is Irish. It just seems that way. But now let me introduce the head of the American Labor movement, whose mother and father were born right here in Ireland—George Meany, who is traveling with us. And I would like you to meet the only man with us who doesn't have a drop of Irish blood in his veins, but who is dying to—the head of protocol of the United States, Angier Biddle Duke."

Dublin, Ireland, June 1963: "When my great-grandfather left here to become a cooper in East Boston, he carried nothing with him except two things: a strong religious faith and a strong desire for liberty. And I am glad to say that all of his great-grandchildren have valued that inheritance. If he hadn't left, I'd be working over here at the Albatross Company."

Chapter Twenty-two
Hot Doggerel and Lusty Limericks
Introduction

American dictionaries define the word "doggerel" as a "comic or burlesque verse, usually loose or irregular in measure." The definition is further embellished with such adjectives as "rude" and "crude." Fortunately, the classic poets of Ireland and their Irish-American counterparts, neither of whom were averse to writing an occasional bit of doggerel, were unable to consult modern dictionaries, else posterity would have been the loser.

Doggerel, created by knowledgeable authors who are also gifted with an innate talent for humorous composition, takes on a lasting quality because it has something to say, however mirthfully it is stated. It is the antithesis of the limerick which does not pretend to be anything but sheer nonsense. But let it be said that doggerel, as well as its poor relation, the limerick, must be as meticulously crafted as is conventional poetry, if it is to be accepted by a succession of generations.

The selections in this modest offering need no comments to make them enjoyable. Some of them are translations from the Irish, as are various contributions in other chapters, and are so noted. A few are from very early times and others date from later periods. For example, *"Pangur Bán"* is a translation by Robin Flower of a manuscript found in the monastery of St. Paul in Carinthia, dating approximately from the ninth century, and reminding us how far afield the Irish monks traveled.

Dr. Douglas Hyde, the most eminent of Irish translators, is represented here with "I Shall Not Die for Thee," a superbly crafted satire on "lost love," the age of the original possibly dating back to the eleventh century. One suspects, too, that the anonymous quatrain, "How Colleen Lost Her Teeth," was also translated from the Gaelic.[1]

Some of the doggerel in this chapter is quite contemporary, and others nearly so. "The Tides of Love" might well have been written yesterday, al-

---

[1] There are still many thousands of poems, songs, and stories in the archives of libraries and institutions that, for the writer with a knowledge of Irish, represent a wonderfully fertile field for translation.

though it is some forty years old. The lament with the fifteen-word title, "My Darling, I Was Captured by Cannibals, Who Poached the Eyes You Loved So Well," written at the turn of the present century, is another clever satire on love. The author, Rupert Brooke, demonstrates a rare degree of skill as he carefully constructs his lines, leading to the final, delightfully witty parody of "eternal" love.

Clearly, the Irish authors were master craftsmen whose work was anything but "rude" or "crude." Doggerel may not have been invented in Ireland, but it might as well have been: they seem to hold a monopoly on the genre.

Another facet of Irish poetry—and may the saints forgive me for including it in the category—has swept the world because of its cleverness and rambunctious nonsense. That classification refers to the limerick. The limerick is a kind of humorous verse of five lines in which the first and second lines rhyme with the fifth; and the shorter third line rhymes with the shorter fourth line. This form is named after County Limerick.

Wherein lies the lilt of a limerick?

> Well, it's partly the shape of the thing
> That gives the old limerick wing:
> These accordion pleats,
> Full of airy conceits,
> Take it up like a kite on a string.

According to legend, the limerick stems from the olden days in North Munster where, at social gatherings, groups would sing "Will You Come Up to Limerick?" In later years, the form was taken up by sailors, travelers, and others, and disseminated throughout the world. As the years passed, the limerick grew increasingly obscene until today, there remains only a small selection of those that may be considered "proper." That is not to say, however, that they are no longer funny—many of them are. But with the exception of a few that may be termed "mildly naughty," they were omitted from this anthology. In any event,

> A limerick packs laughs anatomical
> Into space that is quite economical:
> But the good ones I've seen
> So seldom are clean,
> And the clean ones so seldom are comical.

Following is a collection of "clean ones"—doggerel and limericks—which I trust you will agree are comical indeed.

—H.D.S.

"The Young Celtic Poets"

Those dear young Gaels of Ireland
Are the lads who drive me mad;
For half their words need footnotes,
And half their rhymes are bad.[2]

—Patrick Ireland

*

"Pangur Bán"

I and Pangur Bán my cat,
'Tis a like task we are at:
Hunting mice, is his delight,
Hunting words I sit all night.

'Tis a merry thing to see
At our tasks how glad are we,
When at home we sit and find
Entertainment to our mind.

'Gainst the wall he sets his eye,
Full and fierce and sharp and sly;
'Gainst the wall of knowledge I
All my little wisdom try.

So in peace our task we ply,
Pangur Bán, my cat and I;
In our arts we find our bliss,
I have mine and he has his.[3]

—Robin Flower (1819-1873)

*

"The Village Schoolmaster"

Beside yon straggling fence that skirts the way,
With blossom'd furze unprofitably gay,
There, in his noisy mansion, skill'd to rule,
The village master taught his little school.

A man severe he was, and stern to view;
I knew him well, and every truant knew;
Well had the boding tremblers learn'd to trace
The day's disasters in his morning face.

---

[2]A parody of the lines appearing in G. K. Chesterton's "The Ballad of the White Horse."
[3]Translated from the Old Irish.

Full well they laughed, with counterfeited glee
At all his jokes, for many a joke had he;
Full well the busy whisper, circling round,
Convey'd the dismal tidings when he frown'd.

Yet he was kind: or if severe in aught,
The love he bore to learning was in fault;
The village all declar'd how much he knew;
'Twas certain he could write, and cypher too.

Lands he could measure, terms and tides presage,
And even the story ran that he could gauge.
In arguing too, the parson own'd his skill,
For e'en though vanquished, he could argue still.

While words of learned length and thundering sound
Amaz'd the gazing rustics rang'd around,
And still they gaz'd, and still the wonder grew,
That one small head could carry all he knew.

—Oliver Goldsmith

*

"The Rakes of Mallow"

Beauing, belling, dancing, drinking,
Breaking windows, damning, sinking,
Ever raking, never thinking,
    Live the rakes of Mallow.

Spending faster that it comes,
Beating waiters, bailiffs, duns,
Bacchus' true-begotten sons,
    Live the rakes of Mallow.

One time naught but claret drinking,
Then like politicians thinking
To raise the sinking funds when sinking,
    Live the rakes of Mallow.

When at home with dadda dying,
Still for Mallow water crying;
But where there's good claret plying,
    Live the rakes of Mallow.

Living short but merry lives;
Going where the Devil drives;
Having sweethearts, but no wives,
    Live the rakes of Mallow.

Then to end this raking life,
They get sober, take a wife,
Ever after live in strife,
    And wish again for Mallow.

—Anonymous (circa 1790)

*

"A Glass of Beer"

The lanky hank of a she in the inn over there
Nearly killed me for asking the loan of a glass of beer;
May the Devil grip the whey-faced slut by the hair,
And beat bad manners out of her skin for a year.

That parboiled ape, with the toughest jaw you will see
on virtue's path, and a voice that would rasp the dead,
Came roaring and raging the minute she looked at me,
And threw me out of the house on the back of my head!

If I asked her master he'd give me a cask a day;
But she, with her beer at hand, not a gill would arrange!
May she marry a ghost and bear him a kitten, and may
The High King of Glory permit her to get the mange!

—James Stephens (1882-1950)

*

"The Tides of Love"

Flo was fond of Ebenezer—
    "Eb," for short, she called her beau.
Talk of Tides of Love, great Caesar!
    You should see them—Eb and Flo.

—Thomas A. Daly (1871-1948)

*

"I Shall Not Die For Thee"⁴

For thee I shall not die,
    Woman high of fame and name;
Foolish men thou mayest slay,
    I and they are not the same.

Why should I expire
    For the fire of any eye,
Slender waist or swan-like limb,
    Is't for them that I should die?

---

⁴Translated from the Old Irish.

The round breasts, the fresh skin,
  Cheeks crimson, hair so long and rich;
Indeed, indeed, I shall not die,
  Please God, not I, for any such.
The golden hair, the forehead thin,
  The chaste mien, the gracious ease,
The rounded heel, the languid tone,
  Fools alone find death from these.

Thy sharp wit, thy perfect calm,
  Thy thin palm like foam of sea;
Thy white neck, thy blue eye,
  I shall not die for thee.

Woman, graceful as the swan,
  A wise man did nurture me,
Little palm, white neck, bright eye,
  I shall not die for thee.

—Douglas Hyde

*

"Satisfied"

Tell me no more I am deceived,
That Chloe's false and common;
I always knew, at least believed,
  She was a very woman.
As such I liked, as such caressed,
She still was constant when possessed,
  She could do more for no man.

But oh, her thoughts on others ran,
  And that you think a hard thing;
Perhaps she fancied you the man,
  And what care I one farthing?
You think she's false, I'm sure she's kind;
I take her body, you her mind,
  .Who has the better bargain?

—William Congreve (1670-1729)

*

"False Though She Be"

False though she be to me and love,
    I'll ne'er pursue revenge;
For still the charmer I approve,
    Though I deplore her change.
In hours of bliss we oft have met:
    They could not always last;
And though the present I regret,
    I'm grateful for the past.[5]

                        —William Congreve

✻

"Petticoats Down to My Knees"

When my first troubles in life I began to know,
    Spry as a chick newly out of the shell,
Nothing I longed for so much as a man to grow,
    Sharing his joys and his sorrows as well.
Now that the high tide of life's on the slack again,
    Pleasure's deep draught drained down to the lees,
Dearly I wish I had the days back again,
    When I wore petticoats down to my knees!

Well do I mind the day I donned trousereens,
    My proud mother cried, "We'll soon be a man!"
Little we know what fate has in store for us—
    Troth, it was then that my troubles began.
Cramped up in clothes, little comfort or ease I find,
    Crippled and crushed, almost frightened to sneeze!
Oh to have back my old freedom and peace of mind,
    When I wore petticoats down to my knees!

Now must I walk many miles for an appetite,
    And after all find my journey in vain—
Oh for the days when howe'er you might wrap it tight,
    My school lunch was ate at the end of the lane!
Now scarce a wink of sleep on the best of nights,
    Worried in mind and ill at ease,
Headache or heartache ne'er troubled my rest of nights,
    When I wore petticoats down to my knees!

Once of my days I thought girls were nuisances,
    Petting and coaxing and ruffling your brow,
Now Love, the rogue, runs away with my few senses,
    Vainly I wish they would fondle me now!
Idols I worship with ardor unshakeable,
    But none of all half so fitted to please

---

[5]Congreve apparently wrote this piece as a postscript to the preceding "Satisfied."

As the poor toys full of sawdust and breakable,
  When I wore petticoats down to my knees!

Little I cared then for doings political,
  The ebb or the flow of the popular tides,
Europe might quake in convulsions most critical—
  I had my bread buttered well on both sides.
Now must I wander for themes for my puny verse
  Over earth's continents, islands and seas;
Small stock I took of affairs of the universe,
  When I wore petticoats down to my knees!

Life is a puzzle and man is a mystery,
  He that would solve them a wizard need be;
Precepts lie thick in the pathways of history,
  This is the lesson that life has taught me.
Man ever longs for the dawn of a golden day,
  Visions of joy in futurity sees,
Ah! he enjoyed Life's cream in the olden day,
  When he wore petticoats down to his knees!

—Francis A. Fahy

∗

"My Darling, I Was Captured by Cannibals, Who Poached the Eyes You Loved So Well"

The limbs that erstwhile charmed your sight
  Are now a savage's delight;
The ear that heard your whispered vow
  Is one of many *entrées* now;
Broiled are the arms in which you clung,
  And devilled is the angelic tongue;
And oh! my anguish as I see
  A Black Man gnaw your favorite knee!
Of the two eyes that were your ruin,
  One now observes the other stewin'.
My lips (the inconstancy of man!)
  Are yours no more. The legs that ran
Each dewy morn their love to wake,
  Are now a steak, are now a steak!...
O love, O loveliest and best,
  Natives this *body* may digest;
Whole, and still yours, my *soul* shall dwell,
  Uneaten, safe, incoctible.

—Rupert Brooke (1887-1915)

∗

"How Colleen Lost Her Teeth"

Colleen is toothless, yet when she was young
   She had tooth enough, and too much tongue.
What can I now of toothless Colleen say?
   Just that her tongue has worn her teeth away.

—Anonymous, County Leinster (circa 1870)

*

"Tim the Dragoon"

Be aisy an' list to a chune
That's sung of bowld Tim the Dragoon—
   Sure, 'twas he'd niver miss
   To be stalin' a kiss
Or a brace, by the light of the moon, *Aroon**
With a wink at the Man in the Moon!

Rest his sowl where the daisies grow thick;
For he's gone from the land of the quick:
   But he's still makin' love
   To the leddies above,
An' be jabbers! he'll tache 'em the thrick, *Avick*†
Niver doubt but he'll tache 'em the thrick!

'Tis by him the dear saints'll set sthore,
And'll thrate him to whiskey galore:
   For they've only to sip
   But the tip of his lip,
An' bedad! they'll be askin' for more, *Asthore*‡
By the powers, they'll be shoutin' "Ancore!"

—William Ireland

*

---

*A secret or pet name.
†Lad.
‡My beloved; my treasure.

The Anonymous Land of Laughable Limericks

The reader will find no signatures to the limericks which follow. This is not to say that the Irish have a peculiar passion for anonymity. Indeed, they prefer to see their names affixed to their creations: preferably emblazoned in bold capital letters. Very few of these lines, however, can be traced to their sources, and, regrettably, the authors must remain anonymous. More's the pity, too! They were exceptionally clever writers whose compositions have endured the test of decades and even centuries of telling and retelling.

Backbiter
A bishop residing in Meath
Sat down on his set of false teeth;
    Said he, with a start,
    "O Lord, bless my heart!
I've bitten myself underneath!"

*

Trouble in Paradise
God's plan made a hopeful beginning,
But men spoiled his chances by sinning.
    We trust that this story
    Will end in God's glory,
But, at present, the other side's winning.

*

Burrp!
There was an old man of Kilkenny
Who ate sixty-five eggs for a penny.
    When they asked, "Are you faint?"
    He replied, "No, I ain't,
But I'd rather I hadn't et any."

*

Get Me Behind Me
As a beauty I am no star,
There are others more handsome by far;
    But my face, I don't mind it,
    For I am behind it:
It's the people in front get the jar!

*

Cemented Relations
There was an old maid of Vancouver,
Who captured a man by maneuver;
   For she jumped on his knee
   With a chortle of glee,
And nothing on earth could remove 'er.

*

From Mirth to Birth
An amoeba named Sam and his brother,
Were having a drink with each other;
   In the midst of their quaffing
   They split their sides laughing,
And each of them now is a mother.

*

The Canny Canner
A canner, exceedingly canny,
One morning remarked to his granny:
   "A canner can can
   Anything that he can,
But a canner can't can a can, can he?"

*

The Candle Cook
There was a young woman named Riley,
Who valued old candle-ends highly;
   When no one was looking
   She used them for cooking.
"It's wicked to waste," she said dryly.

*

Ruinous Rhymes
A young poet whose name was McMann,
Wrote verse that never would scan.
   When they said, "But the thing
   Doesn't move with a swing,"
He said, "Yes, but I always like to get as many
words into the last line as I possibly can."

*

Tragedie l'Amour
There was a young man from the West
Who loved a fair lassie with zest.
　　So hard did he press her
　　To make her say, "Yes, sir,"
That he broke the cigar in his vest.

＊

Vexing Vision
There was a young lady of Flint
Who had a most horrible squint.
　　She could scan the whole sky
　　With her uppermost eye,
While the other was reading small print.

＊

Pained Posterior
A faith healer whose name was O'Neil,
Said, "Pain in itself isn't real.
　　Yet, if I sit on a pin
And it punctures my skin,
I dislike what I think that I feel."

＊

Polly Wants a Cracker—Period!
A certain old maid of Cohoes,
In despair taught her bird to propose.
　　But the parrot, dejected,
　　At being accepted,
Shrieked words too profane to disclose.

＊

Delightful Confirmation
There were two young ladies of Birmingham,
And this is the story concerning 'em:
　　They each made so free
　　As to sit on the knee
Of the bishop as he was confirming 'em.

＊

The Tutor's Tooters

A tutor who tooted the flute,
Tried to teach two young tooters to toot.
    Said the two to the tutor:
    "Is it harder to toot, or
To tutor two tooters to toot?"

*

A Mathematician
Counts His Blessings

There was an old fellow of Trinity
Who solved the square root of infinity.
    But it gave him such fidgets
    To count up the digits
That he dropped Math and took up Divinity.

*

Spitework!

There was a young lady of Glasgow
Whose party proved quite a fiasco.
    At nine-thirty about,
    The lights all went out,
Through a lapse on the part of the Gas Co.

*

Call Me Skinny

An old fellow whose name was McQueen
Grew so abnormally lean,
    And flat and compressed
    That his back touched his chest,
And sideways couldn't even be seen.

*

The Grave Student

A studious colleen named Breeze,
Weighed down with B.A.'s and M.D.'s,
    Collapsed from the strain.
    Said her doctor, " 'Tis plain
You are killing yourself by degrees."

*

The Gracious Guernsey
The cautious collapsible cow
Gives milk by the sweat of her brow.
　　Then under the trees
　　She folds her front knees
And sinks fore and aft with a bow.

*

Peek-a-Boo!
A lass in the village of Bligh,
Was so exceedingly shy,
　　That undressing at night
　　She turned out the light
For fear of the All-Seeing Eye.

*

Self-Starter
There once was a pious young priest
Who lived almost wholly on yeast.
　　"For," he said, "it is plain
　　We must all rise again,
And I want to get started, at least."

*

Termite Haven
There once lived a certain Miss Gale
Who turned exceedingly pale;
　　For a mouse climbed her leg
　　(Don't repeat this, I beg),
And a splinter got caught in its tail.

*

Dimwitty Kitty
There was a kind curate of Kew
Who kept a large cat in a pew.
　　There he taught it each week
　　A new letter of Greek,
But it never got further than *Mu*.

*

Ida's Last Stand
A peculiar old lady was Ida;
She'd scream at the sight of a spider.
   She would faint at a lamb
   And run wild from a ram,
But fearlessly tackle hard cider.

        ✻

Dinner al Fresco
There was a disgusting old man
Who used to eat catch-as-catch can.
   He covered his vest
   With remains of the best
Of gravy and chicken and ham.

        ✻

The Toe iv Me
Boot to Ye!
Augustus Fitzgerald Moran
Fell in love with Patricia McCann.
   With a yell and a whoop
   He cleared the front stoop
Just ahead of her papa's brogan.

        ✻

Miss O'Brien Goes to Zion
There once was a girl named O'Brien
Who taught holy hymns to a lion.
   Of the lady there's some
   In the lion's tum-tum;
The rest twangs a harp up in Zion.

        ✻

Shipboard Shenanigans
There was a young matron named Harrison
Who craved an affair with a Saracen.
   So once on a liner
   She took up with a Shriner
Who suffered, I fear, by comparison.

        ✻

O Solo Mi-yowww!
  Of a sudden the great prima donna
  Cried "Gawd, my voice is a goner!"
      But a cat in the wings
      Said "*I* know how she sings,"
  And finished the solo with honor.

*

Infernal Internals
  There was a young lady of Hyde;
  Of eating green apples she died.
      Within the lamented
      They soon had fermented
  And made cider inside her inside.

*

Heartaches and Bellyaches
  There was a fair maid who would sigh,
  "Ah, love is a torture," she'd cry.
      Said her pa, "Tommyrot!
      'Tisn't love that you've got—
  'Tis a mixture of pickles and pie!"

*

O, Those Wasted Years
  There was a young lady named Florence
  Who for kissing professed great abhorrence.
      But when she'd been kissed
      And found what she'd missed,
  She cried till the tears came in torrents.

*

Interfaith Understanding
  A Baptist young lady named Alice
  Once wet in a Catholic chalice.
      'Tis the padre's belief
      It was done for relief,
  And not out of Protestant malice.

*

Life in the Raw
To an artist a husband named Bicket
Said, "Turn yourself round and I'll kick it!
  You have painted my wife
  In the nude to the life:
Do you think, my dear sir, that was cricket?"

*

Excommunicated
There was an old monk of Siberia
Whose life it grew drearier and drearier.
  Till he broke from his cell
  With a hell of a yell,
And made off with the Mother Superior.

*

A Punster from Munster
A cheese that was aged and gray,
Was walking and talking one day.
  Said the cheese, "Kindly note
  My mom was a goat,
And I'm made out of curds, by the whey!"

*

The Faithful Flock
There were three little birds in a wood,
Who always sang hymns when they could.
  What the words were about
  They could never make out,
But they felt it was doing them good.

*

As Show Folk Say: "Hamois!"
There once was a naughty young chamois
Who went for a walk with his mamois.
  When she said, "My dear child,
  I fear you are wild,"
The wicked young goat exclaimed, "Damois!"

*

The Toungled Tang
There was an old lady of Tring
Who, when somebody asked her to sing,
Replied, "Isn't it odd
I can never tell 'God
Save the Weasel' from 'Pop Goes the King.' "

*

Cure for Insomnia
Mike Flanagan frequently chose
To sleep standing up on his nose.
When asked for a reason,
Said he thus got a season
Of restful and peaceful repose.

*

Sanitary Janitary
There once was a fellow named Greening,
Who fell down four flights without meaning.
The janitor swore
As G. hit the floor:
"This'll take the whole afternoon cleaning!"

*

Fast Lady of the Evening
There was a young woman named Bright
Whose speed was faster than light.
She set out one day
In a relative way,
And returned on the previous night.

*

The Valiant Bridegroom
Said an ardent young bridegroom named Trask:
"I will grant any wish that you ask."
Said his bride, "Kiss me, dearie,
Until I grow weary"—
But he died of old age at the task.

*

Unsullied Conscience
A scrupulous priest of Kildare
Used to pay an old sinner to swear.
   For an hour or two
   He would paint the air blue
While the padre would wrestle with prayer.

*

Under the Anheuser Bush
There was a young girl named Anheuser
Who thought that no man could surprise her.
   But Old Overholt
   Gave her virtue a jolt,
And now she is sadder Budweiser.

*

Heeding the Headless
Cleopatra, who thought they maligned her,
Resolved to reform and be kinder.
   "If I'm peevish," she said,
   "And cut off your head—
Won't you give me a gentle reminder?"

*

The Thrifty Farmer
A farmer's wife, Maggie McGowan,
Once said to her better half, "How in
   The world can I wear
   My new hat to the Fair,
When you've used it for milking the cow in?"

*

Vertigo
A sensitive girl named O'Neill
Once went up in a big ferris wheel.
   But when halfway around
   She looked down at the ground,
And it cost her a two-dollar meal.

*

Thoughtful Golfer
A golfer whose name was Muldoon,
Always played golf with a spoon.
  "It's handy," said he,
  "For the brandy, you see,
Should anyone happen to swoon."

*

Sneaky Snacker
There was a fat lady named Maude
Who was a contemptible fraud.
  To eat at the table
  She *never* was able,
But out in the pantry—oh, Lord!

*

Space Odyssey
There was a young lady named Stella,
Fell in love with a bowlegged fella.
  The venturesome chap
  Let her sit in his lap,
And she fell clean through to the cella.

*

Bored Bottoms
There once was a preacher unkind
Who preached out of time and of mind.
  His hearers, alack,
  Got a pain in the back,
And put pillows behind the behind.

*

An Eye for Decor
An Irishman, Paddy McGrew,
Painted his children sky-blue.
  When his wife cried, "My dear,
  Don't you think they look queer?"
He said, "Quiet—or the next will be you!"

*

Nasal Mystery
There was a young lady of Kent
Whose nose was most awfully bent.
 One day, I suppose,
 She followed her nose,
And God only knows where she went!

*

O, I C!
(This story I tell you is true:)
Sue tried to catch the 2.2.
 Said a porter, "Don't worry
 Or flurry or scurry;
It's a minute or 2 2 2.2."

*

Sailing Down the Alimentary Canal
I sat next to the Duchess at tea;
It was just as I feared it would be:
 Her rumblings abdominal
 Were simply phenomenal,
And everyone thought it was me!

*

The S-s-stutterer
There was a young priest of Calcutta
Who spoke with a terrible stutter.
 At breakfast he said,
 "Give me b-b-b-bread
And b-b-b-b-b-b-butter."

*

Irish Enterprise
There was a young girl of Kilkenny
Who was worried by lovers so many,
 That the saucy young elf
 Simply raffled herself,
And the tickets were two for a penny.

*

Absinthe Makes the
Heart Grow Fonder

There was an old fellow of Trinity,
A doctor well versed in Divinity.
    But he took to free thinking
    And then to deep drinking,
And was forced to leave the vicinity.

*

Those Horrible Hubbies

There was an old woman of Thurston
Who thought her third husband the worst one.
    For he rightly was reckoned
    Far worse than the second,
And the second was worse than her first one.

*

Madam, Your Drawers!

There was a young lady of Tottenham,
Her manners—she'd wholly forgetten 'em.
    While at tea, at the Vicar's,
    She took off her knickers,
Explaining she felt much too hot in 'em.

*

You Know Me—Eddie's Friend!

There was a young man so benighted,
He never knew when he was slighted.
    He went to a party
    And ate just as hearty
As if he'd been really invited.

*

Molar Mauler

In the Irish village of Cosham,
Jack took out his dentures to wash 'em.
    But his wife said, "Now, Jack,
    You put them right back,
Or I'll jump on the things and I'll squash 'em."

*

Pickled Perkins' Gherkins

Let us weep for the maiden named Perkins
Who was terribly fond of small gherkins.
   She went out to tea
   And ate fifty-three,
Which pickled her internal workin's.

*

What Price Integrity!

There was a young lady from Kent
Who always said just what she meant.
   People said, "She's a dear,
   So unique—so sincere!"
But they shunned her by common consent.

*

Banker's Approval

There once was a lass with such graces,
That her curves cried aloud for embraces.
   "You look," said McGee,
   "Like a million to me,
Invested in all the right places."

*

Squeaky Shoes Among the Pews

A young lady named Tricia O'Hare
Tried to steal out of church during prayer.
   But the squeak of her shoes
   Awakened all in the pews,
So she sat down again in despair.

*

Double Slip

A sweet girl whose name was O'Dell,
While walking down Chestnut Street, fell.
   She got up with a bound
   And looked all around,
And said in her dear voice, "Oh, hell!"

*

Cheers for the Ears
There was a young man of Devizes
Whose ears were of different sizes.
   The one that was small
    Was of no use at all,
But the other won several prizes.

       *

The Twickenham Walker
There was a young lady of Twickenham
Whose shoes were too tight to walk quick in 'em.
   She came back from her walk
    Looking white as a chalk,
And took 'em both off and was sick in 'em.

       *

Degrees of Blarney
A blarneyin' bucko named Pat,
To girls he proposed this and that.
   When he spoke about "this"
    He meant cuddle and kiss,
But Lord knows what he meant by his "that."

       *

The Flying Friar
A fat friar who lived in Dundalk
Proclaimed he could fly like a hawk.
   Cheered by all the townspeople
    He jumped from the steeple,
But the splashdown proved it just talk.

       *

Pollination of a Rose
A lovely young rose of Tralee
Was naughty while out on a spree.
   Now she writes to the papers,
    Deploring such capers,
And signs herself, "Mother Machree."

       *

Bloomer Girl

A lassie named Gwendolyn Landon
Had feet too narrow to stand on;
  So she stood on her head
  'Til the day she was wed,
And was known for her reckless abandon.

*

Warm Response

A senile old lady of Eire
Sat contentedly close to the fire.
  When told, "You're too hot,"
  She'd retort, "No, I'm not!"
And heatedly call you a liar.

*

Bury the Sherry, Dear

A colleen from old Londonderry,
On Guinness was loving and merry.
  She dallied with sin,
  On bourbon and gin,
But was rigid and frigid with sherry.

*

Gladys's Additive

A matron named Gladys O'Toole,
Boiled her husband in oil—'twas cruel.
  She said, "In my car
  This mix will go far,
And he'll be of some use—the old fuel!'

*

Lawn Food

A shy girl was Mollie McClure,
With a mind that was holy and pure.
  She fainted away
  In a delicate way
If anyone mentioned manure.

*

Modesty
"I've observed the bird and the bee,"
Said a sweet little rose of Tralee.
   "Their ways are so strange,
   I could never arrange
To let anyone try that with me."

*

Divine Innocence
Some verses like these, I surmise,
Were not meant for heavenly eyes.
   Saints Peter and Paul
   Don't get them at all,
And Our Father's aghast with surprise!

Chapter Twenty-three
The Wee People
Introduction

When we speak of the "wee people," we are referring to the *slooa shee* (the fairy host), representing various members of the Irish spirit world. There are, for example, the trooping fairies who dance in the forest glades and by the river banks, but are never alone. Sometimes they are gathered by the thousands: you can tell their presence by the rustling of the leaves and the sighing of the wind. But at other times they may be fewer than a dozen. Then there are the solitary fairies—the leprechauns, or fairy shoemakers, and the pookas and banshees. The pooka can take the form of many animals and can foretell the future, provided you are careful to please the creature in everything you do and say. The banshee, also a solitary fairy, attends the old Irish families and *keens* (howls) before a death.

Who are the *deenee shee* (fairy people)? Irish antiquarians tell us that the fairy people were once thought to be the gods of pagan Ireland, the *Tuatha De Danan,* who gradually diminished in size over the centuries when they were no longer fed sacrificial offerings. With the advent of Christianity in sixth-century Ireland, the Church swept aside the former pagan demonology and instituted its own. The old gods were termed "fairies," fallen angels who were not good enough to be saved, nor bad enough to be lost.

The fairies are quick to take offense, and must be addressed or mentioned only in a most respectful manner. The peasantry of old spoke of them in whispers, or not at all. When it was indeed necessary to refer to the *deenee shee,* it was best to allude to them as "the gentry," or *daoine maithe,* "the good people." But "the gentry" were not always good, as any Irish priest will darkly affirm. Lacking a conscience as we conceive it, they might commit deeds which would be judged as evil in human perspectives, but which, on their own terms, were completely devoid of malice. If they liked a human they protected him; if not, they brought misery, sometimes paralyzing him and his cattle with fairy darts.

The *slooa shee* have their merry side, too. When they are happy, they sing. Irish folklore is replete with tales of unfortunate maidens who heard their beautiful songs and pined away and died of an inexpressible longing. But they do not confine their activities to luring colleens away with their music. Occasionally they are not very nice (according to our way of thinking) and will engage in a wee bit of child stealing, or enslave a mortal who offended them. They will also punish the eavesdropper who is foolish enough to sing their songs; they grow furious when they hear their lovely music on inept, human lips.

There are few humorous folk tales about the fairy host, for the stories were born in fear, not humor. The present author does not believe in the creatures, of course. However, should one of them happen to read or hear about this short introduction, let it be understood that he has written these words in a most respectful manner, and a cup of fresh milk has been placed on his windowsill in the traditional sign of respect, and as a good-will sacrificial offering.

—H.D.S.

*

The Trooping Fairies

"The Fairies"

Up the airy mountain,
  Down the rushy glen,
We daren't go a-hunting
  For fear of little men;
Wee folk, good folk,
  Trooping all together;
Green jacket, red cap,
  And white owl's feather!

Down along the rocky shore
  Some make their home,
They live on crispy pancakes
  Of yellow tide-foam;
Some in the reeds
  Of the black mountain lake,
With frogs for their watch-dogs
  All night awake.

High on the hill-top
  The old King sits;
He is now so old and gray
  He's nigh lost his wits.
With a bridge of white mist
  Columbkill he crosses,
On his stately journeys
  From Slieveleague to Rosses;
Or going up with music

On cold starry nights,
To sup with the Queen
Of the gay Northern Lights.

They stole little Bridget
For seven years long;
When she came down again
Her friends were all gone.
They took her lightly back,
Between the night and morrow,
They thought that she was fast asleep,
But she was dead with sorrow.
They have kept her ever since
Deep within the lake,
On a bed of flag-leaves,
Watching till she wake.

By the craggy hill-side,
Through the mosses bare,
They have planted thorn-trees
For pleasure here and there.
Is any man so daring
As dig them up in spite,
He shall find their sharpest thorns
In his bed at night.

Up the airy mountain
Down the rushy glen,
We daren't go a-hunting
For fear of little men;
Wee folk, good folk,
Trooping all together;
Green jacket, red cap,
And white owl's feather!

—William Allingham (1824-87)

*

"The Priest's Supper"[1]

It is said by those who ought to understand such things, that the good
people, or the fairies, are some of the angels who were turned out of
heaven, and who landed on their feet in this world, while the rest of their
companions, who had more sin to sink them, went down further to a worse
place. Be that as it may, there was a merry troop of the fairies, dancing and
playing all manner of wild pranks, on a bright moonlight evening toward
the end of September. The scene of their merriment was not far distant

[1] Thomas Crofton Croker, 1828. *Fairy Legends and Traditions of the South of Ireland.*

from Inchegeela, in the west of County Cork—a poor village, although it had a barrack for soldiers. But great mountains and barren rocks, like those round about it, are enough to strike poverty into any place. However, as the fairies can have everything they want for wishing, poverty does not trouble them much, and all their care is to seek out unfrequented nooks and places where it is not likely anyone will come to spoil their sport.

On a nice green sod by the river's side were the little fellows dancing in a ring as gaily as may be, with their red caps wagging about at every bound in the moonshine, and so light were these bounds that the lobs of dew, although they trembled under their feet, were not disturbed by their capering. Thus did they carry on their gambols, spinning round and round, and twirling and bobbing and diving, and going through all manner of figures, until one of them chirped out:

> "Cease, cease with your drumming,
> Here's an end to our mumming;
>   By my smell
>   I can tell
> A priest this way is coming!"

And away every one of the fairies scampered off as hard as they could, concealing themselves under the green leaves of the lustmore, where, if their little red caps should happen to peep out, they would only look like its crimson bells; and more hid themselves at the shady side of stones and brambles, and others under the bank of the river, and in holes and crannies of one kind or another.

The fairy speaker was not mistaken; for along the road which was within view of the river, came Father Horrigan on his pony, thinking to himself that as it was so late he would make an end of his journey at the first cabin he came to. According to this determination, he stopped at the dwelling of Dermod Leary, lifted the latch, and entered with "My blessing on all here."

I need not say that Father Horrigan was a welcome guest wherever he went, for no man was more pious or better beloved in the country. Now it was a great trouble to Dermod that he had nothing to offer his reverence for supper as a relish to the potatoes, which "the old woman," for so Dermod called his wife though she was not much past twenty, had down boiling in a pot over the fire. He thought of the net which he had set in the river, but as it had been there only a short time, the chances were against his finding a fish in it. "No matter," thought Dermod, "there can be no harm in stepping down to try. Maybe, as I want the fish for the priest's supper, then one will be there before me."

Down to the riverside went Dermod, and he found in the net as fine a salmon as ever jumped in the bright waters of "the spreading Lee." But as he was going to take it out, the net was pulled from him. He could not tell how or by whom, and away got the salmon, and went swimming along with the current as gaily as if nothing had happened.

Dermod looked sorrowfully at the wake which the fish had left upon the water, shining like a line of silver in the moonlight, and then, with an angry motion of his right hand, and a stamp of his foot, gave vent to his feelings by muttering, "May bitter bad luck attend you night and day for a blackguard schemer of a salmon, wherever you go! You ought to be ashamed of yourself, if there's any shame in you, to give me the slip after this fashion! And I'm clear in my own mind you'll come to no good, for some kind of evil thing or other helped you. Did I not feel it pull the net against me as strong as the devil himself?"

"That's not true for you," said one of the little fairies who had scampered off at the approach of the priest, coming up to Dermod Leary with a whole throng of companions at his heels; "there was only a dozen and a half of us pulling against you."

Dermod gazed with wonder on the tiny speaker, who continued: "Make yourself noways uneasy about the priest's supper; for if you will go back and ask him one question from us, there will be as fine a supper as ever was put on a table spread out before him in less than no time."

"I'll have nothing at all to do with you," replied Dermod in a tone of determination. He paused and then added, "I'm much obliged to you for your offer, sir, but I know better than to sell myself to you, or the like of you, for a supper; and more than that, I know Father Horrigan has more regard for my soul than to wish me to pledge it forever, out of regard to anything you could put before him—so there's an end to the matter."

The little speaker, with a pertinacity not to be repulsed by Dermod's manner, continued, "Will you ask the priest one civil question for us?"

Dermod considered for some time, and he was right in doing so, but he thought that no one could come to harm out of asking a civil question. "I see no objection to do that same, gentlemen," said Dermod; "but I will have nothing in life to do with your supper—mind that."

"Then," said the little speaking fairy, while the rest came crowding after him from all parts, "go and ask Father Horrigan to tell us whether our souls will be saved at the last day, like the souls of good Christians; and if you wish us well, bring back word what he says without delay."

Away went Dermod to his cabin, where he found the potatoes placed out on the table, and his good woman handing the biggest of them all, one like a beautiful laughing apple, smoking like a hard-ridden horse on a frosty night, over to Father Horrigan.

"Please, Your Reverence," said Dermod, after some hesitation, "may I make bold to ask your honor one question?"

"What may that be?" said Father Horrigan.

"Why, then, begging Your Reverence's pardon for my freedom, it is, if the souls of the good people are to be saved at the last day."

"Who bid you ask me that question, Leary?" said the priest, fixing his eyes upon him very sternly, which Dermod could not stand before at all.

"I'll tell no lies about the matter, and nothing in life but the truth," said Dermod. "It was the good people themselves who sent me to ask the question, and there they are in thousands down on the bank of the river, waiting for me to go back with the answer."

"Go back by all means," said the priest, "and tell them, if they want to know, to come here to me themselves, and I'll answer that or any other question they are pleased to ask, with the greatest pleasure in life."

Dermod accordingly returned to the fairies, who came swarming round about him to hear what the priest had said in reply; and Dermod spoke out among them like the bold man he was. But when they heard that they must go to the priest, away they fled, some here and more there, and some this way and more that, whisking by poor Dermod so fast and in such numbers that he was quite bewildered.

When he came to himself, which was not for a long time, back he went to his cabin, and ate his lone potatoes along with Father Horrigan, who made quite light of the thing. But Dermod could not help thinking it a mighty hard case that his reverence, whose words had the power to banish the fairies at such a rate, could not, at the least, have gotten back the fine salmon that the good people had taken away from him in such a rude manner.

—Thomas Crofton Croker (1798-1854)

*

"The Stolen Child"[2]

Where dips the rocky highland
    Of Sleuth Wood in the lake,
There lies a leafy island
    Where flapping herons wake
The drowsy water-rats.
There we've hid our fairy vats
Full of berries,
And of reddest stolen cherries.
Come away, O human child,
With a fairy hand in hand,
For the world's more full of weeping than
        you can understand.

Where the wave of moonlight glosses
    The dim gray sands with light,
Far off by Furthest Rosses
    We foot it all the night,
Weaving olden dances,
Mingling hands, and mingling glances,
    Till the moon has taken flight;
To and fro we leap,
    And chase the frothy bubbles,
    While the world is full of troubles,
And is anxious in its sleep.
Come away! O, human child!
To the woods and waters wild,

---

[2]W.B. Yeats, *The Celtic Twilight*, 1893. The areas mentioned in "The Stolen Child" are in the Sligo vicinity. The place called Furthest Rosses, author Yeats assures us, is a noted fairy locality. It is there, at a certain rocky atoll, where one dares not fall asleep, for he may awaken without his full senses, the fairies having carried off his soul.

With a fairy hand in hand,
For the world's more full of weeping than
    you can understand.

Where the wandering water gushes
  From the hills above Glen-Car,
In pools among the rushes,
  That scarce could bathe a star,
We seek for slumbering trout,
  And whispering in their ears;
    We give them evil dreams,
Leaning softly out
  From ferns that drop their tears
    Of dew on the young streams.
Come! O human child!
To the woods and waters wild,
With a fairy hand in hand,
For the world's more full of weeping than
    you can understand.

Away with us he's going,
  The solemn-eyed;
He'll hear no more the lowing
  Of the calves on the warm hill-side.
Or the kettle on the hob
  Sing peace into his breast;
Or see the brown mice bob
  Round and round the oatmeal chest.
For he comes, the human child,
To the woods and waters wild,
With a fairy hand in hand,
For the world's more full of weeping than
    he can understand.

          —William Butler Yeats (1865-1939)

*

The Solitary Fairies

Master and Man[3]

    Billy Mac Daniel was once as likely a young man as ever shook his brogue during a *patron* [a festival held in honor of some patron saint], emptied a quart, or handled a shillelagh; fearing for nothing but the lack of a drink; caring for nothing but who should pay for it; and thinking of nothing but how to have fun over it. Drunk or sober, a word and a blow was ever the

---

[3]Croker, *op. cit.* (*Fairy Legends and Traditions of the South of Ireland,* Thomas Crofton Croker).

way with Billy Mac Daniel; and a mighty easy way it is of either getting into or of ending a dispute. More's the pity that, through the means of his thinking and fearing and caring for nothing, this same Billy Mac Daniel fell into bad company; for surely the good people are the worst of all company anyone could come across.

It so happened that Billy was going home one clear, frosty night not long after Christmas. The moon was round and bright; but although it was as fine a night as a heart could wish for, he felt pinched with cold. "By my word," chattered Billy, "a drop of liquor would be no bad thing to keep a man's soul from freezing in him; and I wish I had a full measure of the best."

"Never wish it twice, Billy," said a little man⁴ in a three-cornered hat, bound all about with a gold lace, and with great silver buckles in his shoes, so big that it was a wonder how he could carry them. He held out a glass as big as himself, filled with as good liquor as ever eye looked on or lip tasted.

"Success, my little fellow," said Billy Mac Daniel, nothing daunted, though well he knew the little man to belong to the good people. "Here's your health, and thank you kindly, no matter who pays for the drink." He took the glass and drained it to the very bottom without ever taking a second breath to it.

"Success," said the little man, "and you're heartily welcome, Billy. But don't think to cheat me as you have done others—out with your purse and pay me like a gentleman."

"Is it I pay you?" said Billy. "Could I not just take you up and put you in my pocket as easily as a blackberry?"

"Billy Mac Daniel," said the little man, getting angry, "you shall be my servant for seven years and a day, and that is the way I will be paid. So make ready to follow me."

When Billy heard this he began to be very sorry for having used such bold words toward the little man, and he felt himself, yet could not tell how, obliged to follow the little man the livelong night about the country, up and down, and over hedge and ditch, and through bog and brake, without any rest.

When morning began to dawn, the little man turned round to him. "You may go home, Billy," he said. "But on your peril, don't fail to meet me in the Fort-field⁵ tonight. If you do, it may be the worse for you in the long run. If I find you a good servant, you will find me an indulgent master."

---

⁴Whether "the little man" in this tale refers to a leprechaun or a clurichaun is best left to the experts to decide. Some folklorists hold that they are one and the same spirit, in different moods and shapes. In any case, they are all old, withered, and solitary, quite unlike the sociable trooping fairies. The leprechaun is a mischievous creature, often with an eye for a pretty girl, whom he does not mind stealing away for his own. The clurichaun makes himself at home in gentlemen's wine cellars, and is sometimes thought to be a leprechaun on a spree. He is unknown in Connaught and the North.

⁵Forts (*Cusheen Loo,* in Irish), also called "raths," are circular ditches enclosing a little field. Farmers do not work these raths, nor does anyone else, for if a human digs into the earth he will soon come to stone chambers, their beehive roofs and walls made of unmortared stone. Here in these fields the ancient Celts fortified themselves

Home went Billy Mac Daniel, and though he was tired and weary enough, never a wink of sleep could he get for thinking of the little man. But he was afraid not to do his bidding, so up he got in the evening, and away he went to the Fort-field. He was not long there before the little man came toward him. "Billy," he said, "I want you to saddle one of my horses: we are going on a long journey tonight. And you may saddle another for yourself—you may be tired after your walk last night."

Billy thought this very considerate of his master, and thanked him accordingly: "But," said he, "if I may be so bold, sir, I would ask which is the way to your stable, for never a thing do I see but the fort here, and the old thorn tree in the corner of the field, and the stream running at the bottom of the hill, with the bit of bog over against us."

"Ask no questions, Billy," said the little man, "but go over to that bit of bog and bring me two of the strongest rushes you can find."

Billy did so, wondering what the little man would be at. He picked two of the stoutest rushes he could find, with a little bunch of brown blossoms stuck at the side of each, and brought them back to his master.

"Get up, Billy," said the little man, taking one of the rushes from him and striding across it.

"Where shall I get up, please Your Honor?" said Billy.

"Why, upon horseback, like me, to be sure," said the little man.

"Is it after making a fool of me you'd be," said Billy, "bidding me get a horseback upon that bit of rush? Maybe you want to persuade me that the rush I pulled out but a while ago out of the bog over there is a horse?"

"Up! up! and no words," said the little man, looking very angry. "The best horse you ever rode was but a fool to it." So Billy, thinking all this was a joke, and fearing to vex his master, straddled across the rush. "Borram! Borram!" cried the little man (which in English means to become great), and Billy did the same after him. Presently the rushes swelled up into fine horses, and away they went at full speed. But Billy, who had put the rush between his legs without much minding how he did it, found himself sitting on horseback the wrong way, which was rather awkward, with his face to the horse's rump; and so quickly had his steed started off with him that he had no power to turn around, and there was nothing therefore for it but to hold on by the tail.

At last they came to their journey's end, and stopped at the gate of a fine house. "Now, Billy," said the little man, "do as you see me do, and follow me close. But as you did not know your horse's head from his tail, mind that your own head does not spin round until you can't tell whether you are standing on it or on your heels."

The little man then said some queer kind of words, out of which Billy could make no meaning, but he contrived to say them after him for all that—and into the fine house they went through the keyhole of a door, and

---

and their cattle, retreating in winter into the stone chambers, where they were also buried. The fairies have taken up their abode in the underground chambers, guarding them from all disturbance. Flint arrowheads are occasionally found near the raths; these are called "fairy darts" which are flung at humans, or even cattle, who intrude.

through one keyhole after another, until they got into the wine cellar, which was well stored with all kinds of wine.

The little man fell to drinking as hard as he could, and Billy, no way disliking the example, did the same. "The best of masters are you, surely," said Billy to him, "no matter who is the next; and well pleased will I be in your service if you continue to provide plenty of drink."

"I have made no bargain with you," said the little man, "and will make none; but up and follow me." Away they went, through keyhole after keyhole.

When they came back to the Fort-field the little man dismissed Billy, bidding him to be there the next night at the same hour. Thus did they go on, night after night, shaping their course one night here, and another night there; sometimes north, and sometimes east, and sometimes south; until there was not a gentleman's wine cellar in all Ireland they had not visited, and could tell the flavor of every wine in it as well; aye, better than the butler himself.

One night when Billy Mac Daniel met the little man as usual in the Fort-field, and was going to the bog to fetch the horses for their journey, his master said to him, "Billy, I shall want another horse tonight, for we may bring back more company than we take." So Billy, who knew better than to question any order given to him by his master, brought a third rush, much wondering who it might be that would travel back in their company, and whether he was about to have a fellow servant. If I have, thought Billy, he shall go and fetch the horses from the bog every night, for I don't see why I am not, every inch of me, as good a gentleman as my master.

Well, away they went, Billy leading the third horse, and never stopped until they came to a snug farmer's house, in the County Limerick, close under the old castle of Carrigogunniel, that was built, they say, by the great Brian Boru. Within the house there was great carousing going forward, and the little man stopped outside for some time to listen. Suddenly, turning around, he said, "Billy, I will be a thousand years old tomorrow."

"God bless us, sir, will you?" said Billy.

"Don't say those words again, Billy," said the little old man, "or you will be my ruin forever. Now Billy, as I will be a thousand years in the world tomorrow, I think it is full time for me to get married."

"I think so too, without any kind of doubt at all," said Billy, "if ever you mean to marry."

"And to that purpose," said the little man, "have I come all the way to Carrigogunniel; for in this house, this very night, is young Darby Riley going to be married to Bridget Rooney; and as she is tall and comely, and has come of decent people, I think of marrying the girl myself, and taking her off with me."

"And what will Darby Riley say to that?" said Billy.

"Silence!" said the little man, putting on a mighty severe look. "I did not bring you here with me to ask questions." Without further argument, he began saying the queer words which had the power of passing him through the keyhole as free as air, and which Billy thought himself mighty clever to be able to say after him.

In they both went, and for the better viewing of the company, the little man perched himself up as nimbly as a cocksparrow upon one of the big beams which went across the house over all their heads, and Billy did the same upon another facing him; his legs hung down as untidy as could be. It was quite clear he had not taken pattern after the way in which the little man had bundled himself up together. If the little man had been a tailor all his life he could not have sat more contentedly upon his haunches.

There they were, both master and the man, looking down upon the fun that was going forward. Under them were the priest and piper, and the father of Darby Riley, with Darby's two brothers and his uncle's son. There, too, were both the father and the mother of Bridget Rooney, and proud enough the old couple were that night of their daughter, as good right they had; and her four sisters, with brand new ribbons in their caps, and her three brothers all looking as clean and clever as any three boys in Munster; and there were uncles and aunts, and gossips and cousins enough besides to make a full house of it. Plenty was there to eat and drink on the table for every one of them, if they had been double the number.

Now it happened, just as Mrs. Rooney had helped his reverence to the first cut of the pig's head which was placed before her, beautifully bolstered up with savories, that the bride gave a sneeze, which made everyone at the table start, but not a soul said, "God bless us." All thinking that the priest would have done so, as he ought if he had done his duty, no one wished to take the word out of his mouth, which, unfortunately, was preoccupied with pig's head and greens. After a moment's pause, the fun and merriment of the bridal feast went on without the pious benediction.

Of this circumstance both Billy and his master were no inattentive spectators from their exalted stations. "Ha!" exclaimed the little man, throwing one leg from under him with a joyous flourish. His eye twinkled with a strange light, while his eyebrows became elevated into the curvature of Gothic arches. "Ha!" said he, leering down at the bride, and then up at Billy, "I have half of her now, surely. Let her sneeze but twice more, and she is mine, in spite of priest, mass book, and Darby Riley."

Again the fair Bridget sneezed, but it was so gently, and she blushed so much, that few except the little man took, or seemed to take, any notice. No one thought of saying, "God bless us."

Billy all this time regarded the poor girl with a most rueful expression of countenance. He could not help thinking what a terrible thing it was for a nice young girl of nineteen, with large blue eyes, transparent skin, and dimpled cheeks, suffused with health and joy, to be obliged to marry an ugly little bit of a man who was a thousand years old, barring a day.

At this critical moment the bride gave a third sneeze, and Billy roared out with all his might, "God save us!" Whether this exclamation resulted from his soliloquy, or from the mere force of habit, he never could tell exactly himself. But no sooner was it uttered than the little man, his face glowing with rage and disappointment, sprang from the beam on which he had perched himself, and shrieking out in the shrill voice of a cracked bagpipe, "I discharge you from my service, Billy Mac Daniel—take *that* for your wages," he gave Billy a most furious kick in his lower back, which sent his unfortunate servant sprawling upon his face and hands right in the middle of the supper table.

If Billy was astonished, how much more so was every one of the company into which he was thrown with so little ceremony. But when they heard his story, Father Cooney laid down his knife and fork, and married the young couple out of hand, with all speed. And Billy Mac Daniel danced the Rinka at their wedding, and plenty did he drink at it too, which was what he thought more of than dancing.

—Thomas Crofton Croker

*

The Kildare Pooka[6]

Mr. H—— R——, when he was alive, used to live a good deal in Dublin, and he was once in a great while out of the country on account of business. But the servants were kept on at the big house at Rath, all the same as if the family was at home. Well, they used to be frightened out of their lives after going to their beds, with the banging of the kitchen door, and the clattering of fire irons, and the pots and pans and dishes. One evening they sat up ever so long, keeping one another in heart with telling stories about ghosts and witches, when—what would have it?—the little scullery boy that used to sleep over the horses and could not get room at the fire, crept into the hot hearth, and when he got tired listening to the stories, sorra fear him, but he fell dead asleep.

Well and good. After they were all gone and the kitchen fire raked up, he was woke with the noise of the kitchen door opening, and the trampling of an ass on the kitchen floor. He peeped out, and what should he see but a big ass, sure enough, sitting on his curabingo and yawning before the fire. After a little while the creature looked about him and began scratching his ears as if he was quite tired, and says he, "I may as well begin first as last."

The poor boy's teeth began to chatter in his head. "Now he's goin' to ate me," says he.

But the fellow with the long ears and tail on him had something else to do. He stirred the fire and then he brought in a pail of water from the pump, and filled a bog pot that he put on the fire before he went out. He then put his hand—foot, I mean—into the hot hearth and pulled out the little boy, who let out a roar of fright. But the pooka—for that is what it was, naturally, or unnaturally—only looked at him and thrust out his lower lip to show how little he valued him. Then he pitched him into his pew again.

---

[6]Patrick Kennedy, *Legendary Fictions of the Irish Celts* (New York: Macmillan Publishers, Inc., 1937).

Well, the creature then lay down before the fire till he heard the boil coming on the water, and maybe there wasn't a plate, or a dish, or a spoon on the dresser that he didn't fetch and put into the pot, and wash and dry the whole bilin' of 'em as well as e'er a kitchen maid from that of Dublin town. He then put all of them up in their places on the shelves—and if he didn't give a good sweepin' to the kitchen, leave it till again. Then he comes and sits *fornent* the boy, let down one of his ears and cocked up the other, and grinned.

The poor boy strove to cry out, but not a sound 'ud come out of his throat. The last thing the pooka done was to rake up the fire and walk out, giving such a slap o' the door that the boy thought the house couldn't help tumbling down.

Well, to be sure if there wasn't a hullabullo next morning when the poor fellow told his story! They could talk of nothing else the whole day. One said one thing, another said another; but a fat, lazy scullery girl said the cleverest thing of all. *"Musha!"* says she. "If the *pooka* does be cleaning up everything that way when we are asleep, what should we be slavin' ourselves for doing his work?"

"Seadh go deimhin" (yes, indeed), says another; "them's the wisest words you ever said, Kauth. It's meself won't contradict you."

So said, so done. Not a bit of a plate or dish saw a drop of water that evening, not a whisk was laid to the floor, and everyone went to bed soon after sundown. Next morning everything was as fine as fine in the kitchen, and the lord mayor might eat his dinner off the floor. It was great ease to the lazy servants, you may depend, and everything went on well till a foolhardy gag of a boy said he would stay up one night and have a chat with the pooka.

He was a little daunted when the door was thrown open and the ass marched up to the fire. "Sir," says the boy when he at last picked up his courage, "if it isn't takin' a liberty, might I ax who you are, and why you are so kind as to do half of the day's work for the girls every night?"

"No liberty at all," says the pooka. "I'll tell you, and welcome. I was a servant in the time of Squire R's father, and was the laziest rogue that ever was clothed and fed, and done nothing for it. When my time came for the other world, this is the punishment that was laid on me—to come here and do all this labor every night, and then go out in the cold. It isn't so bad in the fine weather; but if you only knew what it is to stand with your head between your legs, facing the storm from midnight to sunrise, on a bleak winter night."

"And could we do anything for your comfort, my poor fellow?" says the boy.

"Musha, I don't know," says the pooka, "but I think a good quilted frieze coat would help to keep the life in me them long nights."

"Why then, in troth, we'd be the ungratefullest of people if we didn't feel for you."

To make a long story short, the next night but two, the boy was there again, and if he didn't delight the poor pooka, holding up a fine warm coat before him, it's no mather! Betune the pooka and the man, his legs was got into the specially-made four arms of it, and it was buttoned down the breast and the belly, and he was so pleased he walked up to the glass to see how he looked. "Well," says he, "it's a long lane that has no turning. I am much obliged to you and your fellow servants. You have made me happy at last. Good night to you."

So he was walking out, but the other cried, "Och! sure you're going too soon. What about the washing and sweeping?"

"Ah, but you may tell the girls that they must now take their own turn. My punishment was to last till I was thought worthy of a reward for the way I done my duty. You'll see me no more."

And no more they did, and right sorry they were for having been in such a hurry to reward the ungrateful pooka.

—Patrick Kennedy

*

The Piper and the Pooka[7]

In the old times, there was a half fool living in Dunmore, in the County Galway, and although he was excessively fond of music, he was unable to learn more than one tune, and that was the "Black Rogue." He used to get a good deal of money from the gentlemen, for they used to get sport out of him. One night the piper was coming home from a house where there had been a dance, and he was half drunk. When he came to a little bridge that was up by his mother's house, he squeezed the pipes on, and began playing the "Black Rogue" (*an rogaire dubh*). A pooka[8] came behind him, and flung him up on his own back. There were long horns on the pooka, and the piper got a good grip of them, and then he said—

"Destruction on you, you nasty beast, let me home. I have a tenpenny piece in my pocket for my mother, and she wants snuff."

"Never mind your mother," said the pooka, "but keep your hold. If you fall, you will break your neck and your pipes." Then the pooka added, "Play up for me the 'shan Van Vocht' (*an t-seannbhean bhocht).*"

"I don't know it," said the piper.

"Never mind whether you do or you don't," said the pooka. "Play up, and I'll make you know."

The piper put wind in his bag, and he played such music as made himself wonder.

---

[7]The author-translator, Douglas Hyde, ranks among the great scholars of Ireland. Writing under his Gaelic name, An Craoibhinn Aoibhinn, he was the author of many works, including *A Literary History of Ireland* (1899) and *Love Songs of Connaught* (1894). Dr. Hyde was largely responsible for the revival of the Irish language and literature through his founding of the Gaelic League in 1893. He was President of Ireland from 1938 to 1945. (See Biographical Index of Authors, in this volume.)

[8]Dr. Hyde used the Gaelic *puca* in this literal translation of an ancient folk tale. The Anglo-Irish form, pooka, is used here for the sake of conformity. Whatever the spelling, the pooka is half-spirit, half-animal (of many species), the forefather of Shakespeare's Puck.

"Upon my word, you're a fine music master," says the piper then; "but tell me where you're for bringing me."

"There's a great feast in the House of the Banshee, on the top of Croagh Patric tonight," says the pooka, "and I'm for bringing you there to play music. Take my word, you'll get the price of your trouble."

"By my word, you'll save me a journey, then," says the piper. "Father William put a journey to Croagh Patric on me because I stole a white gander from him last Marinmas."

The pooka rushed him across hills and bogs and rough places, till he brought him to the top of Crough Patric. Then the pooka struck three blows with his foot, and a great door opened, and they passed in together, into a fine room.

The piper saw a golden table in the middle of the room, and hundreds of old women (*cailleacha*) sitting round about it. The old women rose up and said, "A hundred thousand welcomes to you, you pooka of November (*na Samhna*). Who is this you have with you?"

"The best piper in Ireland," said the pooka.

One of the old women struck a blow on the ground, and a door opened in the side of the wall, and what should the piper see coming out but the white gander which he had stolen from Father William.

"By my conscience, then," says the piper, "myself and my mother ate every taste of that gander, only one wing, and I gave that to *Moy-rua* (Red Mary), and it's she told the priest I stole the gander."

The gander cleaned the table, and carried it away, and the pooka said, "Play up some music for these ladies."

The piper played up, and the old women began dancing, and they danced till they were tired. Then the pooka said to pay the piper, and every old woman drew out a gold piece and gave it to him.

"By the tooth of Patric," said he, "I'm as rich as the son of a lord."

"Come with me," says the pooka, "and I'll bring you home."

They went out then, and just as he was going to ride on the pooka, the gander came up to him and gave him a new set of pipes. The pooka was not long until he brought him to Dunmore, and he let the piper off at the little bridge. Then he told him to go home, and says to him, "You have two things now that you never had before—you have sense and music (*ciall agus ceol*).

The piper went home and he knocked on his mother's door, saying, "Let me in. I'm as rich as a lord, and I'm the best piper in Ireland."

"You're drunk," said the mother.

"No, indeed," said the piper, "I haven't drunk a drop."

The mother let him in, and he gave her the gold pieces. "Wait now," said he, "till you hear the music I'll play."

He buckled on the pipes the gander had given him, but instead of music, there came a sound as if all the geese and ganders in Ireland were screeching together. He awakened the neighbors, and they were all mocking him, until he put on the *old* pipes, and then he played melodious music for them; and after that he told them all he had gone through that night.

The next morning, when his mother went to look at the gold pieces, there was nothing there but the leaves of a plant.

The piper went to the priest and told him his story, but the priest would not believe a word from him, until he put the new pipes on him—and then the screeching of the ganders and geese began.

"Leave my sight, you thief," said the priest.

But nothing would do the piper till he put the *old* pipes on him to show the priest that his story was true.

He buckled on the old pipes, and he played melodious music, and from that day till the day of his death, there was never a piper in the County Galway as good as he was.

—Douglas Hyde

*

The Banshee at the Bridge

"The banshee,⁹ Misther Harry? Well, sir, as I was strivin' to tell ye, I was goin' home from work one day, from Mr. Cassidy's that I tould ye of, in the dusk o' the evenin'. I had more nor a mile—aye, it was nearer two mile—to thrack to where I was lodgin' with a dacent widdy woman I knew, Biddy Maguire by name, so as to be near me work.

"It was the first week in November,¹⁰ an' a lonesome road I had to travel, an' dark enough, with threes above it; an' about halfways there was a bit iv a bridge I had to cross, over one o' them little sthrames that runs into the Doddher. I walked on in the middle iv the road, for there was no toe-path at that time, Misther Harry, nor for many a long day afther that. But, as I was sayin', I walked along till I come nigh upon the bridge, where the road was a

---

⁹The banshee, the female apparation who wails before the death of a human (but only for members of old Irish families), is sometimes accompanied by a coach-a-bower—a huge black coach which is pulled by headless black horses, and driven by a *dullahan,* a headless phantom. *Duffy's Sixpenny Magazine* (Dublin) tells us that "the sinister, coffin-mounted coach rumbles to the door of a dying Irishman or Irishwoman, but should anyone be so foolhardy as to open it, a basin of blood will be thrown in his face." The origin of the *dullahan* is obscure. According to Thomas Crofton Croker, it is believed to have emanated from Norway where, folklore has it, the heads of corpses were cut off to enfeeble their ghosts. However, W. B. Yeats offers the suggestion, that the *dullahan* may have descended from the giant of Irish mythology who swam across the Channel with his head in his teeth.

¹⁰Many Irish folktales dealing with fairies are laid in November, the third fairy festival of the year. The first is May Eve which, however, occurs only every seventh year when they fight furiously for the harvest—the choicest ears of grain, of course, belong to them. The fighting can be detected in the whirling of the wind and the debris of the fields and woods flying about. Witnessing this, the peasantry respectfully remove their hats and murmur, "God bless the good people."

The second of the fairy festivals occurs on Midsummer Eve. At this time, when the bonfires are kindled on every hill in honor of Saint John, the fairies are at their merriest—and usually most lustful. Sometimes, on Midsummer Eve, they will steal away beautiful girls for their brides.

The November Eve festival sees them at their wickedest—and gloomiest—for this is the first night of winter, according to the old Gaelic reckoning. On this night, the fairies dance with the ghosts, the pooka is abroad, and witches make their spells. After November Eve the blackberries are no longer wholesome because the pooka has spoiled them.

bit open, an' there, right enough, I seen the hog's back o' the ould-fashioned bridge that used to be there till it was pulled down years ago, an' a white mist steamin' up out o' the wather all around it.

"Well, now, Misther Harry, often as I'd passed by the place before, that night it seemed sthrange to me, an' like a place ye might see in a dhrame; an' as I come up to it I began to feel a cowld wind blowin' through the hollow o' me heart. *Musha* Thomas, sez I to meself, is it yerself that's in it, sez I. So I put a bould face on it, an' I made a sthruggle to set one foot afore the other, ontil I came to the rise o' the bridge. And there, God be good to us! in the cantle o' the wall I seen an ould woman, as I thought, sittin' on her hunkers, all crouched together, an' her head bowed down, seemin'ly in the greatest affliction.

"Well, sir, I pities the ould craythur, no matther the mortial fright I was in, so I up an' sez to her, 'That's a could lodgin' for ye, ma'am.' Well, she tuk no more notice o' me than if I hadn't let a word out o' me, but kep' rockin' herself to an' fro, as if her heart was breakin'. So I sez to her again, 'Eh, ma'am, is there anythin' the matther with ye?' An' I made for to touch her on the showldher, ownly somethin' stopped me, for as I looked closer at her I saw she was no more an ould woman nor she was an ould cat.

"The first thing I tuk notice to, Misther Harry, was her hair that was sthreamin' down over her showldhers, an' a good yard on the ground of aich side o' her. O, but that was the hair! The likes iv it I never seen on mortial woman, young or ould, before nor sence. It grew as sthrong out iv her as out iv e'er a young slip iv a girl ye could see; but the color iv it was a mysthery to describe. The first squint I got iv it I thought it silvery gray, like an ould crone's; but when I got up beside her I saw, by the glance o' the sky, it was a sort iv an Iscariot color, an' a shine out iv it like floss silk. It ran over her showldhers and the two shapely arms she was lanin' her head on, for all the world like Mary Magdalen's in a picther. And then I persaved that the gray cloak and the green gownd undernaith it was made of no earthly matherial I ever laid eyes on.

"Now I needn't tell ye, sir, that I seen all this in the twinkle of a bedpost—long as I take to make the narration iv it. So I made a step back from her, an' I sez out loud, 'The Lord be betune us an' harm!' An' with that I blessed meself.

"Well, Misther Harry, the word wasn't out o' me mouth afore she turned her face on me. *Musha,* Misther Harry, but 'twas that was the awfullest apparition ever I seen, the face iv her as she looked up at me! God forgive me for sayin' it, but 'twas like no face I could mintion—as pale as a corpse, an' most o' freckles on it, like the freckles on a turkey's egg; an' two eyes sewn in with red thread, from the terrible power o' cryin' they had to do; an' such a pair iv eyes as they wor, Misther Harry, as blue as two forget-me-nots, an' as cowld as the moon in a bog-hole iv a frosty night, an' a dead-an'-live look in them that sent a cowld shiver through the marrow o' me bones. By the mortial! ye could have rung a taycuful o' cowld paspiration out o' the hair o' me head that minute, so ye could.

"Well, I thought the life 'ud lave me intirely when she riz up from her hunkers, till, bedad! she looked mostly as tall as Nelson's Pillar. An' with those two eyes gazin' back at me, an' her two arms stretched out before her, an' a *keine** out iv her that riz the hair o' me scalp till it was as stiff as the hog's bristles in a new hearth broom, away she glides—yes, *glides*—around the angle o' the bridge, an' down with her *into the sthrame* that ran undhernaith it.

" 'Twas then I began to suspect what she was. I made a great sthruggle to get me two legs into a fast throt, in spite o' the spavin o' fright the pair o' them wor in. How I brought meself home that same night the Lord in heaven ownly knows, for I never could tell. But I must ha' tumbled agin the door, and shot in head foremost intò the middle iv the floor, where I lay in a dead swoon for mostly an hour. The first I knew was Mrs. Maguire stannin' over me with a jorum o' punch she was pourin' down me throath to bring back the life into me, an' me head in a pool iv cowld wather she dashed over me in her first fright.

" 'Arrah, Misther Connolly,' sez she, 'what ails ye, to put the scare on a lone woman like that?' sez she.

" 'O, glory be to God!' sez I. 'But I thought I was in purgathory at the laste, not to mintion an uglier place,' sez I, 'ownly it's too cowld I find meself, an' not too hot,' sez I.

" 'Faix, an' maybe ye wor more nor halfways there, ownly for me,' sez she. 'But what's come to you at all, at all? Is it your own fetch† ye seen, Misther Connolly?''

" 'Aw, *naboslish* [don't mind it]!' sez I. 'Never mind what I seen.'

"So, by degrees, I began to come to a little; an' that's the way I met the banshee, Misther Harry!"

"But how did you know it really was the banshee after all, Thomas?"

"Begor, sir, I knew the apparition of her well enough, but 'twas confirmed by a sarcumstance that occurred the same time. There was a Misther O'Nale was come on a visit, ye must know, to a place in the neighborhood—one o' the ould O'Nales iv the County Tyrone, a rale ould Irish family—an' the banshee was heard *keinin'* round the house that same night, by more than one that was in it; an' sure enough, Misther Harry, he was found dead in his bed the next mornin'. So if it wasn't the banshee I seen that time, I'd like to know what else it could a' been."

—John Todhunter (1809-73)

---

*The Celtic form for *keen*: to wail or howl in mourning for the dead.
†Spirit.

Chapter Twenty-four

Proverbs, Maxims, and Sayings[1]

Introduction

The humor of Ireland is no recent growth, as may be ascertained by the folklore, traditional songs, poems, and proverbs of the country. It is, in fact, one of Ireland's ancient characteristics, well illustrated in some of its early literature which has not been translated to this day. It is often thought that the most striking feature of older Celtic literature is its sadness, an opinion held for many years because of the emphasis placed on the melancholy side of those early Celtic writings. The subject matter of this book suggests otherwise.

Most of the proverbs, some of which are very ancient, are characteristic enough to show that the early Irish were naturally joyous, as a primitive people usually are, for sadness generally comes with civilization and knowledge. The fragments of folklore that have so far been rescued impress us with the idea that its originators were homespun, cheerful, and mirthful. Certainly, their proverbs demonstrate that the early humor of the Irish Celts is amusing in conception and in expression, especially when it is sharpened into satire.

The selections which follow have not been separated into classified categories for the simple reason that they defy accurate classification. However, as the authors have long since gone to their reward, and their original meanings forever shrouded, the proverbs and sayings can mean what we wish them to mean—and that, perhaps, is precisely what the ancient scribes intended.

—H.D.S.

---

[1]The sayings represented in this chapter have been gleaned from a number of sources: mainly from the collected and uncollected work of the eminent Irish scholar and folklorist, Dr. Douglas Hyde, and from the translations of Francis A. Fahy, Patrick J. McCall, and Joseph O'Leary, all of whom are also represented in other sections of this book. Other contributions were unearthed from old Irish publications, including the *Penny Journal* and *Duffy's Sixpenny Magazine*. Several additional maxims—among the best in this collection—were found in the yellowed pages of the *Dublin University Magazine* for 1839 and 1878.

A man ties a knot with his tongue that his teeth will not loosen.

Honey is sweet, but don't lick it off a briar.

The doorstep of a great house is slippery.

Laziness is a heavy burden.

You'd be a good messenger to send for death (said of a slow person).

Better the end of a feast than the beginning of a fight.

Let him cool in the skin he warmed in.

A man is shy in another man's corner.

The pig in the sty doesn't know the pig going along the road.

'Tis on her own account the cat purrs.

Cows far from home have long horns.

A black hen lays a white egg (*i.e.,* do not judge by appearances).

'Tis a very good story that fills the belly.

He knows more than his "Our Father."

A soft word never yet broke a tooth.

He comes like the bad weather (*i.e.,* uninvited).

Who lies down with dogs will get up with fleas.

The pig does not look up to see where the acorns are falling from

The eye of a friend is a good looking-glass.

'Tis the fool has luck.

What the pooka writes, he himself can read.

A blind man can see his mouth.

Don't leave a tailor's remnant behind you.

'Tis a wedge of itself that splits the oak.

The three sharpest things of all—a thorn in mire, a hound's tooth, and a fool's retort.

The jewel most rare is the jewel most fair.

He that loses the game, let him talk away.

A heavy purse makes a light heart.

He is like a bagpipe—he never makes a noise till his belly's full.

Out of the kitchen comes the tune.

Falling is easier than rising.

A woman has an excuse readier than an apron.

The secret of an old woman is scolding (*i.e.,* no secret at all).

A bad wife takes advice from every man but her own husband.

The daughter of an active old woman makes a bad housekeeper.

Never take a wife who has no faults.

She burnt her coal and did not warm herself (said when a woman makes a bad marriage).

A ring on the finger and not a stitch of clothes on the back.

A hen with chicks never yet burst her craw.

A big belly was never generous.

One bit of a rabbit is worth two of a cat.

When the hand ceases to scatter, the mouth ceases to praise.

Big head and little sense.

The tail is part of the cat (*i.e.*, a man resembles his family).

A cat's milk gives no cream (said of a stingy person).

Butter to butter is no relish (said when two men dance together or two women kiss each other).

One cockroach knows another.

A heavy load are your empty guts.

The young thorn is the sharpest.

Sweet is wine, bitter its payment.

An alm from his own share, to the fool.

Better a wren in hand than a crane promised.

A closed hand gets but a shut fist.

They are not all big men who reap the harvest.

Easy, oh woman of three cows (against pretentious people)!

Fair words won't feed the friars.

Never poor till one goes to Hell.

Not worried till married.

Three without rule—a wife, a pig, and a mule.

When your hand is in the dog's mouth, draw it out gently.

After their feeding, the whelps begin to fight.

The four drinks—the drink of thirst, the drink without thirst, the drink for fear of thirst, and the drink at the door.

A woman is more obstinate than a mule—a mule than the Devil.

All the world would not make a racehorse of a jackass.

When the goat goes to church, he never stops till he goes up to the altar.

A strip of another man's leather is very soft.

'Tis a bad hen that won't scratch for herself.

Better riding a goat than the best marching

Death is the poor man's doctor

There's no good crying when the funeral is gone.

Though near to a man his coat, his shirt is nearer (*i.e.,* blood is thicker than
 water).

What cannot be had is just what suits.

An unlearned king is a crowned ass.

Nora having a servant and herself begging (shabby gentility).

A man without dinner—two for supper.

The man without a resource is hanged.

Poor women think buttermilk good.

Harsh is the poor man's voice—he speaks all out of place.

A wet mouth does not feel a dry mouth (*i.e.,* plenty does not understand
 want).

'Tis a fine horse that never stumbles.

A hen carried far is heavy.

The day of the storm is not the day for thatching.

Winter comes on the lazy.

A crow thinks its own young white.

Putting on the mill the straw of the kiln (*i.e.,* robbing Peter to pay Paul).

What goes to length goes to coldness.

Better the good that is than the double good that was.

A good retreat is better than a bad stand.

Not better is food than sense at time of drinking.

Thy complexion is black, says the raven.

Better be sparing at first than at last.

Whoever escapes, the peacemaker won't.

I would take an eye out of myself to take two out of another.

Melodious is the closed mouth.

Alas for a house that men frequent not.

It's many the skin that sloughs off youth.

Time is a good storyteller.

The quills often took the flesh with them.

One debt won't pay another.

There never came a gatherer but a scatterer came after him.

There's none for bad shoes like the shoemaker's wife.

No man ever gave advice but himself were the better for it.

A man of learning understands the half-word.

O'Brien's gift and his two eyes after it (*i.e.,* regretting it).

God put the blight on the potato, but England put the hunger upon Ireland.

Contention is better than loneliness.

Biographical Index of Authors

ALLINGHAM, WILLIAM: Born in Donegal, in 1824, Allingham was best known for his short lyrics, most notably *The Fairies,* beginning "Up the airy mountain, Down the rushy glen." The poet died in 1889.

BARRETT, EATON STANNARD: Satirist and poet, he was one of the wittiest writers of his time. Born in Cork in 1786, he graduated from Trinity College, Dublin, and became a barrister in London. Some of his satires had great vogue, especially *All the Talents,* a pungent attack against the British administration in Ireland. He was the author of various humorous novels, plays, and poems, but could write well on serious subjects. Barrett died in Glamorganshire, Wales, on March 20, 1820.

BOUCICAULT, DION: The real name of this popular dramatist and actor was Dionysius Lardner Boucicault. He was born in Dublin on December 26, 1822, and wrote *London Assurance* at Coventry Gardens, when only nineteen years old. His Irish dramas were well known and some scholars still consider them as the best of their kind. He is remembered for such of his works as *The Wearin' o' the Green, The Sidewalks of New York* and many others of his more than 300 songs, humorous novels, poems, and dramas, in many of which he acted on the stage. The most notable of these was his play, *The Colleen Bawn,* which enjoyed a half-century of popularity. His 1859 melodrama, *The Octoroon,* was successfully revived in New York in 1961. He spent many years in the United States, where he died in September 1890.

BOURKE, JAMES JOSEPH: He was born in Dublin, on September 17, 1837. His poems were very widely known and appreciated by Irish people everywhere. Over his signature, "Tiria," he wrote mainly for Irish newspapers, and was often quoted in American publications by lecturers and comedians. He died in 1901.

BOYLE, WILLIAM: There were few Irish authors whose writings were more racy than his, though he was never vulgar. He was born in 1853 in Dromiskin, County Louth, and was educated at St. Mary's College, Dundalk.

CANNING, THOMAS: A soldier who served with the Sixty-first Regiment, he was the author of *Detached Pieces in Verse*, published in Cork in 1800 or thereabouts.

CANNING, GEORGE: He was born in London on April 11, 1770. His father and mother were Irish, and he insisted that he was an Irishman born out of Ireland. After a brilliant parliamentary career, he became prime minister in 1827, but only held the position for about three months, his death occurring on August 8th of that year. His witty essays were written in early life for *The Microcosm* and *Anti-Jacobin*.

CARLETON, WILLIAM: Author of the *Traits and Stories of the Irish Peasantry*, he was recognized as one of the greatest delineators of Irish character. Born in Prillisk, County Tyrone, in 1794, Carleton was the son of a peasant. His best-known work, mentioned above, appeared in 1820, and after that date scarcely a year passed without a new work of his appearing. He wrote largely for the *Dublin University Magazine* and was granted a Civil List pension of two hundred pounds by Lord John Russell. He died near Dublin on January 30, 1869.

COLEMAN, PATRICK JAMES: He was a native of Ballaghadeerin, County Mayo, where he was born on September 2, 1867. He matriculated in London University, and in 1888 went to America. There, he occupied a position in the journalistic world of Philadelphia, and was regarded as one of the more gifted Irish-American poets.

CROKER, THOMAS CROFTON: He was born in Cork, in 1798. An antiquarian of note, he was one of the first to collect Irish folklore. From 1825 to 1828 he compiled *Fairy Legends and Traditions of the South of Ireland*. In 1829 he completed *Legends of the Lakes*, and in 1837 published his popular *Songs of Ireland*. He died in 1854.

CURRAN, JOHN PHILPOT: This noted orator and wit was born in Newmarket, County Cork, on July 24, 1750. His patriotism endeared him to generations of his countrymen, and his eloquence and humor made his name widely familiar until the turn of the twentieth century. He is currently being "rediscovered" in Ireland.

DAWSON, ARTHUR: A baron of the Exchequer in Ireland, Dawson was born about 1700. He graduated with a B.A. from Dublin University. Because of his austere appearance and regal bearing, his keen sense of humor always evoked surprise among those who did not know him well. He died in 1775, leaving a note for his friends in which he insisted that they seek him out as soon as they arrived in Heaven so that they might enjoy a few companionable drinks together.

DeQuincy, J.: A solicitor's clerk in Limerick, he wrote humorous verse in the Irish papers in the mid-1800s. As so often happens, he received scant recognition for his talents until long after his death. Little is known about him.

Downey, Edmund: Author of the well-known stories that were signed, "F. M. Allen," such as "Through Green Glasses" and others. These richly humorous Irish tales are perhaps better known, but can hardly be considered superior to his excellent sea stories. He was born in Waterford in 1856, the son of a shipowner and broker. He came to London in 1878 and was for a time employed by Tinsley, the publisher, and later entered the publishing field on his own. He died in 1923.

Dufferin, Lady: Born in 1807, she was the daughter of Thomas Sheridan—son of Richard Brinsley Sheridan, whose work also appears in this volume. She and her two sisters were noted for their beauty; one of them, Mrs. Norton, was well known as a poetess, as was Lady Dufferin. Her first husband was Pryce Blackwood (afterward Lord Dufferin). She then married the Earl of Gifford. She died on June 13, 1867. In addition to their humor, her poems were often exquisite in their pathos or grace.

Ettingsall, Thomas: A fishing tackle manufacturer of Wood Quay, Dublin, he was born about the close of the eighteenth century, probably in 1798 or 1799. He wrote for the *Irish Penny Journal* (1840) and the *Dublin Penny Journal* (1832). He collaborated with H. B. Code in the authorship of *The Angling Excursions of Gregory Greendrake,* which was published in Dublin in 1824. He died in poverty about 1850.

Fahy, Francis Arthur: One of the most humorous of all Irish poets, and one of the raciest (even more so than William Boyle, whose contributions also appear in this work). Born in Kinvara, County Galway, on September 29, 1854, he went to London as a Civil Service clerk in 1873. He wrote many poems for the Irish papers, signed "Dreoilin" (the Wren), and in 1887 published a collection of his *Irish Songs and Poems* in Dublin. Some of his songs were set to music, and a number of his poems were included in an anthology, *Songs of the Four Nations,* in 1895.

Farquhar, George: This once-noted dramatist was born in Derry in 1678, the son of a clergyman. He studied at Dublin University, but did not graduate. He went on the stage in 1695 and, although successful as an actor, left the theater to write plays; among them are *The Beaux Stratagem, The Inconstant,* and *The Recruiting Officer.* He died in April 1707.

Ferguson, Sir Samuel: Regarded as one of the greatest of Irish poets, he was born on March 10, 1810, graduated from Dublin University, and became a lawyer. He was one of the leading contributors to *Blackwood's Magazine,* and published several volumes of very admirable poetry, and some graphic stories of ancient Ireland. He died on August 9, 1886.

French, William Percy: He was born at Clooniquin, County Roscommon, on May 1, 1854, and graduated from Dublin University. He was one of the most clever of the Irish humorists of his day, and was the author of many verses, stories, and essays. Most of his writings appeared in a small Dublin comic, *The Jarvey,* edited by himself. Some of his songs became very popular, and he was also the author of the librettos of two operas.

GOLDSMITH, OLIVER: The leading facts of Goldsmith's career are almost too well known to need even bare mention. He was born in Pallas, near Ballymahon, County Longford, on November 10, 1728. He entered Dublin University and graduated with a B.A. in 1749. After wandering about Europe, he settled down in London to a literary life, his first experiences being those of a badly-paid hack. He died on April 4, 1774. Details of his hectic life may be found in most encyclopedias.

GRAVES, ALFRED PERCEVAL: The author of *Father O'Flynn* and other compositions, he was considered the most popular of the humorous Irish songwriters, with the possible exception of Samuel Lover (see separate listing). He not only produced many good songs in the lighter vein, but also wrote excellent ones of a serious character. He was the son of the Bishop of Limerick, and was born in Dublin in 1846. A graduate of Dublin University, he held the position of Inspector of Schools. He resided for some years in Taunton, but later moved to London, where he accomplished much to make Irish music and Irish character better known. He died in 1912.

GRIFFIN, GERALD: Born in Limerick on December 12, 1803, he traveled to London in his youth to carve out his fortune. He wrote some fine Irish stories and some beautiful poems, as well as a fairly good play. But, just as he was succeeding in literature, he withdrew from the world, joining the order of Christian Brothers. He died in Cork on June 12, 1840. His best known book is *The Collegians, or the Colleen Bawn,* adapted by Boucicault into a highly successful play. (See Boucicault.)

HALPINE, CHARLES GRAHAM: Author of two volumes of important verse, some of which is very humorous. He was born at Oldcastle, County Meath, in 1820, and was the son of a Protestant clergyman. He came to the United States in the 1850s and fought through the Civil War, gaining the rank of colonel. He died as a result of an overdose of chloral, used to induce sleep, on August 3, 1868.

HYDE, DOUGLAS, LL.D.: Born in Kilmactranny, County Sligo, about 1860. As a child he lived in Frenchpark, County Roscommon, where his father, Reverend Arthur Hyde, had his ministry. A graduate of Dublin University, he had a brilliant career there. He was one of the foremost Irish writers of his time, and a master of the Gaelic tongue. He won fame as a scholar, and was an enthusiast in folklore studies, publishing fine collections of Irish folk tales and popular songs of the west of Ireland. He was also a clever writer of verse, both in Irish and in English. He died in 1949.

KENEALY, EDWARD VAUGHAN HYDE, LL.D.: Born in Cork on July 2, 1819, he graduated with an LL.D. from Dublin University in 1850. He was called to the English Bar in 1847, and had a somewhat stormy career as a member, being finally disbarred because of his conduct in the then-famous Tichbourne case. He wrote much for the celebrated magazine *Fraser,* in its early years; also for *Bentley's Miscellany,* and published various collections of poetry. Kenealy was a vigorous journalist, and a man of undoubtedly great ability. He entered Parliament in 1875, despite his earlier disbarment. He died on April 16, 1880.

KICKHAM, CHARLES JOSEPH: He was a poet of the people and a novelist of some power. To get a genuine impression of the home life of the Munster people, his stories, *Sally Cavanagh* and *Knocknagow, or the Homes of Tipperary,* must be read. He was born in Mullinahone, County Tipperary, in 1828, and became a Fenian. He was connected with *The Irish People,* the Fenian journal, and was arrested in 1865 and sentenced to a prison term of fourteen years. He lost his sight during imprisonment and was shattered in health. Yet, even in the depths of his despair, he was somehow able to create humorous pieces, as well as trenchant ones. He died on August 22, 1882, mourned by the Irish as both a writer and a patriot.

LEFANU, JOSEPH SHERIDAN: Born in Dublin in August 1814, he was graduated with a B.A. from Dublin University in 1837. He was called to the Bar, but devoted himself to literature and journalism. He owned two or three Dublin papers, and was editor of *The Dublin University Magazine,* also his property, where most of his novels and poems first appeared. He was one of the most enthralling of novelists, his *Uncle Silas, In a Glass Darkly,* and others, being examples of his literary power. His poems, such as "Shamus O'Brien," were also very well known. He died on February 7, 1873.

LEVER, CHARLES JAMES, M.D.: This novelist, once among the most widely read of Irish writers, was born in Dublin on August 31, 1806, and graduated with an M.B. from Dublin University in 1831. He took his M.D. degree at Louvain and became a doctor in Ireland, but also practiced abroad for a time successfully. He was editor of *The Dublin University Magazine* from 1842 to 1845, and wrote much for it, as he did for *Blackwood's Magazine* and other leading periodicals. He served as English Consul in Italy, and died at Trieste on June 1, 1872. He authored numerous popular novels.

LOVER, SAMUEL: He was poet, painter, musician, dramatist, and novelist— and successful in all departments. His work in each was excellent, and he might have been considered great, had he confined himself to any one of them. He was born in Dublin on February 24, 1797, and was first notable as a painter of miniatures. His weak eyesight, however, compelled him to give up the art. He wrote several plays, one or two tremendously popular novels, and some hundreds of songs, most of which he set to music himself. He died on the island of Jersey, July 6, 1868.

LUTTRELL, HENRY: At one time, Luttrell was one of the most popular men in London society, and was known for his powers of repartee. He was born in 1766 or 1767, in Dublin, and was for a time a member of the Irish Parliament. After the Union, he went to England, where he was a frequent guest at many brilliant social functions. He died in Brompton Square, December 19, 1851. His "Advice to Julia" and "Crockford House" are examples of his cleverness with light, satirical verse.

MAGINN, WILLIAM, LL.D.: One of the greatest scholars and humorists Cork has produced, he was born in that city on July 10, 1793. He was graduated with an LL.D. from Dublin University in 1819. He was, from its commencement, the most brilliant contributor to *Blackwood's Magazine*, and also edited *Fraser* on its appearance in 1830. His fatal propensity for liquor prevented his doing himself justice, though he wrote many inimitable pieces. He was one of the most lovable of men. He died August 21, 1842.

MAHER, WILLIAM: A Waterford clothier, he is now considered the most likely author of *"The Night Before Larry Was Stretched."* One thing is certain: Dean Burrows of Cork did *not* write it, as has often been claimed. Walsh's *Ireland Sixty Years Ago* (published in 1847) credits Maher, who flourished about 1780, as the true author.

MAHONEY, REVEREND FRANCIS SYLVESTER: Usually better remembered as "Father Prout," the name he took as his pseudonym in writing. He was of the Kerry family, but was born in Cork in 1804-1805, as is frequently said. He was educated for the priesthood at Amiens and Paris, and joined the Jesuit order. After some years, however, he practically gave up his functions and led a Bohemian life. He was a well-received contributor to *Fraser*, where his "Reliques" appeared. In later life, he served as Paris correspondent of *The Globe* (which he partly owned) and as Roman correspondent of *The Daily News*. Before his death, which occurred in Paris, May 18, 1866, he repented of his disregard for his sacred calling. He was buried in his native city. It is extremely difficult to make extracts from Mahoney's prose because of the superabundant classical allusions and references which it contains. The fact that he could write very funny poems and stories is surprising, as he was not a very agreeable man. In fact, according to his contemporaries, he was a most unpleasant individual.

MANGAN, JAMES CLARENCE: One of the first of the early Irish poets, he was held to be the greatest of them by many of his countrymen. Born in Dublin on May 1, 1803, he was the son of a grocer. He wrote innumerable poems for the Irish periodicals of his time, notably *The Nation* and *Dublin University Magazine*. He knew various languages, but his pretended translations from Turkish, Coptic, Hebrew, Arabic, and Persian are so many jokes. He was most unfortunate in life, mainly through his addiction to alcohol. He had a wonderful personality, which attracted many other writers to him, and his great poetical gifts are gradually becoming evident to English critics. He was greatly encouraged by his admirers, but to little avail. He died in a Dublin hospital on June 20, 1849.

MATHEW, FRANK: A solicitor, and a nephew of the eminent English judge, Sir James Mathew, he was born in 1865. His first literary work was a biography of his illustrious relative, Father Mathew, *The Apostle of*

Temperance. His excellent Irish stories, which appeared in *The Idler,* were collected in a volume titled *At the Rising of the Moon.*

McCALL, PATRICK JOSEPH: A genuinely Irish poet whose original poems and translations from the Gaelic are very characteristic. He was the son of a Dublin grocer (the author of a memoir of Mangan), and was born in Dublin, March 6, 1861. McCall was educated at the Catholic University School in his native city, and for some years was a frequent and welcome contributor to the Dublin Nationalist Press. A good selection of his poems was published under the title *Irish Noines* in the 1880s. His stories appeared mostly in *The Shamrock,* of Dublin.

McKOWEN, JAMES: Born in Lambeg, near Lisburn, County Antrim, on February 11, 1814. McKowen received only an elementary education. He was first employed in a thread factory, afterwards working as a linen bleacher for many years. He wrote principally for North Ireland papers, and was exceedingly popular with Ulster people, although several of his works later found a much wider audience. He died April 22, 1889.

MOORE, THOMAS: Son of a Dublin grocer, he was born in that city on May 28, 1779. He graduated from Dublin University and studied law in London. He began to write poetry and prose in his early youth, but his first great success was occasioned by his *Irish Melodies,* which made its initial appearance in 1806. According to press reports of the day, "Moore was a great hand with the ladies." He died on February 26, 1852.

O'CONOR, CHARLES PATRICK: Born in County Cork in or about 1837, he went to England in his youth. He wrote some good verse, and was granted a Civil List pension of fifty pounds a year. Most of his contributions were to Irish papers. His complete works were published by himself.

O'DONNELL, JOHN FRANCIS: An Irish writer best remembered to his countrymen as a poet, he was born in Limerick, 1837, and began to write for the press at the age of fourteen. In 1861 he went to London, where he wrote for various journals, including those of Charles Dickens. He died on May 7, 1874. A selection of his poems was published in 1891 by the Southwark Irish Literary Club.

O'FLAHERTY, JOHN: Born in 1794, Dublin, where his father was a pawnbroker in Ross Lane, he was apprenticed to a bookseller and eventually turned to journalism. He was on the staff of Dublin's *Morning Post,* and afterwards edited the *Wexford Evening Post.* He died in May 1828. He published three volumes of verse, and some of his songs enjoyed wide popularity, especially "The Humors of Donnybrook Fair," which was taken from his *Trifles in Poetry* (1813).

O'KEEFE, JOHN: This once-popular dramatist was born in Dublin on June 24, 1747, and first intended to be an artist because of the skill he displayed at a very early age. But he preferred the stage and was, for a time, a successful actor. Moving to London, he earned repute as a dramatist, writing numerous plays, chiefly operas and farces, which had great vogue. He is remembered especially for his *Wild Oats*, a comedy which, after these great many years, is still occasionally seen on the stage. O'Keefe lost his eyesight many years before his death in Southampton, February 24, 1833.

O'LEARY, JOSEPH: He is the author of *The Tribute,* a collection of prose and verse which was published anonymously at Cork in 1833. He was born in that city about 1790, and was a contributor to the "scurrilous" *Freeholder,* and other papers of Cork and Dublin. He came to London in 1834 and served as parliamentary reporter for the *Morning Herald.* Between 1840 and 1850 he disappeared, and is believed to have committed suicide in the Regent's Canal. "Whiskey, Drink Divine" first appeared in *The Freeholder* in 1820. The poem is again published in this present volume for the first time in the United States.

O'LEARY, PATRICK: One of the foremost writers in Old Irish of the nineteenth century, he was a resident of West Cork and was born in that city, circa 1830. He translated his own works into English, and was a regular contributor to *The Gaelic Journal* and Gaelic societies throughout the world. He died in 1903 or thereabouts.

O'RYAN, JEREMIAH: Born near Bansha, County Tipperary, about the close of the eighteenth century, and died in March 1855, he is generally known as "Darby Ryan of Bansha." Some of his works were collected and published in Dublin in 1861.

PORTER, REVEREND THOMAS HAMBLIN, D.D.: Born about 1800, he died sometime between 1865 and 1869, but little is known about him. He graduated with a D.D. from Dublin University in 1836, and wrote a few pieces which were published in Dublin magazines. *The Nightcap* appeared about 1820. A dour man, he is said to have amazed his colleagues with his keen sense of humor, which only was manifested in his writings.

ROCHE, SIR BOYLE: Born in 1740, somewhere in the south of Ireland. A soldier, he distinguished himself in the American Revolutionary War. He entered the Irish Parliament, and was created a baronet in 1782 by the British government for his unwavering support. He was pensioned for his service in voting for the Union, and died in Dublin, June 5, 1807. He was noted for his very carefully prepared blunders in speech—the "Irish bulls" of note; a number of which appear in this volume.

SHALVEY, THOMAS: A market-gardener in Dublin, he wrote some amusing poems for James Kearney a vocalist who sang at several music halls in Dublin and surrounding areas. Kearney was very popular and some of his best songs were written for him by Shalvey. He was born around the first part of the eighteenth century and died in 1848 or 1849. Little is known about him, for Kearney received nearly all of the acclaim.

SHERIDAN, RICHARD BRINSLEY: Born in October 1751 in Dorset Street, Dublin, the son of a noted actor and manager, he was a dramatist, orator, drunkard, and spendthrift whose name figures very prominently in the memoirs of his time. His wit, as well as his cash, was often squandered in every direction. Critics often reproached him for making every one of the characters in his plays as witty as himself. He was an important personality in the politics of his day, and sat in the English Parliament for many years. He died in debt and poverty on July 7, 1816, and was accorded a grand burial in Westminster Abbey.

STEELE, SIR RICHARD: Born in Dublin, in 1671 or 1672, he was educated at the Charterhouse School, London, and at Oxford. In 1709, he commenced the publication of *The Tattler,* and followed it with *The Spectator* and other journals, all of which are quoted to this day. He also wrote several comedies and other works. He entered Parliament in 1713, and held one or two government offices. He died in Wales, September 1, 1729.

STERNE, REVEREND LAURENCE: Born in Clonmel, County Tipperary, on November 24, 1713, he graduated with an M.A. from Cambridge in 1740. His father was an Army officer. He was ordained about 1741 and, after some years of inactivity at home and travel abroad, wrote his great work. *Tristram Shandy,* which appeared at intervals between 1759 and 1767. His *Sentimental Journey* appeared in 1768. He died in March of that year.

SULLIVAN, TIMOTHY DANIEL: A well-known politician of his time, he was born in Bantry, County Cork, in 1827. He was one of the most widely read of the Irish verse writers, and wrote several songs which have deeply impressed themselves on Irish memories. But he excelled in the writing of political skits, which at one time formed one of the chief features of the *Nation,* a newspaper of note then edited by him.

SWIFT, REVEREND JONATHAN, D.D.: This greatest of satirists in the English tongue was born in Hoey's Court, Dublin, on November 30, 1667. He graduated with a B.A. from Dublin University in 1686, and a D.D. later at Oxford. Ordained in 1694, he published *The Tale of a Tub* in 1705. *Gulliver's Travels* followed in 1726-27, and innumerable other works came from his pen. He was one of Ireland's champions of independence, and had an extraordinary popularity with the people. He died on October 19, 1745.

WADE, JOSEPH AUGUSTINE: An unfortunate Irish genius, he was born in Dublin in 1796, the son of a dairyman on Thomas Street. As a poet and musician Wade has been highly praised. He composed some excellent songs, some of them marvelously witty, but was very erratic in his career. He made large sums of money when he applied himself, but died in poverty September 29, 1845.

WALLER, JOHN FRANCIS, LL.D.: Born in Limerick in 1809, he was connected with the Wallers of County Tipperary. He graduated with an LL.D. from Dublin University in 1852, and held an important government position in Dublin for many years. He was editor of *The Dublin University Magazine* for some time and published several volumes of clever pros, and verse.

He was considered one of the best of Irish songwriters. Waller died on January 19, 1894.

WINSTANLEY, JOHN: A Fellow of Trinity College, Dublin, he was born in 1678 and died in 1750. His poems first appeared in 1742, and in a second series published after his death by his son.

"ZOZIMUS": He was the once-celebrated blind beggar of Dublin who possessed a remarkable ability to recite poems. Many anecdotes and poems, including "Whiskey and Wather" which appears in this volume, have been attributed to him. However, they could not have been written by him anymore than the other pieces assumed to be his compositions merely because he recited them. "Whiskey and Wather," for example, was taken from a song book published in Dublin. But "Zozimus," whose real name was Michael Moran, did bring them to fame through his superior recitations.

Glossary of Gaelic and Anglo-Irish Words and Phrases

Abu: Our "boy"; our man; our hero.
Achora: Friend.
Acushla: Little darling. See *Macushla.*
Alanna: Child.
Amadan (Also *Omadhaun*): Fool; simpleton.
A mhic (Also *Mic*): My son; Oh, son. *Mic* is the vocative of Mac
Aroon: A secret or pet name.
Asthore: My beloved; my treasure.
Aulaun: A lout.
Avick (*Avic*): See *A mhic.*
Avochal: My boy.
Avourneen machree: Darling of my heart.

Bad cess: Bad luck. The word *cess* is believed to be a corruption of the English word, "success." It is almost always preceded by the descriptive "bad."
Baithershin: So be it; that is possible.
Banshee: An attendant fairy in Irish folklore who follows the old families, and none but them, and wails just before a family member dies. Derived from *ban* (*bean*, a woman, and *shee (sidhe),* a fairy. See *Keen.*
Bawnditch (*Badhun*): An enclosure or wall around a house. Derived from *ba, cows,* and *dhun,* a fortress. Properly, cattle-fortress.
Bedad: An exclamation similar to the English "by gosh," or "by God," and sometimes thought of as "be damned."
Beimedh a gole: Let us be drinking!
Black and Tans: Auxiliaries, organized by England's parliament to suppress Irish resistance to British rule. The Black and Tans, so named from the mixture of police and army uniforms they wore, terrorized Ireland in 1920, but succeeded only in strengthening the Irish will to resist. See *Sinn Fein.*

Blarney: Flattering or wheedling talk, or cajolery; to ply or beguile with blarney: "He blarneys the colleens with the most outrageous statements." In addition to the customary definitions, blarney, in the United States, also means the glib defense of one's position; a clever, quick, witty response to gain an end or some advantage. It is the good humor with which it is said that keeps blarney from being vulgar or crude.

Blarney stone: A stone in Blarney Castle, in the hamlet of Blarney, County Cork. Whoever kisses the Blarney stone, which is placed in an almost inaccessible position near the top of the thick stone wall of the fifteenth-century castle, is said to acquire marvelous powers of persuasion and skill in flattery; that is, the lucky person has been endowed with the "gift of blarney."

Blatherskite: A person given to voluble, empty talk; a chatterbox.

Boccagh (also *Geochag*): A beggar.

Bodach: A clown.

Boreen: A country lane, or path.

Bosthoon: A blockhead.

Bouchal: Boy.

Brogan: In Ireland, a shoe or boot. In the United States, a heavy or extra-large shoe or boot. (See *Leprechaun*: the fairy shoemaker, for derivatives.)

Bunnaun: A cudgel.

Cailin deas: See *Colleen dhas*.

Caish: A pig.

Canavaun: Blossom of the bog.

Casogue: A coat.

Cauth: A girl's name; Kate (diminutive of Katherine).

Cead mille failte (pronounced *cade meelya falltha*): A hundred thousand welcomes.

Ceanabhan: See *Canavaun*.

Cess: See *Bad cess*.

Coatamore: See *Cothamor*.

Colleen: A young girl; an Irish girl; a girl's name.

Colleen dhas: A pretty girl.

Colloguing: Talking.

Coolyeens: Curls.

Cothamor: An overcoat.

Creepie: A three-legged stool.

Croosheening: Whispering.

Cruistin: Throwing.

Curse of the Irish: Addiction to alcohol.

Dáil Éireann and the Seanad Éireann: The two-chambered legislative assembly that governs the Republic of Ireland. The lower house may amend, but not veto, bills initiated by the democratically-elected upper house. Executive power is vested in the prime minister; the president signs and promulgates the laws.

Daltheen: A puppy.

Daoine maithe: The good people (meaning the fairy creatures of Irish folk lore).

Deeneeshee (*Daoine sidhe*): Fairy people, in Irish folklore, including the leprechauns, pookas, and banshees.

Deeshy: Small.

Dhioul: Devil.

Dhudeen: A short-stemmed tobacco pipe.

Dilse: Love.

Doreen (*Deorin*): A small drop.

Eire: Ireland. Related to the poetic Erin and the literary form, Hibernia (Latin).

Emerald Isle: Ireland. The euphemism takes its name from the large central plain which extends to the Irish Sea between the Mourne Mountains in the North and the mountains of Wicklow in the south. While the highlands of the north, west, and south, whose rim roughly encloses the plain, are generally barren, the central plain itself is extremely fertile and the climate is temperate and moist, warmed by southwesterly winds. The rains, which are heaviest in the west (some areas have more than eighty inches annually), are responsible for the brilliant green of the Emerald Isle.

Fenian Movement: Organized in the United States by Irish immigrants who arrived here between 1845 and 1851 in the wake of mass starvation, disease, and British persecution in Ireland. In the United States, the Irish-Americans, under the Fenian banner, continued their bitter opposition to the British government, while helping to feed and clothe their less fortunate kinsmen in Ireland.

Flaitheamhail: See *Flaugholoch*.

Flaugholoch (*Floohool*): Generous, satisfying.

Foosther: Diversion.

Fornent (*Fornenst*): This Gaelic word has several shades of meaning, depending upon the context in which it is used: in front of, opposite, opposite to, facing, across from, against, close to, etc.

Gaelic: The Celtic languages, a subfamily of the Indo-European languages spoken in Ireland, Highland Scotland, and on the Isle of Man. Generally, the form spoken in Ireland is known as Irish, that of Scotland as Scottish or Scottish Gaelic, and that on the Isle of Man as Manx. "Erse" is sometimes used as a synonym for "Gaelic."

Galloglasses: Mercenary footsoldiers. Many of the *galloglasses* came to Ireland in the thirteenth century as a military body, the units serving the most powerful chiefs in the north of Ireland. In time, the *galloglasses* became the core of the leading families of the country.

Ganconer (*gean-canach*): Love-talker; a fairy in Irish folklore who appears in lonesome valleys, usually with a *dhudeen* (tobacco pipe) in his mouth, and who makes love to milkmaids and other girls of the countryside.

Garda Siochana: Civic Guard in the Republic of Ireland.

Geochagh: See *Boccagh*.

Girsha (*Geersha*): Girl.
Gom (*Gommach*): A fool.
Gombeenman: A usurer. During Ireland's potato famine of the 1840s, for
   example, in the absence of their staple, the potato, which had been des-
   troyed by blight, the people ate meal instead. This meal (among other
   foods and supplies) was purchased from the hated *gombeenman* at out-
   rageous prices, or on exorbitant credit terms, and often both.
Gommach: See *Gom*.
Goulogue: A forked stick.
Grawls: Children.

Home Rule: A nineteenth-century Nationalist movement to end the union
   with Great Britain, through a separate Irish parliament, led by the brilliant Charles Stewart Parnell. The constitutional Home Rule movement,
   frustrated by internal divisions and resisted by the British government,
   was supplemented and finally superseded by the *Sinn Fein*. See *Sinn
   Fein*.

I.R.A.: See *Irish Republican Army*.
Irish Republican Army (I.R.A.): A national organization devoted to the in-
   tegration of Ireland as a complete and independent entity, organized by
   Michael Collins from the remnants of rebel units dispersed after the ill-
   fated Easter rebellion of 1916. With the establishment of the Irish Free
   State in 1922, the I.R.A. became the stronghold of intransigent opposition to Ireland's dominion status and to the separation of northern
   Ireland. During the early years of the Free State, the I.R.A. was responsible for numerous bombings, raids, and street battles. As a result, it
   gradually lost the popular Free State support it had enjoyed, and was
   eventually outlawed by both Irish governments and became a secret organization, agitating to end the separation of northern Ireland (Ulster).

Keen (*Caoine*): The funeral cry or wail of lament for the dead, practiced by
   the Irish peasantry. Said to be an imitation of the wail of the banshee.
Kippeen (*Cipin*): Cudgel, or club; a stick.
Knapawn: A huge potato.
Knasster: A large potato, but not as big as a knapawn.

Lawhee: Kindly.
Lenaun: Fairy guardian.
Leprechaun (*Lepracaun*): One of the fairy creatures, or "wee people" of
   Irish folklore. Derived from the Irish *leith brog*, meaning the one-shoe-
   maker, since he is generally seen working at a single shoe. It is spelled in
   Irish, *leith bhrogan*, or *leith phrogan*. The Anglo-Irish word, "brogan,"
   meaning "shoe," is derived from these Gaelic sources.
L.O.I.: See *Orangeman*.
Loodeen: The small toe.
Loughs: Rivers. The Shannon is the longest river, or *lough* in Ireland, and is
   its principal source of electric power. Others include the beautiful *loughs*
   of Allen, Ree, and Derg.

Lusmores: The flowers known as foxgloves.

Ma: My.

Ma bouchal: My boy.

Macushla (From the Old Irish form, *Mo Cuishle):* My darling. (See *Acush-la.)*

Malarkey: Speech or writing designed to obscure, mislead, or impress: ("The politician's campaign promises were just a lot of malarkey.") However, when an Irishman employs malarkey to win a lady's favor, the usual definition do not apply. Malarkey is then defined as overzealous blarney.

Mavrone: An exclamatory term, similar to "my goodness!" etc.

Mick: A derogatory, slang term meaning "Irishman," "shanty Irishman," or an Irish immigrant: derived from the surname prefix, "Mc," meaning "son." However, many first-generation Irish-Americans of the late-nineteenth and early-twentieth centuries themselves adopted the word and often used it against each other in anger or scorn. See *A mhic.*

Mickey: Form of Irish surname prefix, "Mc" (see *A Mhic*). The "mickey" referred to the white, or "Irish" baked potato with which the Irish immigrants were associated in their native country. The sweet potato was known as a "sweet mickey." There was no derogatory connotation to the word, and it has long since become obsolete.

Mille murdher: An exclamation of surprise or indignation, meaning "a thousand murders."

Molly Maguires: A secret organization of Irishmen in the Scranton anthracite districts of Pennsylvania. For several years, from about 1865 to 1875, it dominated the coal mining industry. Its members united to improve their working conditions, but so oppressive were the industrialist mine owners that the Mollies, as they were called, soon resorted to violence and murder to achieve their ends, brought on, in large part, by brutality of the police who were entirely controlled by the mine owners. In turn, the Molly Maguires retaliated by intimidating or killing the police. The Mollies reached the height of their power in 1875, when they managed to organize a strike in a region otherwise virtually unorganized. Their power was finally broken by the spying activity of James McParlan, an Irishman employed by the Pinkerton Detective Agency on behalf of the industrialists who were not so much frightened by the Molly Maguires' violence as by their success in organizing a strike. Twenty of the Mollies were hanged. McParlan's secret reports were released for study in 1947.

Moryah: Forsooth.

Murrain: The rot or blight, labeled the "potato murrain," which resulted in Ireland's devastating potato famine of the 1840s. Among the first crops affected were those around Dublin, where the disease was said to have begun from seed imported from the United States. Much of the suffering, death, and disease arose from Britain's refusal to aid the starving masses, and from Parliament's repeated attempts to minimize the desperate plight of the Irish people in the eyes of other nations, thus forestalling relief shipments of food and medicine to that stricken country.

Musha: An exclamatory word with many shades of meaning: in truth, really, etc. ("*Musha,* I never said my wife *looks* good; I said she *cooks* good!")

Nationalist: An Irishman, usually Roman Catholic, who is opposed to union with Britain. (Orangemen and Unionists are usually Protestant. See *Orangeman.*)

Ochone (*Och hone; Ochone*): Oh, dear! Oh, my! etc.
Ollaves: Judges.
Omadhaun *(Amadan):* A fool.
Orangeman: Usually a Protestant of Scotch Presbyterian faith; a member of the Loyal Orange Institution (L.O.I.), an Irish society organized in the north of Ireland, and largely flourishing in Ulster. It was established in 1795 to defend the laws and rule of England, and to maintain in Ireland the Protestant ascendancy in the face of the rising agitation of the Catholic Emancipation. Its name is taken from the family of King William III of England (William of Orange), who defeated King James II on July 12, 1690, and who landed in England on November 5, 1688. As anniversaries of these two dates, holiday celebrations are made by the L.O.I., at which time members of the order wear orange-colored flowers, orange sashes, and join in parades.

Paddy: The nickname for Padraic, the Gaelic form of Patrick, the patron saint of Ireland. Because so many Irishmen bore the name, the term became generic for all Irishmen before and after the turn of the present century.
Paddy wagon: The name given to the police vehicle that transported intoxicated Irishmen to jail. It began when the Irish immigrants who inhabited the slums of New York City and Boston, suffering from terrible poverty and degrading exclusion from much of America's work force, sought forgetfulness in drink—giving rise to the expression, "The curse of the Irish."
Pogue: A kiss.
Polthogue: A blow.
Pooka (*Phooka*): A legendary Irish spirit, mischievous but not malevolent, corresponding to the English *Puck.* (From the Gaelic *púca.*)
Poteen (*Potheen*): Illicitly distilled whiskey (in Ireland). Poteen corresponds to the American "moonshine" for which the distiller's tax has not been paid and which, therefore, is illegal.
Praties: Potatoes.

Raumach: Rubbish; nonsense.

Saustagh: Suitable.
Seestheen: A seat made of straw or ropes of hay.
Shebeen: A tavern, or house, where liquor is sold illegally. *Shebeening* is the act of visiting one or more *shebeens* on a drinking bout.

Sheehogue *(Sidheog):* A fairy in Irish folklore; a diminutive of *shee* as in banshee. (See *Deenee shee.)*

Shillelagh *(Shillelah; Shillaly):* A cudgel, traditionally of blackthorn or oak; named after the Irish town. The shillelagh is sometimes jocularly called the "Irish boxing glove."

Shoch *(Shough):* A puff, draw, or whiff, as in smoking tobacco.

Sinn Fein: ("Ourselves.") A movement devoted to the ideals of Irish independence from Britain rather than merely to a separate parliament, as had been advocated earlier (see *Home Rule). Sinn Fein* supported the Easter rebellion of 1916, which was suppressed but developed into guerrilla warfare, mainly led by General Michael Collins (see *Irish Republican Army).* To suppress the Irish freedom fighters, Britain created the *Black and Tans* (see separate listing). However, it was the *Sinn Fein,* under its leader, Eamon de Valera, which ultimately won Ireland its independence from Britain.

Slainte: Health, as in a drinking toast.

Slooa shee: The fairy host representing various members of the Irish spirit world.

Spalpeen: While this word denotes a lad or boy, it is more often used to mean a rascal. In the 1800s, however, *spalpeen* also referred to a migrant farmworker. There was no pejorative connotation to the term. A farmer on poor, unproductive land, who could not raise a sufficient crop to pay rent to his absentee landlord in England, would help other farmers with their harvests in order to meet his payments.

Sthronsuch: A lazy thing. ("You *sthronsuch,* sleeping the morning away when you should be working!")

Vanithee *(Ban-a-t'yee):* Woman of the house.

Waumasing: Strolling.

Wirra: The exclamation, *Oh!* Some writers use the word to denote "woe."

General Index

1/05